NEITHER EAST NOR WEST

NEITHER EAST NOR WEST

Iran, the Soviet Union, and the United States

EDITED BY
Nikki R. Keddie and
Mark J. Gasiorowski

Yale University Press New Haven and London

Designed by James J. Johnson and set in Times Roman types by The Composing Room of Michigan, Inc.

Printed in the United States of America by Vail-Ballou Press, Binghamton, New York

Library of Congress Cataloging-in-Publication Data

Neither East nor West : Iran, the Soviet Union, and the United States
    edited by Nikki R. Keddie and Mark J. Gasiorowski.
        p.   cm.
    Includes bibliographical references.
    ISBN 0–300–04656–1 (alk. paper). — ISBN 0–300–04658–8 (pbk. : alk. paper)

    1. Iran—Foreign relations—Soviet Union.   2. Soviet Union—Foreign relations—
Iran.   3. Iran—Foreign relations—United States.   4. United States—Foreign relations—
Iran.   5. United States—Foreign relations—Soviet Union.   6. Soviet Union—Foreign
relations—United States.   I. Keddie, Nikki R.   II. Gasiorowski, Mark J., 1954– .
DS274.2.S65N45   1990
327.55047—dc20   89–25077
                                                                               CIP

The paper in this book meets the guidelines of permanence and durability of the Committee on Production Guidelines for Book Longevity of the Council on Library Resources.

10   9   8   7   6   5   4   3   2   1

Contents

Contributors

MURIEL ATKIN is Associate Professor of history at George Washington University. She is the author of *Russia and Iran, 1780–1828* (Minneapolis: University of Minnesota Press, 1980) and *The Subtlest Battle: Islam in Soviet Tajikistan* (Philadelphia: Foreign Policy Research Institute, 1989).

MAZIAR BEHROOZ is a candidate for a Ph.D. in history at the University of California, Los Angeles.

JAMES A. BILL is Professor of Government and the director of the Reves Center for International Studies at the College of William and Mary. His most recent book is *The Eagle and the Lion: The Tragedy of American-Iranian Relations* (New Haven: Yale University Press, 1988).

RICHARD W. COTTAM is University Professor of political science, University of Pittsburgh. He is the author of *Iran and the United States: A Cold War Case Study* (Pittsburgh: University of Pittsburgh Press, 1988).

ROBERT O. FREEDMAN is Peggy Meyerhoff Pearlstone Professor of Political Science and dean of graduate studies at Baltimore Hebrew University. His published writings include *Soviet Policy toward the Middle East since 1970* (New York: Praeger, 1982).

MARK J. GASIOROWSKI is Associate professor of political science at Louisiana State University. He has published an article on the coup d'état in Iran of 1953 in the *International Journal of Middle East Studies* and has just completed a book on American foreign policy toward Iran under the Shah.

FRED HALLIDAY is Professor of international relations at the London School of Economics. He is the author of *Revolution and Foreign Policy: The Case of*

South Yemen, 1967–1987 (Cambridge: Cambridge University Press, 1989) and *From Kabul to Managua: Soviet-American Relations and the Third World* (New York: Pantheon, 1989).

RICHARD HERRMANN is Associate professor of political science at Ohio State University. He is the author of *Perceptions and Behavior in Soviet Foreign Policy* (Pittsburgh: University of Pittsburgh Press, 1985).

ERIC HOOGLUND is Visiting Associate Professor of political science at the University of California, Berkeley. He is the author of *Land and Revolution in Iran, 1960–1980* (Austin: University of Texas Press, 1982) and *Crossing the Waters: The Arab Immigration to the United States before 1940* (Washington: Smithsonian Institution Press, 1987).

NIKKI R. KEDDIE is Professor of history at the University of California, Los Angeles. She is the author of *Roots of Revolution: An Interpretive History of Modern Iran* (New Haven and London: Yale University Press, 1981) and *Religion and Politics in Iran: Shi'ism from Quietism to Revolution* (New Haven and London: Yale University Press, 1983), and the editor with Juan R. I. Cole of *Shi'ism and Social Protest* (New Haven and London: Yale University Press, 1986).

BRUCE R. KUNIHOLM is Professor of public policy and history and the director of the Institute of Policy Sciences and Public Affairs at Duke University. He is the author of several books on American policy in the Near East, including *The Origins of the Cold War in the Near East: Great Power Conflict and Diplomacy in Iran, Turkey, and Greece* (Princeton: Princeton University Press, 1980), and is working on a book about the relations between the United States and Turkey.

R. K. RAMAZANI is the Harry F. Byrd, Jr., Professor of Government and Foreign Affairs at the University of Virginia. His two latest books are *Revolutionary Iran: Challenge and Response in the Middle East* (Baltimore: Johns Hopkins University Press, 1986) and *The Gulf Cooperation Council: Record and Analysis* (Charlottesville: University Press of Virginia, 1988).

GARY SICK is Adjunct Professor of Middle East politics and a fellow of the Research Institute on International Change at Columbia University. He served on the staff of the National Security Council under Presidents Ford, Carter, and Reagan and is the author of *All Fall Down: America's Tragic Encounter with Iran* (New York: Random House, 1985).

Acknowledgments

This book is based on a conference, "Iran, the U.S., and the U.S.S.R.," held at U.C.L.A. in April 1988. Thanks are due to the financial sponsors, the Ford Foundation and the University of California Institute for Global Cooperation and Conflict and its director at the time, Herbert York. Thanks go especially to the chief active sponsor, the U.C.L.A. Center for International and Strategic Affairs, and its director, Michael Intriligator, and also to cosponsors, the U.C.L.A. von Grunebaum Center for Near Eastern Studies, and its director, George Sabagh, and the University of California, Santa Barbara Global Peace and Security Program, and its director, John Ernest.

Also very helpful were Gerri Harrington, Karl Arnold, Jonathan Friedlander, Afshin Matin-Asgari, Brett Henry, and Ann Florini. Leslie Evans did extensive work editing the manuscripts before they went to Yale manuscript editor Cecile Watters. Charles Grench, our Yale editor, was as helpful as always. Fred Kameny saw the book through production. Jane Bitar and the efficient staff of Word Processing for Social Sciences and Humanities retyped the entire manuscript.

Thanks are also due to other scholars who participated in the conference in various capacities: Shahrough Akhavi, Shaul Bakhash, Jahangir Behrouz, Igor Belyaev, Leonard Binder, Nancy Gallagher, Hans Rogger, William Miller, Mehdi Noorbakhsh, and Hashem Pesaran.

Owing largely to the help of authors and editors, the transition from conference to book has been unusually smooth and trouble-free. For purposes of a book there had to be some changes in the papers that were included. Because of the rapidly changing nature of the topic, it was felt necessary to have some chapters updated by their authors at the last opportunity in late July 1989, after the Iranian presidential elections and constitutional change but before the Lebanese hostage crisis.

NEITHER EAST NOR WEST

Introduction

NIKKI R. KEDDIE

This book deals with the relations of Iran, the United States, and the Soviet Union between 1945, when the Cold War began, and 1988–89, when it was dramatically attenuated. Not entirely by chance, Iranian events played an important role both in shaping the hostile relations between the United States and the Soviet Union soon after World War II and in contributing to a world situation in the late 1980s in which peaceful solutions came to the fore in many parts of the world. In 1946, the United States reacted strongly to the delayed withdrawal of Soviet troops from Iranian Azerbaijan and Kurdistan, where they had supported local movements for ethnic autonomy. Even though the importance of this reaction may have been exaggerated (as suggested in chapter 3 by Richard Herrmann), there is no doubt that this was one of the first postwar incidents in which the Soviets were seen by the American public and government as an active, expansionist force that the United States must actively counter. The widespread belief that the United States had prevented large areas of Iran from falling to communist rule laid a basis for American interventionism in Iran and elsewhere.

In 1988 and 1989, actions by Iran were important in stimulating hopes for peace throughout the world, and the Soviet-American relationship regarding Iran strengthened suggestions that the Cold War might be ending. The last period of the Iran-Iraq war, covered especially in the chapters by Robert Freedman, Gary Sick, Fred Halliday, and Richard Cottam (5, 10, 11, and 12), saw a significant rapprochement of Soviet and American policies, even though the

1

Soviets were unwilling to apply sanctions against Iran to U.N. Resolution 598 on ending the Iran-Iraq war. In other words, Soviet policy was not as anti-Iranian as American policy was, but it was not pro-Iranian either, and the Soviets were not willing to help Iran enough to endanger their long-standing ties to Iraq. Tehran's inability to get the kind of aid from the Soviets that the Iranians wanted (and frequently announced that they wanted) was clearly one factor in Iran's economic and military collapse, which led to its pursuit of a cease-fire and peace in August 1988. The Iran-Iraq war was one of several foreign conflicts in which the Soviets under Mikhail Gorbachev actively sought peace, in part to save money on arms sent abroad.

Between the conflict of 1946 and the cooperation of 1988 to end its war with Iraq, Iran was the scene of several events central to the Cold War. But Iran's importance to struggle between great powers was nothing new. In the modern period alone, Iran was a focus of conflict in the nineteenth century between Russia and Great Britain, which feared Russian advances toward India. Much of the exaggerated British rhetoric in this period expressing fears of Russian expansion sounds similar to what was heard in the United States during the Cold War, as is suggested in chapter 4, by Muriel Atkin. In the early twentieth century various Western powers vied for influence in Iran, with Great Britain and Nazi Germany emerging as the most important contestants in the interwar period.

The reasons for Iran's importance to the major powers are not far to seek. Its long borders on Russia and the Persian Gulf made Iran a possible target for Russian expansion, and it abutted the routes to British India. The British had an exaggerated fear during much of the nineteenth century that Russia would take over more Iranian territory or use trade and transport to move closer to the Gulf and to India. In fact, both Britain and Russia wanted to keep Iran as one of several buffer zones that would prevent them from coming into direct contact and likely conflict where the Indian and Russian empires approached each other. This desire of both countries on the one hand to gain as much political and economic advantage as possible and on the other to avoid the conquest or partition of Iran was responsible for keeping Iran from colonial rule, while at the same time placing it from the early nineteenth century until the Bolshevik Revolution largely under the indirect control of the British and the Russians (each of whom had periods of dominance).

This position under the strong influence of two hostile parties taught Iranian rulers that their best chance to retain meaningful independence was to play one party against the other in time-honored manner. Although there is nothing peculiarly Iranian about this means of maneuvering (it is often the only tactic open to a weak party), the Iranians have proved to be very good at it, and they have often been aided by the conviction of foreigners that Iranians are irrational, incomprehensible, and not to be taken seriously. As recently as the Iran-Contra affair, the Iranians were able to obtain large amounts of arms from the United States in return for almost nothing that the United States cared about (see chapter 7, by James Bill), and in the view of Robert Freedman, they were able to play comparable games with the Soviets from a position of extreme weakness (see chapter 5).

Perhaps Iran's long history of subjection to outside conquerors and dominant powers is partly responsible for the cultural features that foreigners find so baffling. Indirection and an avoidance of speaking frankly offer protection against menacing rulers and outsiders. In addition, numerous experiences with foreigners who undermined popular Iranian movements and leaders have lent weight to ideologies and movements that center on the need to suppress foreign influence. The most notable examples of these are the movements led by Mohammad Mosaddeq against the British oil concession and the Islamic Revolution of Ayatollah Khomeini, marked by the slogan "neither East nor West." There is nothing irrational about a dominated Third World country seeking to suppress the influence of great powers, although the conviction that this suppression can be complete and will solve all problems is unrealistic and illusory, whether it comes in nationalist or religious guise.

After the Bolshevik Revolution, Soviet Russia renounced virtually all loans and concessions in Iran, and the Soviets were not a major player there between the wars. Iran's value to the outside world had increased markedly in 1908 with the discovery of oil, which came to be effectively monopolized by the Anglo-Iranian Oil Company (AIOC), most shares of which were bought by the British government. Great Britain, with both oil and the Persian Gulf to consider, was the most interested party in Iran in the interwar years, and a British general was the main influence behind the scenes in bringing about the coup d'état of Reza Khan in 1921. In 1925 Reza himself named the first shah of the Pahlavi dynasty after deposing the Qajars. He was far from being a mere tool of the British, however, and he emulated Ataturk in Turkey by undertaking a series of reforms to increase national strength, unity, and independence, and decrease the power of decentralizing leaders tied to the old socioeconomic system—especially the clergy and tribal leaders. Like Ataturk's reforms, Reza Shah's program of modernization provided for a degree of liberation for women, already advocated by progressive women earlier in the century. Partly to free himself of British power and partly under the influence of the Nazis' Aryan nationalism, Reza Shah also allowed German economic and political influence in Iran to grow in the 1930s.

This increase in German influence contributed to the reassertion of Soviet and British control in mid-1941, after Hitler attacked the Soviet Union. The British and Soviets wished to use Iran as the best available supply route from the West to the Soviet Union, and they demanded among other things that Iran expel German nationals who they believed were agents. In the face of Russo-British occupation and control, Reza Shah abdicated and was forced into exile by the British, to be succeeded by his young son Mohammad Reza. Although this reintroduced more decentralized, parliamentary government under the constitution of 1906–07, which had seldom been enforced, it also gave extraordinary political power to the British and Soviet forces now occupying Iran, as well as to the American forces who joined them after the United States entered the war in December 1941.

Conflict between the great powers for the control of Iran was renewed in 1946, when the Soviets failed to live up to an agreement specifying the date of their withdrawal from northern Iran. (Richard Herrmann gives details about this period in chapter 3.) Although Soviet attempts to influence events in Iran were what rated headlines abroad, more important in the long run was the steady increase in American power over Iran's central government, economy, and military. To Iranian nationalists, however, the United States was not yet a major source of concern, because once the Soviet troops had left, the British were a more obvious target. Particular causes for anger were their monopoly control of oil and the continued dramatic growth of British oil profits while Iranian royalties remained very low. American oil companies elsewhere in the Middle East had begun so-called 50-50 deals, and some American diplomats in fact encouraged the Iranians to demand a better deal from the British. The nationalist movement culminated in the nationalization of the Anglo-Iranian Oil Company in early 1951, and in the prime ministership of Mohammad Mosaddeq. The United States was hostile toward Mosaddeq, especially after Dwight Eisenhower and his secretary of state, John Foster Dulles, took office in early 1953, and later in the year it adopted a British plan to overthrow him. Oil theoretically remained "nationalized," but all major decisions were now to be made by an international consortium in which the AIOC had a 40 percent share and American companies another 40 percent.

The restoration to power of the Shah in 1953 resulted in the de facto abandonment of constitutional parliamentary rule. Although parliaments remained, they were essentially handpicked by the Shah and those around him, and never again were there independent prime ministers at odds with the Shah. The dictatorial power of the Shah rested largely on the backing given him by the United States, which included major support from the military and secret police (see chapter 6, by Mark Gasiorowski). The Shah became a kind of American, or Anglo-American, surrogate in the Gulf, especially after the British withdrew their forces there. Active in the North Yemeni civil war of the 1960s on the royalist-Saudi side, the Shah was even more involved with sending troops to put down leftist rebels in the Dhofar province in Oman. At the same time, the United States sent advisers to help train the Shah's principal secret police, SAVAK, a job also undertaken by Israel. (Although the large Israeli advisory and military role in Iran is not extensively considered in this book, it was if anything more important than that of Germany in the 1930s and caused far more internal resentment.)

After 1946 the United States built up its power and influence in Iran to the point where the dictatorial Shah was widely and plausibly considered to be essentially an American tool. The Soviets, however, were much less successful in influencing Iran, despite their location on Iran's border. The record indicates that far from being reckless and expansionist, the Soviet Union did not pay careful enough attention to Iran to understand what was happening there, and almost never took any action that might risk confrontation with the United States. Even its support of the Marxist Tudeh Party was sporadic and often abandoned when the alternative of improving relations with the Iranian government presented itself. The whole history of Soviet relations with Iran from 1946 to 1988 suggests that the dominant Soviet goal was to be on good terms with those in power—whether it was the Shah or the mollas—and that whenever better relations with Iran's government became possible, direct criticism of it was usually muted. The Soviets believed that a leftist, revolutionary orientation was attainable in Iran only in the period immediately after World War II, and perhaps again just after the revolution of 1979; even at these moments there was no encouragement of guerrillas or of violent activities such as those undertaken by the Islamic leftist Mojahedin-e Khalq or the Marxist Feda'iyan-e Khalq.

Notwithstanding the usual picture of the Soviet Union and communism as aggressive and revolutionary, the postwar history of Iran both under the Shah and under Khomeini offers no real evidence that the Soviets tried effectively to convert Iran to communism or to a leftist, united-front government. The apparent exceptions to this occurred in the military, where both in the mid-1950s and in the 1980s communist cadres were uncovered. But the evidence that the Soviets were unwilling to take actions that risked confrontation with the West, and their lack for more than forty years of any effective plan to increase their real influence in Iran, call into question whether the communist groups in the army would have been used except in the most improbable circumstances. When the Tudeh had significant popular support (ca. 1943–55), the Soviets did not build on it with effective mass movements. Partly because the Tudeh followed misguided Soviet analyses, they failed to take advantage even of the major anti-imperialist movement that occurred when Mosaddeq was in power.

Instead, the Tudeh withheld support from Mosaddeq at critical times, such as during the 1953 coup against him.

The period from 1946 to 1978 was therefore characterized by a decline in British influence, a dramatic rise in American influence, a significant growth in Israeli influence (largely clandestine), and a sporadic Soviet influence that never came close to bringing about a coup or revolution or to influencing the government strongly. To a degree the Soviets were content to have good relations with the Shah, as they did in the 1970s, with substantial economic cooperation, trade, and small sales of arms.

The sixties and especially the seventies in Iran may have seemed a period of relatively satisfactory relations from the viewpoint of the great powers, but the Iranian population generally did not see things this way. Iran had a long history of outside control, but also of mass resistance to this control. In 1891–92 the Iranians, led by bazaar merchants and the clergy, launched a nationwide movement against a British monopoly concession to Iranian tobacco. The movement became so widespread and unified that the Shah was forced to cancel the concession. In 1905–11 a revolution led by the bazaar, intellectuals, and parts of the clergy succeeded in gaining from the Shah a constitution and parliament. Like the earlier movement, this one was largely directed against foreign control of Iran. Several uprisings after World War I were similarly directed against foreign control, as was the oil nationalization after World War II; in all these movements arbitrary rulers in Iran were also a target.

Many Iranians never forgave the United States for supporting the overthrow of Mosaddeq. A movement led by the clergy against the government that took place in 1962–63, a decade after the overthrow, was generally dismissed in the West as simply a reactionary religious movement against reform, but in fact it was underpinned by strong anti-American sentiment. Ayatollah Khomeini, who now emerged as the leader of the antigovernment clergy, did join in clerical objections to women's suffrage, but he was careful not to take a position on land reform, thus suggesting that he was concerned with popular support. His chief target was the Iranian government's subservience to the United States and Israel, a point he stressed again in 1964 just before he was exiled, when an unpopular agreement on the status of forces was passed by the Iranian parliament; this greatly expanded diplomatic immunity by granting it to the American military and their families.

Hostility toward American control of Iran was a prominent feature of the revolution of 1979, along with hostility toward Iranian ties to Israel. Relations with the United States worsened further after the crisis that began in late 1979 when the Iranians held U.S. officials hostage. Although the revolution's slogan "neither East nor West" has had different meanings at different times (as Maziar

Behrooz shows in chapter 1), for much of the time it has been especially an anti-American slogan.

Yet the highly ideological nature of the Iranian Revolution has often aligned its leaders against almost all foreign powers, and it was not only the United States but also the Soviet Union that contributed to Iran's losses in the war with Iraq. Although Iraq was the aggressor in the war, this was not enough to win for Iran the sympathy of other governments. In addition to Iraq and its Arab allies, Iran in the end found itself taking on France, a chief supplier of arms to Iraq, and the United States, which massively entered the Gulf and the tanker war in Iraq's behalf. At the same time, Iran was alienating the Soviet Union, with which its relations had already deteriorated since 1983, when leaders of the Tudeh Party were arrested and Soviet leaders were expelled. Iran was also aiding anti-Soviet rebels in Afghanistan and long resisted Soviet efforts to get Iran to settle the war with Iraq on the basis of the status quo ante. Adding to Iran's problems were Iraq's use of poison gas and its missile attacks on Iranian cities. It should have been clear to Iran that it was not large or strong enough to win a war against its adversary, both superpowers, and a host of other hostile nations.

Iran tried during the war to compensate in part for its difficulties with the United States and the Soviet Union by cultivating relations with other powers, and it has continued to do so since the war (a point dealt with only peripherally in this book). These other powers include Japan, which buys much oil from Iran and has economic projects there, West Germany, and Italy. Dramatic incidents cut Iran's ties to France, Great Britain, and Canada for a time, but these were restored in 1988—only to be set back in early 1989 by the controversy surrounding Salman Rushdie, which for a time hurt prospects for increased trade and economic relations. Diversified relations with much of the Third World and with Eastern Europe have continued. Iran is thus not the pariah nation it may have appeared to be from the point of view of the United States. The cease-fire with Iraq and the Soviet withdrawal from Afghanistan lifted some of the obstacles to stronger links between Iran and the superpowers, and links with the Soviets in particular were strengthened in early 1989.

As the 1980s neared an end, the first signs of better relations with the United States appeared in the summer 1989 Lebanese hostage crisis. Relations with the Soviets have improved, but although, on the one hand, Mikhail Gorbachev is moving for peace and goodwill all over the world, on the other he and his supporters are cutting back on uneconomical expenditures abroad, and it is just such expenditures that Iran wants most from the Soviet Union. In the past unfulfilled Soviet-Iranian projects, such as restored deliveries of Iranian natural gas to the Soviets, essentially foundered on Iran's expectations that the Soviets would make investments or set prices that benefited Iran but were unprofitable for themselves. At the same time, the adherents of one school of Soviet thought, reflecting a particular interpretation of the Soviet-American rapprochement, would like the Soviet Union and the United States to cooperate in fighting the dangers of Khomeinism felt in some Muslim parts of the Soviet Union. (This was essentially the position taken by Igor Belyaev at the conference on which this book is based.) But the dominant Soviet trend is toward improving economic and political ties to Iran, not toward joining the West in criticizing or pressuring it. The Soviets appear not to have made a point of Iran's executions of Tudeh and other leftists in late 1988.

American relations with Iran have been tense ever since the revelations of the Iran-Contra affair, particularly in view of the need felt afterward for the United States to end the mistrust the affair caused among "moderate" and anti-Iranian Arab states (discussed by Eric Hooglund in chapter 8). There continue to be strains between Iran and the United States, and to a much lesser degree, between Iran and the Soviet Union. It seems, however, probable that if the lessening of tensions worldwide continues this will be reflected in the state of affairs between Iran and the superpowers: first, because Iran is impoverished and it is expensive to have conflicts with two countries that are uniquely positioned to make its life harder, and second, because improved Soviet-Amerian relations remove much of the impetus that in the past led the United States and the Soviet Union each to encourage hostile acts by Iran toward the other.

There is also a little-noted confluence of similar economic forces in all three countries that has been moving them toward peace and reduced expenditure on armaments. In each case a military buildup undertaken in the past has caused growing domestic economic problems. This has been most noticeable in the Soviet Union, where the stress is now on organizing the economy rather than on military expenditures; as with the United States, many of the arms produced at home have been sent abroad. There seems little doubt that Gorbachev's reforms are motivated largely by a desire to create a viable economy, and that the Soviet Union's reduction or abandonment of some weapons systems and its willingness to end wars in the Third World stem from the need to redirect investment and effect dramatic economic changes. (Naturally, there are also other, more ideological components to the new policies.) In relation to Iran, this policy means that the Soviets preferred to see an end to the war with Iraq, that they did not provide arms to either side to the degree that this was politically possible, and that they did not give Iran all the economic concessions it wanted.

The United States is also feeling an economic pinch, caused partly by huge and often wasteful expenditures on armaments. This helped make President Reagan and his supporters mitigate their anti-Soviet ideology and consider Soviet proposals to reduce arms, which were in any event favorable to the United States. Because the Soviet economic crisis is worse than the American one, the United States has been able to profit from the Soviet Union's willingness to concede points, without having to concede as much. In a sense the Soviets are helping the United States to deal with its budgetary problems, for the United States can abandon or slow the development of weapons systems without worrying about countervailing Soviet military strength. With regard to Iran, economic change and the new Soviet foreign policy positions, especially on Afghanistan, should mean that the United States has less incentive than before to maneuver in behalf of installing an Iranian government friendly to the United States and hostile to the Soviets, or to supply with armaments any government that claims anti-Soviet credentials. A Soviet-American agreement not to intervene in Iran of the kind suggested by Bruce Kuniholm (see chapter 9) may become a real possibility, given more rational policies by the United States in the future. And if Iran adopts for its foreign policy the rational basis suggested by R. K. Ramazani (chapter 2), better relations with the United States can be possible in any case.

Just as the Soviet Union and the United States moved in the late 1980s toward partial disarmament, peace, and moderation largely because of their economic and military overextension, Iran's international position may well become moderated because of similar problems. For all its occasional rhetoric, Iran seems to have accepted the reality of Islamic revolution in only one country, even though maverick groups may still carry out extreme acts abroad. Most of Iran's leaders see the importance of economic reconstruction, and even though Iran now stresses economic ties with Eastern Europe and Asia, increased Western ties in the future seem probable. Like the Soviet Union and the United States, Iran is faced with a recent heritage of economic policies that were not very successful, and it is also faced with some basic decisions, particularly as regards the relative roles in the economy of government and the private sector.

In addition, Iran has been caught since the late 1980s in a battle of succession and ruled by a factionalized government. Without venturing to predict what the final outcome will be, I note that Iran's situation is quite different from that of well-known dictatorships after World War II, when most foreigners would have been hard put to name anyone strong in the countries other than their dictators. In Iran, Khomeini was not a true dictator: he usually gave his views at the end of a long and largely public debate if he gave them at all. The electorate, the parliament, and several men in public positions have all played a major role in Iran. Power already centered in Hashemi-Rafsanjani and Khamene'i even before they were elected president and *faqih*. They still must deal with the "radical" faction and it is not possible to predict the outcome with certainty. There may be major changes, but, as in China and the Soviet Union, the new leaders began by proclaiming their fidelity to Khomeini's heritage. For the near future, change in the system seems far more likely to come from within than by any overthrow, especially in the absence of a significant organized opposition.

Predictions are always hazardous. It is not to be ruled out that Iran's development will be unexpected or that the Cold War will revive and Iran will again be seen as a prize in the Great Game. The major dangers and negative consequences to the great powers of playing with Third World nations would seem to have been adequately demonstrated in the case of Iran, however, and it is to be hoped that the more peaceful and constructive trends that have recently begun in the world will continue and will have an increasing impact on relations between the great powers and Iran. For all the strong rhetoric that sometimes emanates from Iran, its government since 1988 has not been adventurist in foreign policy. Better Iranian relations with the United States and continued improvement of relations with the Soviet Union remain possible, given flexibility on all sides.

The View from Tehran

1

Trends in the Foreign Policy of the Islamic Republic of Iran, 1979–1988

MAZIAR BEHROOZ

The 1979 revolution in Iran opened a new chapter in the conduct of Iranian foreign policy. With the establishment of the Islamic Republic of Iran (IRI) the nation's foreign policy changed from a basically pro-Western stance to one summed up by the slogan "neither East nor West" (*nah sharq, nah gharb*).[1] Yet, this slogan, which was introduced to Iranian society by the new Islamic leadership, has not had the same meaning for the different factions that have taken their turn in ruling the country. Rather, the foreign policy of the IRI since the 1979 revolution has embodied a series of inconsistent goals that, depending on the ruling faction of the day, have reflected differing interpretations of the slogan.

Although the Islamic leadership that took over after the collapse of the imperial regime was made up of different factions, all of them had come to accept Ayatollah Khomeini's version of an Islamic state, which was based on the notion of the "rule of the jurisprudent" (*velayat-e faqih*). These groups, who in fact had little in common in their worldviews, together made up the new ruling Islamic elite. They included, first, the Islamic "liberals," or the secular Islamic activists who had been involved in the nationalist opposition to the Shah's regime, and, second, the clerics, who tended to view the Islamic state as a more theocratic entity.

The foreign policy of the IRI may be divided into three periods:

1. The period of the "liberals," February 1979–June 1981, when the so-

called liberal faction of the new Islamic elite was in charge of IRI foreign policy. This period may be further subdivided into the Provisional Government period (February–November 1979), when Mehdi Bazargan and his allies were in charge of IRI foreign policy, and the presidency of Abol Hasan Bani-Sadr (January 1980–June 1981), whose departure marked the end of liberal rule.

2. The period 1981–84, when an isolationist trend dominated the IRI's foreign policy. This period saw a process of consolidation, competition, and the polarization of two ruling *maktabi* (committed and doctrinaire) factions, mainly over domestic issues. At this time the "neither East nor West" policy was implemented according to a strict isolationist interpretation.

3. The period of pragmatists, 1984–89, which has witnessed the coming to power of a reformist faction with a pragmatic approach to foreign policy. This faction has operated under a new set of rules and has adopted a more open-door approach to foreign powers.

This chapter will initially analyze Khomeini's view on foreign policy. Then it will discuss IRI foreign policy–making in the three periods and will conclude by addressing certain important questions about the future path of IRI foreign policy.

Khomeini's Views on Foreign Policy

With regard to the superpowers, Khomeini said, "We must settle our accounts with great and superpowers, and show them that we can take on the whole world ideologically, despite all the painful problems that face us,"[2] and he declared, "We will not agree to be dominated by America or by the Soviet Union. . . . The superpowers wish to dominate human beings."[3] In Khomeini's theory, a state ruled by an Islamic jurisprudent (*faqih*) was the means by which a just society could be established. Iran had become the first true modern Islamic state, but the "Islamic Revolution" could not be limited to that country alone. Khomeini's foreign policy doctrine, based on the slogan "neither East nor West," should be understood within the context of his trans-Iranian goals. Not only must the IRI remain independent of the superpowers, but it must seek to promote just Islamic societies in other regions.

In elaborating Iran's foreign policy in 1980, Khomeini said, "We say we want to export our revolution to all Islamic countries as well as to the oppressed countries. . . . We want all nations and governments to sever the control of superpowers over their resources. Export of our revolution means that all nations grow aware and save themselves."[4] Thus, his foreign policy formula for the IRI had two interconnected dimensions: first, its independence vis-à-vis the great powers, and second, the promotion of Islamic movements in other areas, or what became known outside of Iran as its attempt to export the "Islamic Revolution." Not surprisingly, this outlook has alarmed several other nations.

To Khomeini's views on the foreign policy of the IRI must be added the factor of Israel and South Africa. These two states, according to him, permit no compromise as far as an Islamic state is concerned.

Khomeini's views are often echoed by the IRI's media and its top leaders. Ayatollah Mohammad Hosain Beheshti wrote in 1980, "Islam recognizes no borders. . . . The foreign policy of the IRI, therefore, cannot be based on isolation. Our policy must tell us what to do beyond the borders and what relations to have with the people beyond these borders."[5] And the daily *Jomhuri-ye Islami* stated in 1985, "In the view of the Islamic Republic of Iran, there is no difference between Eastern and Western colonialism. The domineering powers, as we pointed out before, despite all their differences and rivalries are coherent and share the same direction in one thing: that is, combating the Islamic and independence-seeking movements."[6]

It is not clear which countries fall in the categories of East and West. One would think that the Islamic leaders were referring to the Eastern and Western blocs, or the Soviet Union's East European socialist allies and America's allies, the West European capitalist democracies and Japan. But in practice, although acting hostilely toward the United States and, to a lesser extent, the Soviet Union, the IRI has tried to maintain, as much as possible, normal relations with the allies of the superpowers.

The meaning of exporting the "Islamic Revolution" is also unclear. Does it merely mean, as Khomeini implied, that the IRI should set an example so that other countries will become aware of their situation as colonies of East and West? Or does it mean the active promotion of Islamic movements, as happened when the IRI supported the attempted coup in Bahrain in January 1980, IRI supporters bombed Kuwait in December 1983, the Islamic Revolutionary Guards (*pasdaran-e enqelab-e islami;* hereafter, the Guards) were sent to Lebanon, and the IRI became involved in the hostage situation in Lebanon? Even the country's constitution is ambiguous on this subject. This document, which outlines the main governing laws of Iran, also sets the general foreign policy objectives of the Islamic state. Article 154 says, "While refraining from all interference in domestic affairs of other nations, the Islamic Republic shall support any struggle of deprived people against the oppressing classes anywhere on the face of the earth."[7] This, of course, is a paradox: IRI must refrain from interfering in the domestic affairs of other countries and, at the same time, support movements in other countries to overthrow their governments.

Foreign Policy—Making in the Islamic Republic of Iran

The Period of the Liberals (February 1979–June 1981)

The affairs of the new Islamic state, following the success of the revolution, were entrusted to Mehdi Bazargan and his allies. The Provisional Government was in fact a coalition between the Islamic liberal Freedom Movement and the secular National Front, which participated as a junior partner and whose leader, Karim Sanjabi, was the foreign minister of the Provisional Government during the first few months. Yet the Freedom Movement and its leader, Bazargan (who had formed his government on the basis of a mandate from Khomeini), clearly enjoyed hegemony in the cabinet—and indeed, the National Front elements soon left it.

The Provisional Government had its own interpretation of "neither East nor West." According to this interpretation, the IRI should remain an independent political entity (as Khomeini wished), but should be more receptive to the West in order to check the influence and threat of the East. The following recollection of an American policymaker about the views of Ibrahim Yazdi (the Provisional Government's foreign minister after Sanjabi) on this subject helps explain the Provisional Government's perception of foreign policy:

> In foreign affairs, Yazdi outlined a policy of strict nonalignment which he compared to the U.S. isolation of the past. They would not seek stability through a military buildup. He stressed the deep popular resentment and hatred toward the United States for its unconditional support of the shah since 1953, but he felt that friendly future relations were possible if Americans stopped interfering in Iranian affairs. He said Iran had "no better memories" of the Russians than of the Americans . . . [but] "at least Americans believe in God."[8]

People like Yazdi and Bazargan were among those whom the U.S. policymakers chose to call the moderates of the new Islamic leadership. And it was this group that American officials thought would replace the imperial regime.

There is an abundance of evidence regarding the Provisional Government's pro-West tendencies in the *Documents from the Nest of Spies* (*Asnad- e Laneh-ye Jasusi;* hereafter Documents), selected from the papers seized from the U.S. embassy after the takeover by the Muslim Students Following the Imam's Line (SFIL) in November 1979.[9] The Documents acknowledge the U.S. embassy personnel's awareness of a difference of opinion between Khomeini and the Provisional Government on the issue of relations with the United States.

The embassy reported on 31 May 1979: "PGOI [the Provisional Government] and Khomeini differ on value of U.S. ties. Khomeini's open anti-Americanism has sparked increase in anti-American activity."[10] This was at a time when the embassy observed that both Ibrahim Yazdi and Abbas Amir-Entezam (the Provisional Government's spokesperson) had publicly expressed their government's wish to continue contacts with the West and had hoped that relations with the United States would "soon take a turn for the better."[11] The last U.S. ambassador to Tehran, William Sullivan, suggested to his superiors that both Bazargan and Entezam displayed much distrust of the Soviets and desired to maintain close relations with the United States.[12]

Signs of the Provisional Government's positive attitude toward America, but within the context of "neither East nor West," can also be seen in its approach to the United States toward the end of its period of rule. The meeting between Bazargan and Zbigniew Brzezinski in Algiers on 1 November 1979, one of the factors contributing to the downfall of the Provisional Government, further explains the foreign policy objectives of the liberals. The IRI delegation to Algeria that took part in the meeting with Brzezinski included Bazargan, Yazdi, and Mostafa Chamran (the defense minister). According to Brzezinski, the issue of the Shah and his return to Iran, although publicly stressed by Iran, was not a major concern, indicating that Bazargan's main objective was a strategic one. Brzezinski reported that the overall relationship between the two countries was discussed.

The Provisional Government did not last long after the Algiers meeting. Following the admission of the Shah to the United States and the takeover of the U.S. embassy in Tehran on 4 November 1979, the Bazargan government collapsed, with both domestic and foreign policy factors contributing to its downfall. Domestically, many paralegal institutions had been created by the new Islamic elite after the revolution. These institutions, which existed alongside and parallel to the old imperial ones, were autonomous and independent from the Provisional Government. It may be that a kind of dual power was in place, with the Provisional Government controlling the old state apparatus. The paralegal institutions (such as the Guards and the security committees, or *komiteh*) were a rallying ground for those in the ruling elite who opposed Bazargan and his policies. The clergy-dominated Islamic Republic Party (IRP) was the manifestation of this group, and powerful personalities such as Ayatollah Beheshti, Ali Akbar Hashemi-Rafsanjani, Ali Khamene'i, Javad Bahonar, and Hasan Ayat were among its leaders. The IRP opposed the Provisional Government's interpretation of "neither East nor West" and any reconstruction of relations with the United States. It may be that the IRP was shrewdly playing along with the mass anti-Americanism then rampant and Khomeini's distrust of the United

States. In any event, the differences between the Provisional Government and the IRP ranged from economic to foreign affairs issues, and it was two of the latter that played a direct role in the Provisional Government's demise: the Shah's admission into the United States and the Brzezinski-Bazargan meeting in Algiers. A recently published book in Iran on the foreign policy of the IRI reflects the views of the group that opposed the Provisional Government. *Reviewing the IRI Foreign Policy* states: "Then the foreign policy of Iran reached a point where the prime minister of the Provisional Government met with Carter's National Security Advisor [Brzezinski] and in order to justify his action, suggested: 'We must reconstruct our foreign policy which has been damaged during the revolution by apologizing to the United States for the slogan "Down with America." ' "[13]

The collapse of the Provisional Government was followed in a few months by the presidency of Bani-Sadr, although he had already clashed with Khomeini over foreign policy. During the period between the fall of Bazargan's government and the presidential election in December 1979, the Revolutionary Council was directing the affairs of the state and had chosen Bani-Sadr to take charge of the foreign ministry. When, in December 1979, the subject of the American hostages came before the U.N. Security Council, Bani-Sadr suggested that Iran participate. This ran counter to the publicly stated position of Khomeini, who absolutely rejected it and sent a message to Bani-Sadr threatening him with dismissal. Subsequently Bani-Sadr resigned from his post.[14]

During Bani-Sadr's administration (January 1979–June 1981) three major foreign policy issues preoccupied his government: the Iran-Iraq war, the U.S. embassy hostages, and the Afghan war. On the first issue, the IRI faced the difficult situation of fighting Iraq while under strong U.S. and international pressure to release the American hostages. The Islamic elite believed that both superpowers were involved in the war despite their public claims of neutrality, and Bani-Sadr devoted much energy to Iran's war efforts. On the hostage issue, the IRI was in a direct confrontation with the United States. The American efforts to isolate the IRI internationally in order to secure the release of the hostages were successful, and this frustrated Bani-Sadr's initiatives in foreign policy. On the Afghan issue, the IRI was in an indirect confrontation with the Soviet Union, whose military occupation of Afghanistan gave rise to friction between the two countries. Thus at a time of isolation from the West, a possible opening to the East was closed off by the Afghan war. No matter how Bani-Sadr interpreted "neither East nor West," objective conditions left him little room to maneuver, and his administration remained relatively isolated on the international scene.

Bani-Sadr's foreign policy objectives remained basically the same as those of the Provisional Government except that he was perhaps more suspicious of the United States. He favored close relations with Western European countries, which he hoped would join with Iran to resist U.S. hegemony.[15]

Bani-Sadr's preoccupation with the American hostages, which soon became the indicator of who was in charge of foreign policy, was the most time-consuming aspect of his administration. His plans for centralizing government and ending the dual power, for economic growth and stabilization, and for reforming the armed forces went hand in hand with the need to normalize Iran's foreign relations. But the hostage situation restrained his actions. He blamed the hostage-taking for Iran's economic isolation, feared more direct U.S. retaliatory action against Iran, was displeased with the SFIL's autonomy, and needed the billions of dollars in frozen Iranian assets in American banks. But his efforts to secure the release of the hostages and take command of foreign policy were resisted by his opponents in the IRP, with Khomeini's help. Bani-Sadr wanted the fate of the hostages to be decided by the Revolutionary Council, but on 23 February 1980, Khomeini undercut his position and decided that the Majles, whose election was set for March 1980, should rule on the issue, a decision that put off resolution of the situation indefinitely. On 6 March the SFIL defied Bani-Sadr and refused to hand over the hostages to the Revolutionary Council.

After the Majles elections in March and May 1980, Bani-Sadr found himself in a weakened position because his opponents had gained a strong majority. From this point on his situation worsened. The Majles rejected all his choices for prime minister and he was forced to accept Mohammad Ali Raja'i, a rival and IRP member, for the post. Next came the question of cabinet ministers: Bani-Sadr thought that competence and experience should be the criteria for choosing them, but Raja'i insisted on their ideological devotion to the system. Raja'i proposed a cabinet of twenty-one members in September 1980, and Bani-Sadr rejected seven of them, including the foreign minister. In the end, he rejected at least six candidates for the foreign ministry and the post remained vacant throughout his administration.[16]

After the hostage crisis was resolved, Bani-Sadr moved to end Iran's isolation in the international community, and high-ranking IRI delegations were sent abroad. But these efforts were limited by his opponents, who had their own agenda on foreign as well as domestic issues. This opposition, which went under the unofficial title of maktabi, centered around the clergy-dominated IRP.

As noted earlier, the maktabis had formed their own paralegal governing organs to function alongside the old imperial structures, which were controlled by the liberals. The SFIL members were in close association with the maktabis, and after the takeover of the U.S. embassy, they selectively used the documents they found to expose the pro-West tendencies of the liberals. Hence, after the collapse of the Provisional Government, documents were published connecting top members of the Freedom Movement (such as Amir-Entezam, Yazdi, and Bazargan) to foreign powers. Bani-Sadr's connections to foreigners were exposed only after his dismissal, and such connections on the part of clerics like Beheshti were not aired. Thus, during the hostage crisis the maktabis unofficially played an important role in the foreign policy of the IRI by using popular anti-American feeling against the liberals. The maktabis eventually won the struggle and managed to oust the liberals and take control of the state apparatus as a whole. Following the June 1981 crisis, Bani-Sadr was ousted from power, and severe repressive measures were taken against the opposition.

The Maktabi Period (1981–84)

From 1981 to 1984, the IRI underwent a deep internal crisis that included repression of the opposition. The maktabis were strongly influenced by the SFIL—a reality that manifested itself in Iran's foreign policy. The maktabis, naturally, had their own interpretation of "neither East nor West," and it was very narrow: the IRI adopted a strict isolationist foreign policy; hence this period may also be called the isolationist period. A high-ranking IRI leader, Ayatollah Mohammad Hosain Ali Montazeri, expressed the sentiments of this period very well. In a speech delivered to a group of theology students, he said that the IRI should not be fooled by either the West or the East because the West had helped establish and maintain Israel and the East had massacred the clergy in Afghanistan.[17]

The causes of the IRI's isolation from the West were both historical and contemporary. The major historical factor was the United States' support of the Shah's dictatorship, including the U.S.-planned coup of 1953; its active part in implementing the Shah's land reform program; its training and support for the Shah's military and security forces; and its support of the imperial regime during the revolutionary struggle of 1978–79. Moreover, the IRI constantly feared intervention in Iran from the United States. Other factors that helped promote the isolationist trend were (1) the IRI's attempts to export Islamic revolution, which were perceived by the West as efforts to undermine the stability of pro-West governments in the region; (2) the role of some Western powers, especially France, in supplying the Iraqi war effort and providing sanctuary for exiled IRI opposition figures; (3) the anti-Americanism of some IRI foreign policy–makers; and (4) the Reagan administration's emphasis on restoring America's prestige abroad and combating terrorism with force. These factors, as well as the fact that the liberals had become notorious for their pro-

West tendencies, kept the IRI from undertaking any rapprochement with the West.

The causes of the IRI's isolation from the East were somewhat different. To begin with, the Soviet Union certainly did not share the same historical background as the United States as far as Iran was concerned. Any direct Soviet involvement in Iranian affairs had ended with the aborted 1946 Azerbaijan venture. The Soviets' interests were manifested indirectly either through the Tudeh Party or through diplomatic means. Although some strong anti-Soviet elements within the ruling elite could point to instances of Soviet damage to Iranian national interests, they were not thought to be comparable to those of the United States. Other causes for the isolation of the IRI from the East were (1) the Soviet Union's military support to Iraq; (2) the Soviet military occupation of Afghanistan; (3) the activities of the Tudeh Party of Iran; and (4) the hostility toward the Soviet Union felt by some circles within the ruling elite. The Soviet Union considered both Iran and Iraq to have anti-imperialist tendencies and therefore took a neutral position toward the war. Nevertheless, this did not prevent it from fulfilling its military obligations toward Iraq, which proved to be a major impediment to close relations with the IRI.

The Afghan war was an even more contentious issue. The occupation of Afghanistan by an atheist state and the Afghan mujahedin's resistance were reason enough to involve the IRI in the struggle, undeterred by the fact that the United States was also deeply involved. Iran's support for some mujahedin factions and its demand that the Soviet Union evacuate Afghanistan remained major problems between the two states.

The activities of the Tudeh became another source of tension after the party was attacked and disbanded by the government in 1982–83. The confessions of the Tudeh leaders after their arrests further aggravated Iran-Soviet relations, especially when party members implied in their statements that they had been spying for the Soviet Union. Nevertheless, it must be noted that Iran-Soviet relations never reached the same level of antagonism as did relations between Iran and the United States. The Soviet Union always kept its embassy in Tehran open and fully operational, and the level of trade between the two countries was significant and continued to grow up to the time of the Tudeh arrests. After the arrests and the confessions of 1983, however, the volume of trade was reduced by 50 percent and fell to its lowest point.[18] This is how Ali Akbar Nateq-Nuri, minister of state, summarized Iran-Soviet relations in 1982–83: "The East initially thought that the Islamic revolution would turn to them after it had cut its ties with America. They only understood the 'nor West' portion of the Iranian people's slogan 'Neither East nor West.' The existence of such mercenaries as the Tudeh supported their belief. But as time passed, they began to realize that this revolution will not compromise with the East while it is fighting the West."[19]

The decision to attack the Tudeh was part of a larger plan apparently made in 1980. According to this fifteen-point plan, the opposition political parties were ranged into three categories, which the IRI would attempt to dismantle consecutively. The Tudeh's name fell in the third category, which meant that its turn would come after the more dangerous organizations were destroyed. Hence the assault on the Tudeh was not surprising and had little to do with the IRI's foreign relations.[20] The timing of the attack on the Tudeh was apparently associated with the defection, in 1982, of Vladimir Kuzichkin, a senior diplomat in the Soviet embassy in Tehran. The operation was run by British intelligence, which subsequently debriefed Kuzichkin. It seems that Kuzichkin knew the names of a number of Soviet agents in Iran, and according to the *New York Times,* this information was passed to the IRI through the CIA.[21] The fact that the Tudeh came under attack after this event shows that the IRI leadership must have sensed an immediate threat from Tudeh penetration of the government and moved quickly to contain the damage.

Another important component of the IRI's isolationist policy was the notion of exporting Islamic revolution. The advocates of isolationism believed that their Islamic Revolution could be maintained only through its expansion in the Moslem world, if not the world in general. Of course, the notion was not new. The policy had been part of Khomeini's worldview and was promoted by the maktabis during the liberal period. The only difference now was that the maktabis were in full control of the Islamic state. Neither was the idea of exporting their revolution a uniquely Iranian policy. Other revolutions had passed through a similar stage—for example, the French and Russian revolutions. The IRI supporters' activities in the region directed at this end included attempts made on objectives in Kuwait that led to the car bombing at the U.S. embassy; the efforts to overthrow the government of Bahrain and the renewal of Iranian claims on that island; the annual clashes with the Saudi regime during the hajj ceremonies; and IRI support for the Hizbollah (party of god) of Lebanon, which led to the car bombing of U.S. military installations and gradually gave the Hizbollah a dominant role in Lebanese affairs.[22]

The maktabis included a range of people who basically opposed the liberals' conduct of foreign and domestic affairs. Their main organizational base was the IRP, through which they controlled the paralegal structures noted earlier. But the unity of the maktabis was both temporary and fragile, and survived only as long as the liberals posed a threat. As soon as the liberal factor was removed, a process of polarization in domestic and foreign affairs began to take shape in the maktabi ranks.

The isolationist wing of the maktabis was basically in charge of foreign affairs from mid-1981 to 1984. The advocates of this policy were the SFIL and such personalities as Mir-Hosain Musavi, Ali Akbar Mohtashami, Hadi Ghaffari, and Hojjat al-Islam Mohammad Musavi Khoeiniha.

The Pragmatist Period (1984–89)

By 1984, a new trend, and therefore a new interpretation of "neither East nor West," had begun to take shape. A more pragmatic approach to the conduct of IRI foreign relations was adopted by a faction within the ruling elite. Only beginning in this period, it was later consolidated and continues to dominate IRI foreign policy to the present day. Pragmatism represented a reaction to the isolationist policy of the preceding years. Although no one event in 1984 can be singled out as the turning point, Khomeini's speech on 28 October 1984 to a group of IRI foreign representatives signaled the legitimization of the new trend: "The superpowers and the United States thought that Iran . . . would be forced into isolation. That did not happen and Iran's relations with foreigners increased. Now, they argue that relations with governments are of no use and our relations should be established with the nations. . . . This is contrary to wisdom and *shari'a*. We must have relations with all the governments."[23]

Clearly Khomeini was turning against isolationism. The seeds of the trend had been planted during previous years, but only now had it enough strength to claim Khomeini's support, and personalities such as Ali Akbar Velayati, the foreign minister, and Ali Akbar Hashemi-Rafsanjani, the Speaker of the Majles, had become its advocates. Conflict over the new interpretation could be detected in August 1984 in Majles discussions. The elections of the second Majles ended in June of that year and subsequently the cabinet stood for a new vote of confidence. During this process, Velayati came under limited but sharp attacks from some Majles members for his handling of IRI foreign policy. Mortaza Razavi, a member from Tabriz, criticized his loose interpretation of exporting revolution and his ministry's new approach to the West (in this case, the visit of West Germany's foreign minister to Tehran). Another member, Hadi Ghaffari, objected to Velayati's open-door policy and the fact that the Majles was not kept involved in shaping IRI foreign policy.[24] And a statement was distributed in the Majles strongly criticizing the government's foreign policy and comparing it to that of pro-Western governments.[25]

To put the development of the new trend in perspective, one should note the negative effects of the isolationist policy on the conduct of the Iran-Iraq war. After the victory of the battle for Khorramshahr (the only major city occupied by Iraq), which signaled the expulsion of Iraqi forces from Iranian territory

(1982), the IRI leadership made the decision to advance into Iraq and overthrow the Ba'ath regime. The principal question was whether the IRI could, with its limited economic and military resources, continue the war and at the same time confront both the West and the East. The isolationists' answer was positive, but the advocates of the new trend thought otherwise. To this must be added the growing economic difficulties faced by the IRI. Therefore, an objective need for revising the IRI's foreign policy was a strong factor in forcing a new interpretation of "neither East nor West." The IRI had to break out of its isolation in order to overcome its internal economic difficulties and to continue the war. The situation called for a pragmatic approach to foreign policy.

The first signs of the reinterpretation in regard to the East were the steps taken to try, once again, to normalize relations with the Soviet Union. By April 1985, the anti-Soviet propaganda had been toned down and negotiations started to reopen Tass offices in Tehran with an increased Soviet diplomatic staff.[26] The IRI also indicated its acceptance of the Soviet position that the Tudeh affair was a purely internal matter, thus removing a major source of tension in Iran-Soviet relations. Rafsanjani summed up the relationship between the two countries in 1985 as follows: "The relations with the Soviet Union have improved a little. . . . some problems are being removed. . . . we are informed that Soviet arms supplies to Iraq have been reduced somewhat. . . . We shall try to cooperate more in trade and industrial fields."[27] Rafsanjani insisted, however, that reaching an agreement over Afghanistan was not possible.

Economically, the chilly relations of preceding years began to change, though at a slow pace. The Soviet Union agreed to open its market to some Iranian goods, to send back the experts needed to finish industrial projects in Iran, and to accommodate other IRI economic demands. For its part, the IRI sent economic delegations to the Soviet Union and other East European countries.[28]

The new approach toward the West first became apparent in August 1984, when Velayati was criticized by Majles deputies for his attempts to move closer to the Western European countries. But the primary manifestation of the new trend was the "Irangate" affair. On the Iranian side, Irangate represented their approaching the West in general, and the United States in particular, in the hope of receiving assistance for the IRI's war efforts and its economic crisis. As early as 1985 pamphlets proposing the need for closer relations with the United States were distributed among the highest levels of IRI leadership; one official said the pamphlets argued that a closer relationship would help Iran break free from its cultural and economic poverty. Interestingly, the pamphlets were written by those who had supported taking the U.S. hostages.[29] The short-term objective of the Irangate contacts seems to have been to get badly needed weaponry in order to continue the war with Iraq. The Iranian military had been trained and supplied by the United States before the revolution, and its dependency on the Americans was a reality the IRI policymakers could not ignore. The long-term objective seems to have been to open a dialogue with the United States, which it was hoped would lead to closer relations between the two countries. One of the pamphlets stated, "We must go to those who had the most cultural and economic relations with us before the revolution." The IRI's attempts to help solve the TWA hijacking in 1985 also was part of the new pattern.

The revised approach was the result of a process of polarization within the maktabi ranks and the gradual emergence of two factions within the ruling elite. Rafsanjani described the factions in 1986 as (1) those in support of nationalization of most industries and (2) those in support of the private sector.[30] Although he described them only in economic terms, from 1986 onward, the factional differences began to surface in a large range of issues. They had to do mainly with domestic problems rather than foreign policy, because the latter was heavily influenced by the war factor, on which Khomeini had taken a firm position: Iran must devote all resources and sacrifice other interests to advance the war effort. Since the Iran-Iraq war was instrumental in determining foreign policy, open debates and disagreements were rare and foreign policy usually escaped the factional infighting.

The two factions, which can be called statist-reformist (pro-state) and conservative (pro–private sector), entered a decisive period of struggle in 1987 and 1988. Before this period they had competed for Khomeini's support, but now it became evident that he was taking the side of the statist faction. The abolition of the IRP, Khomeini's religious decrees (fatvas), and the recent parliamentary elections have all testified to this fact.[31] What had started as the polarization of the maktabis ended with the domination of the statists within the state apparatus. Yet it is important to note that the statists' control of foreign policy preceded their eventual control of the state. As mentioned before, the rapprochement with the West and the East between 1984 and 1986 was a clear sign of shifting policy. Therefore, though the internal consolidation of the statists was not complete until 1987–88, they had dominated the IRI's foreign policy as early as 1984.

Personalities such as Ayatollah Azari Qomi, President Ali Khamene'i, and the majority of clerics in the Guardian Council (*shora-ye negahban*) belong to the conservative faction. But the statist faction, as we shall see below, has had a more complex structure. Personalities like Rafsanjani and Velayati have joined such isolationist advocates and "radical" personalities as Musavi, Khoeiniha, Ghaffari, and Ali Akbar Mohtashami in forming the statist faction. Hence it has actually been a fragile coalition formed around current issues. It is composed of the advocates of the isolationist policy, who form the "radical" wing, and those who embraced the new pragmatic line in 1984. Between 1984 and the first half of 1988 domestic issues were of more importance and, because of the war, foreign policy was less a source of confrontation. Thus the two groups have formed the two wings of a coalition and established a united front against the conservative faction. The pragmatic wing was in charge of foreign policy and advocated a rapprochement toward both the West and the East while it united with the radicals in confronting the conservatives.[32]

The rapprochement could not have been achieved without Khomeini's consent and support. The Irangate affair was a good example of this. Today it has become clear that those who planned the general policy outline of Irangate believed they could count on Khomeini's support, and in fact they received it. When the Irangate policy came under heavy attack from the conservative faction, Khomeini intervened directly and silenced the voices of criticism.[33] Hence the faction that had proposed the venture was able to survive the political storm that followed it and was even able to eliminate the rival radical Hashemi group that had exposed the Iran–United States contacts.[34]

The pragmatists, like the other factions, have their own, less ideological interpretation of "neither East nor West," which they do not hesitate to exercise both in foreign and domestic policy disputes. With Khomeini's backing, the pragmatists managed to turn the Irangate affair to their own advantage. Thus, though Irangate turned out to be a nightmare for American policymakers, the pragmatists used it to get some badly needed military hardware, to eliminate the radical Hashemi group, and to reassure the Iranian public that it was only the United States, and not the IRI, that sought rapprochement by delivering weapons, cake, and a Bible. The worsening relations with the United States that followed Irangate were basically the result of a shift in American foreign policy, not a major shift in the IRI's position. Attesting to the shift in U.S. policy were the reflagging of Kuwaiti tankers, the deployment of the U.S. armada in the Persian Gulf, the naval battles between the IRI and the United States, and the shelling of Iranian oil facilities in the Persian Gulf. One American scholar characterized the shift in American policy as follows: "Crude anti-Sovietism and blindness to the real forces shaping Iran's foreign policy have moreover allowed us to be manipulated by others against our interest. In the Iran-Contra affair, we were exploited by Israelis and Iranian leaders alike."[35]

A look at the foreign policy of the IRI between 1986 and 1988 reveals that unlike the United States the major emphasis was on rapprochement with the West, not confrontation. Iran's limited response to U.S. harassment in the Persian Gulf, although partly caused by the few options open to IRI policymakers, also had strong roots in the new rapprochement policy. Further evidence were the steps taken to normalize relations with Britain and France, and the IRI's increasing willingness to solve the hostage dilemma in Lebanon.

The same policy may also be seen in relation to the East, with the difference that perhaps because of the new Soviet leadership, the East has been much more receptive. The Soviet media in 1987 contained numerous reports on the changing attitude in Iran. On 20 March 1987, *Pravda* cited media coverage in Iran about the need to expand economic relations between the two countries. *Pravda* also quoted Mohammad Javad Larijani (the IRI's deputy foreign minister and a pragmatist) as suggesting that the IRI and the Soviet Union "take common stands against the intrigues of American imperialism in the region. Second, we're neighbours, and this opens up good prospects for trade, economic, scientific, technical and cultural exchanges. Relations between us are beginning to develop once again. . . . the existing obstacles are temporary in nature. Sooner or later they will disappear, while the bonds of good-neighbourliness with the Soviet Union will remain."[36]

On 9 August 1987, *Izvestia* reported that "talks on the expansion of Soviet-Iranian trade ties are now under way."[37] The expansion included a gas pipeline, rail transport, a new rail route in Central Asia, and possibly a new oil pipeline from Iran through the Soviet Union to the Black Sea. And finally, on 5 December 1987, *Pravda* quoted the IRI ambassador to Moscow as saying, "We value highly our ties with the Soviet Union and would like to develop them."[38] When the Soviet involvement in Afghanistan reached an end, an additional obstacle to Iran-Soviet rapprochement had been removed.

A challenging test for the rapprochement policy toward the East developed in early 1988, when an unruly mob attacked the Soviet embassy in Tehran. Apparently the attack was prompted by the disclosure that the missiles that were hitting Tehran during the final phase of "the war of the cities" were Soviet-made and had recently been supplied to Iraq. Yet the pragmatists' grip on power was so strong they managed to contain and control public rage. Rafsanjani publicly accepted the Soviet explanation that the missiles were actually short range and that Iraq had managed to alter their capabilities with the help of some Western countries. Following this explanation, the anti-Soviet rage abated, and it appears that by 1988 the IRI's relations with the East were improving rapidly.

With the end of the Iran-Iraq war, new prospects have opened in the foreign policy of the IRI. The war was always a major obstacle to rapprochement with West and East. It was an even stronger factor in Iran–United States relations, since America openly sided with Iraq in the Persian Gulf confrontations of 1987 and 1988. With the war over and the era of Iran's reconstruction approaching, the pragmatists are showing even stronger signs of seeking rapprochement with the West. For example, the daily *Ettela'at* (which is published under the supervision of Khomeini's son, Ahmad Khomeini, and edited by Mohammad Doa'i, a Majles deputy and member of Khomeini's staff) recently wrote that the reestablishment of relations with the United States is necessary, adding, "Now the time has come for the lack of logical and correct relations between Iran and America to be removed."[39]

The IRI's foreign policy and the interpretation of the fundamental foreign policy slogan "neither East nor West" have gone through three major shifts since the establishment of the Islamic Republic. The slogan had a more pro-Western bias during the liberal period and stood for isolationism during the maktabi period. Today, during the reformist period, especially under Rafsanjani's pragmatic guidance, the slogan seems to advocate rapprochement with both the West and the East. But the policy is already threatening to break up the reformist coalition that has taken shape around domestic issues. This is to suggest that the more radical elements in the reformist faction or the former isolationists may no longer remain united in face of the new situation. Before the end of the Iran-Iraq war, objective limitations were imposed upon the rapprochement policy. Now that these limitations are disappearing, the policy may become a major national issue. Disagreements within the reformist faction are already surfacing. The resignation of the Musavi cabinet in September 1988, on the ground that many of its members would not receive confirmation from the Majles, as well as Khomeini's refusal to accept the resignation were signs of short-term future changes.[40] There have also been reports that Musavi wrote a secret letter to Khamene'i giving as the main reason for his resignation the failure to consult him on the peace process. He is said to have complained that decisions on foreign policy had been made without his knowledge.[41]

Conclusions

The foreign policy of the IRI under the slogan "neither East nor West" has played an important role for the ruling elite, both domestically and internationally. Domestically, it has helped present an alternative to the pro-Western policies of the imperial regime. It has also helped the IRI disarm its opposition by projecting to the Iranian people a politically independent and "anti-imperialist" image. Being able to project such an independent image of the state has been an important issue in domestic Iranian politics since the 1979 revolution. Internationally, the slogan has presented the IRI as a nonaligned government that not only consistently resists the domination of the two world blocs but also challenges their interests, both in the region and worldwide. Yet, as discussed above, the IRI's foreign policy has had three distinguishable phases, each of which has claimed allegiance to Khomeini's interpretation of "neither East nor West."

Answering the following questions can help us understand the dynamism of IRI foreign policy and its probable future path: What is the relationship between the trends in IRI foreign policy and Khomeini's views? How is the IRI's foreign policy likely to be affected by domestic economic conditions in Iran and the ideology of the IRI? And which direction will Iranian foreign policy take in the immediate future? To answer the first question, the factions that have taken their turn in running the Iranian state had Khomeini's backing and sought their legitimacy in his support. All the other legitimizing factors (such as the people's vote or the Majles) were secondary to Khomeini's authority, which stood above the IRI's constitutional limits. Khomeini's authority could indeed break the constitutional barriers of the IRI if the situation called for it as has been demonstrated throughout the existence of the IRI. It is quite possible that changes in IRI foreign policy in fact reflected changes in Khomeini's view. Of course, this does not mean that one man—Khomeini—decided the fate of a nation independently of the objective circumstances. What it does mean is that the trend that received Khomeini's support and consequently maintained the initiative also commanded the state.

Certainly the practicality of a faction's policy has had a direct effect on this complex process. Thus, in November 1979 the Provisional Government simply lost Khomeini's support while its rival faction managed to gain his backing for the hostage-taking policy. The importance of this point can be seen by examining the process by which various trends have managed to dominate foreign policy decision making. Khomeini was the ultimate authority and the factions sought his approval for their legitimacy, but the factions shaped Khomeini's view and in turn were affected by the outcome of his decision. The validity of this notion can be realized by comparing Khomeini's view with that of the various phases. Khomeini's initial interpretation of "neither East nor West" seems to have been closer to the isolationist trend.[42] This included the American hostage issue, the "Great Satan" image of the United States, and the anti-Sovietism of 1982–84. Yet, as is becoming evident, the trend toward rapprochement is changing IRI foreign policy to one of normal (if not good) relations with both the West and the East.

To answer the second question—how foreign policy will be affected by domestic economic conditions and IRI ideology—two factors must be noted. First, the IRI has been built upon Islamic tradition, which is generally seen as guaranteeing the right to private property. Indeed, none of the Iranian leaders has ever denied this principle. An Islamic state that does not radically break with this tradition is unlikely to break with the capitalist economic system. It seems likely, then, that a capitalist IRI in the long run will remain within the world capitalist system. One scholar has suggested, "During the two and a half years that have elapsed since the revolution, despite all the rhetoric, very little has been done to fundamentally alter the dependent capitalist economic structure inherited from the old regime."[43]

These factors should guarantee the IRI's ties with the West and provide a strong anticommunist element in IRI foreign policy. Ibrahim Yazdi's statement that "at least Americans believe in God" was not an empty phrase. Similar beliefs were echoed by Rafsanjani when he said: "We do not have ill feelings that he [Reagan] has sent a Bible. He is, after all, a Christian and believes in the Bible and knows that, as Moslems, we accept Jesus and the Bible in principle. He, therefore, found a common denominator between himself and us."[44] Therefore, though the IRI leadership may want to create an independent (*mostaqell*) Iran, both politically (*estellal-e siyasi*) and economically (*khodkafa'i-e eqtesadi*), this may not become a reality. And how a dependent economy will affect the political independence of the IRI only time will tell.

In answering the third question, concerning the future direction of Iran's foreign policy, one must consider the factor that will affect the country's short-term future more than any other—namely, its postwar reconstruction. With the Iran-Iraq war at an end, the reconstruction policies of the immediate future are becoming an important foreign policy issue. It is evident that Iran by itself cannot repair the damage to its economy, which is estimated to have run in the hundreds of billions of dollars; the country will need all the help it can find. At the time of the cease-fire, the Islamic leaders realized this fact very clearly, and there soon began talk of collaboration with both the West and the East and even of allowing investments by multinational corporations.

Nevertheless, although the need for cooperation with the outside world will moderate IRI foreign relations, it will also widen the gap between those who wish to conduct the reconstruction with outside involvement and those who wish to do the job by relying on Iran's very limited domestic resources. In this context, factional tension intensified in 1988–89. In a September 1988 speech Khamene'i, a conservative, complained that the same people who wanted the IRI to confront the Iraqi army with Molotov cocktails now were saying that reconstruction must be achieved by relying only on Iran's domestic resources.[45] At the opposite end of the spectrum, Musavi warned about the dangers of dependency on the multinationals, and added, "If we become careless and build up a debt of a few tens of billions of dollars in a few years, then America does not have to fear our political and Islamic slogans since it will have all the levers for the control of our revolution."[46] As of 1989, the pragmatists occupy the center of the spectrum, and their task is either to find a common denominator between the two extremes or to side with one of them against the other. Domestically they sided with the isolationists up to the summer of 1988. But on reconstruction they have tended to lean toward the conservatives. Up to late 1988, Khomeini gave his support to the pragmatists. But his remarks on reconstruction in October of that year showed a hard-line approach. In a later message to the people he rejected cooperation with the "criminal Soviet Union" and the "world-devouring United States," and added, "As long as I live, I will not allow the real direction of our policies to change."[47] It is not clear how much of this was rhetoric and how much was real, however, for Khomeini sided with the pragmatists on most issues.

Epilogue

The Satanic Verses

The crisis over Salman Rushdie's *The Satanic Verses* in early 1989 suddenly gave a new direction to the foreign policy of the IRI. After violent demonstrations in Pakistan and India denouncing Rushdie, Khomeini in February 1989 issued a decree calling for Rushdie's death. A few days later, on 22 February, Khomeini openly attacked those liberals who tried to mislead the revolution.[48] Following these events some twelve West European governments reduced their diplomatic missions in Tehran to express their objections to Khomeini's actions.

If nothing else, the Salman Rushdie crisis showed, once again, Khomeini's essential and decisive role in the decision-making processes of the IRI. But why did he decide to take such an extreme action? Did not this mean a complete reversal of the rapprochement policy and thus a strong setback for the pragmatists? What factors, other than the book itself, effected such a sudden shift of policy, and how strategic was this policy reversal?

Khomeini's initial angry reaction to *The Satanic Verses* and his death decree for Rushdie may have been more of an emotional outburst than a preplanned move against the pragmatists. A similar outburst had occurred a few weeks earlier. In that case Khomeini had asked for the severe punishment of five radio officials who were responsible for a disrespectful program regarding the daughter of the Prophet Mohammad. A woman interviewed on the program had suggested that her role model was a Japanese television personality and not the prophet's daughter, Fatima. In his angry response, Khomeini called for the death of those responsible if it was intentional and heavy punishment if it was not. A few days later he forgave all of them.

Whether the outburst against Rushdie was deliberate or spontaneous, the outcome was advantageous to the radical-statists and their isolationist policy. In terms of the IRI's relations with the West, it looked as if whatever the pragmatists had planned during the last few years was destroyed overnight. All the preparations for normalization with the West were swept aside by the Rushdie storm. On the other hand, not surprisingly, the crisis resulted in closer relations with the East.

Despite the turn of events in the IRI's foreign policy and Khomeini's apparent tough anti-Western rhetoric, one must note that domestically the power base of the advocates of the pragmatic approach was hardly touched. Khomeini may have discarded, for the time being, the pragmatic approach, but he did not move against the pragmatists in any other form. This left them in a strong position.

The most obvious feature of the early 1989 developments was Khomeini's vacillation: It was he who supported the rapprochement efforts of the pragmatists. It was he who accepted peace with Iraq and shocked the radical-statists. And in early 1989 it was he who changed direction again and seemed to be supporting the isolationists. Yet this history of vacillation between loyal IRI factions also suggested that the latest shift in government policy might not be long term either. The death decree, although damaging to the IRI's relations with the West, might very well have helped the state satisfy supporters who were both fanatical and disappointed with the war's outcome and the rapprochement policy.

There is a point in revolutionary movements when the leaders whose lives have been devoted to the revolution may stand in its way; they may, at times, start to damage the system they want to save. Mao Zedong had reached such a stage toward the end of his life. Brezhnev's prolonged illness allowed his aides to manipulate his authority. It is entirely possible that Khomeini reached such a point as well. Because of his authority and his special position in the IRI ruling elite, Khomeini's vacillation between different policies left Iran with no firm long-term policies while he was alive.

The Post-Khomeini Period

In the aftermath of Khomeini's death on 3 June 1989, there have been strong signs that the pragmatists have resumed their drive for the implementation of their program. To begin with, Khamene'i was selected to replace Khomeini as faqih. This move was a political compromise between the factions more than anything else. That Khamene'i was a political choice is clear, for he does not have the religious authority required to be Khomeini's replacement. Khamene'i and the conservatives have no great differences with the pragmatists over foreign policy, but they are in opposition to the radicals on almost every issue.

The IRI constitution was modified in a referendum held on 28 July 1989, the same day as the presidential election. The most important element of change was the concentration of power in the office of the president and the elimination of the prime minister's post (the radicals' power base). Rafsanjani won the presidency by an overwhelming majority. In the Majles, the powerful position of the head of the foreign affairs subcommittee was taken away from Sadeq Khalkhali, a radical, and given to Said Raja'i-Khorasani, a pragmatist and former IRI ambassador to the United Nations.

Regarding the Soviet bloc, relations have already improved dramatically. The multimillion-dollar agreements signed between the IRI and the USSR would have been inconceivable only two years ago. Regarding the West, Rafsanjani did not waste much time and sent out friendly signals only five days after Khomeini's death. In an interview with foreign reporters in Tehran he talked about the IRI's desire to have normal relations with the West if domination was not part of the deal.[49] As of August 1989, the domination of the pragmatists appears to be strong.

Notes

1. What Iranians actually say is *nah sharqi, nah gharbi,* literally "neither Eastern nor Western."

2. R. K. Ramazani, "Khumayni's Islam in Iran's Foreign Policy," in *Islam in Foreign Policy,* ed. Adeed Dawisha (London: Cambridge University Press, 1983), 21.

3. Ibid., 17.

4. *Jomhuri-ye Islami,* 21 Oct. 1980.

5. *Iran Press Digest,* 26 May 1987 (hereafter *IPD*).

6. *Jomhuri-ye Islami,* 5 Feb. 1985.

7. *The Constitution of the Islamic Republic of Iran* (Tehran: Islamic Propagation Organization, n.d.), 70.

8. Gary Sick, *All Fall Down: America's Tragic Encounter with Iran* (New York: Penguin Books, 1986), 168–69.

9. The Muslim Students Following the Imam's Line (SFIL) were responsible for the takeover of the U.S. embassy in Tehran in 1979. They were under the political guidance of Habibollah Payman, the leader of the Moslem Combatants, and Hojjat al-Islam Musavi Khoeiniha, a member of the IRP Central Committee. The SFIL were able to confiscate hundreds of documents following the embassy takeover. Although they were only a few hundred in number, by their use as a political tool, the documents played an important role in Iranian politics. For more, see Mohsen M. Milani, *The Making of Iran's Islamic Revolution: From Monarchy to Islamic Republic* (Boulder, Colo.: Westview Press, 1988), 274–76; *IPD,* 14 Jan. 1986.

10. *Documents of the Nest of Spies* (*Asnad-e laneh-ye jasusi*) (N.p.: Muslim Students Following the Imam's Line, n.d.), 15:59.

11. Ibid., 34:138.

12. Ibid., 18:25.

13. Quoted in *Iran Almanac and Book of Facts* (Tehran: Echo of Iran, 1987), 83.

14. Ibid., 84.

15. Shaul Bakhash, *The Reign of the Ayatollahs* (New York: Basic Books, 1984), 98.

16. Ibid., 108.

17. *Kayhan* (Tehran), 1 Jan. 1983.

18. *IPD*, 16 July 1985. Some Soviet embassy personnel were also asked to leave Iran.

19. *Kayhan* (Tehran), 3 May 1983.

20. For the document regarding the plan to attack the opposition, see *Kar* (the publication of the Organization of Iranian People's Feda'i Guerrillas), 26 May 1981.

21. *New York Times,* 20 Nov. 1986.

22. R. K. Ramazani, *Revolutionary Iran: Challenge and Response in the Middle East* (Baltimore: John Hopkins University Press, 1988), 32–54.

23. *Kayhan* (Tehran), 29 Oct. 1984.

24. *Etella'at* (Tehran), 23 Aug. 1984.

25. *IPD,* 18 Sept. 1984.

26. Ibid., 23 Apr. 1985.

27. Ibid., 12 Feb. 1985.

28. Ibid., 18 Feb. 1986.

29. This point was made by Asqarizadeh, who was a member of the SFIL, in *Kayhan* (Tehran) 28 Dec. 1986. See *Aqazi,* nos. 3–4 (Winter–Spring 1986–87): 19.

30. For an analysis of factionalism in the IRI, see Shahrough Akhavi, "Elite Factionalism in the Islamic Republic of Iran," *Middle East Journal* 2 (Spring 1987): 181–201.

31. Khomeini's decrees, in his capacity as both a *marja'-e taqlid* (source of emulation) and the Supreme Religious Leader (*vali-ye faqih*), made two important points. First, the state may regulate the activities of the private sector, and second, the state (that is, *velayat-e faqih*) has the ultimate power compared to the traditional Islamic laws (*shari'a*).

32. Ahmad Ashraf, in a recent interview, has categorized the factions the same way, under slightly different names. He calls them the conservative/traditionalists, the pragmatic/moderates, and the radicals. See *Middle East Report,* no. 156 (January–February 1989): 13.

33. *Kayhan* (Tehran), 22 Nov. 1986. Rafsanjani suggests that Khomeini knew about the affair by saying: "Of course, that day, we could arrest them [the McFarlane group], put them on trial and have them shot as spies. But such action did not fit into our plan. Therefore after a consultation in presence of the Imam, we decided to let the gentlemen leave in good health." See *Kayhan Hava'i,* 24 Dec. 1986.

34. The Hashemi group was the core of an organ named Liberation Movement Support Center. The head of the group was Mehdi Hashemi, who was a distant relative of Ayatollah Montazeri and a close childhood friend of his son Mohammad. The group is credited with exposing the McFarlane mission to Tehran (1986). Subsequently, Hashemi and his accomplices were arrested, on different charges, and Mehdi was executed. For more on this group and its history, see "On Mehdi Hashemi and His Group," *Iran Press Digest,* no. 43 (November 1986).

35. Nikki R. Keddie, "Iranian Imbroglios: Who's Irrational?" *World Policy Journal* 5 (Winter 1987–88): 31.

36. *Current Digest of the Soviet Press,* 22 Apr. 1987.

37. Ibid., 9 Sept. 1987.

38. Ibid., 26 Jan. 1988.

39. *Iran Times,* 26 Aug. 1988.

40. *Kayhan Hava'i,* 14 Sept. 1988.

41. This was reported in *Le Monde,* 15 Oct. 1988. See *Iran Times,* 21 Oct. 1988. Musavi has denied writing this letter.

42. See nn. 1 and 2.

43. M. H. Pesaran, "The System of Dependent Capitalism in Pre- and Post-Revolution Iran," *International Journal of Middle East Studies* (November 1982): 14.

44. *IPD*, 3 Feb. 1987.

45. *Iran Times*, 9 Sept. 1988.

46. *Kayhan Hava'i*, 5 Oct. 1988.

47. *New York Times*, 5 Oct. 1988.

48. *Iran Times*, 24 Feb. 1989.

49. Ibid., 16 July 1989.

2

Iran's Resistance to the U.S. Intervention in the Persian Gulf

R. K. RAMAZANI

Not since the Vietnam war had the United States deployed such massive naval forces as in the Persian Gulf between 22 July 1987, when the United States began to escort American-flagged Kuwaiti oil tankers, and 20 August 1988, when the cease-fire in the Iraq-Iran war took effect. Nor had any Third World nation so fiercely resisted American military, economic, and diplomatic pressures as had revolutionary Iran.

Contrary to general perception, Iran's acceptance on 18 July of U.N. Security Council Resolution 598 calling for a cease-fire and withdrawal of forces to recognized international frontiers did not simply reflect the battlefield setbacks that had started with the Iraqi recovery of the Fao Peninsula the previous April. Nor did it reflect a breakdown of Iran's resistance to the U.S. military intervention in the Persian Gulf. Rather, it reflected Ayatollah Khomeini's overriding concern with the survival of the revolution, which could be threatened by the alienation of the masses from the revolutionary government because of its failure to meet its promises of economic betterment and social justice.

The U.S. Decision to Intervene

To justify its controversial decision to intervene in the Persian Gulf, the Reagan administration tried to blame Iran for the tragic deaths of thirty-seven American servicemen killed by Iraq on the USS *Stark* in May 1987. President Reagan stated on 19 May, "Iran was the real villain in the piece"[1] and depicted the country as a threat to Western freedom, security, and oil supplies. He asked rhetorically three days later, "Why did this happen? Why to them? Could anything be worth such a sacrifice?" and answered, "Peace is at stake here, and so, too, is our own security and our freedom. Were a hostile power ever to dominate this strategic region and its resources, it would become a chokepoint for freedom—that of our allies and our own. And that is why we maintain a naval presence there." On 29 May, he told the American people, "Everyone can remember the woeful impact of the Middle East oil crisis of a few years ago [actually, fourteen]: the endless, demoralizing gas lines, the shortages, the rationing, the escalating energy prices, double digit inflation and the enormous dislocation that shook our economy to its foundation."[2]

These deep concerns with freedom, security, and oil, the Reagan administration claimed, underpinned its commitment to the high-minded principle of freedom of navigation. But this principle sounded like a hollow slogan. According to the Department of State, before the American reflagging of the Kuwaiti ships, "the percentage of ships hit [was] still very small—less than 1 percent of those transiting the Gulf."[3] Moreover, Iran had attacked only half as many tankers as Iraq—and those in retaliation for Iraqi attacks on Iranian oil exports. Because Iran must export its oil by sea, it is committed to free navigation, whereas Iraq is unconcerned about this principle because it exports all its oil overland.

The U.S. decision to intervene in the Persian Gulf largely reflected the misapplication of the rancid formula of containment of the Soviet Union and communism. Every doctrine in American diplomacy since World War II—the Truman, Eisenhower, Nixon, and Carter doctrines—represented an obsession with the Soviet threat to the Middle East. The Carter Doctrine specifically committed the United States to the defense of the free flow of Gulf oil supplies to world markets in the face of a Soviet threat. Ironically, the Reagan administration's decision to intervene in the Gulf came at a time when Moscow was offering to protect Kuwait's export of oil supplies rather than threatening to disrupt it. For months, Washington had failed to respond to a Kuwaiti request for protection. But when President Reagan learned that Kuwait and the Soviet Union had reached a deal to be signed in ten days, he rushed into the decision to reflag eleven Kuwaiti tankers on 7 March 1987, only five days later. The former secretary of defense Caspar Weinberger believed that an American refusal to honor the Kuwaiti request, in the face of the Kuwaiti appeal to Moscow for help, "would have created a vacuum in the Gulf into which Soviet power would shortly have been projected."

Iran's Perception of U.S. Intervention

How did the leaders of revolutionary Iran see the U.S. decision to intervene in the Persian Gulf? Between March 1987, when reports of Kuwait's request for superpower protection of its oil shipping began to appear, and 22 July 1987, when the United States began escorting Kuwaiti tankers flying American flags, Iranian leaders believed that a Soviet-American "conspiracy" against Iran was being hatched. On 7 May 1987, Ali Akbar Hashemi-Rafsanjani, the Speaker of the Majles, said that "the collusion between the United States and the USSR over the Persian Gulf is a conspiracy against Iran. . . . This latest move, and the use of the superpowers' flag to allow passage of ships off Iran's shores is a flagrant intervention and disgrace."[4]

Ayatollah Mohammad Hosain Ali Montazeri saw an even more extensive conspiracy—one involving a coalition between the Gulf Arab states and the superpowers and directed against both Iran and Islam. He said on 22 April 1987 that some of the Persian Gulf states "who claim to be Muslims, instead of stretching their hands of brotherhood toward Iran, one day go to America and another day to the Soviet Union. They lease ships from them and abjectly request entry for American and Soviet fleets into the Persian Gulf. What they are doing is similar to what the Jews of Medina did at the time of the most noble prophet . . . when they sided with the infidels against Islam and Muslims."[5]

The Iranian Foreign Ministry saw the superpower intervention in the Gulf region largely in temporal rather than religious terms. On 22 April 1987, it reiterated that the task of maintaining the security of the Persian Gulf rests "solely with regional countries and that Iran which has the longest shore shoulders the greatest part of the task of maintaining security of the region." It also implied a threat to the states supporting Iraq in the Gulf, saying that the "Persian Gulf states will enjoy security as long as the security of the Islamic Republic is respected." It warned finally that "interference of the superpowers in the region will not only increase the danger of regional clashes but will also be detrimental to those countries who requested protection from the superpowers."[6]

Finally, and most important, U.S. intervention in the Persian Gulf was perceived as an attempt by the United States to "impose peace on Iran," to borrow the words of Ayatollah Montazeri, just as it had imposed war. In the minds of revolutionary Iranians, the Iraq-Iran war was really the "American war" and U.S. intervention was intended to ensure that the war would continue until an "American peace" was imposed on Iran. The standard Iranian government publication, *The Imposed War,* describes the American motives in these terms:

> Following the victory of the Islamic Revolution of Iran, which created a
> center of social, cultural and political dynamism in the region, the U.S.

deputized the Baghdad regime to invade Iran and overthrow its fledgling government, thus attempting to contain the growth of the Islamic Revolution and prevent it from flourishing in the region and disseminating its liberating message to the farthest corners of the globe, inspiring the deprived masses to break the centuries-old yoke of superpowers' dominance.[7]

Such a perception rejects the standard Western interpretation that the Iranians saw the American imposition of the war simply as a means of pressuring Iran to free the American hostages. As early as 1981, I argued that the fear of the Iranian revolutionaries about an American encirclement of the revolution first surfaced during the seizure of power by the revolutionary forces in February 1979 when, for the first time, the United States declared it would itself defend its vital interests in the Gulf region's oil supplies by military force "if appropriate."[8] This crucial declaration by Secretary of Defense Harold Brown, during his visit to the Middle East (9–19 February 1979), rang the alarm bells in Iran. The militant revolutionaries, in particular, saw in this declaration an early expression of American hostility toward the Iranian Revolution, partly because it was accompanied by Washington's search for a new pro-American military alignment among the regional states, now that the Shah's regime had collapsed. In addition to offering an unprecedented amount of military and economic aid to "pro-Western countries of the Middle East," the defense secretary proposed the formation of a U.S.-sponsored "consultative framework" envisaging military cooperation among Egypt, North Yemen, Jordan, Sudan, Israel, and, if possible, Saudi Arabia. From the Iranian perspective, the U.S. intervention in the Gulf, staring in 1987, was the natural outgrowth of the fall of the surrogate regime of the Shah and Washington's determination to contain the Iranian Revolution with the help of subservient Gulf Arab states if possible and unilaterally if necessary.

The Nature of Iran's Resistance

Except for such widely read but uninformed pundits on Middle Eastern affairs as Charles Krauthammer, who—in advocating an iron-fist U.S. policy in the Gulf—equated revolutionary Iran with Grenada,[9] any serious student of Iran could have predicted that the Iranians would fiercely resist U.S. intervention in the region. The Iranian leaders warned the United States in no uncertain terms before the start of the U.S. convoy operations in July 1987 that they would not be deterred from pursuing their Gulf policies, especially in retaliating against Iraq's disruption of Iran's oil exports. Prime Minister Mir-Hosain Musavi said on 6 May that the "Islamic Republic will not retreat from its declared policies regarding the Persian Gulf under any circumstances. There will be security for all countries or for none. The presence of the big powers' fleets will not weaken our resolve in implementing the 'eye for an eye' policy."[10] Hashemi-Rafsanjani, who had all along hoped that logistical difficulties and congressional opposition would deter the United States from intervening, stressed, "We should be ready so that if any country in the south of the Persian Gulf were to place bases, ports, and jetties at the disposal of the United States, we should go and occupy that place and drive out the Americans."[11]

Naturally, the Iranian leaders attributed their resolve to resist U.S. intervention to the nature of the Iranian Revolution and regretted that Washington had not learned any lessons from its bitter experience with Iran. Ayatollah Khomeini spoke of the nation's sense of sacrifice and martyrdom, saying:

> A nation that seeks martyrdom, a nation whose individual members lose their limbs and then complain by saying: O God, did you not consider me worthy of taking my life? is not afraid of their [superpowers'] actions. Do not frighten such a nation with your possible deeds: go and do what ever damn thing you want to do and cannot do. These superpowers intend to dominate the world; and some destitute members of the Gulf, such as Kuwait, are afflicted by this temptation, imagining that by falling into America's lap things will end [khalas]. This is a mistake.[12]

Ayatollah Khomeini attributed Iran's resolute resistance not only to Shi'i-based fearlessness but to the nation's will to defy the "bullies" of world politics. President Reagan's ill-advised characterization of Iran as a "barbaric country" on 26 May 1987 stirred Khomeini's deep sense of patriotism.[13] On 29 May he said,

> I suppose you have heard recently that the U.S. President has said that the people of Iran are barbarians. If by barbarians you mean that they rise against your interests and oppose your desires, then you call them barbarians if you feel like. And if by barbaric, you in fact mean something else, you are talking nonsense. Is a barbarian someone who does not allow others, the bullies, to violate his rights, or someone who intends to violate others' rights? One should not make uncalculated remarks. . . . A regime that comes from the opposite corner of the world to this corner to threaten that we should do such-and-such; it is not barbaric? Or is the barbarian the one who says: Let us live freely in our land in our country?[14]

Ever since the Arab invasion of Iran in the seventh century, the relative weight of "Iranianness" and "Islamicness" in the Iranians' sense of national identity has been a fundamental concern of the country's political culture. On the surface, the process of Islamicization since the eruption of the revolution has set the issue to rest. Yet the facts speak differently. In spite of the campaign of Islamicization, the nationalist epic of the poet Firdausi, *Shahnameh*, is still recited in Iranian "coffee-houses" (*qahveh-khaneh*) and "houses of strength" (*zurkhaneh*). The age-old debate between the proponents of "nationalism" (*melligera'i*) and Shi'ism (*Shi'agari*) has also deepened as never before.[15] The kind of Islamic thought that dominates the thinking of the clerical ruling elite disparages Iran's pre-Islamic history and modern secular nationalism. Yet both Shi'ism and nationalism continue to underpin the country's fierce sense of independence, which has been, for half a millennium, the hallmark of its foreign policy.[16] Only since the revolution, however, has this ancient dedication to resisting foreign control enjoyed such widespread support from the now-politicized masses of the Iranian people.

A longstanding mixture of history and mythology, facts and fiction, realism and idealism, has underpinned the perception that Iran's primacy in the Persian Gulf is the sine qua non of its overall freedom from foreign control,[17] and the Iranian Revolution added a new sense of religious primacy to this perception.[18] As early as 1983, the Iranian leaders warned the United States against intervention in the Gulf, proclaiming that the resistance of the Iranian people could result in a reenactment of the "epic of Karbala" at the Strait of Hormuz.[19] The Iranian Revolution is perceived as an "Islamic Revolution," and the Gulf remains the *Persian* Gulf in spite of the rise of the "Islamic Republic." Iranian authors today no longer gloss over the Achaemenid and Sassanian periods of Iran's dominance over the Gulf. The Ministry of Foreign Affairs more than ever before is opposed to any designation other than the "Persian Gulf" for the strategic waterway. In the words of a contemporary Iranian writer: "The United States must recognize that the Persian Gulf is not an 'American lake.' [It] will always remain the Persian Gulf, and the powerful Islamic Republic will oppose any foreign intervention in the Gulf from a position of strength."[20]

Military Resistance

Revolutionary Iran resisted the U.S. intervention in the Persian Gulf partly by military means. Before 24 July 1987, when Iranian mines struck the *Bridgeton* (a Kuwaiti supertanker flying the American flag), the country's military actions, as well as its declaratory policy, were directed against both superpowers. The first superpower vessel to be attacked by Iran was a Soviet freighter, *Ivan Koroteyev,* on 6 May 1987. Although some believed that the attack by

Iranian speedboats was an unauthorized and intemperate action by Revolutionary Guards operating on their own,[21] others thought it was a deliberate act
intended to warn both Moscow and Washington not to become deeply involved
in the Iraq-Iran war.[22] Before the start of the American convoy operations,
another Soviet vessel, *Marshal Chuikov*, struck an Iranian mine on 17 May as it
approached Kuwait. This was one of the three vessels leased to Kuwait by the
Soviets on the basis of an agreement reached between the two countries on 1
April 1987.[23]

Once the U.S. naval escort of reflagged Kuwaiti ships began, the Iranian
military resistance focused on a variety of these "American" vessels. The
Bridgeton was the first reflagged Kuwaiti supertanker to be struck by an underwater mine. It ripped a hole in the ship's hull, setting back Kuwait's shuttle of
crude oil and causing some embarrassment to U.S. officials, although none of
the crewmen aboard the twelve-hundred-foot tanker was injured. Prime Minister Mir-Hosain Musavi called the incident "an irreparable blow to America's
political and military prestige," adding that "the U.S. schemes were foiled by
invisible hands. It proved how vulnerable the Americans are despite their huge
and unprecedented military expedition to the Persian Gulf to escort Kuwaiti
tankers."[24] Hashemi-Rafsanjani claimed on 16 August 1987 that Iran had a
factory "that could produce mines like seeds."[25] On 20 August, Kamal
Kharazi, spokesman for the Iranian Supreme Defense Council, reportedly said
that although Iran had placed mines in the Persian Gulf, their use "was not
designed to block freedom of navigation." Rather, they were intended only to
protect Iranian coastal installations, and he added that "as long as there are
foreign forces in the Gulf it is quite natural to use such means to block approaches."[26]

The crippling of the *Bridgeton* was more significant for Iran and a greater
setback for Kuwait and the United States than has been realized. To Iran, this
was its "first victory" against U.S. intervention in the Persian Gulf. To Kuwait,
it was a serious blow to the export of its crude oil, most of which was to be
shuttled by the *Bridgeton* to safer waters beyond the Strait of Hormuz. Of the
eleven reflagged tankers, only the *Bridgeton* was capable of carrying crude oil;
the others carried refined petroleum products. In view of the symbolic significance of the damage to the ship, the Kuwaiti officials, after months of repair,
decided to withdraw the tanker from shuttle service, fearing that the "Iranians
might have their finger on her. They might want to hit her again for publicity."
For the United States, however, this decision removed from the scene one of the
original reasons for the reflagging operation.[27]

The initial U.S. underestimation of Iran's mine-laying capability continued to haunt Washington in spite of a subsequent increase in American mine-

sweeping equipment and additional support from its allies. Even five months after the *Bridgeton* was struck, American sources were reporting that "the mine threat continues to bedevil the U.S. military mission in the gulf. Serious questions remain of whether the Western fleets will be able to halt Iran's mine-laying operations. There are alarming indications both that the Iranians are building new mines and that they may be acquiring new, so-called influence mines from Libya which can be activated by sound waves or the vibrations of passing ships."[28] This news made clear Iran's determination to resist U.S. intervention in the Gulf in spite of an American attack on an Iranian vessel. On 21 September, the day before President Ali Khamene'i was scheduled to address the U.N. General Assembly, a U.S. Navy helicopter attacked the *Iran Ajr*. Three Iranian crewmen were killed and two others were lost at sea. Later the United States destroyed the ship and returned twenty-six surviving crewmen to Iran. The Reagan administration said that the vessel had been laying underwater mines fifty miles from Bahrain. Strangely enough, however, the videotape that was supposed to prove that the Iranians had been caught red-handed was never produced, ostensibly because of technical failures.

In testing the limits of the American intervention, Iran hit another American-flagged Kuwaiti ship. On 16 October 1987 an Iranian missile struck the *Sea Isle City* while it was in Kuwaiti territorial waters. The Iranians knew that the United States was committed to protecting such ships while they were in international shipping lanes, but would its protection extend to the territorial waters of a coastal state? Iran got its answer on 19 October, when the United States retaliated by destroying one Iranian derelict oil rig and blowing up two other rigs. Predictably, Iran in turn retaliated three days later by firing a missile into Kuwait's Sea Island oil terminal, the main Kuwaiti installation for handling supertankers. From this time on, Iran carefully avoided American-flagged Kuwaiti ships and concentrated on vessels carrying Kuwaiti and Saudi oil and petroleum under other flags. For example, on 16 November 1987, in an angry reaction to the perceived American-inspired Amman summit meeting in which the Arab states denounced Iran in unprecedentedly harsh terms, Iran attacked the U.S.-managed Liberian-registered tanker *Lucy* and the U.S.-owned supertanker *Esso Freeport*, which was registered in the Bahamas, as it sought to leave the Gulf with a cargo of Saudi Arabian crude oil.[29]

The objectives, strategy, and tactics of revolutionary Iran in resisting American intervention have been implicit in the preceding discussion. The country's principal objective was to resist American intervention without being distracted from its continuing war with Iraq. At sea, this meant that Iran was determined to strike at Iraq by hitting ships carrying the crude oil and petroleum products of Kuwait and Saudi Arabia, Iraq's main bankrollers and logistical supporters.

Iranian deployment of missiles concerned American policymakers the most. Iran had previously hit Kuwait with rockets, but on 4 September 1987, it hit the southern coast of Kuwait for the first time with a surface-to-surface missile. Although two Kuwaiti ships flying American flags (*Surf City* and *Chesapeake City*) were nearby, they were not targeted—the Iranian objective was to harass Kuwait. Some believed that the Iranian attack represented the first hostile use of Chinese-made Silkworm missiles in the war; others thought the missile might have been Soviet-made, either a Scud or a Styx missile.[30] Although both Iran and China denied dealing in Silkworm missiles, on 25 September Chinese premier Zhao Zhang said that China would attempt to prevent export of its weapons, presumably by third countries, to Iran and Iraq.[31] The deployment of Silkworm missiles by Iran was said to have been one of the rationales for the Reagan administration's decision to intervene in the Gulf. Neither the Iranian nor the Chinese denials satisfied the administration's demand for the discontinuation of Chinese-Iranian missile deals. In fact, because of its continued concern about this weapons system, the administration announced on 22 October 1987 that it was putting curbs on the export of some high-technology products to China, presumably a "proportional response" to the continuing sale of Chinese Silkworm missiles to Iran. This marked the first time that Washington imposed new restrictions on China since relations had begun to improve during the Nixon administration.[32]

From the Iranian perspective, Tehran's relations with Beijing held a much greater importance than the acquisition of Silkworm missiles. As early as 1985, when Hashemi-Rafsanjani visited the People's Republic, it was clear that the Iranian clerical leaders viewed the country as an important counterweight to the rival superpowers. And friendly relations with China were in keeping with Iran's emphasis on the importance of Third World nations in its foreign policy. The idea of what I have called "third-power policy" has historically been attractive to Iranian policymakers; only the favored third power has differed from time to time according to changing circumstances. The constitutionalists, and later the Mosaddeqists, favored the United States, as did Mohammad Reza Shah in the 1940s and after, but his father, Reza Shah, had cultivated close ties with Germany during his rule.

In military terms, also, China was important to Iran as the source of weaponry other than Silkworm missiles. So deep was the military relationship between the two countries that in 1986 China and North Korea provided nearly 70 percent of all Iranian military imports. Shortly after the United States imposed the ban on the export of some high-technology products to China, Iran received a shipment of artillery pieces and shells from China, and Reagan administration officials said on 27 October 1987 that one hundred sophisticated Chinese C-801 antiship missiles either had been delivered or might be on the way to Iran. These missiles are faster and more accurate than Silkworms. Iran already had a hundred in stock in 1987, and Chinese technicians had trained Revolutionary Guardsmen to assemble, fire, and maintain them.[33]

In 1986, Iran purchased $600 million worth of arms from China, and the figure for 1987 was probably $1 billion. Representative Les Aspin's criticism of China revealed the range of arms Iran purchased from the People's Republic; they included "artillery shells, mortar rounds, anti-tank weaponry and perhaps even aircraft."[34] Iran received more Chinese arms early in 1988, although Reagan administration officials were divided on whether China had abandoned its sales of Silkworms to Iran and did not know whether these new shipments dated from before Chinese assurances that it was not selling such weapons to Iran. Finally, on 9 March 1988, the United States lifted the high-tech trade impediments against China because Washington had "every reason to believe the Chinese have lived up to their assurances" about not selling antiship missiles such as Silkworms to Iran. This move eased the Iran-related Sino-American tensions, but it failed to get China's unconditional support for a U.S.-backed arms embargo against Iran through the United Nations.[35]

Diplomatic Resistance

The same agility, flexibility, and innovativeness that characterized revolutionary Iran's fierce resolve to resist U.S. intervention in the Persian Gulf by military means also marked its diplomatic actions. During the 1987–88 period, the United States tried to induce its friends and allies to impose diplomatic and economic pressures on Iran as it had done during the 1979–81 hostage crisis. The difference now was that its diplomatic and economic pressures were paralleled by the unprecedented buildup of a Western armada in the Persian Gulf. Predictably, in 1987–88, as in 1979–81, Iran played its Soviet card, especially after July 1987, when the United States began its naval escort of Kuwaiti tankers. Revolutionary Iran's foreign policy doctrine of "neither East nor West" has not precluded a little tilting toward either side if it has served its national interests.

Although in late 1986, after a six-year suspension, Iran resumed the activities of the Soviet-Iranian Permanent Commission for Joint Economic Cooperation by signing its first economic cooperation protocol with Moscow,[36] Soviet-Iranian relations did not really begin to warm up until after the U.S. intervention in the Gulf. The Pentagon gave Soviet and Iranian leaders a com-

mon cause, one that Iran deftly exploited in resisting American military, economic, and diplomatic pressures inside and outside the United Nations. Outside
the world organization, unprecedented ties in the economic and technical fields
were forged between Tehran and Moscow in spite of continuing differences
over Afghanistan and the sustained supply of Soviet arms to Iraq. Inside the
U.N. Security Council, the Soviet Union blocked the imposition of an arms
embargo on Iran sought by the Reagan administration.

After the Arab states of the Persian Gulf created the Gulf Cooperation
Council (GCC) in 1981, Iran tried to walk a tightrope between intimidating its
members and ingratiating itself with them, depending on the position of each on
the Iraq-Iran war. Tehran's relations with the United Arab Emirates were friendly and those with Oman were improving, these countries having been more
dovish than either Saudi Arabia or Kuwait in GCC circles. But its relations with
Saudi Arabia and Kuwait were frequently jeopardized because of their open
support for Iraq's war efforts, and Iran resented the Saudi- and Kuwaiti-led
efforts of the GCC aimed at putting diplomatic pressure on Iran by encouraging
an anti-Iranian stance within the Arab League and the U.N. Security Council.
The GCC states, in 1984, 1986, and 1987, influenced the adoption of anti-
Iranian resolutions by the Security Council, and they did the same thing in the
Arab League over the years. At the instigation of the GCC states, the Arab
summit meeting at Amman in November 1987 condemned Iran in the harshest
language ever used by the league. The Arab leaders stated: "The conference
condemns Iran's occupation of part of Iraqi territory and its procrastination in
accepting Security Council Resolution 598. They call on Iran to accept the
resolution and implement it in toto, according to a sequence of its operative
paragraphs," which meant according to the interpretation of the resolution by
the Iraqi regime.[37] What took foreign and Arab observers by surprise was that
Syria, Iran's major Arab ally in the war against Iraq, joined in the condemnation. Unnoticed, however, were the repeated trips of Syrian officials to Tehran.
Momentarily trapped between their alliance with Iran and their expedient support of Iraq, they sought to explain to Iranian leaders their stance at the Amman
summit. By taking advantage of this Syrian predicament, the Iranian leaders
used the Syrian mediation to woo the GCC states.

Syrian mediation efforts between Iran and the GCC states redounded to
Iran's advantage in two major ways. First, the Arab consensus reached during
the Amman summit broke down after only three months. Resentful of the
mediation efforts of its archrival Syria, the Iraqi regime ended its short-lived
propaganda truce with Syria in February 1988 when Iraqi officials described the
Syrian diplomatic moves in favor of Iran as "treacherous," and President Saddam Hussein accused Syria of returning to a "presummit atmosphere" and of

reneging on the strong anti-Iranian consensus reached in Amman. The Syrians, he said, "should at least not ally themselves with the enemies of the Arab nation."[38] Second, the Syrian mediation efforts reinforced Iran's own longtime diplomatic efforts to maintain a dialogue with the GCC, especially with its more sympathetic members.[39] King Fahd's remarks at the GCC summit in December 1987 echoed the Arab tough line against Iran that had been taken at the Amman summit, but the final communiqué of the GCC summit spoke much more softly about Iran.

More constructively, King Fahd and the other GCC leaders "authorized" the president of the United Arab Emirates to explore a diplomatic initiative between Iran and the GCC members. The Syrians quickly seized this opening and intensified their behind-the-scenes mediation efforts between Iran and the GCC. They dispatched Vice President Abdul Halim Khaddam and Foreign Minister Farouk Charaa to the Gulf. Although Iran disappointed the GCC states by insisting that the war with Iraq was not negotiable, the renewed dialogue with the GCC was a major diplomatic achievement for Tehran, especially against the backdrop of bitter antagonism between Tehran and Riyadh after the tragic incident at Mecca in July 1987. Just as Iran befriended the Soviet Union and China to counter American pressure, it kept its alliance with Syria and its dialogue with the United Arab Emirates and Oman, partly as a counterweight to the formation of a durable pro-Iraqi and anti-Iranian Arab coalition.

Outside the Arab world, Iran intensified its close ties with other Third World nations also as a means of neutralizing U.S. efforts to isolate Iran internationally. For years revolutionary Iran had forged close economic, commercial, and technical ties with Islamabad and Ankara, partly for the strategic reason of resisting Soviet pressures. It also established with Pakistan and Turkey an Economic Cooperation Organization in 1985 similar to the old Regional Cooperation for Development (RCD) of the 1960s. But the close ties with Pakistan and Turkey could also be used to counter American as much as Soviet pressures, and in 1987, Iran began to do so. The revelation that in 1986 Iran had exported about $500 million worth of crude oil to the United States prompted the House and Senate to vote overwhelmingly to ban imports, particularly of oil, from Iran. The Reagan administration at first resisted the ban partly because it believed that it might contravene the U.S.-Iran Algiers agreement that had settled the hostage crisis, but later it succumbed to congressional pressure. On 26 October 1987, only four days after Iran's missile attack on Kuwait's Sea Island oil terminal, the administration imposed an embargo on U.S. imports from Iran and a ban on fourteen kinds of "militarily useful" items previously exported to Iran. In justifying the ban, President Reagan cited Iran's "continued aggression" against nonbelligerent nations and its refusal to accept U.N. Resolution 598. He also said that the ban would "remain in place so long as Iran persists in its aggressive disregard for the most fundamental norms of international conduct."[40] The Iranians scoffed at the ban, pointing out that they had themselves banned U.S. imports as early as 1983 and that the U.S. economic sanctions would have little or no adverse effects on Iran, because they were not formally coordinated with other nations.

No other aspect of Iran's diplomatic resistance to the U.S. intervention in the Persian Gulf was so deftly conducted as its unprecedented moves in the United Nations. The Western media universally considered Iran's nonrejection of U.N. Resolution 598 of 20 July 1987 with suspicion and its continuous talks with the secretary-general as nothing but a stalling tactic to give it time to stock up on ammunition for another land offensive against Iraq sometime before April 1988. Objectively speaking, however, the Iranian decision to adopt a diplomatic option as a possible means for ending the war reflected a combination of diplomatic and strategic factors.

Diplomatically, after the Iraqi invasion of Iran in September 1980, the revolutionary regime had for all practical purposes boycotted the U.N. Security Council. The council had failed to acknowledge Iraq's responsibility for starting the war and had not called on Iraq to withdraw its forces from Iran's territory. Still worse, over the years in resolution after resolution, the council had shown a definite bias against Iran. In contrast, Resolution 598 seemed to respond to the Iranian demand for a determination of who started the war. Before the resolution was adopted, Prime Minister Musavi said on 24 June 1987 that unless the United Nations acted to "change its direction and expose the aggressor, condemn the aggressor, and suggest a way of trying the aggressor . . . a resolution by the Security Council will be considered worthless."[41] But since paragraph 6 of Resolution 598 provided for an "impartial body" to determine who started the war, Iran saw no reason to reject it out of hand and entered into negotiations with the secretary-general.

Strategically, Iran opted for a diplomatic as well as military approach to the war in 1987 because its leaders recognized in February of that year that Iran needed a new strategy. The massive Karbala Five offensive, unlike similar land offensives launched in 1984 and 1986, had failed in spite of the deaths of some forty-five thousand Revolutionary Guards. The need for a new strategy was first voiced by Hashemi-Rafsanjani on 9 February 1987 when he said, "To tell the truth, we cannot see a bright horizon now, so far as ending the war in its present form is concerned."[42] He spelled out the new form he had in mind later in the year when everyone expected another massive Iranian offensive. He said on 13 November, "We do not launch a Karbala 5-type offensive, after which the Iraqis can have a long rest and our enemies have the opportunity to prepare themselves for later occasions. We should be able to carry out *numerous and consecutive* Karbala-type operations at any time."[43] This new strategy required even more men and money than earlier ones, and it lay behind the message of 13 November 1987 issued by the Supreme War Support Council to the Iranian people. In addition to calling for massive recruitment efforts, the council asked the Iranian people to participate in a "financial jihad": "Those who are unable to go to the fronts—such as women, the sick, and those with other excuses—should contribute with a financial jihad. People with the means should accept the financial cost of at least one fighter."[44]

By negotiating with the United Nations, Iran deprived the United States of the opportunity to add the threat of a U.N.-sponsored arms embargo on Iran to the military pressures engendered by its intervention in the Persian Gulf. Contradicting rumors about conflict among the Iranian leaders, the U.N. secretary-general said on 16 September 1987, "In Iran I met with the four personalities who are supposed to decide on foreign policy. The four leaders said exactly the same thing. They have a unified position."[45] They told him that if an impartial body were established they would be prepared to observe informally the call for a cease-fire while that commission investigated who started the war. For all practical purposes, in its guidelines of 15 October 1987 to the secretary-general, the Security Council tilted toward the Iranian interpretation of Resolution 598—that is, "the observance of a cease-fire" should start concurrently with the "setting into motion" of such an investigative commission. Iraq adamantly insisted, however, that Resolution 598 must be accepted and implemented by Iran in toto, according to the sequence of its operative paragraphs. This meant that Iran must accept the cease-fire and withdraw its forces from Iraqi territory even before the investigation started.

Iran Ends the War: An Internal Assessment

Why did Iran finally decide to accept Resolution 598? If, indeed, as early as 9 February 1987 Hashemi-Rafsanjani had acknowledged that the war was not winnable, why did it take Iran almost a year to accept the resolution after its adoption? To address these questions even tentatively, one must assume that a complex combination of external and internal pressures ultimately led to Iran's acceptance of the cease-fire. On balance, however, it appears to have been the weight of internal factors that proved decisive.

To consider the external factors first, they fall into two major categories. Although the Iraqi pressures were considerable, they were not decisive. Neither the Iraqi missile bombardment of Iranian cities between February and April 1988 nor the Iraqi battlefield successes at Fao, at Majnoon Islands, and at

Shalamcheh seem to have forced Iranian leaders to accept the cease-fire, although admittedly the missile attacks dented Iranian morale and battlefield losses robbed Iran of major bargaining leverage in the postwar peace negotiations. A report asserting that the United States warned Iran, through German foreign minister Hans-Dietrich Genscher in March 1988, that a continuation of the war would result in Iraqi attacks that would cause the collapse of the Iranian military establishment cannot be verified.[46] Whether true or not, the fact remains that Iran did not take steps to end the war in the five months between Genscher's alleged visit to Tehran and Iran's acceptance of Resolution 598.

What is more, the American military intervention in the Gulf was no more influential than the Iraqi battlefield successes in nudging Iran toward a decision to end the war. As already noted, the realistic Iranian leaders, headed by Hashemi-Rafsanjani, had opted for a two-pronged strategy, *including diplomacy,* about six months before the adoption of Resolution 598. They did not reject the resolution out of hand after it was adopted, and they entered into earnest negotiations about the resolution with U.N. secretary-general Javier Pérez de Cuellar in September 1987. The American military intervention influenced the Iranian decision only insofar as the Iranian leaders, according to their own admission, were concerned that the military skirmishes might lead to a war with the United States. This concern was evident particularly in the wake of the American destruction of much of Iran's naval forces and the Sirri and Sassan oil fields in retaliation for the mining of the USS *Roberts* in April 1988. Although Iran did latch onto the tragic downing of its passenger plane by the USS *Vincennes* on 3 July 1988 in announcing its acceptance of the cease-fire on 18 July, it was rationalizing, rather than giving the reason for, its decision.

To overrate the influence of the American military intervention on the Iranian decision, furthermore, is not only to downplay the major roles played by the Soviet Union (both in the adoption of Resolution 598 and in nudging Iran toward its acceptance), the GCC nations, and the U.N. secretary-general but also to underestimate the importance of the Reagan administration's own diplomatic initiatives. As early as 1985, I suggested the need for an American peace strategy that would include support for the role of the United Nations.[47] But as is well known, the Reagan administration did not seriously pursue such a course until January 1987, when the fall of Basra seemed imminent.

More important, to overrate the influence of external pressures, whether Iraqi or American, is to downplay the decisive influence Iran's domestic conditions exerted on its decision finally to accept the U.N.-brokered cease-fire. Since the beginning of the Iranian Revolution, and most particularly since the fall of Mehdi Bazargan and Abol Hasan Bani-Sadr, two major tendencies have competed for the control of Iran's foreign policy—revolutionary idealism and revolutionary realism.[48] Ayatollah Khomeini used to call these tendencies "two ways of thinking," and Hashemi-Rafsanjani labels their proponents as "factions." As the leading realist among the Iranian political elite, Hashemi-Rafsanjani acknowledged for the first time in February 1987 that the war was unwinnable. He was later able to persuade the other three Iranian leaders concerned with foreign policy decision making (President Khamene'i, Prime Minister Musavi, and Foreign Minister Velayati) to accept a diplomatic option for ending the war. Although the four leaders spoke with one voice about Iran's conditions for accepting Resolution 598, ideological factions, headed by Interior Minister Ali Akbar Mohtashami, opposed the diplomatic option and the resolution from the start. Even after Khomeini accepted it, Minister Mohtashami seemed to acknowledge Khomeini's decision only grudgingly, judging by his statement of 12 September 1988 to the Majles. He merely deferred to Ayatollah Khomeini's decision, saying that he was not opposed to the wishes of the "absolute imam."

The fundamental question then is: Why did Khomeini accept Resolution 598? To comprehend his decision, one must realize that Khomeini fitted neither of the categories suggested above. As the supreme arbiter of Iranian affairs, he looked after the country's overall national interest. His conception of the "national interest" took into account Iran's need for power as a nation-state, but its hallmark was the overriding goal of creating an ideal Islamic state led by the *faqih*. The survival of the revolution was the essential prerequisite for achieving that goal, and to ensure the survival of the revolution, he acted as the supreme balancer among political factions. As he said, "For the sake of maintaining a balance among various factions, I have always issued both bitter and sweet instructions, because I consider all of them as my dear ones and children."[49] His decision to accept Resolution 598 in 1988 happened to favor the position of the realists, whereas his decision to continue the war in 1982 had happened to support the position of the ideological factions. In his judgment, both decisions were in the interest of the survival of the revolution. In his words, "At the very hour our nation saw the interest of the survival [*baqa'*] of the revolution in the acceptance of the resolution, it had once again fulfilled its obligation."[50] In other words, Khomeini accepted Resolution 598 because he believed that Iran was in danger of losing both the revolution and the war.

What did he see as a threat to the survival of the revolution? The answer may lie in his fear that the masses would become alienated from the revolutionary government as a result of ever-increasing socioeconomic hardships. The grave economic conditions that threatened to fuel popular alienation were twofold. First, oil revenues, the backbone of the Iranian economy, fell drastically because of an unprecedented fall of oil prices worldwide in 1986 and because of an equally unprecedented increase in Iraq's capability for disrupting Iranian oil exports in 1987. As a result, the revolutionary government's ability to meet the demands for both guns and butter had hit its lowest point by July 1988. The second source of potential alienation of the masses, particularly the poorer classes, was the lack of significant progress in fulfilling the revolutionary promises of greater social justice and economic betterment. For years, the conservative members of the Guardian Council had vetoed the reform bills necessary for the fulfillment of these promises. By 1988, however, because of the increasing economic hardships, the blocking of the reforms seemed certain to precipitate even direr consequences. Ayatollah Khomeini, therefore, lowered the boom on 6 January 1988 by issuing a decree subjecting the decisions of the Guardians to the review of a thirteen-member council "in the interest of the Islamic country."

Reconstruction and the Rushdie Affair

For almost nine months between Khomeini's acceptance of Resolution 598 on 18 July 1988 and his imposition of a death sentence on Salman Rushdie, author of the controversial novel *The Satanic Verses*, on 14 February 1989, the realist factions seemed to be riding the crest of success. Throughout the period between the settlement of the hostage dispute with the United States (January 1981) and the acceptance of the cease-fire (July 1988), these factions had tried to terminate Iran's international isolation. Their open-door foreign policy, however, had met with only limited success for two reasons: Iran's adamant continuation of the war and its reputation as a supporter of international terrorism.

Emboldened by Khomeini's decision to end the war, the realist factions used the issue of postwar reconstruction to breach Iran's international isolation. Diplomatic relations with Western countries were resumed or expanded. More important, new economic ties were either envisaged or forged with Western countries. Despite the opposition of the ideological factions to the idea of importing foreign capital and know-how, the realist factions actively supported the proposal. In addressing the objections of the ideological factions, President Khamene'i, for example, said on 7 October 1988 that in face of Iran's shortages it "should use foreign resources. . . . We cannot prolong the issue of reconstruction for 100 years."[51] Hashemi-Rafsanjani, to cite another example, said on 21 October 1988 that "we should absorb skilled manpower from abroad and programs should be designed to encourage the return to Iran of skilled Iranians now residing abroad."[52] Along the same lines, in addressing a group of foreign and Iranian researchers and university professors ten days later he was reported to have said, "Iranian scientists—whether they believe in the revolution or not—cannot find a more suitable place than their own homeland to serve."[53]

What concerned the ideological factions most of all was the possibility that the realist factions' efforts to renew and expand diplomatic and economic ties with the West might ultimately lead to the improvement of relations with the United States. Even before President George Bush apparently extended an olive branch to Iranian leaders in his inaugural address, the ideologues interpreted Ayatollah Khomeini's statements to mean, in the words of Interior Minister Mohtashami, "that America cannot return to this country." He added, "This nation will not play into the hands of criminal America."[54]

The fear of the ideological factions that the realist factions were throwing Iranian doors wide open to the West was put effectively to rest on 7 March 1989. Iran severed diplomatic relations with Britain at the expiration of the Majles's week-long grace period during which the two countries failed to resolve their three-week dispute over the Rushdie affair. The laboriously worked-out memorandum of understanding that Iran and Britain had signed on 9 November 1988, which was to be the basis of their newly resumed diplomatic relations, was scrapped, for all practical purposes. In announcing the break, the Iranian Foreign Ministry said that it considered itself "not just the executor" of Iranian foreign policy "but in a larger scope the executor and protector of the foreign policy of the Islamic world against blasphemy"; thus it regarded "defending Islam and its values as a divine and legal responsibility."[55] This statement was fully in keeping with Khomeini's perception that the publication of *The Satanic Verses* reflected "the Western powers' hatred of the Islamic world and Islamic jurisprudence [*feqahat*]. . . . The issue for them is not that of defending an individual: The issue for them is to support an anti-Islamic and anti-value attitude which has been masterminded by those institutions which belong to Zionism, Britain, and the United States, and which have placed themselves against the Islamic world through ignorance and haste."[56]

As a devout Muslim, Khomeini, like many Muslims, truly believed that Rushdie's work was a "blasphemous book." But as the supreme leader of Iran, he perceived the imposition of a death sentence on the author as helpful to the consolidation of the Islamic Revolution. In ending the war with Iraq for the sake of the survival of the revolution, his decision favored the position of the realist factions, and in imposing the death sentence on Rushdie, his decision supported the ideological factions in their opposition to Iran's expanding ties with other, particularly Western, countries. This interpretation of Khomeini's actions as representing a balancing act between factions seems to be supported by the following paragraph from a "very important" (Iranian appellation) address by

Ayatollah Khomeini to the instructors and students of religious seminaries and Friday and congregational imams:

> It is not necessary for us to pursue the establishment of extensive ties, because our enemies might imagine that we have become dependent on and attach so much importance to their existence, to the degree that we quietly condone insults [like Rushdie's] to our beliefs and religious sanctities. This [Rushdie's book] is an example for those who continue to believe this, and say that we must revise our politics, principles, and diplomacy, that we have blundered and must not repeat previous mistakes; those who still believe that extremist slogans, or war, will cause the West and East to be pessimistic about us, and that ultimately all this has led to the isolation of our country; those who believe that if we act in *a pragmatic way* they will humanely reciprocate and will mutually respect nations, Islam and Muslims—to them this [*The Satanic Verses*] is an example.[57]

Khomeini's admonition to the realist, or pragmatic, factions not to forge extensive ties with Western countries was obviously music to the ears of the ideological factions. The break of diplomatic relations with Britain on 7 March 1989 seemed to carry Khomeini's admonition to its logical conclusion, causing alarmists in the West to despair of the possibility of developing any constructive relations with revolutionary Iran so long as Ayatollah Khomeini was alive. His depiction of the Rushdie novel as an anti-Islamic Western conspiracy was seen as a backlash against the efforts of those realistic leaders who pushed for new ties with the West in their quest for postwar reconstruction. It was also seen as the return of revolutionary Iran to its nearly confrontational stance against the rest of the world.

And yet, four points of caution are in order as a corrective to such an exaggerated interpretation. First, revolutionary Iran's bark has consistently been worse than its bite. Second, there is nothing new about the tendency of Iranians to interpret events as conspiracies against their country by foreign powers. Rushdie, therefore, is seen as a foreign or Western "agent" or "mercenary" rather than as a bold novelist. This tendency has deep roots in Iranian political history, particularly that of the past two centuries: Iran has been the object of repeated invasion, partition, occupation, and intervention. Third, the apparent rise in the fortunes of the ideological factions and the check on the expansion of ties with Western powers could not last. Indeed, in the months following the death of Khomeini on 3 June 1989, the realists led by Rafsanjani and Khamene'i have been chosen for the top positions and have dominated policy decisions.

Fourth, the revolutionary promises of a better life and greater social justice for the poor paradoxically compel any revolutionary government to forge ties with both the East and the West, but particularly with the West. With the rare exception of a few zealot ideologues, the slogan of "neither East nor West" is understood among the Iranian political elite to mean no Eastern or Western *domination* of Iran rather than no relations with either bloc. This understanding is the by-product of a decade of revolutionary experimentation with reducing Iran's dependency on both East and West, a dependency that the revolutionaries insist is inherited from the prerevolutionary era and that economic realities suggest cannot be wished away for a long time to come. Most of these realities compel more extensive relations with the Western world where Iran's best markets, most of its sources of hard currency, and most desirable capital goods and technology happen to be located. Moreover, because of the country's historical mistrust of and political and ideological differences with Moscow, Iran's commercial, economic, and technical relations with the Soviet Union remain relatively limited despite some improvements since 1986 resulting largely from their common opposition to Western military intervention in the Persian Gulf.

Is Iran Turning East?

Moscow's position on the Rushdie affair and an unprecedented improvement in Soviet-Iranian relations intensified the fear of the alarmists in the West. On 28 February, two weeks after Khomeini pronounced his death sentence on Rushdie, the Soviet Union broke its silence on the affair. Soviet Foreign Ministry spokesman Genady Gerasimov said that the Soviets had "gained the impression that the Iranian government wants a solution and believes that the Soviet Union could have a positive role in achieving this."[58] Suspecting that Moscow was poised to exploit the strain between Iran and the West, State Department spokesman Charles E. Redman said on 2 March, "There is nothing here that involves mediation," adding that "from our perspective, the solution to the Rushdie case is very simple. Iranian death threats are unacceptable. We've encouraged other countries around the world to speak up on this. The United States has spoken up. And it is high time the Soviets spoke up."[59] When the Soviet ambassador did speak up, he said that the Rushdie affair "is something that reflects once more the importance of respect for all general human rights." He then asked rhetorically, "For example, religious feelings, is it a general human right? Yes. Or freedom of expression. Is it a general human right? Of course. But the skill, the science, the art, is to be balanced. Our position was formulated on the basis of this general approach."[60]

What lay behind this "neutral" position was the Soviet desire not to jeopardize Moscow's budding relations with Tehran. Planned before the Rushdie fracas, the visit of Foreign Minister Eduard Shevardnadze to Iran on 25–27 February 1989 made him the first member of the Soviet Politburo to call on Khomeini. Discussed long before Khomeini's death (3 June 1989), Hashemi-Rafsanjani's official visit to the Soviet Union on 20–23 June made him the first high-ranking Iranian leader to visit the Soviet Union since the revolution. The Kremlin treated the Majles Speaker like a head of state, Gorbachev labeling his visit "a landmark event," and assuring his Iranian guests that there could not and would not be anything in Soviet policy now that would damage Iran's interests. He added, "We explicitly declare that our country supports your anti-imperialist revolution." For emphasis, Hashemi-Rafsanjani singled out one point in his first round of talks with Gorbachev. He said, "The important development in our country after the revolution is that the people and the authorities decide for themselves without [allowing] the intervention of any foreign elements." Clearly, Hashemi-Rafsanjani was moved by the respectful reception he had. He said, "I have been in Moscow for only 24 hours. . . . But I already feel almost at home," and he voiced the idea of a joint Soviet-Iranian space flight.[61]

This is no place to analyze at length the wide variety of economic, commercial, scientific, cultural, consular, and other agreements and understandings that the Soviet and Iranian leaders officially initialed after many months of preparation. But briefly stated, the reconstruction programs will involve cooperation between the two countries until the year 2000 at a cost of possibly $7–8 billion. The political understanding involved a variety of issues, including peace negotiations with Iraq, Afghanistan, the Palestinians, Lebanon, South Africa, the Nonaligned Movement, the United Nations, and North-South relations. Information on two issues of perhaps the greatest importance, however, was almost nonexistent. Hashemi-Rafsanjani said nothing to reveal the Soviet-Iranian understanding on the arms issue. He emphasized the principle of self-sufficiency in Iran's defense buildup, admitting only that "we do have certain technical needs" that Iran hoped would be satisfied by "various sources." The major specific news was furnished on 26 June 1989 by the Abu Dhabi *Al-Ittihad,* which reported that Moscow would supply Tehran with about one hundred advanced tanks, setting the irreversible termination of the Iraq-Iran conflict as a condition for supplying Iran with advanced aircraft. The Kuwaiti *Al-Qabas* of the same date, however, said that the Soviet Union agreed to provide Iran with sophisticated weapons in return for a promise from Hashemi-Rafsanjani that Iran would not interfere in the Soviet Muslim areas, suggesting that Iran had been behind the unrest in Uzbekistan.

Although the official communiqué as well as other sources frequently mentioned the principle of noninterference in internal affairs, there was no reliable indication as to whether the Kremlin ever accepted Iran's repeated cancellations of Articles 5 and 6 of the 1921 treaty, which the Soviets interpret as giving them the right to intervene in Iran militarily if they judge their security to be threatened from Iran. Only the Abu Dhabi *Al-Ittihad* reported that the Soviet Union and Iran agreed to change the text of the treaty, presumably resulting in a new treaty of "friendship and cooperation" similar to the Soviet-Iraqi treaty. The issues of arms transfers and of cancellation of Articles 5 and 6 of the 1921 treaty thus remain to be clarified.

The major significance of Hashemi-Rafsanjani's visit to the Soviet Union for Iran's foreign policy in general and its relations with the United States in particular, however, was almost universally overlooked. As I argued in the *Washington Post* of 2 July 1989, this visit might well signify the beginning of Iran's reentry into the international community, signaling the desire of the Iranian leaders to base their country's future relations with other nations, including the United States, on the concept of equilibrium rather than on the idea of a struggle between good and evil. There appears to be no doubt that Soviet-Iranian economic, commercial, cultural, scientific, and technical relations will expand in the next decade and that the Soviets hope this will lead to increasing political influence in Iran.

Yet, paradoxically for revolutionary Iran, the road to Washington may well turn out to be through Moscow. In following the fundamental tenet of its own foreign policy, Iran will have to balance its cooperation with the East with cooperation with the West to avoid a dominant influence by or dependency on either bloc. This is the real meaning of Iran's "neither East nor West" principle as interpreted by every major Iranian leader over the past decade. Even Khomeini admitted in his will that Iran's need for foreign aid is an "undisputed fact." The opportunity for the United States to normalize relations with Iran is reinforced by other factors as well. With Soviet power too close for comfort, historical memories too bitter to forget, and Western technology and markets for oil too beneficial to ignore, political prudence as well as economic profit demand a turn to the West after an excursion in the East.

Given this opportunity, President Bush will be remiss if he confines his initiative to the olive branch he offered in his inaugural address. The situation now calls for a more creative and less cautious move on the part of the United States for a constructive dialogue with Iran based on mutual interest and respect. There is no better place to start than in the Persian Gulf, where the psychological wounds inflicted on Iran as a consequence of American military intervention are the deepest. A reduction of U.S. forces in the Gulf to the pre-escort level; a more generous American offer of compensation for the families of the 250 Iranian citizens who perished in the accidental shooting down of an Iranian passenger plane by the USS *Vincennes;* an American offer to help rebuild the three Iranian oil rigs the U.S. forces destroyed in October 1987 and to reconstruct the Sirri and Sassan oil fields they destroyed in April 1988—these and similar magnanimous gestures would go a long way toward the realization of the reciprocal goodwill President Bush was hoping for when he said, "Goodwill begets goodwill."[62]

Notes

1. *Washington Post,* 20 May 1987. For a detailed discussion of the reasons for Kuwait's request for reflagging of its oil tankers and the American response, see R. K. Ramazani, "The Iran-Iraq War and the Persian Gulf Crisis," *Current History* (February 1988): 61–64, 86–88.

2. *New York Times,* 30 May 1987.

3. United States Department of State, *U.S. Policy in the Persian Gulf,* Special Report No. 166, July 1987, 10.

4. Foreign Broadcast Information Service, *Daily Report, South Asia,* 8 May 1987 (hereafter cited as FBIS-SA).

5. Ibid., 23 Apr. 1987.

6. Ibid.

7. Islamic Republic of Iran, War Information Headquarters, Supreme Defense Council, *The Imposed War: Defence vs. Aggression* (Tehran: N.p., April 1984), in Arabic, English, and Persian, 7–8. See also Daftar-e Siyasi-ye Sepah-e Pasdaran-e Enqelab-e Islami (Political Bureau of the Islamic Revolutionary Guard), *Gozari bar do sal jang* (A review of two years of war) (N.p., n.d.). One of the most useful research tools for sources in the Persian press is the two-volume index, Vezarat-e Ershad-e Islami (Ministry of Islamic Guidance), *Fehrest-e maqalat-e jang-e tahmili dar matbu'at-e jomhuri-ye Islami-ye Iran* (Index to articles on the imposed war in the press of the Islamic Republic of Iran) (N.p., n.d.).

8. R. K. Ramazani, "The Genesis of the Carter Doctrine," in *Middle East Perspectives: The Next Twenty Years,* ed. George S. Wise and Charles Issawi (Princeton: Darwin Press, 1981), 165–80, and *The United States and Iran: The Patterns of Influence* (New York: Praeger, 1982), 163–64.

9. *Washington Post,* 23 Oct. 1987.

10. FBIS-SA, 7 May 1987.

11. Foreign Broadcast Information Service, *Daily Report, Near East and South Asia,* 5 June 1987 (hereafter cited as FBIS-NES).

12. Ibid., 1 June 1987.

13. For President Reagan's remark, see *New York Times,* 27 May 1987.

14. For the text of Ayatollah Khomeini's message, see FBIS-NES, 1 June 1987.

15. For a useful source on Ayatollah Khomeini's own views on nationalism, see the eleventh volume in the series of collections entitled *Dar jostoju-ye rah az kalam-e Imam, Melligera'i* (In search of the path from the word of the imam, "nationalism") (Tehran: Mo'asseseh-ye Amir Kabir [Ministry of Islamic Guidance], 1983–84). For an analysis of the interrelationship of nationalism and revolutionary Islam, see Reza Davari, *Nasionalism va enqelab* (Nationalism and revolution) (Tehran: Vezarat-e Ershad-e Islami, 1986–87).

16. See R. K. Ramazani, *The Foreign Policy of Iran, 1500–1941: A Developing Nation in World Affairs* (Charlottesville: University Press of Virginia, 1966), *Iran's Foreign Policy, 1941–1973: A Study of Foreign Policy in Modernizing Nations* (Charlottesville: University Press of Virginia, 1975), and *Revolutionary Iran: Challenge and Response in the Middle East* (Baltimore:

Johns Hopkins University Press, 1986; paperback ed., with an epilogue on the Iranian-American arms deal, 1988).

17. R. K. Ramazani, *The Persian Gulf: Iran's Role* (Charlottesville: University Press of Virginia, 1972), esp. 1–27.

18. Ramazani, *Revolutionary Iran,* esp. 19–31.

19. For the text of the most important policy statement to date by revolutionary Iran on the Persian Gulf and the Strait of Hormuz, see ibid., esp. 275–81.

20. Mohandes Sayyed Ali Musavi Qomi, *Khalij-e Fars dar gozar-e zaman* (The Persian Gulf in the course of time) (Tehran: Bonyad-e Nabovvat, 1987–88), 19–20.

21. *Washington Post,* 14 May 1987.

22. Ibid., 9 May 1987.

23. The other two Soviet vessels leased to Kuwait were the *Marshal Maikov* and the *Marshal Bugrumyan.* See *New York Times,* 18 May 1987.

24. *Washington Post,* 25 July 1987.

25. Ibid., 17 Aug. 1987.

26. Ibid., 21 Aug. 1987.

27. Ibid., 28 Nov. 1987.

28. Ibid.

29. Ibid., 17 Nov. 1987.

30. Ibid., 5 Sept. 1987.

31. Ibid., 27 Sept. 1987.

32. *New York Times,* 23 Oct. 1987.

33. Ibid., 28 Oct. 1987.

34. *Washington Post,* 25 Dec. 1987.

35. China will support such an embargo if "the overwhelming majority" of the U.N. Security Council goes along. Ibid., 10 Mar. 1988.

36. R. K. Ramazani, "Iran," in *1987 Yearbook on International Communist Affairs,* ed. Richard F. Staar (Stanford: Hoover Institution Press, 1987), 432–36.

37. *New York Times,* 9, 10, and 12 Nov. 1987.

38. *Washington Post,* 3 Feb. 1988.

39. Ramazani, *Revolutionary Iran,* esp. 137–43. See also Ramazani (with the assistance of Joseph A. Kechichian), *The Gulf Cooperation Council: Record and Analysis* (Charlottesville: University Press of Virginia, 1988), esp. 190–96.

40. *Washington Post,* 27 Oct. 1987.

41. FBIS-NES, 24 June 1987.

42. *Economist* (London), 14 Feb. 1987, 30.

43. Emphasis added; ibid., 16 Nov. 1987.

44. Ibid., 13 Nov. 1987. An individual's share of financial jihad amounted to 2,000 tomans for a soldier. Ayatollah Khomeini volunteered to pay for fifty fighters. President Khamene'i complained that the poor paid, but the rich held back.

45. *New York Times,* 17 Sept. 1987.

46. FBIS-NES, 7 Sept. 1988.

47. R. K. Ramazani, "Iran: Burying the Hatchet," *Foreign Policy* (Fall 1985), 52–74.

48. For details on these two tendencies, see R. K. Ramazani, "Iran's Foreign Policy: Contending Orientations," *Middle East Journal* (Spring 1989), 202–17.

49. FBIS-NES, 24 Feb. 1989.

50. Ibid.

51. Ibid., 11 Oct. 1988.

52. Ibid., 21 Oct. 1988.

53. Ibid., 1 Nov. 1988.

54. Ibid., 19 Oct. 1988.

55. *Washington Post,* 8 Mar. 1989.

56. *BBC Summary of World Broadcasts,* 24 Feb. 1989.

57. Emphasis added; ibid. For a slightly different version of this paragraph, see FBIS-NES, 24 Feb. 1989.

58. *Washington Post,* 1 Mar. 1989.

59. *New York Times,* 3 Mar. 1989.

60. Ibid.

61. Foreign Broadcast Information Service, *Daily Report, Soviet Union,* 22 June 1989, 25.

62. For the text of President Bush's inaugural address that included this plea for goodwill, see *Department of State Bulletin,* April 1989, 1–3. For suggestions about nourishing goodwill toward Iran, see my op-ed pieces in *New York Times,* 10 Aug. 1989, and *Boston Globe,* 20 Aug. 1989.

II | Iran and the Soviet Union

3

The Role of Iran in Soviet Perceptions and Policy, 1946–1988

RICHARD HERRMANN

Although most Americans seem convinced that they know what Soviet policy toward Iran has been in the postwar era, this conviction is no substitute for historical reality and is often at odds with reality. Americans tend to assume that the Soviets have sought, and still seek, to dominate Iran and the Persian Gulf and that Soviet policies are fundamentally aggressive and conquest-oriented, being deterred only by fear of the United States and its allies. Although this perception has some elements of truth, it is inadequate to explain any of the major developments in U.S.-Soviet relations. Even the crisis of 1945–46—when the Soviets supported autonomist movements in Azerbaijan and Kurdistan and refused to withdraw their troops on the promised date—turns out on closer examination not to have been the victory for American policy that is usually presented. Soviet policy toward Mosaddeq's nationalist government cannot be understood in terms of a bipolar paradigm, nor can Soviet policy toward the Shah or the Islamic regime, both of which varied from unfriendly to friendly.

In effect, Soviet policies toward Iran have been far more variable and tentative than the usual picture of single-minded domination aims would suggest. Americans have underestimated the importance that geostrategic security considerations have played in shaping Soviet policy and have been insensitive to the fears that major American influence in the Persian Gulf generate in Moscow. Today the independent and nonaligned policy of the Islamic Republic greatly complicates, if it does not directly contradict, the bipolar assumptions of the Cold War and challenges traditional Soviet and American strategies. Iran is likely to threaten American and Soviet interests. But as perceptions in Moscow change, allowing for a new conception of U.S.-Soviet security relations and a less East-versus-West understanding of regional conflicts, Iran need not be the source of a new Cold War.

I do not intend to retell the well-known tale of Soviet efforts in the "Great Game" of U.S.-Soviet rivalry in the Middle East.[1] In fact, I intend to challenge the basic Cold War story line. I plan to proceed by first looking at the 1946 conflict over the Soviet withdrawal from Azerbaijan. Following the 1946 case, I examine Soviet policy in the heart of the Cold War years from 1949 to 1962. After this, I deal with the development of détente and the very complex relationship that the Soviet Union developed with Iran in the late 1960s and early 1970s. In the final section, I discuss Soviet policy during the Iranian Revolution. This section will deal with the revolutionary period itself, with the postrevolutionary period (1980–87), and finally with the perceptions of Iran that compete in Moscow in the late 1980s and that are likely to affect Soviet diplomacy in Gorbachev's era of "new thinking."

Why Did Stalin Withdraw in 1946?

The motivations and grand design of Stalin's diplomacy have been the subject of well-rehearsed debates between traditional and revisionist historians. But whether Moscow had a forward-looking design bent on conquest, was terrified of capitalist encirclement, and determined to secure Soviet defenses or was simply trapped in an action-reaction cycle of mutual fear and escalation, the Soviet Union's actions toward Iran in 1945–46 were forceful and interventionist. The Red Army, which had been in Iran during the later years of the war, was used to protect and support both Kurdish and Azerbaijani separatist movements. Soviet troops intercepted Iranian forces marching to quell these separatist attempts and remained in Iran as Moscow insisted on oil concessions from Tehran. In the minds of many Americans and Iranians, Stalin's plan to establish puppet states on the Soviet Union's southern frontier, to pressure Turkey, and to drive the Western powers from the area was obvious.[2]

The traditional view of the 1946 case ends with an American victory. In this view, standing behind brilliant Iranian diplomacy, Washington used the United Nations and the leverage of military threats to force the Soviet Union to retreat. The pullback of the Red Army, which began in May 1946, was predicated on a successfully negotiated oil agreement between Moscow and Tehran.[3] By the end of the year, Iran had reestablished control in both territories. Its Majles then refused to accept the oil arrangement, thus expelling the Russians without actually surrendering any lasting concession. The masterful diplomacy of Iran's prime minister Qavam as-Saltaneh and Washington's tough line were given the primary credit for Stalin's defeat.[4]

Although the traditional interpretation of Soviet strategy has some merit, particularly in its more complex and subtle form, it is not altogether persuasive.[5] An interpretation that emphasizes Moscow's concern for security fits the evidence just as well. George Kennan, who at the time was no dove, thought that the proximity of northern Iran to Soviet oil, as well as the potential strategic value of Iranian oil in the hands of Soviet adversaries, worried Soviet leaders.[6] More recently, Richard W. Cottam has argued that although the direct threat to Baku may have been small, the image of a British-dominated Iran may have loomed large in Moscow. It would fit the historical memory of competition with London in this area of the world.[7] Marshall Shulman's classic reappraisal of Stalin's foreign policy in Europe may be equally apt with respect to Iran:

> The serious weakening of the British and French positions . . . led to a period of active probing by the Soviet Union to establish the outer periphery of its new sphere of control. The militancy with which this was done in the early Cominform period created the impression in the West that this constituted the revival of a world revolutionary drive. This impression was probably mistaken, for the key to the action now appears to have been the consolidation of Soviet control over territory gained since 1939 and an essentially reactive response to ward off an anticipated effort by the West to recover these territories.[8]

Americans often dismiss as naive any interpretation of Soviet strategy that emphasizes defensive motives. In 1946, however, what was considered far-fetched, if not dangerously romantic, was the notion that the United States could make the Soviets withdraw. Washington had no conventional military options in the area. The U.S. ambassador, George Allen, knew that if Moscow decided to play tough he could not promise the Iranians much help other than to protest in the United Nations. The State Department concluded that there was nothing Washington could do to enhance appreciably Iran's ability to resist.[9] Worse still, Washington could not expect to enjoy any support from Great Britain. Even if London had wanted to shore up Iranian independence, which it probably did not, it had no resources to offer. London would settle for a division of Iran, acknowledging the Soviet influence in the North as long as it was able to retain control in the South.[10]

President Harry Truman recalled in 1952 that he had threatened Stalin in 1946 and that this display of strength forced the Soviet dictator to concede. The Soviet retreat had to be a product of resolute American resistance. What else could have caused it? This question, of course, was precisely the puzzle that perplexed American analysts in 1946.[11] They knew there had been no credible American coercion and no American threats. Historians have found no evidence to corroborate President Truman's memory but have instead unearthed a good deal of information to suggest that his recall was heavily influenced by the ideology of the Cold War.[12]

In fact, American support for Iran in 1946 was meager at best. Washington refused Qavam's request for combat material and military equipment. It agreed to extend credit for the purchase of surplus weapons only in the fall of 1946, after the major Soviet-Iranian deal had been struck and the Soviet withdrawal had begun. It did not commit military advisers to Iran for yet another year, starting in late 1947.[13] Washington held Moscow accountable in the United Nations, but a diplomatic tongue-lashing hardly seemed like the kind of pressure that would make Joseph Stalin even blush, much less retreat.

If the United States did not make threats, other than to protest in the United Nations, and could not and did not deliver a credible and effective force to Iran, then why did the Soviet Union pull back? The main explanation probably rests with Soviet priorities. The southern front, and Iran in particular, was not at the center of Soviet concerns. The European theater was top priority. Because Iran was a second priority, it is possible that the meager costs Washington could threaten were enough to dissuade the leaders in Moscow. But if this is so, why did they intervene in the first place? Surely, they knew Washington would complain in diplomatic circles. If northern Iran was not worth at least defending Soviet credibility as a great power, then why waste the energy and potential embarrassment?

On the other hand, if Stalin considered the threat of an Anglo-American dominated Iran to be serious enough to call for Soviet interference in Azerbaijan and Kurdistan, then what changed in 1946 that could have reassured him that a withdrawal was safe? Iran did agree to an oil concession. But if this was the critical concern, then why did Stalin refrain from enforcing this outcome after the Majles double-crossed him? The Red Army was still ready to march, and the Kurds, if not the Azeris, could be expected to fight. Anyway, oil would hardly assuage Soviet concerns about security. Moscow did not need Iran's oil in 1946. What would reassure Stalin were political acts that would reduce the image of an Anglo-American conspiracy to control Iran.

In this regard, two developments may be relevant. First, with the ascension of Qavam as-Saltaneh to the post of prime minister, Moscow had a leader in Iran that it could view as independent of British or American control. At the time, some Americans considered Qavam a Soviet puppet.[14] He was perceived in Washington, as well as by the U.S. ambassador in Tehran, as likely to be much too forthcoming with the Russians.[15] His credibility as a nationalist may have deflated Soviet fears. Second, the United States stuck to an evenhanded approach to Soviet concerns. Instead of pressuring the Iranians to take a tough and threatening position toward the Soviets, Washington encouraged Qavam to appease Moscow's oil demands and not antagonize Stalin.[16]

The Soviet Union did not want Great Britain or the United States to control Iran. It took direct and brutally imperial actions to ensure that its southern flank was not an outpost for a hostile great power. On this point there is little disagreement. Whether Moscow actually aspired to dominate Iran as a springboard for the conquest of all of Southwest Asia is a matter of dispute—in many ways one that cannot be resolved. Those who hold the expansionist view can explain Soviet retreats, as in 1946, as caused by American pressure. When this seems incredible, as I implied above, they can argue that Moscow desires the spoils of war without the costs of war and is unwilling to accept even minor costs. Moscow's passivity, they might suggest, is simply Soviet patience. The leaders in the Kremlin decided to wait for a still more inviting opportunity. This teleological argument has a reasonable place in the planning of prudent policy options, but it renders the academic proposition invulnerable. The best we can do is trace the pattern of Soviet behavior over the subsequent forty years and see if it exploited other opportunities in Iran when they came along or simply reacted to threats on its southern frontier as they were perceived.

The Cold War, 1949–1962: Soviet Strategy and Action

A United Front with Anti-Imperial Forces

It was not long after the war that leaders in Moscow described the United States as their greatest threat. The United States was described as building a set of regional outposts from which to pressure the Soviet Union and attack socialism. It was within this general picture that Soviet leaders saw Iran. The United States was seen as determined to control Iran, both to loot its natural resources and to capitalize on its proximity to the Soviet Union's southern republics. Not surprisingly, Moscow expressed great displeasure and protested vigorously whenever the American-Iranian military connection improved and Tehran's behavior fit Cold War expectations.

Moscow complained bitterly about the outlawing of the Tudeh Party in Iran in 1949.[17] It also protested the extension of U.S. military aid to Iran in 1952 and denounced Tehran's regime harshly when it decided to join the Baghdad Pact in October 1955. In 1958–59, as Washington and Iran moved toward signing a joint defense agreement, Moscow did more than protest. It tried to persuade Tehran to forgo this choice. Its blandishments and threats had no effect on Iran's decision, although they may have helped the Shah to get a better deal from Washington, but they did reflect Moscow's strong opposition to America's military presence in Iran. None of this, of course, is exceptional. Who could expect anything but opposition to the development of any enemy military presence directly on one's southern frontier? What is interesting is that Moscow confined its opposition to tough talk and ferocious propaganda.

The Cold War had the effect of inducing a simple geostrategic conception of regional events. Complicated political situations were reduced to simple-minded logic such as "the enemy of my enemy is my friend" and the "friend of my enemy is my enemy." The litmus test for regional parties in Soviet eyes came to be their attitude toward "Western imperialism" and, more important, the United States. When Arab or Iranian nationalism led to opposition to Anglo-American influence, Moscow celebrated the "just cause" and claimed to be its greatest defender.[18] To the extent that Gamal Abdul Nasser's Suez victory in 1956 and Iraq's revolution in 1958 diminished the strength of the "anti-Soviet" alliances they were very good things. If they could all unite into a powerful regional movement and expel the West completely, that would be even better. To the extent that they also opposed the Soviet Union's influence and domestic Communist parties, they, of course, were misguided and still under the sway of reactionary ideas. Moscow often complained about the anticommunist actions of Arab and Iranian nationalists, but for the most part it did not make aid and support contingent on this ideological score.[19] The litmus test was anti-imperialism and geostrategic utility.

When Mohammad Mosaddeq came to power and endorsed nationalization of the British-controlled Iranian oil industry, there was some ambivalence in Soviet descriptions and perhaps a bit of hope that this nationalist would reverse the escalating American presence. When he endorsed the 1952 extension of U.S. military aid to Iran and made his continuing optimism about U.S.-Iranian relations clear, Soviet propaganda increasingly dismissed him as little more than an agent of the big bourgeoisie.[20] The Tudeh Party continued to work with Mosaddeq's National Front on an informal and tacit basis, implying, despite their real differences, that there was still some hope for a united-front strategy in which "reactionary" forces could be defeated.[21]

Verbal Activism and Soviet Acquiescence to the Overthrow of Mosaddeq

Although the Tudeh Party was an important actor in Iran in the early 1950s, the real covert action came from Washington and London. Operation

Ajax was fairly simple.[22] The Shah would fire Mosaddeq, appoint Gen. Fazlollah Zahedi prime minister, have him declare martial law, and that would be that. The troublesome nationalist would be gone, the oil issues could be resolved on terms agreeable to the West, and a regime would be in place that would establish strict order and eliminate any chance that communists might exercise influence in Tehran. The operation failed when Mosaddeq refused to play his role, had the Shah's messenger arrested, and watched as the Shah fled the country. The nationalists rallied around their leader and crowds came into the street to protest the Shah's intrigue with foreigners. At this point the Tudeh Party escalated the situation by fostering violent demonstrations in Tehran and attacking religious institutions and symbols of the Pahlavi regime.

These disturbances, and Mosaddeq's decision to keep the troops loyal to him in the barracks, gave Zahedi a chance to rescue Operation Ajax. He ordered his troops to quell the violence in the streets and declared martial law. Tudeh followers, who had originally come into the streets in conjunction with the nationalist opposition to the Shah's plot, were told by the party to get off the streets as the violent developments, being fueled by American agents acting as provocateurs, were creating a pretext for Zahedi's move. With the Tudeh abandoning the streets, Zahedi's forces took control.[23]

Although the Tudeh played a role in the events of August 1953, it did not make a bid for power, and there is no evidence that Moscow was involved in any of the action. Soviet propaganda had been alluding to the possibility of an American-orchestrated coup for some time, and after the initial collapse of the Ajax plan *Pravda* simply reported the coup failure in a straightforward way.[24] When the second part of the drama unfolded, *Pravda* took a very negative line. The United States, its reporter said, had been unsatisfied with a client state and wanted an absolute puppet regime.[25] This regime, *Pravda* continued, was based on horrifying terror and reflected Washington's "barefaced colonial policy" of opposing any Iranian leader who advocated progressive change, his country's freedom, or national independence. Besides this predictable verbal blast, the Soviet Union simply stood aside.[26]

The Tudeh had come into the streets, but the stimulus for this had been Washington's decision to attack the charismatic symbol of Iranian nationalism, not Soviet covert activities. When the Tudeh was crushed and Mosaddeq arrested, Moscow protested loudly but did nothing. In the same week that *Pravda* denounced the U.S. role in Iran and described the Iranian regime as nothing more than a puppet of Washington's anti-Soviet terrorist policy, *Pravda* announced with delight that, after several months of negotiations, letters were exchanged on 3 September 1953 agreeing to a large increase in Soviet-Iranian trade.[27] At this time the Malenkov transition to a post-Stalin foreign policy had just begun and there was hope of diminishing American hostility with a Soviet policy more amenable to compromise. With the rise of Khrushchev, Moscow's interest in competing in the Third World grew, as did its perception that non-aligned and nationalist movements could help shift the "correlation of forces" away from the postwar American hegemony. As Arab nationalists would find out throughout the rest of the decade, however, the Soviets might verbally condemn American actions and call for a united front against imperialism, but when the chips were down the Soviet Union was unwilling, unable, or perhaps both, to defend its credibility with costly and determined actions.[28]

Détente in Soviet-American and Soviet-Iranian Relations

Play Acting Cold War Roles and Building Stable Relationships

In the 1960s and early 1970s Moscow was consistently critical of both Iran's growing military dependence on Washington and the development of its impressive military arsenal. The script became entirely routine. The United States, in its rapacious pursuit of oil and its never-ending militaristic fascination with blocs and military supremacy, used Iran as a link in its network of Middle Eastern clients. Despite the well-rehearsed propaganda, Soviet officials spared Iran from some of the criticism directed at other American clients, such as Saudi Arabia, and developed a policy toward Iran that was quite complex. By the mid-1970s Soviet writers described Moscow's relationship with Iran as very good. And it was.

Before the Iranian Revolution, the Soviet Union was the largest market for the export of Iranian manufactured goods. At the same time, Iran had become the largest market for Soviet nonmilitary goods in the Middle East.[29] With over three thousand Soviet advisers in Iran, the extent of Soviet scientific and technical assistance was obvious. At the time, this was the largest contingent of Soviet technicians anywhere in the Third World.[30] The well-publicized Iranian-Soviet gas arrangements were only the most visible evidence of the substantial and very stable Soviet investment in the Shah's regime.

In 1966 Moscow agreed to make Soviet arms available to Tehran, and in the five years from 1966 to 1970 it sold approximately $344 million worth of military hardware to Iran.[31] This represented only 12 percent of Iran's military imports, however, compared to the 85 percent share held by Washington. During the Nixon-Kissinger years of 1970–76, Iranian military imports skyrocketed, nearly quadrupling the purchases of the previous five years. With the gates to the American arsenal wide open for the Shah, Moscow had a difficult time competing. In the latter part of the seventies, but still before the revolution, Moscow was able to regain a small 2 percent ($210 million) share of the Iranian arms market, and it encouraged its East European allies actively to court the Shah in order to establish new sources of oil.[32]

The dual character of Soviet policy toward the Shah's regime is easier to describe than it is to explain. Positive Soviet-Iranian relations developed, despite the continuing American dependence on Iran as a strategic "pillar." They also developed in spite of Soviet support for Nasser in the 1960s, for Iraq in the early 1970s, and for other regional adversaries of the Shah, such as the rebels in Dhofar. Moscow might have been trying to entice the Shah to abandon the Western connection, but the carrots and sticks it used hardly seemed credible in this regard. And if American power deterred or frightened the Soviets, then why would Moscow further enhance the Iranian military capacity with aid and arms sales? The answers to these questions are complicated and deserve more elaboration than I can give here, but both the complexity of Iranian policy and the emergence of the Brezhnev strategy for détente deserve special consideration.

Americans may have felt that the Shah's regime reflected Washington's will to contain communism and stood as a pillar of anti-Soviet stability, but it is unlikely that this romantic image prevailed in Moscow. Beginning in 1962, Soviet policy toward the Shah's regime began to develop in a complex way. The major impetus for the break with the classic Cold War perspective was the Shah's decision to accept a mutual nonaggression arrangement with Moscow and his pledge never to allow rockets aimed at the Soviet Union to be deployed on Iranian soil.[33] In the beginning of the next decade, Iran and the Soviet Union signed a mutual friendship treaty to accompany their burgeoning trade. Western experts on Iran doubted that confrontation with the Soviet Union was very high on the Shah's foreign policy agenda.[34] Soviet planners probably came to the same conclusion. The Shah had dreams of Iranian regional hegemony and preeminence in the Indian Ocean, as well as grandiose economic aspirations, but these were for himself and not for the United States. As he became stronger he would become more independent and pursue his own imperial ambitions. In the process Tehran would do many things that Moscow disagreed with, but to the extent that they were part of Tehran's agenda and not Washington's they would be of lesser geostrategic importance. Although the Shah advertised his anticommunism when in Washington, he also flirted with Moscow in order to hike American anxiety and open American pocketbooks. At the same time he was careful to reassure Soviet leaders that he would not allow Iran to be used as a springboard for an attack on the Soviet Union. Iranian air and sea forces, as mighty as they were, were not deployed to meet a Soviet challenge in the North but rather to pursue the Shah's southern ambitions.[35]

There is little evidence that the Iranian armed forces ever alarmed Soviet planners. Even at the height of the Iranian buildup, the twenty-four divisions in the Soviet southern command included only one tank division. Moreover, nearly all of these divisions were kept at the lowest level of readiness (category three) with most of their equipment presumably present and their manpower in some form of reserve.[36] The United States had tried to develop a major military force in Pakistan beginning in 1954, but even the American officers involved never felt that the Pakistani forces would be used against anyone but the Indians, despite all the rhetoric about containing communism.[37] The Shah's forces in Iran also may have been very potent against regional adversaries, but they were likely to fight the Russians only in American imaginations.

The deterrent effect of the Shah's forces and the American nuclear umbrella may have had less to do with the Soviet Union's constrained and positive relationship with the Shah than did the Shah's policies of reassurance. His direct agreements with Moscow coupled with his own policies of regional aggrandizement (which would distract him from serving in any American anti-Soviet crusade) may have convinced Moscow that there was not too much to fear strategically and quite a bit to be gained by dealing with the presumably stable dictator. Nowhere is this clearer than in Moscow's reaction to the Shah's bloody games in Iraqi Kurdistan.

Testing the Limits of Détente: The Shah's Game in Kurdistan

In 1972, shortly after détente had been the theme of a Moscow summit, the Nixon administration agreed to a political escapade that was a classic hardball geostrategic maneuver. The Ba'ath regime in Iraq agreed to a national compromise with the Kurdish Democratic Party (KDP) in March 1970. The National Accord, along with the rising oil prices, led to promising forecasts for Iraqi development.[38] In October 1971 an attempt was made on Kurdish leader Mulla Mustafa al-Barzani's life, and conflict among Kurds and Arabs began to simmer again.[39] Before this, in August, the Shah had asked the United States to join with him in his efforts to intervene in Iraq and use the Kurdish "card," as the Shah called Barzani's movement, to destabilize Iraq.[40]

In the first few months of 1972 the fighting in Kurdish areas slowly escalated, presumably with Iranian aid flowing to the Kurds, despite the fact that even as late as 15 May 1972 the Ba'ath was still seeking a national front arrangement that would include the Iraqi Communist Party and the KDP.[41] It was roughly at this time that the United States became fully involved in the plan and endorsed the Shah's Kurdish policy, providing $16 million to the Kurdish forces.[42] The fighting would preoccupy the Shah's adversary in Baghdad and destabilize what Cold War–minded Americans regarded as a Soviet client in the Middle East. Israel would push the plan along to weaken its Arab enemy. The United States and the Shah agreed ahead of time that if the Kurds should actually be successful and threaten to achieve independence, support would be withdrawn so as not to create difficulties for the Shah in Iranian Kurdistan.[43]

If Soviet leaders saw Iran in classic Cold War terms, one would expect them to counter this Iranian-American-Israeli adventure quickly. They would not tolerate subversive operations through ethnic minority groups that not only lived on their southern border but also resided in the Soviet Union. The Soviet Union did come to Iraq's defense, but slowly and in a complex way.[44] For nearly two years it preached a policy of national reconciliation and tried to mediate a new agreement among the Kurds, the Ba'ath, and the Iraqi communists.[45] Finally, in March 1974, after the Kurdish leaders declared their autonomy in a zone encompassing the Kirkuk oil fields and had promised Washington a friend in OPEC once they were free, Moscow dropped its efforts to reestablish a national compromise and helped Iraq turn the tide on the battlefield.[46] With the military tide shifting, the Shah agreed to negotiate, and both sides compromised in the Algiers Accord in early 1975. Despite the Soviet aid that had made it possible for Iraq to achieve a negotiated outcome that was acceptable to its interests, Iraqi leaders complained that Soviet support had been late and reluctant.[47] After all, in the midst of the struggle, in October 1972, Moscow had signed a friendship treaty with Tehran; and during this period Soviet trade with Iran was greater than that with Iraq.[48]

There is no reason to assume that Moscow was deterred by Washington or lacked the ability to intervene earlier and settle the Kurdish case on its own terms. Soviet troops had just withdrawn from Egypt and could have been dispatched to Iraq. Even the Soviet press knew that Washington would not fight for the Kurds.[49] Moreover, the Soviet international public relations position as the defender of an ally facing externally supported subversion was very strong. When we consider that this came on the heels of the Soviet expulsion from Cairo and that it presumably came at a time when Moscow was looking to secure its remaining relationships in the Arab world, it reveals both how little threat leaders in Moscow felt from Tehran and how important they considered their relationship with the Shah to be.

The Kurdish case was a small incident in an era defined in Moscow as one of peaceful coexistence. The Shah's friendship and nonaggression policies may have calmed lingering Soviet fears of Cold War encirclement, but they probably seemed almost insignificant in comparison to the effect Willy Brandt's *Ostpolitik* in Europe had. With the essential postwar status quo in Europe accepted by all of the key European states and the United States, Soviet leaders felt that the preconditions for a modus vivendi with the West were in place. The Soviet strategic nuclear arsenal had come of age, and, according to Soviet analysts, the United States had been compelled to accept the reality of parity and the end of postwar American hegemony.[50] The Brezhnev conception of détente forecast a period of continued change and revolution in the Third World as national liberation forces riding the wave of mass-based nationalism achieved independence from neocolonialism. In some cases, the Soviet Union would help if counterrevolutionaries were being bolstered with external support. In most cases it would certainly applaud. In the case of Iran, however, there is no evidence that Soviet leaders felt these trends would affect the Shah's stability or understood the forces that consumed his regime.

The Iranian Revolution and Soviet Foreign Policy

Late, but Clear Support: Soviet Hopes for the
Anti-American Revolution

Judging from the daily Soviet press, leaders in Moscow were slow to see the signs of revolution in Iran. The Soviet dailies did not cover the January 1978 protest in Qom, nor did they have much to say about the February riots in Tabriz. It was still a time to advertise the great cooperation and friendship in Soviet-Iranian relations and to worry about pollution in the Caspian Sea.[51] Even after the huge demonstrations in June and July and the September violence on Black Friday in Jaleh Square, *Izvestia* simply ran a Tass report announcing that American officials were getting nervous about the events in Iran and planned to look into them.[52] By the end of October the Soviet press had changed. There was still no criticism of the Shah nor any hint that his regime might ultimately collapse, but there was a direct discussion of the social and economic "antagonisms" in Iran. These were attributed to a number of factors, such as the development of an isolated and corrupt bureaucracy, excessive military spending, and repression, but for the most part they were explained as the consequences of rapid modernization and the Shah's ambitious programs for social change.[53]

At some point in November 1978, Soviet leaders evidently decided that the Shah's regime would fall. When they did, their press abandoned the "backlash against rapid modernization and its negative side effects" script. Soviet writers explained that the "modernization" talk was nothing but a sham and a forgery. The problem was the Shah's vassal-like subservience to Washington and his personal corruption and ruthlessness. His regime was defended with the iron fist of SAVAK butchers and American agents. All the social antagonisms of the economy were still mentioned as well, but now the opposition was not against modernization but against American imperialism and the fascist monarch.[54]

Although the Soviet Union did not stimulate the Iranian Revolution, it is hardly surprising that it would applaud the Shah's demise and encourage the revolutionary regime to follow an anti-American course. As argued above, Moscow had never been happy with the American influence in Tehran. The threat it perceived from Iran may not have been very intense, but if this threat could be reduced still further without any major Soviet activity, why should Moscow object? The geostrategic loss for the United States was obvious. Soviet planners did not need to believe that Moscow's influence in Tehran would increase to welcome the revolutionary anti-American developments.[55] The key lessons, they explained, were that American puppets who were hated by their people could not be kept in power regardless of how hard Washington tried.[56]

Soviet writers like to exaggerate Moscow's role in defending the Iranian Revolution. It is true that from November 1978 through February 1979 Moscow repeatedly warned the United States against directly intervening, but it is very doubtful that this Soviet posture actually deterred an American attack.[57] Contingency plans for intervention were being considered in Washington, but ultimately a coup operation was not given the final go-ahead. The key variables in these decisions, however, related to the situation on the ground in Iran and not to fears about Soviet pique.[58] In January 1979 the Soviet press and radio warned of an imminent American coup in Iran.[59] The U.S. State Department lodged a protest about the Soviet media, complaining that it was inciting violence in Tehran.[60] The possibilities of a coup were being actively pursued by Gen. Robert Huyser and seriously considered in Washington by National Security Adviser Zbigniew Brzezinski. It is possible that the attention paid by the Soviet media made this a more risky American option, but it is doubtful that the Soviet reports of these activities were responsible for inciting anti-Americanism among Iranians as the State Department protests claimed. More likely, Soviet propagandists were trying to convince revolutionary Iranians that Moscow was in their corner.

The Soviet Union applauded the Iranians who were risking their lives to promote massive social and political change. For the Iranians, however, the Russians were latecomers to the revolution and had done nothing in the early days. Worse still, they had for fifteen years enjoyed a comfortable relationship with the Shah and had shown no sympathy for Islam in Central Asia. To maintain the Soviet-Iranian relationship that had developed in the 1970s, Moscow would have to find a way to ingratiate itself with the revolutionary regime and portray itself as the regime's defender.

Support, but Not Control: Anti-Americanism Was Enough

A few important Americans, who were wedded to a bipolar paradigm, suspected Moscow's hand somewhere behind the robes of the mollas.[61] Certainly Soviet radio propaganda was supportive of the revolution. As time went by, the KGB conspiracy theory looked increasingly silly and almost no one subscribed to it. Instead, the fear was that if an Islamic republic was formed, Iran would eventually go communist.[62]

Whether the Soviet Union's strategy was defensive or expansionist, leaders in Moscow would welcome the collapse of "America's Shah." If it was expansionist and reasonably opportunistic, however, we might expect the Soviet Union to have tried to exploit the Iranian Revolution more fully and even to exert direct influence on Tehran. At the military level, the absence of Soviet action was overdetermined: any use of force against Iran would have been costly, dangerous, and politically unwise. The Iranian resistance could never have defeated the Red Army, but it could have made such an adventure costly. Needless to say, such a gross use of force would have evoked universal condemnation in the region and might possibly have led to a coalescing of anti-Soviet forces. If the Soviets had chosen to act with enough force to intimidate the whole region and set off a rush to Moscow to appease the new regional hegemon, then they would also have had to anticipate a major American and West European response and perhaps even a nuclear exchange.

The American position in Southwest Asia was very weak. It had no viable conventional option against a determined Soviet attack, and its nuclear threat, therefore, was of uncertain credibility, given the standard logic of extended deterrence in an era of mutual assured destruction. American defense planners at first argued that the West had no options in the Gulf and therefore predicted a Soviet conquest of the world without their having to fire a shot—unless, of course, massive new expenditures were made to improve American logistic abilities.[63] Whether anything could be done to make up for an eight-thousand-mile disadvantage in proximity was never quite clear. Other studies suggested that the Soviet Union could not occupy northern Iran without major losses and that neither huge expenditures nor increased aid to conservative Arab regimes that might be hostile to Israel was necessary.[64]

The American fascination with the Soviet military threat to Iran was symptomatic of a weakness in American political and strategic analysis. U.S. policymakers apparently contemplated military tactics and "war games" without ever considering the details of Iranian politics, the profound social and political changes taking place in the region, or the complicated pattern of actual Soviet diplomacy.[65] Moreover, the war games approach missed the essential characteristic of the superpowers' competition in the Cold War era. The contest was not on the battlefield but in the manipulation of political events. George Kennan warned in the 1940s that the threat was not military but political. The contest would be based on the details of the social and political relationships in Iran that American military scenarios seemed determined to ignore.

Subversion from the Left: The Tudeh Party as an Instrument

Soviet propaganda in 1979–80 often called for unity and cooperation among the disparate elements that made up the revolution, but it rarely simplified the situation and suggested that this cooperation was already present or could be easily achieved.[66] There were many elements within the revolutionary opposition, and most Soviet articles began with some effort to emphasize this complexity and identify the key players. Iranian experts like Yelena Doroshenko were undoubtedly the best at this, but even key commentators in *Kommunist* like Pavel Demchenko drove home the point that a wide range of views existed in Tehran.[67]

There also was very little effort to pretend that the revolution had been a socialist one. The revolution was described as having progressive aspects, and hope was evident that trends for progressive social change might continue in later stages of the process, but nearly all Soviet articles were heavily qualified. They stressed how much confusion was still evident in Tehran, how many things still needed to be done, and how difficult it was to predict the future direction of Iranian politics. Some analysts exaggerated the role played by leftist groups, but nearly everyone returned to an explanation of why the clergy had played the central role in the revolution.[68] No one in the Soviet press expressed any surprise that Islam had been the glue that held the opposition together. The Shah, they said, had destroyed all other organizations that might have served as revolutionary institutions. And besides, the standard line continued, most Iranians had not yet had any access to ideological systems other than religious and nationalistic-religious ones. The revolution, the Soviets explained, was spontaneous and broadly popular, and the clergy was well positioned to channel its fury.

In this environment the Tudeh Party could only support the Khomeinists and preserve the central anti-imperialist achievement of the revolution. Soviet policy endorsed the Tudeh decision. After the Tudeh was crushed in 1983, leading party members testified at their trials that they had served as Soviet agents and had plotted to overthrow the Islamic regime. They confessed that their support for the Islamic government had always been tactical, with a long-run aim of infiltrating the security forces and the army and then pushing the clerical regime aside and seizing power for themselves and their foreign (Soviet) masters. These "confessions" were obtained under horrifying conditions and may have reflected the suspicions and propaganda needs of the clerical leaders in Iran far more than the actual intentions of the Tudeh.[69] But, just the same, it is possible that Tudeh and Soviet leaders hoped for the continuation of the revolution into the social and economic arena sometime in the future.[70] What is important, however, is that there is no evidence of serious Soviet actions to support a Tudeh bid for power, nor is there any evidence that anyone in Moscow seriously thought that the Tudeh could be a viable option in anything but the very long term.

Even the most optimistic Soviet analysts in regard to the Tudeh's role in Iran saw no chance for any short-term advantage beyond securing the anti-American direction of the revolution. S. Aliyev, for instance, claimed that it was hard to overvalue the importance of the continued growth in the workers' consciousness that might enable left-wing forces to struggle for further social progress some time in the future. But, Aliyev lamented, this task "seemed incredibly difficult" unless the left-wing parties united into a mass party.[71] This development seemed unlikely. Aliyev concentrated on the reemergence of the Tudeh Party, but other Soviet specialists, like Doroshenko, did not even mention the Tudeh, instead pointing out the role of the left-Islamic Mojahedin-e Khalq during the revolution.[72]

Moscow's relationship with the "progressive Muslims" following Ali Shariati and Ayatollah Sayyed Mahmud Taleqani was not strong, nor were its ties to the Mojahedin-e Khalq. Consequently, Moscow's options for acting through leftist movements in Iran that had large popular bases were limited and very long range. In the short term, the Soviet Union tried to develop economic relations with the Islamic regime, supported the regime when the West tried to pressure it economically, and behaved correctly in diplomatic terms.[73] No one in the West can know what Moscow's long-run aims were, but there is no evidence that it intended to challenge the Islamic regime from the left in the immediate postrevolutionary period.

Exploiting Ethnic Nationalism as an Instrument of Soviet Policy

If Moscow had wanted to take advantage of the instability in Iran and do more than enjoy Washington's loss, if it had wanted to gain positive influence of its own, then its most obvious avenue would not have been through the Left but through ethnic and national minorities. After all, this was the instrument it had used in 1946. In 1979, the opportunities were ripe. In February, Ayatollah

Ezzedin Hosaini demanded autonomy for the Kurds, and in March and April fighting broke out in Kurdistan and Turkmenistan. In Kurdistan there were strong nationalist leaders, and among the Turkoman tribes, powerful left-oriented leaders. During the year, Arabs and Baluchi tribesmen in Iran also sought a new relationship with the central government. This led to heavy fighting and the declaration of a state of emergency in Baluchistan in the late fall. Fighting broke out in Tabriz in December 1979, as Azerbaijanis also insisted on new terms for association with the Islamic Republic. Ayatollah Khomeini and Sadeq Qotbzadeh accused the Soviet Union of providing aid to the Kurds, but it is unlikely that much Soviet material assistance was provided to any of these minorities.[74]

In the spring of 1979 Soviet radio broadcasts to Iran did not report on the "just cause" of the minority demands or on the need for the Islamic regime to accept their autonomy. To the contrary, these broadcasts tended to attribute the fighting to CIA-SAVAK provocateurs and other pro-Shah elements.[75] The argument was that the counterrevolutionaries wanted to create the conditions of civil war. Amidst the turmoil, the United States and reactionary Iranian forces would intervene to topple the revolutionary Islamic regime and install a new version of the old order. The key prescriptive part of the message was designed to encourage unity and the subjugation of the national question to the higher purpose of consolidating the revolution. Preserving the anti-imperial (meaning anti-American) character of Iran was clearly Moscow's first priority. Some Soviet writers called the desires of the Kurds, the Baluchis, the Turkomen, and the Arabs "legitimate" and encouraged the Iranian regime to find a way to accommodate cultural autonomy and national self-expression, but this was always within the context of the regime's need to resolve discord and protect the geostrategic achievement of the revolution.[76]

The public sympathy offered by Soviet propaganda to the minorities in Iran was revealing. When internal tension threatened the revolutionary regime, and when this regime was perceived to be pursuing an anti-American course, Moscow criticized the ethnic strife and tried to stifle the political mobilization of ethnic minorities when this mobilization was based on separatist or nationalist themes. In the fall of 1979, however, the Bazargan government moved to reopen more normal contacts with Washington and even to obtain military spare parts. At this point, Soviet commentators like Aleksandr Bovin began to express their "anxiety," "alarm," "uncertainty," and "disappointment" with the course of the revolution.[77] Along with this came a concern for the persecution of the minorities, especially the Kurds.[78] Some articles recalled the great achievements accomplished in Kurdistan in 1946, and many criticized the Iranian use of force in the area.[79] They usually concluded that the Kurds would not be defeated by arms and that the only viable solution was a political settlement that met Kurdish demands.

Mehdi Bazargan and Ibrahim Yazdi's trip to Algeria, their meeting with Brzezinski, and the hostage crisis that soon followed ended the Islamic Republic's flirtation with Washington. It also marked the end of any obvious Soviet concern about Iranian minorities. At the end of the year, ethnic violence in Azerbaijan and Baluchistan was intense. Moscow condemned the separatist efforts in both places as fratricidal wars unleashed by the CIA and SAVAK.[80] These were cases where the Soviet Union may not have wanted to support the minorities for reasons entirely intrinsic to the specific peoples. The Azeris might excite Soviet Azeris and consequently might represent a more dangerous national group to support. Moscow did not have a history of supporting Baluch separatism and may have also concluded that this group had no chance of success inside Iran.[81] The Kurds, who had been worthy of at least sympathy in the late summer and fall, were swept off the Soviet agenda as the hostage crisis once again exaggerated the anti-American aspects of political developments in Iran. It also gave Moscow yet another chance to prove its great friendship for the revolution and its utility as a common foe of imperialism.[82]

The Iran-Iraq War: Opportunities and Threats

Both the military situation and the Soviet Union's behavior toward minorities in Iran suggest that Moscow did not exploit the opportunities available in 1978–80. Soviet objectives appeared to be limited to ensuring that the United States would not stage a comeback in Iran. It is possible, of course, that this restraint was simply patience, as Moscow waited for Iran to fall apart and become a still more inviting and low-cost target of opportunity. If the Soviets were waiting for a better chance to move into Iran, they did not have to wait for long: Iraq attacked Iran in full force in September 1980.

When Saddam Hussein made his bid for predominance in the Persian Gulf and decisive leadership of the Arab world, he presented the Soviet Union with a choice. It could support his attack, revive the ethnic issues in Iran, and help tame the Islamic Republic or it could condemn the attack, back Tehran with air support and fresh supplies, and hope to win favor with the regime in Iran, and perhaps even bring a new government to power in a defeated Iraq. If Moscow had been waiting for an opportunity, either tactic might have made sense. Another tactic for helping to ripen future opportunities would have been to aid both sides and promote continuation of the war. When the two were exhausted, Moscow could then move with "internal" communist revolutions of the East European variety in Baghdad and Tehran. The risks associated with any of these options were fairly modest in relation to the potential geostrategic gains.[83] Moscow, however, chose to avoid them all, opposing the war from the outset and calling for its immediate cessation. It also endorsed the legitimacy of the existing territorial boundaries and called on Iraq to pull back from Iranian territory.

The war in the Gulf allowed the United States to justify the commitment of still more naval forces to the area. It also put the regimes in Baghdad and Tehran at risk and opened uncontrolled and unpredictable possibilities for an American comeback in Southwest Asia. These were the concerns all Soviet comments emphasized.[84] Leaders in Moscow may have been unhappy with the theocracy in Iran and the persecution of leftists and national minorities. They may even have been disappointed that the prospect of a socialist Iran was growing increasingly dim. But these concerns were all of secondary importance. The central strategic issue was the anti-imperial and anti-American posture of the regime in Tehran. Once this had been clarified with the taking of American hostages, Moscow had no interest in Saddam Hussein's fears of Khomeini-type movements in Iraq or in his quest for glory—thus the Soviet Union's refusal to sell new weapons to Iraq and its call for an immediate end to the fighting and an Iraqi withdrawal.[85]

Iranian leaders blamed Washington and Moscow for Baghdad's attack. The Soviet brutality against Muslims in Afghanistan and its repeated refusals to let Tehran open consulates in Soviet Central Asia undermined greatly any Soviet plan to court Islamic Iran. The Soviet Union opposed the Gulf war, but as long as the United States was also uninvolved the issue remained a secondary one. Soviet propaganda condemned the growing American armada in the area and Washington's efforts to deploy forces for the Central Command, but all of this was standard Cold War propaganda. The policy was essentially one of detachment. No threat was perceived intensely enough to require action, and no opportunity was inviting enough to excite Soviet adventurism.

Consolidation of the Islamic Regime and Changing Soviet Perspectives

In 1982–83 two important factors changed: Iran reversed Iraq's initial battlefield success, and the clerical regime decided to smash the Tudeh Party in Iran. When Iran reversed the battlefield situation in the spring of 1982, the Soviet Union's policy also began to change. As Iran went on the offensive, Soviet military aid to Iraq resumed.[86] Moscow continued to stress the importance of territorial integrity and called for the war to end, but now it was shoring up Iraq's ability to resist. This, along with other issues, persuaded the regime in

Tehran to crush the Tudeh Party.[87] In February 1983 Nureddin Kianuri, the head of the Tudeh, was arrested and eighteen Soviet diplomats were expelled from Iran. The Soviet Union protested these actions, complained that the CIA had urged on the anti-Soviet campaign, and began to rethink the role revolutionary Islam would play in the geostrategic struggle between the "two social systems."[88]

From 1983 until 1986 Soviet policy toward Iran did not change substantially. Leadership change in Moscow clearly preoccupied the Soviet Union. Moscow continued to criticize Iran's clerical dictatorship and blame extreme conservative and pro-Western bourgeois forces for the failure of Iran's revolution to deal with that country's social needs. At the same time, however, Moscow worked to keep a diplomatic and economic relationship with Tehran and continued to press for a negotiated outcome in the war. In December 1985 Saddam Hussein visited Moscow and managed to persuade Andrei Gromyko to say that Iran's position on the war was unreasonable.[89] But Saddam's discussions were described by the Soviet media as "frank, businesslike, and friendly," code words for substantially heated and disagreeable. One of the issues that Saddam was probably most unhappy about was the Soviet Union's toleration of Syria's and Libya's transshipment of Soviet tanks, guns, and missiles to Iran.[90] Few Arabs found the Soviet official explanation that it could not control the transshipment of its weapons credible.[91] Only two months after Saddam's visit, Soviet First Deputy Foreign Minister Georgii Kornienko arrived in Tehran for talks that the Soviets described as "frank, comprehensive, and constructive."[92] Moscow continued this policy of talking to both sides and pressing for a diplomatic and negotiated outcome throughout 1987.

Gorbachev's "New Thinking" and Soviet Policy

In early 1986 Mikhail Gorbachev called for new thinking in international relations.[93] His ideas about mutual security and the need to understand regional conflicts in terms other than the East-West struggle did not dramatically change Soviet behavior but certainly created new pressures for change. He continued to attack the American policy of a military buildup in the Gulf and put new emphasis on Brezhnev's 1980 idea of a U.N. force to protect shipping in the Persian Gulf. Moscow continued to deal with both sides of the war, despite Washington's efforts to isolate Iran, but did not take advantage of its unique access to both sides. Rather than trying to exclude the United States, as Washington had tried to cut Moscow out of the Arab-Israeli talks at Camp David, Gorbachev stressed the U.N. negotiations and the importance of dealing with both global and regional concerns.

In December 1986 and January 1987 Kuwait asked the United States to protect its shipping. The United States was slow to respond, leading Kuwait to turn to Moscow with the same request. Moscow agreed in April 1987 to reflag three Kuwaiti tankers, prompting an almost knee-jerk American reaction to answer the long-standing Kuwaiti request and reflag eleven Kuwaiti ships. By the fall of 1987 Moscow had increased its combat ships in the Gulf from two to six, which was still substantially fewer than the seventeen combat ships the United States had in the Gulf at this time and the fifteen U.S. support ships located nearby.[94] As the escalatory dynamic became clear, Kuwait asked the Soviet Union for still more help. At this point, however, Moscow for the most part demurred, evidently demonstrating along with its inclusive diplomatic policy a desire to dampen down the Cold War aspects of the conflict and not allow it to interfere with a fledgling Soviet-American détente.

Soviet policy under Gorbachev has continued many of the traditional patterns in Soviet behavior toward Iran but has also given preliminary signals of a desire for change. No one should expect an abrupt change of course, however, for neither the internal bureaucracy of the Soviet Union nor the international environment of the Gulf and Washington has been conducive to a radical departure in Soviet diplomacy. The glasnost that Gorbachev has used to push political change at home allows us to see some of the competing viewpoints that are struggling to affect Soviet decision making. Because Soviet policy is so multidimensional and is affected by so many different institutions, people with different points of view can each have an effect leading to real domestic political constraints and substantial contradictions in policy. It is vital, therefore, for anyone interested in understanding contemporary and future Soviet policy toward Iran to have some sense of the alternative perspectives that compete within the decision-making process. Three outlooks are particularly important.

Competing Soviet Perspectives on the Cold War and Iran

1. The Cold War Still Lives and Islam Serves
   Imperialism's Purpose

For some Soviet observers the traditional bipolar approach to Iran is still convincing. The Islamic Republic, in this view, cannot find a neutral role outside the East-West struggle.[95] Rostislav Ulyanovsky, a secretary in the Central Committee's International Department, and Semen Agayev had some optimism in 1980 that the Islamic Revolution with its anti-American character could serve "progressive" purposes, but by 1985 they had changed their minds.

By then the Islamic Republic Party (IRP) had crushed both the Mojahedin-e Khalq and the Tudeh; it had established a "clerical despotism" that was anticommunist; it was committed to a destabilizing war in the Gulf; and it was supporting the mujahedin's struggle in Afghanistan. The traditionally Cold War–minded, geostrategically oriented Soviet leaders concluded that revolutionary Islam, if not controlled by Washington, at least objectively served Washington's interests.

In the 1950s, Marxist orthodoxy was enforced by describing nationalists as budding socialists and by cramming the complex developments of the Third World into the categories defined by Soviet ideology. In the 1980s, this practice was condemned by everyone writing in the most important Soviet journals and was rejected even by writers widely assumed to be the protectors of the orthodoxy, like Ulyanovsky.[96] The way orthodoxy was developed in the Iranian case was to describe the revolution as a spontaneous mass revolt that was very broadly based and not really led by the Islamic clergy. The clergy had many advantages over any other potential centers of opposition, but Soviet analyses emphasized the important role played by the leftist parties and by the workers in general. The notion was that the reason the clergy was popular was that it articulated the pent-up hatred for American imperialism and the popular hopes for social change.[97] Semen Agayev went so far as to say that the initial revolution was not even an Islamic one.[98] It was a progressive mass revolt that left in its wake three major contenders for power: the liberals, the clergy, and the Left.

For Ulyanovsky, the first task after the ouster of the Shah was to consolidate the anti-imperialist and antimonarchist aspects of the revolution. This meant an alliance between the most anti-American clerical leaders and the Left. This alliance would oppose the "liberals" who were said to be committed to a bourgeois pattern of capitalist development and a positive relationship with Washington. Soviet observers operating in a bipolar perspective did not criticize the Tudeh's decision to align with Khomeini but lamented the fragmentation within the Left and the inability of the three major leftist parties to unite. The Mojahedin-e Khalq, they explained, had prematurely turned to violence and were crushed in 1981, leaving the Tudeh alone to try to steer the course of events along a socially progressive avenue.[99] The Tudeh, of course, was unsuccessful and was crushed in 1983. By 1984, Agayev and Ulyanovsky had decided that the course of events after 1979 was in fact an "Islamic Revolution" and that the popular cause had been defeated by social reactionaries and clerical dictators.[100]

For the most extreme advocates of the bipolar and geostrategic perspective, President Reagan's decision to provide weapons to Iran came as no surprise. Washington, they argued, was trying to use Islamic movements through-out the Middle East to subvert progressive regimes and threaten the Soviet Union.[101] It had picked up where London had left off in its efforts to use Islamic leaders for geostrategic advantage. Igor Belyayev suggested that Washington was trying to stoke direct subversion in Soviet Central Asia and was supporting Islamic fanatics in Syria, Pakistan, and Afghanistan for anti-Soviet pur-poses.[102] Agayev explained that, far from being critical of Iranian-sponsored terrorism, the United States encouraged it and took a very lenient attitude toward it.[103] Washington, he argued, was interested in promoting conflict in the Gulf to perpetuate the pretext for its massive military buildup in Southwest Asia and to generate opportunities for direct intervention.

2. Moscow and Washington Should Collaborate against Islamic Fundamentalism

A second perspective evident in Moscow in the late 1980s also treated Islamic fundamentalism as practiced in Iran as more of a threat to the Soviet Union than an opportunity. This second view, however, never really accepted the optimistic geostrategic forecasts of the bipolar view that prevailed in the Brezhnev days. The best advocate of this perspective was A. Z. Arabad-zhyan.[104] He described the same three major factions in Iran as did those holding the first view, but suggested that the critical errors derived not from the Left's inability to unite but from the liberals' failure to work with the pre-Khomeini Bakhtiar government and the Left's failure to help the liberals. Arabadzhyan began with the assumption that Khomeini had the mass base and that no one in the Left or among the liberals could compete for the role of charismatic leader. What they had to do, he argued, was to work with Bakhtiar to create a bourgeois-democratic order that could contain the chaotic aspect of the mounting revolution and, it was hoped, prevent the clergy from becoming the absolute hegemon of the revolution.

Arabadzhyan is Armenian and this may have heightened his sensitivity to the threatening aspects of Islamic movements. But before we dismiss his views as driven by his ethnic identity, it is important to point out that he held a very prominent position in the Institute for Oriental Studies in Moscow and devel-oped a complex picture of the Islamic elite within Iran. He highlighted impor-tant differences among Shi'i leaders and spoke favorably of some, while voic-ing strong criticism of the policies of Khomeini and the "theocratic regime." He is a sophisticated scholar, ready to treat Islam as an independent political force in the Middle East that is likely to have a huge effect on future political developments. In the long term it might even provide a basis for regional cooperation and an Islamic structure that could wield the influence of a third superpower. This, in any event, is the aspiration he ascribed to Khomeini.

The most important aspect of Arabadzhyan's argument was the geopolitical implication. The Left should have worked with the liberals to stop the mollas. Gone was the notion that the first priority after the revolution was to defeat the liberals so as to expel any lingering pro-American sentiment. In fact, the East-West dimension of his analysis was entirely subordinate to his regional analysis. To contain Islam the superpowers needed to collaborate, and this might indeed keep the United States involved in Iran. The Islamic regime, he concluded, was a theocratic dictatorship with a capitalist content that was both anticommunist and anti-West. It had its own imperial ambitions and was determined to spread the Islamic Revolution in a way that threatened regional stability, as well as American and Soviet interests. To see Iran as an asset in some great power game would be absurd in this vision. It was a source of common threat that, like Maoism in the 1960s, could (and perhaps even should) have the potential of uniting Washington and Moscow in a coordinated effort to stop revolutionary Islam.

3. Pursue Détente with Washington by Putting Regional Conflicts Aside

Superpower condominium is not a concept supported by Soviet officials, but the idea of looking at regional conflicts outside of the East-West context is. Mikhail Gorbachev has argued that reducing complex regional affairs to the East-West terms of the Cold War is an "anachronism," "a relapse into imperial thinking, which denies the right of a majority of nations to think and take decision independently."[105] Yevgeni Primakov, who has been both a leading Soviet specialist on the Middle East and a key adviser to General Secretary Gorbachev, has stressed the importance of not examining regional affairs through an East-West prism and has argued that both superpowers have a common stake in exerting a "restraining" influence on regional events.[106] He does not relate this to a common concern about Islam; he fears that regional violence might draw the two superpowers into a conflict.[107] The threat is not from Iran itself or from any other Third World country but rather from the risk that unpredictable and uncontrollable regional conflicts might upset the military-political stability in the world and pose a threat to universal security. Bipolar conceptions insist on interpreting events in Iran as favoring either the United States or the Soviet Union and thus fostering fears on both sides that Iran may be used by the other to shift the overall East-West balance in Southwest

Asia. Since neither superpower can nor should try to control Tehran, the answer, according to Primakov, is for both to exercise restraint and leave Iran outside any strategies for advantages in the Cold War.

Gorbachev seems to be inclined toward Primakov's perspective, but he does not set policy with unilateral discretion and is constrained by the domestic political power of the geopolitical perspective. Primakov evidences the desire to accommodate all three points of view.[108] The "new thinking" is set forth as an aspiration or goal to be achieved and defends Soviet policy that seeks to cooperate with the United States in the Gulf. Soviet radio propaganda, on the other hand, is still often very critical of American influence, and after the August 1988 agreement for a cease-fire in the Gulf, Soviet radio took the line that Washington is really the "enemy" of both Baghdad and Tehran.[109] The cease-fire was welcomed in Moscow but was immediately attached to the long-standing Soviet demand that Washington withdraw its naval forces from the Persian Gulf and Arabian Sea.[110] A strong emphasis on multilateral and U.N. forces had been evident in Soviet diplomacy since 1987, but this would also have the effect of reducing the unilateral American presence and could serve old-fashioned bipolar aims.[111] Obviously, nothing the Soviets would agree to would be likely to change the logistic edge they enjoy in Southwest Asia.

Persisting Patterns and the Prospects for Change

It is premature to claim that Gorbachev has transformed Soviet policy toward Iran and has liberated it from the geopolitical orthodoxy of the Cold War and the concomitant ideological gymnastics and flexible redefinitions necessary to paint the anti-American trends as "good" and the anti-Soviet forces as "bad." It is also unfair and shortsighted to deny that in 1987–89 Soviet leaders have indicated a desire to modify, and one day entirely to transform, the pattern of Soviet-American relations that has defined the Cold War. The policies pursued in the Gulf are consistent with traditional geopolitical tactics designed simply to drive the United States back; but they are equally consistent with the opening moves one would expect in a genuine Soviet effort to pursue détente. The withdrawal from Afghanistan is perhaps a major move that goes beyond the simple tactical diplomatic maneuvers and evidences a significant interest in mutual accommodation. But Americans should be cautious about accepting an overly romantic vision of the Soviet retreat. Although it has reduced the Soviet troop presence in Afghanistan, it has not signaled a decision to abandon Southwest Asia or to surrender to American interests.[112]

The Soviet decision to withdraw its forces from Afghanistan was coupled with a continuing commitment to provide massive amounts of weaponry to the government in Kabul and also coincided with a major new Soviet diplomatic effort in the Middle East. In February 1989, on the heels of the final exit of Soviet troops, Foreign Minister Eduard Shevardnadze launched a tour of the Middle East, visiting Syria, Jordan, Egypt, Iraq, and Iran. While in Egypt he met with both Israeli foreign minister Moshe Arens and the PLO's Yasir Arafat and announced a new Soviet plan for Middle East peace. While in Iran, he was received personally by Ayatollah Khomeini, becoming not only the first Soviet foreign minister to visit Tehran in seventy years but also the first foreign minister from any country to be received by the imam.

Shevardnadze was carrying a message from Mikhail Gorbachev responding to Khomeini's very unusual letter sent in January to the Soviet general secretary.[113] Khomeini's letter lectured the Russian leader on the need for religion and invited him to study Islam as a way to "fill up the ideological vacuum" of the Soviet system, but it also included an invitation to establish better relations. The *Tehran Times* described Gorbachev's response to the imam as a "tactful maneuver" and pointed out that Khomeini's initiative in January came on the same day the Majles was breaking relations with Britain. The editorial explained Iranian policy this way: "To stave off pressure to isolate it on the international level, the Islamic Republic of Iran will have to strengthen ties with the Pacific Ocean nations as well as edge towards the Eastern Bloc countries on political and military grounds."[114]

Khomeini never abandoned his commitment to a policy of "neither East nor West." His will, read shortly after his death on 3 June 1989, contained very tough attacks on the Soviet system, Soviet intrigues through the Left in Iran, and Moscow's imperial domination over Islamic peoples in Central Asia and Afghanistan.[115] Khomeini, however, was evidently persuaded that better relations with Moscow were both possible and desirable. Iran and the Soviet Union both wanted to see foreign naval forces, especially American and other NATO ships, withdrawn from the Gulf and could find common cause in Afghanistan once the Soviet Union had decided to leave. Neither Moscow nor Tehran wanted to see American influence in Afghanistan expand as Soviet influence declined. Rumors were commonly heard claiming that radical religious leaders like Hojjat al-Islam Mohammad Musavi Khoeiniha had encouraged Soviet diplomats to withdraw, promising them that they would use their influence with Afghan mujahedin based in Iran to ensure that a pro-American outcome did not prevail in Kabul. Of course, Iranian leaders had their own reasons to oppose some of the most prominent Afghan mujahedin in Pakistan who were supported by the Saudi-based Wahhabis whom Iranian leaders condemned as purveyors of "American Islam." Iran might also persuade the Soviet Union to press for the rapid step-by-step implementation of U.N. Resolution 598 and reduce further military aid to Iraq until Baghdad complied with the U.N. proposals.

In the spring of 1989, the speaker of the Iranian Majles, Hashemi-Rafsanjani, accepted a long-standing invitation to visit the Soviet Union. He explained that Khomeini's letter to Gorbachev was the critical catalyst in speeding up the diplomatic process but that Iran's commitment to a nonaligned policy was still in place.[116] What had changed, according to Rafsanjani, was the Soviet Union. Gorbachev had withdrawn his troops from Afghanistan and had accepted a nonaligned and Islamic outcome free from foreign interference in that country.[117] Gorbachev had also decreased Soviet support for leftists and Marxists in Iran and had abandoned Moscow's previous patronizing attitudes toward the Third World.[118] He additionally had eased the pressure against religion in the Soviet Union and had adopted an evenhanded posture in the Gulf, pressing Iraq to abide by the U.N. efforts to implement Resolution 598. Although Rafsanjani's visit was planned well before Khomeini died, the trip itself came less than three weeks after the imam's funeral and acquired additional significance because of Rafsanjani's evident influence in post-Khomeini Iran.[119]

While in the Soviet Union, Rafsanjani visited Moscow, Leningrad, and Baku and spoke to the Azerbaijanis after Friday prayers. Iran and the Soviet Union agreed to a Declaration on the Principles of Relations, a long-term agreement on economic and technical cooperation, and an agreement on new consular arrangements.[120] In the joint communiqué that was issued during the visit, Iran and the Soviet Union declared that their views on the conflict in the Gulf were in "complete unison" and called on all foreign fleets to leave the region and let only the littoral states secure stability.[121] The two countries also announced their support for an "independent, nonaligned, and Islamic Afghanistan which will maintain friendly relations with its neighbors" and agreed to a series of economic arrangements, including some exchange of gas and credits along with joint drilling explorations in the Caspian Sea.[122] Presumably, the Soviet acknowledgment that it would also help strengthen Iranian defenses and the Iranian announcements that a key motive for the visit was to acquire logistic and military equipment implied that some agreement on arms sales and military cooperation was also reached.[123]

The Soviet decision to welcome Rafsanjani on a fairly grand scale and to work hard to improve Soviet-Iranian relations was not surprising although there was no clear indication of what Gorbachev's intentions were. The move was consistent with a Soviet effort to stabilize the conflict in the Gulf by developing leverage with both Iraq and Iran and pushing for the implementation of U.N.

Resolution 598; at the same time, it obviously satisfied the geopolitical concerns of those in Moscow who worry about regional influence vis-à-vis the United States. It also complemented Soviet efforts to manage the political transition in Afghanistan without surrendering the Najibullah regime and added some marginal economic benefits.

The military agreements between Iran and the Soviet Union, which most people assume exist and were signed secretly, raised debate in Moscow and thus highlighted the struggle between old instincts and new thinking. The Soviet Union was ready to court Iran but not at the expense of regional stability and better relations with the West. For example, when Rafsanjani implied that Iranians and Palestinians might kill Americans in retaliation for Israel's killing Palestinians, the Soviet Persian radio broadcasts into Iran strongly condemned this idea.[124] Moscow rejected Iran's criticisms of Arafat's decision to recognize Israel and denounce terror. Moscow instead emphasized the need for compromise and reconciliation and stressed the importance of settling regional conflicts and avoiding East-West confrontations.

The selling of arms to Iran, of course, would certainly raise concerns in Washington and could be seen as the product of old-fashioned power calculations in Moscow. Aleksandr Bovin, a Soviet journalist typically promoting the new thinking, argued that secret arms sales in the short run might look like an avenue to hard currency and influence in Tehran but in the long run would promote restlessness and instability.[125] He criticized those who evidently supported the arms deal, suggesting that they both misread Rafsanjani's interests (which Bovin assumed would soon take Rafsanjani to Western suppliers as well) and held illusions about the regional scene that were hard to reconcile with new thinking. The arms deal, of course, does not appear to be a major initiative, and in regional terms it might even be seen as putting pressure on Iraq to move toward the U.N. position on the implementation of Resolution 598. The Rafsanjani visit signaled a Soviet readiness to develop a mutually beneficial relationship with Iran but did not by itself reveal any larger and more aggressive Soviet ambitions.

The new thinking, of course, is not simply the abandonment of power calculations, nor does it forecast a full-scale Soviet retreat from the Third World as the United States retakes the field. Americans would be foolish to seduce themselves with such romantic visions. Soviet leaders believe that bargains are the products more of leverage than of altruism and are struggling to redefine the mix of pressures and concessions they can use to protect their security and interests. Gorbachev appears to be continuing a cautious and complex approach to Iran that seeks to minimize the American presence, stabilize a positive relationship with Tehran, and at the same time not excite American fears.

For forty years the major Soviet concern in Iran has been American influence. The country has always been seen as an important component in the global competition with the United States. Soviet leaders have never considered Iran to be among the highest security concerns and have always made their policy in Southwest Asia a second- or even third-level priority. In the days of the Shah, the intensity of the perceived threat was not great. Soviet-Iranian relations were quite good despite Tehran's close association with Washington. When the Islamic Revolution came, Moscow was happy to see Western influence diminished. It encouraged the departure and tried to take diplomatic and relatively low-risk steps to ensure that Washington would not stage a comeback in Iran. In 1980, the Soviet Union did not take all the opportunities that were available to expand its influence. No one would have expected this from a country that has focused on Europe as its primary theater of concern. But anyone arguing that Moscow was aggressively opportunistic and trying to gain leverage over the United States and Western Europe through the oil routes of the Middle East would find relatively little supportive evidence in Soviet behavior.

It is impossible to say with certainty whether the pattern of competition with Washington, which has involved tough Soviet propaganda but fairly marginal Soviet sacrifices and commitments, will continue in the era of the Islamic Republic. It is also not clear whether Gorbachev's "new thinking" will mark the end of an era or be short-lived. The rise of mass politics in Iran and its effect on political legitimacy and power have greatly reduced the ability of either superpower to control events or to imagine Iran as a geostrategic asset. The superpowers may hold onto their grandeur, but the Iranian Revolution has forced them both to adjust their policies in the Gulf. We can only hope that Moscow and Washington will have the wisdom to create new strategies for protecting their security that recognize the declining accuracy of bipolar assumptions and the independent concerns and power of regional states.

Notes

1. The "Great Game" is a metaphor used to describe the British-Russian competition during the nineteenth century in Central Asia. See L. Carl Brown, *International Politics and the Middle East: Old Rules, Dangerous Game* (Princeton: Princeton University Press, 1984).

2. Richard W. Cottam, *Iran and the United States: A Cold War Case Study* (Pittsburgh: University of Pittsburgh Press, 1988), 66–67; Richard W. Cottam, *Nationalism in Iran*, 2nd ed. (Pittsburgh: University of Pittsburgh Press, 1978), 70–73, 118–29. Also see Rouhollah Ramazani, *Iran's Foreign Policy, 1941–1973: A Study of Foreign Policy in Modernizing Nations* (Charlottesville: University Press of Virginia, 1975), 96–114, 123; Mark Lytle, *The Origins of the Iranian-American Alliance: 1941–1953* (New York: Holmes and Meier, 1987), 144–52.

3. Ramazani, *Iran's Foreign Policy,* 141–42.

4. See William Taubman, *Stalin's American Policy: From Entente to Détente to Cold War* (New York: Norton, 1982), 131–32.

5. For the best presentation of the traditional view, one that is much more complex and developed than I can summarize here, see Bruce Kuniholm, *The Origins of the Cold War in the Near East: Great Power Conflict and Diplomacy in Iran, Turkey, and Greece* (Princeton: Princeton University Press, 1980), 303–82.

6. Ramazani, *Iran's Foreign Policy,* 106–07. Also see *Khrushchev Remembers: The Last Testament,* trans. and ed. Strobe Talbott (Boston: Bantam, 1974), 335–36.

7. Cottam, *Iran and the United States,* 66–68, 81. Also see Lytle, *Origins of the Iranian-American Alliance.*

8. Marshall Shulman, *Stalin's Foreign Policy Reappraised* (New York: Atheneum, 1966), 258. The notion of consolidation was central to the strategic ideas of Molotov. He did not believe that compromises would elicit positive Western responses, but he did call for a consolidation of the Soviet perimeter of vital interests. See Jack Snyder, "The Gorbachev Revolution: A Waning of Soviet Expansionism?" *International Security* 12, no. 3 (Winter 1987–88): 99–100.

9. Cottam, *Iran and the United States,* 70–73, 78.

10. Ibid., and see James Bill, *The Eagle and the Lion: The Tragedy of American-Iranian Relations* (New Haven: Yale University Press, 1988), 32.

11. The Cold War script was not well learned or formed by 1946. See Deborah Larson, *Origins of Containment: A Psychological Explanation* (Princeton: Princeton University Press, 1985).

12. Ramazani, *Iran's Foreign Policy,* 138–39; Bill, *The Eagle and the Lion,* 37–38; Lytle, *Origins of the Iranian-American Alliance,* 161; Cottam, *Iran and the United States,* 70. Also see John O'Neal, *Foreign Policy Making in Times of Crisis* (Columbus: Ohio State University Press, 1982), 133–34.

13. Ramazani, *Iran's Foreign Policy,* 153–57.

14. Lytle, *Origins of the Iranian-American Alliance,* 158.

15. Ramazani, *Iran's Foreign Policy,* 149.

16. Ibid., 134.

17. Ibid., 170–72.

18. For an easily accessible example of Soviet propaganda, see "Discussion of the Eisenhower Doctrine and U.S. Foreign Policy," *International Affairs* (Moscow) 2 (1957): 60–84. Also see G. Mirsky, "The U.S.A. and the Middle East," *International Affairs* (Moscow) 12 (1959): 17–23; and M. Ivanov, "The International Oil Consortium and the Independence of Iran," *International Affairs* (Moscow) 12 (1959): 66–71.

19. Ideology was not unimportant to the Soviet Union. The relationship with Nasser in the 1950s was very difficult, as was the Soviet relationship with other nationalists who opposed communism. In the early 1960s, Nasser tried socialist innovations and Moscow's relationship with Egypt improved. Moscow's ties to Iraq were severely strained by Arif's anticommunism. In both cases, however, aid continued for geostrategic reasons despite the ideological animosity. See Oles Smolansky, *The Soviet Union and the Arab East under Khrushchev* (Lewisburg, Pa.: Bucknell University Press, 1974).

20. See "Note from the Soviet Government to the Government of Iran," *Pravda,* 23 May 1952, 2; *Current Digest of the Soviet Press* (hereafter *CDSP*) 4, no. 21 (5 July 1952): 14–15. For a study of Soviet images of Mosaddeq, see Shahrough Akhavi, "The USSR, Mossadeq and Khomeini: Soviet Orientation toward Two Iranian Revisionist Regimes" (paper presented at the conference on "Iran, the US, and the USSR" at University of California, Los Angeles, 22–23 April 1988).

21. See Mark J. Gasiorowski, "The 1953 Coup d'Etat in Iran," *International Journal of Middle East Studies* (August 1987). Also see Bill, *The Eagle and the Lion,* 93.

22. On the American operation, see Cottam, *Iran and the United States,* 103–09; Bill, *The*

Eagle and the Lion, 85–89; and Gasiorowski, "The 1953 Coup d'Etat in Iran." For a recent Soviet account of this event, see Fyodor Sergeyev, "Operation Ajax," *International Affairs* (Moscow) 8 (August 1987): 105–15, and 9 (September 1987): 78–89.

23. On the details of the 1953 events, I am grateful for the help of Mark J. Gasiorowski. See his "The 1953 Coup d'Etat in Iran."

24. Tass, "Failure of Attempted Coup d'Etat in Iran," *Pravda,* 17 Aug. 1953, 4; and "Events in Iran," *Pravda,* 18 Aug. 1953, 4; both in *CDSP* 5, no. 33 (26 Sept. 1953): 20–21. Also see Observer, "Failure of American Venture in Iran," 19 Aug. 1953, 4; *CDSP* 5, no. 34 (3 Oct. 1953): 3–5.

25. I. Plyshevsky, "Provocational Statements in Iranian Press," 5 Sept. 1953, 4; *CDSP* 5, no. 34 (3 Oct. 1953): 5, 39.

26. Bill, *The Eagle and the Lion,* 91, 107–08.

27. Contrast I. Plyshevsky, "American 'Aid' to Iran and What Is behind It," *Pravda,* 9 Sept. 1953, 3, with "On Soviet-Iranian Trade Relations," *Pravda,* 6 Sept. 1953, 4; both in *CDSP,* 5, no. 36 (17 Oct. 1953): 12–13.

28. See Smolansky, *The Soviet Union and the Arab East under Khrushchev.*

29. Ramazani, *Iran's Foreign Policy,* 330–33; International Institute for Strategic Studies (hereafter IISS), *Strategic Survey, 1978* (London: IISS, 1979), 53.

30. *Strategic Survey, 1978,* 53.

31. Michael Brzoska and Thomas Ohlson, *Arms Transfers to the Third World, 1971–85* (Oxford: Oxford University Press, 1987), 343.

32. Ibid. As the world price of oil rose, Moscow decided to charge CMEA members a price that more nearly equaled the market value of oil. The East Europeans were encouraged to seek oil from other sources, such as Nigeria and Iran. The Shah visited Poland and Czechoslovakia in the fall of 1977. In Poland the Shah and Empress Farah were lavishly received and given honorary doctorates at the University of Warsaw. *Radio Free Europe: Situation Report* 22, 30 Aug. 1977, 6–9.

33. Ramazani, *Iran's Foreign Policy,* 315–16, 327–28.

34. Richard W. Cottam, *Foreign Policy Motivation: A General Theory and a Case Study* (Pittsburgh: University of Pittsburgh Press, 1977), 93–97. Ramazani, *Iran's Foreign Policy,* 322–25, also gives a complex set of Iranian motives.

35. Efraim Karsh, *The Iran-Iraq War: A Military Analysis,* Adelphi Papers 220 (London: IISS, 1987), 7. For the location of Iranian air and naval bases, see Gwynne Dyer, "Iran," in *World Armies,* ed. John Keegan (New York: Facts on File, 1979), 331. Dyer argues that the Soviet Union was a major concern of the Shah, but the location of bases and naval concentration suggest a southern agenda.

36. IISS, *The Military Balance, 1975–76* (London: IISS, 1975), 9. Also see *The Military Balance* for the years 1976–77, 9; 1977–78, 9; and 1979–80, 10.

37. Paul Hammond, "A Decade of American Military Aid and Influence in Pakistan" (paper presented at the University of Pittsburgh's Faculty Seminar on Strategy and International Security, 1982).

38. See Hanna Batatu, *The Old Social Classes and the Revolutionary Movements of Iraq: A Study of Iraq's Old Landed and Commercial Classes and of Its Communists, Ba'thists, and Free Officers* (Princeton: Princeton University Press, 1978), 1093–94. Also see *New York Times,* 14 Nov. 1971, 21.

39. *New York Times,* 24 Oct. 1971, 8.

40. See "The Pike Papers," *Village Voice,* 16 Feb. 1976, 85, 87.

41. The Ba'ath formed a national front with Barzani at this time and included five Kurds in its cabinet. See *New York Times,* 15 May 1972, 4. The Pike Commission investigating this episode

concluded that "had the U.S. not reinforced our ally's prodding, the insurgents may have reached an accommodation with the central government, thus gaining at least a measure of autonomy while avoiding further bloodshed." See "The Pike Papers," 85.

42. "The Pike Papers." In July 1972 Barzani and the Ba'ath were still trying to contain the mounting tensions. See *New York Times,* 13 July 1972, 5, 12.

43. "The Pike Papers," 85, 87–88.

44. Robert O. Freedman, "Soviet Policy toward Ba'athist Iraq, 1968–1979," in *The Soviet Union in the Third World: Successes and Failures,* ed. Robert Donaldson (Boulder: Westview Press, 1981), 170–72.

45. Howard Hensel, "Soviet Policy toward the Kurdish Question, 1970–75," *Soviet Union/Union Sovietique* 6 (1979): 61–80.

46. On the Kurds, see Richard W. Cottam, "The Case of the Kurds: Minorities in the Middle East" (paper presented at the annual meeting of the American Political Science Association, 1977). On Soviet military involvement, see Alvin Rubinstein, "Air Support in the Arab East," in *Diplomacy of Power: Soviet Armed Forces as a Political Instrument,* ed. Stephen Kaplan (Washington, D.C.: Brookings Institution, 1981), 499–510.

47. The terms of the settlement promised an end to foreign interference. The Shah shut off aid to the Kurds and partly blocked Iran's borders, allowing the Iraqi regime to crush the Kurds brutally. In return, Iraq agreed to stop supporting ethnic minorities in Iran and other opposition forces, Khomeini being the most important of them. The boundary of the Shatt was also changed to the middle of the channel as is the custom in most waterways. From 1966 to 1970 Moscow accounted for 88 percent of Iraq's weapons. In the period 1970 to 1975 this rose to 97 percent. In these five years Soviet aid more than tripled, but still at $2.042 billion was less than a quarter of American aid to Iran in the same period. In 1976–80 the Soviet share dropped to 85 percent as Iraqi imports again doubled. In 1981–85 Iraq tripled its arms purchases, but the Soviet share dropped to 55 percent. See M. Brzoska and T. Ohlson, *Arms Transfers to the Third World,* 344.

48. Robert O. Freedman, "Soviet Policy toward Ba'athist Iraq," 175.

49. A. Ignatov, "Iraq Today," *New Times* 21 (May 1974): 23–24, described the Kurds as "an interim tool." He outlined the Western plan to destabilize Iraq and concluded that the West would use the tool for a while and "then doom this movement to oblivion and liquidate it."

50. For evidence on Soviet views in this period, see Richard Herrmann, *Perceptions and Behavior in Soviet Foreign Policy* (Pittsburgh: University of Pittsburgh Press, 1985).

51. A. Akhmedzyanov: "On the Path of Cooperation," *Izvestia,* 24 Jan. 1978, 5, Foreign Broadcast Information Service, Soviet Union Daily Report (hereafter FBIS SOV), 78–19, F7–8; and "Concern for the Caspian," *Izvestia,* 23 Apr. 1978, 3, FBIS SOV-78–83, F7.

52. Tass, "The United States and Events in Iran," *Izvestia,* 14 Sept. 1978, 4, FBIS SOV-78–185, F9.

53. Aleksandar Bovin, "Iran: Consequences and Reasons," *Literaturnaya Gazeta,* 25 Oct. 1978, 14, FBIS SOV-78–212, F10–13; A. Filippov, "Iran: Days of Tension," *Pravda,* 3 Nov. 1978, 5, FBIS SOV-78–216, F3–5.

54. S. Kondrashov, "Around the Events in Iran," *Izvestia,* 6 Dec. 1978, 3, FBIS SOV-78–237, F1–3; A. Akhmedzyanov, "Iran's Hot Winter," *Izvestia,* 14 Dec. 1978, 5, FBIS SOV-78–244, F4–7.

55. See, e.g., A. Bovin, "Iran in the People's Hands: Inevitable Denouement," *Izvestia,* 13 Feb. 1979, 4, FBIS SOV-79–033; I. Belyayev, "The Tangle of American-Iranian Problems," *SShA: Ekonomika, Politika, Ideologiya* 2 (February 1980): 48–58, JPRS 75485, 58–71.

56. M. Stura, "His Majesty in Flight," *Izvestia,* 25 Jan. 1979, 5, FBIS SOV-79–22, F3–6; A. Bovin, "Iran in the People's Hands," 4.

57. The most important warning was Brezhnev's 19 November 1978 statement that Moscow

would consider any American interference so close to the Soviet border a threat to Soviet security. Leonid Brezhnev, *Pravda,* 19 Nov. 1978, 2, FBIS SOV-78–224, F1.

58. Zbigniew Brzezinski, *Power and Principle: Memoirs of the National Security Adviser, 1977–1981* (New York: Farrar, Straus and Giroux, 1983), 378–88. Also see Robert Huyser *Mission to Tehran* (New York: Harper and Row, 1986).

59. Soviet radio in Persian to Iran, FBIS SOV-79–2, F2–3, FBIS SOV-79–5, F3–4. Also see A. Filippov, "US Military Pressures on Iran," *Pravda,* 11 Jan. 1979, 5, FBIS SOV-79–10, F3; V. Vinogradov, "Iran: Threat of Military Coup," *Krasnaya Zvezda,* 11 Jan. 1979, 3, FBIS SOV-79–10, F1–3; A. Maksimov, "Iran on the Threshold of a Military Putsch?" *Izvestia,* 13 Jan. 1979, 4, FBIS SOV-79–12, F1; V. Ovchinnikov, "What Then Is Interference?" *Pravda,* 13 Jan. 1979, 6, FBIS SOV-79–12, F2–3.

60. *Facts on File, 1979,* 14–16.

61. See Huyser, *Mission to Tehran,* 176, 227, 233; and Gary Sick, *All Fall Down: America's Tragic Encounter with Iran* (New York: Random House, 1985), 106.

62. Huyser, *Mission to Tehran,* 291.

63. See the U.S. Defense Department report entitled "Capabilities in the Persian Gulf," reported by Richard Burt in *New York Times,* 2 Feb. 1980, 1, 4. Also see the statements by Hon. Robert Komer, under secretary for policy, Department of Defense (DOD); Lt. Gen. Richard Lawson, director, Plans and Policy Organization, the Joint Chiefs of Staff; and the report by the Congressional Research Service team and the DOD, all in U.S. Senate, *U.S. Security Interests and Policies in Southwest Asia,* Hearings before the Committee on Foreign Relations, 96th Congress, 2nd Sess., Feb.–Mar. 1980, 285–303, 336–66.

64. See, e.g., Joshua M. Epstein, *Strategy and Force Planning: The Case of the Persian Gulf* (Washington, D.C.: Brookings Institution, 1987), 98–105.

65. One study that explores Soviet military and political options is Thomas McNaugher, *Arms and Oil: U.S. Military Strategy and the Persian Gulf* (Washington, D.C.: Brookings Institution, 1985), 23–47.

66. Pavel Demchenko, "When the People Rise Up," *Pravda,* 24 Jan. 1979, 4, FBIS SOV-79–019, F5–8; Pavel Demchenko, "Krushenie Absolyutizma" (The collapse of absolutism), *Kommunist* 3 (February 1979): 76–83.

67. Pavel Demchenko, "Iran: Stanovlenie Respubliki" (Iran: The making of a republic), *Kommunist* 9 (June 1979): 110–16; Yelena A. Doroshenko, "The Political Traditions of Shi'ism and the Anti-Monarchist Movement in Iran (1978–1979)," *Nardoy Azii i Afriki* 6 (1980): 58–66, JPRS 77532, 71–16; and Doroshenko, "Iran: Moslem (Shi'ite) Traditions and Modernity," *Aziya I Afrika Segodnya* 8 (August 1980): 59–61, JPRS 76721, 25–30.

68. See S. M. Aliyev, "The Iranian Revolution of 1978–1979 and the Working Class," *Rabochiy Klass I Sovremennyy Mir* 5 (Sept.–Oct. 1980): 104–11, JPRS 77230, 9–24. Aliyev explains that "the greatest activity with regard to organizing mass, anti-Shah demonstrations was developed by the Iranian oppositional clergy, which succeeded by the autumn of 1978 in becoming the recognized predominant force in the popular movement" (16).

69. These fears were fueled when the Soviet vice-consul in Tehran, Vladimir Kuzichkin, defected to Britain and gave information on four hundred Soviet agents operating in Iran. Britain and the United States made Kuzichkin's information available to the Iranians.

70. For one interpretation that takes these confessions seriously, see Zalmay Khalilzad, "Islamic Iran: Soviet Dilemma," *Problems of Communism* 33, no. 1 (Jan.–Feb. 1984): 1–20.

71. Aliyev, "The Iranian Revolution of 1978–1979 and the Working Class," 23.

72. Doroshenko, "The Political Traditions of Shi'ism and the Anti-Monarchist Movement in Iran."

73. Soviet imports from Iran held steady after the revolution in 1980, 1981, and 1982.

Iranian imports from the Soviet Union increased from 1 percent to 8 percent of their imports. See Khalilzad, "Islamic Iran: Soviet Dilemma," 12. Soviet aid to Iran also continued with assistance in the building of steel mills, railroad electrification, and power plant construction. After a dispute over price, gas sales to the Soviet Union stopped. See Shaul Bakhash, *The Reign of the Ayatollahs: Iran and the Islamic Revolution* (New York: Basic Books, 1984), 236–39.

74. *New York Times,* 1 Sept. 1979, 5. *Facts on File, 1979,* 445–46; (1980), 644. For the best evidence that small material support was provided to the Kurds in 1979, see Khalilzad, "Islamic Iran: Soviet Dilemma," 9–10.

75. Soviet radio in Persian to Iran, 23 Mar. 1979, FBIS SOV-79–059, H13–14; 26 Mar. 1979, FBIS SOV-79–059, H15–18; 27 Mar. 1979, FBIS SOV-79–061; H13; 28 Mar. 1979, FBIS SOV-79–062, H6–7; 29 Mar. 1979, FBIS SOV-79–065, H14; 3 Apr. 1979, FBIS SOV-79–066; H10; 3 Apr. 1979, FBIS SOV-79–067, H8.

76. A. Akmuradov, "Slander, the Tool of Reaction," *Pravda,* 4 Apr. 1979, 5, FBIS SOV-79–068, H6–7; M. Krutikhin, "Difficult Changes," *Novoye Vremya* 19, 4 May 1979, 12–13, FBIS SOV-79–093, H1–2; Tass, *Pravda,* 7 Sept. 1979, 5, FBIS SOV-79–177, H1.

77. Aleksandar Bovin, "With Koran and Saber!!!" *Nedelya* 36 (4 Sept. 1979): 6, FBIS SOV-79–176, H1–2.

78. For an argument, albeit with weak evidence, that the Soviet Union air-dropped aid to the Kurds, see Khalilzad, "Islamic Iran: Soviet Dilemma."

79. Soviet radio in Persian to Iran, 21 Sept. 1979, FBIS SOV-79–186, H3; A. Filippov, "Situation in Iran," *Pravda,* 14 Sept. 1979, 5, FBIS SOV-79–184, H9; A. Filippov, "Problem Remains Unresolved," *Pravda,* 16 Sept. 1979, 5, FBIS SOV-79–184; G. Chipashivili, "The Struggle Continues!" *Kommunisti* (Tbilsi), 24 Oct. 1979, 3, FBIS SOV-79–251, H4–6.

80. Moscow Domestic Service, 7 Jan. 1980, FBIS SOV-80–005, H1; 10 Jan. 1980, FBIS SOV-80–008, H1.

81. See Selig Harrison, *In Afghanistan's Shadow: Baluch Nationalism and Soviet Temptations* (Washington, D.C.: Carnegie Endowment for International Peace, 1981), 108–18, 137.

82. Moscow allowed Iran to ship goods across the Soviet Union to escape the pressure of Western embargoes during the hostage crisis.

83. In the first opinion they would help topple the regime in Iran. The United States was already aiding forces in Iraq trying to do the same thing and would have few options if Moscow decided to do likewise. Washington could come to the defense of the country holding its diplomats hostage, but we can wonder how credible this about-face would seem in Moscow. The second scenario pits Moscow against an Arab client; but Iraq since 1976 had increasingly moved to diversify its weapons suppliers and was flirting openly with key American officials such as Brzezinski. Moreover, Moscow would simply be coming to the defense of the attacked party and helping it to defend itself. It would have a strong case to make on the international scene and could expect American defense of Iraq to be greatly complicated by Israel's strong objections. And the final scenario would require very little risk-taking at all. The arms market was profitable and both Washington and Tel Aviv were perfectly content, if not happy, to see the war continue.

84. See, e.g., Igor Belyayev, "Surrounding the Iranian-Iraqi Conflict," *Literaturnaya Gazeta,* 1 Oct. 1980, 9, FBIS SOV-80–193, A2–3; P. Demchenko, "Who Is Fueling the Conflicts?" *Pravda,* 18 Oct. 1980, 5, FBIS SOV-80–204; D. Volskiy, "The Persian Gulf: Dreams and Reality," *Novoye Vremya* 46 (14 Nov. 1980); 1–11, FBIS SOV-80–228; A. Kislov, "Washington and the Iraq-Iran Conflict," *SShA* 1 (January 1981): 51–56, JPRS 77507; V. Pustov, "The Pentagon Plugs the 'Gap,'" *Krasnaya Zvezda,* 5 Mar. 1979, 3, FBIS SOV-79–047.

85. At the time of Iraq's attack Baghdad's foreign minister sought support in Moscow. He was refused and told that Soviet deliveries would end if Iraq continued to attack Iran. See *New York Times,* 24 Sept. 1980, 2. Also see Z. Khalilzad, "Islamic Iran: Soviet Dilemma," 15. Shortly after

Iraq's attack, Moscow reportedly offered military aid to Iran. Evidently it was an offer of limited aid to blunt Saddam's attack and secure the stability of the anti-imperialist Khomeini regime. Iran declined the offer. See Roderic Pitty, "Soviet Perceptions of Iraq," *Middle East Report,* March–April 1988, 23–27.

86. See Pitty, "Soviet Perceptions of Iraq," 26, and Khalilzad, "Islamic Iran: Soviet Dilemma," 16.

87. *New York Times,* 5 May 1983, 1; 6 May 1983, 3.

88. See editorial, "Against Iran's National Interests," *Pravda,* 20 Feb. 1983, 4, FBIS SOV-83–036, H6–7. Also see D. Volskiy, "Iran: Revolution at the Crossroads," *Novoye Vremya* 2 (7 Jan. 1983): 13–15, FBIS SOV-83–009; and R. Ulyanovsky, "Moral Principles in Politics, and Policy in the Sphere of Morals: Iran—What Next?" *Literaturnaya Gazeta,* 22 June 1983, 10, FBIS SOV-83–127, H1–8, H6–7. Islam, the standard line went, could play either a progressive or a reactionary role and was now playing a reactionary one. See I. Timofeyev, "Rol' Islama v Obshchestvenno-politicheskoy Zhizni Stran Zarubezhnogo Vostoka" (The role of Islam in the social-political life of oriental countries) *MEiMO* 5 (May 1982): 51–63.

89. Tass, 16 Dec. 1985, FBIS SOV-85–241, H5.

90. There also were reports of the Soviet Union allowing military aid to reach Iran across Soviet territory. See *Kyodo,* 12 Aug. 1985, FBIS SOV-85–156, H7.

91. See "Seminar with Karen Brutents," deputy secretary of the CPSU CC's International Department, *al-Watan,* part 1, 4 Jan. 1986; part 2, 6 Jan. 1986, in FBIS SOV-86–004, 8–21; FBIS SOV-816–26, H3–15.

92. Tass, 2 Feb. 1986, FBIS SOV-86–022, H1.

93. See Mikhail Gorbachev, *Political Report of the CPSU Central Committee to the 27th Party Congress,* 25 Feb. 1985 (Moscow. Novosti, 1986), 78–94. Also see M. Gorbachev, "A Report to the USSR Supreme Soviet Session on the Results of the Geneva Summit," 27 Nov. 1985, in Gorbachev, *The Coming of the Century of Peace* (New York: Richardson and Steirman, 1985), 76–77.

94. On the reflagging competition, see International Institute for Strategic Studies, *Strategic Survey, 1987–1988* (London: IISS, 1988), 75, 127–32.

95. Ulyanovsky argued in July 1982 that the talk about a "Third Way" in Iran had no real basis. It was "politically untenable," he continued, to adopt a "neutral stance regarding the basic manifestations of the present-day class struggle in the international arena." R. Ulyanovsky, "Iranskaya Revolutsiya i ee Osobennosti" (The Iranian Revolution and its peculiarities), *Kommunist* 10 (July 1982): 106–16, 112–13.

96. R. Ulyanovsky, "O Natsional'noy i Revolyutsionoy Demokratii Puti Evolyutsii" (On national and revolutionary democracy: Ways of evolution), *Narody Azii i Afriki* 2 (March–April 1984): 11–12.

97. Ulyanovsky, "The Iranian Revolution and its peculiarities," 107–11.

98. S. Agayev, "On the Concept and the Essence of the Islamic Revolution," *Aziya I Afrika Segodnya* 5 (May 1984): 27–31, JPRS UPS-84–071, 23–33.

99. Agayev claimed that the leftist parties had similar demands and objectives but could not agree on a cooperative line. In discussing support for each party he leaves no doubt that the Mojahedin and Feda'yan are vastly more powerful than the Tudeh. Ulyanovsky makes a similar argument, and agrees that the Tudeh was weak compared to the other leftist parties. See S. Agayev, "The Zigzag Path of the Iranian Revolution," *Voprosy Istorii* 1 (1985): 43–59; *Soviet Review* 28, no. 1 (Spring 1987): 18–45; R. Ulyanovsky, "Sud'by Iranskoi Revolutsii" (The Iranian Revolution's destinies), *Kommunist* 8 (May 1985): 109.

100. Ulyanovsky, "The Iranian Revolution's destinies," and Agayev, "On the Concept and the Essence of the Islamic Revolution."

101. See Igor Belyayev: "Iranian Gambit," *Literaturnaya Gazeta*, 26 Nov. 1986, 9, FBIS SOV-86-228, and "Irangate and the Destroyers of Parity," *Literaturnaya Gazeta*, 10 Dec. 1986, 9, FBIS SOV-86-238. Also see A. Kislov and R. Zimenkov, *The USA and the Islamic World* (New Delhi: Sterling Publishers, 1984).

102. Igor Belyayev, "Islam and Politics," *Literaturnaya Gazeta*, 13 May 1987, 13 and 20 May 1987, 12, FBIS SOV-87-113.

103. S. Agayev, "Live Bombs," *Nauka i Religiya* 5 (May 1987): 44–47, JPRS NEA-87-092, 85–94.

104. A. Z. Arabadzhyan: "The Iranian Revolution: Causes and Lessons," *Aziya I Afrika Segodnya* 3 (March 1986): 32–36, and "The Iranian Revolution: Causes and Lessons," *Aziya I Afrika Segodnya* 4 (April 1986): 19–22, 38, both in JPRS UIA-86-034, 43–53, 77–83.

105. Mikhail Gorbachev, "A Report to the USSR Supreme Soviet Session on the Results of the Geneva Summit," 76–77. Also see Gorbachev, *Perestroika: New Thinking for Our Country and the World* (New York: Harper and Row, 1987), 173–80.

106. Yevgeni Primakov: "USSR Policy on Regional Conflicts," *International Affairs* (Moscow) 6 (1988): 3–9; "New Philosophy of Foreign Policy," *Pravda*, 9 July 1987, 4, FBIS SOV-87-134, CC5-10; "XXVII C, ezd KPSS i Issledovaniye Problem Mirovoi Ekonomiki i Mezhdunarodnye Otnosheniy" (The 27th CPSU Congress and study of problems of the world economy and international relations), *MEiMO* 5 (May 1986): 3–14.

107. When Yelena Doroshenko, a scholar who works at the Institute for Oriental Studies (which Primakov used to direct) examines the Iranian Revolution, the geopolitical aspects are not emphasized. She concentrates on the various factions within the Shi'i clergy and their deep and complex roots in Iranian society. Doroshenko: "The Shi'ite Clergy in Iran," *Nauka I Religiya* 9 (September 1983). 54–56, JPRS 04 019, 23 321 *Shiitshoye dukhovenstvo v souremennom Irane* (The Shi'i clergy in modern Iran), 2nd ed. (Moscow: Nauka, 1985), 178–201.

108. In his treatment of the Iranian Revolution, Primakov takes the roots of Islamic fundamentalism seriously. He dismisses Western views that see the rise of fundamentalism as a rejection of modernity and stresses instead the historical, political, and cultural roots of Islam that have genuine value as guides to social life. Although his analysis of Islam reflects some of the detachment of Doroshenko, he at the same time emphasizes the "bankruptcy" of the efforts to export Islamic revolution and thereby joins some of the concerns of Arabadzhyan. Primakov goes on to identify three trends in the Islamic movement: the bourgeois, the conservative petty-bourgeois, and the radical petty-bourgeois. He then relates these to predictable geopolitical judgments. He concludes by agreeing with the Ulyanovsky argument that "Islamic revolution" as a political and ideological force has no grounds to claim to be a "third way" of development. See Yevgeni Primakov, "Volna 'Islamskogo': Fundamentalizma Problemy i Uroki" (The wave of "Islamic fundamentalism": Problems and lessons), *Voprosy Filosofiye* 6 (1985): 63–73.

109. Moscow Radio in Persian to Iran, 12 Sept. 1988, FBIS SOV-88-179, 18–19.

110. "Statement by the Soviet Government," *Pravda*, 22 Aug. 1988, 2, FBIS SOV-88-162, 35–36. Also see Konstantin Geyvandov, "Common Sense Prevails: The Cease-Fire Agreement in the Iraq-Iran War Has Come into Force," *Izvestia*, 21 Aug. 1988, 5, FBIS SOV-88-163, 12–14.

111. On the role of the United Nations in the Gulf, see Pavel Demchenko, "The Persian Gulf: Cruisers, Tankers, and the Road to Peace," *Pravda*, 12 June 1987, 4, FBIS SOV-87-116. Also see Mikhail Gorbachev, "The Reality and Guarantees of a Secure World," *Pravda*, 17 Sept. 1987, 1–2, FBIS SOV-87-180.

112. For the details of this argument, see Richard Herrmann, "The Soviet Decision to Withdraw from Afghanistan: Changing Strategic and Regional Images," in *Dominoes and Bandwagons: Strategic Beliefs and Superpower Competition in the Eurasian Rimland*, ed. Robert Jervis and Jack Snyder (New York: Oxford University Press, forthcoming).

113. "Message from Ruhollah Musavi Khomeini to Mikhail Gorbachev," Tehran Domestic Service, 8 Jan. 1989; FBIS NES-89–005, 57–59.

114. Editorial, "Gorbachev's Message: A Tactful Maneuver," *Tehran Times,* 27 Feb. 1989, 2; FBIS NES-89–042, 63.

115. "Third Part of Ayatollah Ruhollah Khomeini's Will," Tehran Domestic Service, 7 June 1989; FBIS NES-89–109, 58–64, 56–60.

116. Interview with Hashemi-Rafsanjani, Tehran Domestic Service, 20 June 1989; FBIS NES-89–118, 48–49.

117. News conference with Hashemi-Rafsanjani, Tehran Television, 8 June 1989; FBIS NES-89–111, 31–40.

118. Hashemi-Rafsanjani, "Friday Sermon," Tehran Domestic Service, 30 June 1989; FBIS NES-89–133, 63–67.

119. Rafsanjani after his return to Iran strongly emphasized that the trip and initiative toward the Soviet Union was Ayatollah Khomeini's idea. When talking about the changes in the Soviet Union that led Iran to develop this new relationship, Rafsanjani ended by saying, "Luckily this took place during the Imam's time. If this would have happened after the Imam, it would have been difficult for us, because some would say the No East, No West thesis would be breached." Hashemi-Rafsanjani, "Friday Sermon," Tehran Domestic Service, 30 June 1989; FBIS NES-89–133, 63–67. Rafsanjani may have been responding to Ahmad Khomeini, who upon the Speaker's return from the Soviet Union argued that the "neither East nor West" doctrine was his father's most important testament and called on Iranians to "demand that our officials say no to both the East and West." "Speech by Ahmad Khomeini," Tehran Domestic Service, 27 June 1989; FBIS NES-89–123, 36–37. Just prior to the Ayatollah's death, some observers in the West felt that Ahmad Khomeini might extend the radical religious denunciation of Ayatollah Montazeri to the pragmatic moves of Rafsanjani. In the immediate post-Khomeini period, however, Rafsanjani and Khamene'i seemed to move quickly to assert their authority.

120. "Declaration on the Principles of Relations between the USSR and Iran," *Tass,* 22 June 1989; FBIS SOV-89–119, 23–24.

121. "Joint Communiqué," *Pravda,* 24 June 1989, 4; FBIS SOV-89–121, 19–20.

122. On what was agreed to, see "Interview with Hashemi-Rafsanjani," Tehran Domestic Service, 24 June 1989, 28–30. Hashemi-Rafsanjani, "Friday Sermon," Tehran Domestic Service, 30 June 1989; FBIS NES-89–133, 63–67, and "Interview with Foreign Minister Ali Akbar Velayati," *Keyhan Hava'i,* 12 July 1989, 14–15; FBIS NES-89–136, 47–50.

123. One report said that the agreement included the delivery of tanks, radar equipment, and training. *Al-Ittihad* (Abu Dhabi), 26 June 1989, 1; FBIS SOV-89–122, 21. Editorial, "New Agreements, Old Relations," *Keyhan Hava'i,* 5 July 1989, 22; FBIS NES-89–132, 75–77.

124. Moscow Radio in Persian to Iran, 12 May 1989; FBIS SOV-89–094, 40.

125. Aleksandr Bovin, "International Panorama," Moscow Television, 2 July 1989; FBIS SOV-89–127, 16.

4 Myths of Soviet-Iranian Relations

MURIEL ATKIN

A recurrent theme in discussions of the turmoil in Iran since 1978 has been the question of how the Soviet Union could benefit from the collapse of American influence there. Estimates of Soviet intentions in Iran often cite the history of tsarist and earlier Soviet relations with Iran to explain the present and predict the future. Unfortunately, some of these appeals to history are ahistorical. This misunderstanding of history takes two forms. One is ordinary factual inaccuracy. The other stems from a fundamental conceptual error in the study of tsarist and Soviet foreign policy: the assumption that policy is made largely on the basis of compulsions that hold sway over the centuries, transcending political changes and unaffected by the mundane political processes and personal strengths and weaknesses that influence the making of foreign policy in other countries. These mistaken approaches also reflect, in some cases, a cavalier attitude toward the significance of history—namely, that it is sufficient to cite something that happened, or allegedly happened, in the past, perhaps out of context, perhaps inaccurately, to prove one's interpretation of current events. The problem is not the occasional slip that can happen to anyone but rather a questionable process of inquiry itself. Soviet foreign policy expert Keith Dunn justly warns that "we should avoid believing that an assumption stated at least three times by three different people is no longer an assumption but a proven fact."[1]

In a sense, the heart of the issue is whether one regards tsarist or Soviet foreign policy–making as fundamentally rational or irrational. "Rational" in this context does not mean wise or admirable. What it does mean is that those who make foreign policy at least attempt to assess pragmatically the conditions under which they must operate and on that basis determine what is in the best interests of the country or, less loftily, that particular faction of policymakers. It is an approach encapsulated in a remark attributed to A. M. Gorchakov, Russia's foreign minister for most of the reign of Alexander II. Gorchakov considered Russia a "great, powerless country" and observed that "one can always dress up finely but one needs to know that one is dressing up."[2] In contrast, to believe in the myths about Russian or Soviet foreign policy is to treat this policy as irrational by ascribing powerful influence to instinctual drives or ambitious grand designs that influence the judgment of generation after generation of policymakers far more than a given era's actual conditions. Many a country's foreign policy may be irrational on occasion. But irrationality is credited too often with too much influence in tsarist and Soviet foreign policy either because evidence to explain the real motives is scarce or because belief in certain irrational motives is viewed as a criterion for disapproval of the policies themselves.

This chapter will examine a few of the historical myths that have been revived in recent years to "explain" Soviet relations with revolutionary Iran. The first category is the conceptual myth, as manifested by the Testament of Peter the Great and the drive to warm-water ports. The second deals with inaccurate understandings of real events, namely, the 1921 Soviet-Iranian treaty and the 1940 Nazi-Soviet negotiations on the division of the postwar world.

Before proceeding, there are two points that require clarification. A critique of misconceptions about tsarist or Soviet ambitions regarding Iran is not at all the equivalent of an endorsement of any policy that St. Petersburg or Moscow actually followed. Nor is it a contention that tsarist or Soviet rulers have never had expansionist ambitions toward Iran. Rather, the issue is that one prerequisite for a sound assessment of such policies must be the rejection of spurious evidence.[3] Even someone like Sir Henry Rawlinson, who in the 1860s and 1870s wrote repeatedly to warn of what he perceived to be a Russian threat to the British position in India, rejected the notion that the motives of Russian foreign policy were inherently different from and less rational than those of other countries. He argued that Russia's early nineteenth-century conquests in Iran, the Caucasus, and the Ottoman Empire were not the result of an "insatiate thirst for conquest" but rather were "amply paralleled by our own annexations in India during the same period."[4] When he speculated about the motives for Russia's pursuit in his own day of increased influence or outright rule in Iran, Afghanistan, and Central Asia, he regarded the truth as difficult to discern but suggested causes that depended not on irrational drives but on the kinds of political and military concerns of ordinary statecraft.[5]

The second point is that scholarly works of high quality have already addressed many of the concerns this chapter discusses.[6] It is a sad reflection on the nature of expertise that some of the people who have sought to explain the current and future state of Soviet-Iranian relations have not benefited from these works.

One of the canards most resistant to the weight of evidence is the belief that there is a grand design for Russian expansion formulated in the Testament of Peter the Great and followed by all his successors, including the modern Soviet leadership. Peter the Great wrote no such plan; the Testament exists in several versions, all forgeries, dating from the eighteenth and nineteenth centuries. Scholars have been demonstrating its fraudulence for more than a century.[7] Despite these valiant efforts, belief in the Testament survives. The *Christian Science Monitor* reacted to the Soviet invasion of Afghanistan by stating that "Peter the Great would be proud of his commissar successors in the Kremlin. . . . He would see [them] . . . acting in accordance with the injunction given in his will. . . . Whoever succeeded him, Peter said, should move southward to Constantinople and India, for 'whoever governs there will be true sovereign of the world.'"[8]

Another version of this point in the Testament includes an explicitly Iranian dimension—namely, Russia should make war on Iran and advance to the Persian Gulf in order to gain control over East-West commerce and, on that basis, to dominate Europe.[9] This was the version that *Time* cited when assessing the situation in Iran on the eve of the late Shah's departure into exile. The *Time* article introduced this provision of the Testament with an observation that reflects the belief in inherited drives that transcend normal political considerations: "Things have not changed much since czarist times."[10] A recent account of Soviet-Iranian relations cites the same provision of the Testament to argue that in it Peter "first formulated the guidelines" for Russian attempts to conquer northern Iran from his own day to the end of the second Russo-Iranian war in 1828.[11]

An even more popular legend about Russian intentions toward Iran deals with the quest for warm-water ports. This is not synonymous with a quest for access to the high seas, which many observers have also attributed to St. Petersburg and Moscow. Although some interpretations combine the two presumed motives, high-seas navigation is not contingent upon the acquisition of warm-water ports, as the modern use of icebreakers demonstrates. Alfred Thayer Mahan, whose turn-of-the-century writings on the importance of sea power enjoyed international influence, believed that Russia pursued territorial expansion in order to gain openings to the sea. He included Iran's Persian Gulf coast and the coast of China among the main targets, but did not cast the issue in terms of a quest for warm water. As a fervent believer in the importance of sea power, he concluded that Russia's leaders saw their country as having too small a coastline relative to its large land mass. He further contended that the pursuit of wealth through East-West trade, which he ascribed to Russia, required the acquisition of water routes, which he regarded as inherently superior to land-based means of transportation, including railroads. [12] In general, the access-to-the-high-seas interpretation is more likely to consider the nature of the objectives and pragmatic concerns than the warm-water-ports interpretation, which assumes that invoking the words "warm water" explains all.

The origins of the warm-water-ports theory blur with other European fears of Russian expansion in the direction of the Straits and India. By 1869, it had become an issue in its own right, as indicated when Germany's representative in St. Petersburg explained Russian expansion in Asia in terms not of conscious policy but rather of a force of nature drawn to warm-water ports and fertile southern lands. [13] My unscientific survey of various college-educated Iranians born since World War II is that the legend retains a following, at least among Iranians of that social milieu. It is also widely believed in the West. [14] For example, Alvin Cottrell, a veteran American specialist on Gulf affairs, used this to help explain the presence of the Soviet navy in the Indian Ocean in the 1970s: "Many writers have commented upon the historical continuity between Soviet and Czarist imperialism. The drive for warm water ports and an outlet to the great oceans of the world can be traced back to the days of Peter the Great and Catherine." [15]

The legend has been cited many times since the Iranian Revolution raised the possibility of a shift in Iran's orientation not only away from cooperation with the United States but also toward improved relations with the Soviet Union. During the final days of the Shah's regime, the *Wall Street Journal* identified a "warm-water port on the Persian Gulf" as one of Russia's long-standing objectives in Iran. [16] To some, the Soviet invasion of Afghanistan was especially significant because it brought the Soviet Union "closer to achieving an objective that eluded czars for more than a century . . . [territorial advance] that eventually could yield Moscow direct access to warm-water ports" on the coast of Iran and Pakistan. [17] During 1987 some observers greatly exaggerated the extent to which Iran warmed toward the Soviets. In anticipation of the signing of a Soviet-Iranian friendship treaty in 1987, an event that did not occur, a historian and a journalist predicted that "the new accord could give Moscow what it has wanted since the days of the czars: a strategic corridor to the warm waters of the Indian Ocean" via Iran. [18]

In fact, Russia's rulers never looked at Iran in terms of a route toward warm-water ports. That various Russian rulers had ambitions regarding Iran has been amply documented; but this does not mean that one may ascribe any motive one chooses to those ambitions. The pursuit of warm-water ports was not a Russian ambition with respect to Iran.

The assertion quoted above that this alleged quest dates from the reigns of Peter and Catherine is simply erroneous. Peter's ambitions in Iran centered on the coast of the Caspian Sea. He hoped to trade with Iran and India but expected to do so from this northerly location, not by obtaining direct access to the Persian Gulf. Similarly, Catherine the Great's Iranian ambitions focused on the North—the Caspian coast and Transcaucasia. Only at the end of her reign, when she made war against Iran's new ruler because of competing claims to suzerainty over the Kingdom of Georgia, did she try to conquer more southerly parts of Iran. Even then, the prime objective was not the Gulf coast but Isfahan, the old royal capital on the central Iranian plateau. In any event, the campaign was canceled by Catherine's successor soon after her death, without her troops reaching any part of the Iranian plateau.[19]

Subsequent tsars lacked the naval resources and the serious intention of gaining a port on Iran's southern coast. One of the authors long consulted on Anglo-Russian competition over Iran, Lord Curzon, argued differently. In fact his warning against such aspirations by Russia was cited approvingly in the *Washington Post* article quoted above. Yet Curzon is hardly convincing on this point. He claimed that Russia "yearns for an outlet upon the Persian Gulf and in the Indian Ocean."[20] He offered no substantiation for this assertion, however. Moreover, he himself did not always take this threat seriously. When he discussed this possibility in the first volume of *Persia and the Persian Question*, he added that no British government would allow Russia such an outlet and that the prospect of Russia obtaining one was too unlikely to be worth discussing.[21] Only when he returned to the subject, in the second volume, did he omit his earlier dismissal of this coming to pass. In general, Curzon's depiction of the Russian menace is based on speculation, rumor, and the quotation of the most intemperate statements in the Russian press. The fact that many intemperate statements could indeed be found in the press does not prove that the people who made them determined Russia's policy.

On the rare occasions when Russian officials contemplated their country's prospects in the Gulf, a fair amount of probity colored their judgments. On these occasions, an obsession with warm-water ports was conspicuous by its absence. By the end of the nineteenth century, Russia had agents in various parts of Iran, including the southeastern province of Seistan, much to the chagrin of the British. These agents gathered intelligence and tried to increase

Russia's influence. Although such activities may legitimately be deemed unwelcome by other parties, they are not in themselves proof that St. Petersburg had decided to escalate its involvement in Iran by launching a bold drive beyond the northern provinces, where its influence was already considerable, toward Iran's southern coast. Nor do they constitute motives for such a drive.

In 1890, a time when some Russian businessmen and officials were interested in building a railroad across Iran to the Gulf coast, the head of the Foreign Ministry's Asiatic Department, I. A. Zinov'ev, himself no friend of Britain, argued forcefully against attempting to establish a Russian presence in the Gulf. His position was that while Russia was weak in that region Britain was strong and would surely oppose a Russian attempt to gain a foothold there. The establishment of a naval facility in the Gulf to strengthen Russia's position against the British would be fraught with difficulties, which were, by implication, not worth the cost.[22] In the end, Zinov'ev won the policy debate.

A decade later, Britain's discomfiture in the Boer War encouraged Tsar Nicholas II and some of his officials to look for ways to overcome what they saw as Britain's constant obstruction of Russia's right to pursue imperial grandeur. The solution they envisaged was to profit from Britain's preoccupation elsewhere to enhance Russia's position in Asia, including its position in the Persian Gulf. Thus, new initiatives were contemplated not as the result of some irrational preoccupation with the region but rather as the result of a fortuitous opportunity in a particular historical context.

At that time, Russia sent a small number of ships, both naval and merchant, to Iran's Gulf coast. Russian publications urged the acquisition of a port there. Although that did not happen, two consulates were set up in the region and a shipping line between the Black Sea and the Gulf began operation. Nonetheless, the foreign minister, Count Murav'ev, although in favor of increasing Russian influence in Iran, argued against taking control of a Gulf port on the grounds that the British were too determined to be masters there and Russia lacked the means to defend such an acquisition. According to Murav'ev, the burdens of a Russian foothold on the Gulf would outweigh the benefits because it would cost too much, overextend the government's resources, and be too far from Russia's base of strength. The part of Iran with which Murav'ev favored the development of sea and land communications routes was the North, not the southern coast. The ministers of war and the navy agreed with the gist of Murav'ev's argument about the Gulf.[23] Despite the alarm among some British officials, notably Lord Curzon, then viceroy of India, over Russia's appearance in the Gulf, that presence amounted to very little.[24]

During the same period, the tsar's powerful minister of finance, S. Iu. Witte, advocated ensuring strong Russian influence in Iran and even eventual territorial annexation. But the specific region he valued was the North, which he considered the most attractive on the grounds that it possessed Iran's best economic assets.[25] When Witte became interested in establishing a presence on Iran's southern coast, he was prompted by the same kinds of economic concerns that underlay his attitude toward foreign policy in general—the desire to develop Russia's economy by promoting exports, including exports to Asian markets. This had nothing to do with primeval instincts. Rather, it was an attitude that many of his Western contemporaries shared. His most ambitious plan regarding southern Iran was to build a pipeline from the Baku oil fields in Russia's Transcaucasia to some unspecified place on Iran's Gulf coast.[26] The aim was to give Russia a less costly route to deliver its own oil to Asian markets,[27] thus making its price more competitive, and also to open the door for Russia to compete with Britain for Gulf commerce. In the end, Witte reluctantly abandoned the plan because it interfered with a higher priority, the conclusion of a loan agreement with Iran, which promised to increase Russia's influence over the Tehran government.[28]

In any event, Russia had barely begun to expand its influence in the Gulf when the Russo-Japanese war began in 1904, bringing Russia immense problems, including naval catastrophe and an attempted revolution. These events ended any prospect of further Russian activity in the Gulf, for whatever motive, for the remainder of the tsarist era.

With the establishment of Communist rule in Soviet Russia, the new regime also developed ambitions in Iran. However, these ambitions were motivated by rational, though not necessarily wise or admirable, assessments of the international politics of the day. Soviet leaders tried to establish a modus vivendi with their comparatively weak southern neighbors, to end their own diplomatic isolation, and to revive the waning prospects for revolution in Europe by fomenting anticolonial unrest in Asia; they did not inherit an obsession with warm-water ports. In fact, until the late 1930s, Soviet naval thought focused on the defense of Soviet coastal waters. Through the end of World War II, coastal defense was the most the Soviet Union could have aspired to, given its limited naval resources.[29]

When the Soviet military formulated a contingency plan for an invasion of Iran during World War II (probably in the first half of 1941), the Gulf coast was not a serious target. The plan focused on northern Iran for defensive as well as offensive reasons. Considerations included the risk of an attack on the Baku oil fields from Iranian territory, the possibility of fighting a British force advancing toward Soviet territory via Iraq or northeastern Iran, the attractiveness of Iran's northern provinces as the most economically developed parts of the country, and the significance to the British of northeastern Iran for the defense of India.

The plan provided extremely detailed information on routes the Red Army could take into Iran from the northwest, the Caspian coast, and the northeast. The Persian Gulf coast ranked as a minor consideration in this discussion; in a study that runs to 243 pages in the English translation, the total coverage of the route to the Gulf occupies only a handful of pages. Moreover, this study is vague about objectives on the Gulf coast. All it says is that, in the event of an advance to that region, the Red Army should aim for some town in Khuzistan, rather than another point on the Gulf, but does not specify an objective; it notes that there is oil in the area but does not identify where the main oil installations are or what might be done with them. The generality of this brief section contrasts sharply with the attention to minute detail in the rest of the plan.[30]

Since the 1950s, the Soviet Union has developed a navy that operates in many regions of the globe, including the Persian Gulf. It may be appropriate for the United States to regard this in a negative light, but that does not change the fact that the growth of Soviet naval power is the result not of some age-old drive but rather of specific developments in a particular historical context. These developments include the Soviet determination to acquire the kind of navy that befits a great power, to develop the capacity to strike foreign naval vessels capable of launching an attack on Soviet territory from great distances, to deny unchallenged dominance of the seas to an enemy in time of war, and to use naval forces for purposes that are not only military but also political, such as supporting client states and influencing other countries.[31]

So far is a preoccupation with warm-water ports from being the keystone of Soviet naval policy in the postwar era that one of the major routes the Soviets have developed since the 1960s is an Arctic passage to Siberia and East Asia. By using icebreakers, the Soviets can keep the route open for about one hundred days a year and save time in comparison with the Suez Canal route.[32] Of course, this does not mean that the Soviet navy prefers icy waters, but rather that it readily uses them and is not constantly preoccupied with finding warm-water routes as an end in itself.

In addition to the spurious motives that have been attributed to tsarist and Soviet foreign policy, certain events in Soviet-Iranian relations that have indeed occurred have been mythologized in the sense that they have been expanded to mean more than they really do and have been relied upon to explain too much. Two major examples of this are the 1921 Soviet-Iranian treaty and the 1940 Soviet-German talks about territorial claims in the postwar world.

The belief is widespread that the 1921 treaty, particularly its sixth article, permits the Soviets to send troops into Iran whenever they consider their security threatened from that direction. Typical of this view is the assertion that "relations between the two countries have been bedeviled by the ghost of the

1921 treaty . . . which allowed the Soviet Union to intervene in Iran in the event of a threat against Soviet territory."[33] The *Wall Street Journal*'s interpretation of the treaty presumed even greater latitude for intervention by claiming that the treaty permitted the Soviets to call a domestic attempt to topple the Iranian government a threat to Soviet security and send in troops on that basis.[34] A still broader interpretation, offered during the hostage crisis, posited that the Soviets might send troops into Iran to help that country repulse a hostage rescue operation by the United States and that "in accordance with the 1921 Soviet-Iranian treaty, they [Soviet troops] might continue to stay there after that help was no longer needed."[35]

All of these interpretations of the treaty are inaccurate. The treaty as ratified restricts the conditions for intervention in a way that has long since rendered the relevant provisions obsolete. Moreover, the government of the Islamic Republic of Iran may have a strong case under international law to support its abrogation of those provisions.

The controversial points of the treaty are Articles 5 and 6. Article 5 commits each signatory to ban from its territory "any organizations or groups of persons . . . whose object is to engage in acts of hostility against Persia [Iran] or Russia, or against the allies of Russia [that is, the other Soviet republics]." Article 6 is even more important. It states that if some third party or foreign country should establish a military presence in Iran in order to strike at Soviet Russia and if the Iranian government could not stop such activities, then "Russia shall have the right to advance her troops into the Persian interior for the purpose of carrying out the military operations necessary for its defense."[36]

The Iranian legislature, the Majles, voiced serious misgivings about various provisions of the new treaty, including Article 6, as well as the general status of Soviet-Iranian relations. Therefore the Majles did not ratify the treaty soon after its signing in February 1921 but instead continued to ponder it for the rest of the year. To encourage ratification, and in response to a direct request from the Iranian government for clarification, the Soviets provided a note that sharply restricted the conditions under which Article 6 might be invoked.[37] The note specified that the relevant treaty provisions were "intended to apply only to cases in which preparations have been made for a considerable armed attack upon Russia . . . by the *partisans of the regime which has been overthrown* or by its supporters among those foreign Powers which are in a position to assist the enemies of" Soviet Russia (emphasis added).[38]

The Soviet note met a condition set by the Iranian government for ratification of the treaty. That in itself would give it significance under international law. Moreover, the note became a revision added to the treaty itself.[39] Thus, the restricted definition of the permissible conditions for intervention is the valid one under international law. Since the prospect of armed intervention in the Soviet Union by supporters of the Romanov dynasty or the Provisional Government of March to November 1917, with or without foreign assistance, has long since ceased to be a realistic possibility, Article 6 no longer has any legitimate standing in the conduct of Soviet-Iranian relations.

Furthermore, the government of the Islamic Republic abrogated Articles 5 and 6 in November 1979. Ordinarily one party to a bilateral treaty cannot abrogate any part of the treaty unless the other signatory agrees, which, in this case, the Soviet Union has not done; but an argument can be made for the legitimacy of this particular abrogation. According to the Vienna Convention on the Law of Treaties, there are some occasions when changing circumstances are so at variance with a treaty's original intent and so alter what is required of the signatories that abrogation is permissible. The absence of any credible prospect for restoring Russia's old regime meets the criterion for drastically altered circumstances. In addition, the United Nations Charter prohibits any member from threatening or using force to interfere with a state's sovereignty or territorial integrity and ascribes to the charter precedence over other treaties conflicting with it that have been signed by members of the United Nations. By this standard, too, Article 6 could legitimately be abrogated.[40]

Nonetheless, the Soviet Union has invoked the provision several times since 1921, and the note of clarification has not been cited in response. The most dramatic occasion was in 1941, when it was one of the reasons used to justify the Soviet invasion of northern Iran.[41] The invasion was conducted in concert with Britain, for which the defeat of Nazi Germany was of vastly greater importance than Iranian sovereignty. If British diplomats were aware that Article 6 offered inadequate justification, they would hardly have considered it beneficial to Britain's interests at the time to raise that objection to a joint military action intended to aid the war effort. The Soviets have occasionally referred to Article 6 directly or indirectly since then, from the Azerbaijani crisis of 1945–46 to the era of the Islamic Republic. Moscow set the tone for contemporary allusions to the treaty even before the fall of the Shah. In November 1978, Leonid Brezhnev declared that the Soviet Union would regard foreign intervention in Iran as a threat to Soviet security and coupled that with a reference to the long border between the two countries.[42] Despite the implied threat in this statement and the episodes of mutual recrimination between the Soviet Union and the Islamic Republic since 1979, there have also been important occasions when each country has cultivated good relations with the other, even though they continue to disagree on the status of the 1921 treaty.

The other real event in Soviet-Iranian relations that has been extensively mythologized is the Soviet-German discussion in November 1940 about territorial claims in Eastern Europe and Asia. According to the mythic interpretation of these negotiations, "the Soviets revealed their vast ambitions" in the Persian Gulf.[43] Another commentator warned that in these talks, the Soviet representative, V. M. Molotov, declared that the Persian Gulf was the "focal point of the aspirations of the Soviet Union," which, wrote the commentator, remains the case today. "Any understanding," he added, "of what is happening in Iran today . . . must begin with the historical record."[44]

German records of the negotiations, which have been available in published form in English for forty years,[45] present a different picture altogether, in which Soviet attention was focused on Eastern Europe while Germany tried to deflect that focus to Southern and Central Asia, far from Germany's own expansionist targets in Europe.[46]

By the summer of 1940, Soviet-German relations were showing signs of strain, particularly over the war with Finland, competing interests in Romania, and the Soviet annexation of Lithuania. In November 1940, Molotov traveled to Berlin for talks with Ribbentrop and Hitler. Germany's aim was to persuade the Soviet Union to endorse the Tripartite Pact among Germany, Italy, and Japan and to lure the Soviets into concentrating on the Middle East while Germany strengthened its position in Europe.

Ribbentrop opened the talks by stating that Britain's defeat was assured and that Hitler advocated the rough delineation of postwar spheres of influence for Germany, the Soviet Union, Italy, and Japan. The German sphere was to include Western Europe, those parts of Eastern Europe already assigned to it by prior Soviet-German agreement, and parts of central Africa. Ribbentrop then asked Molotov "whether Russia in the long run would not also turn to the South for the natural outlet to the open sea that was so important."[47] Molotov's nonchalant response was to ask which sea. Again, it was Ribbentrop who demonstrated enthusiasm for Soviet expansion into Iran by advising Molotov that the best access to the sea for the Soviet Union would be "in the direction of the Persian Gulf and the Arabian Sea."[48] Thus, it was Ribbentrop who broached the idea in the first place and who coined the phrase that has been used to symbolize Soviet designs on the Gulf states.

Molotov did not object to letting Ribbentrop offer the Soviet Union a free hand in the Gulf, but neither was he distracted from far higher priorities elsewhere. When he met with Hitler, the points he pressed included Soviet interests in Bulgaria, Romania, and Turkey, the limits of the Japanese sphere in East Asia, and the status of Finland. The tone of the discussion showed signs of displeasure on both sides over these issues.[49] Molotov did not bother to raise the Gulf question at all.

At the final meeting, Ribbentrop offered Molotov encouragement for a new agreement with Turkey on navigation of the Straits and again tried to shift his attention far away, not only in the direction of the Gulf, but also toward the Indian Ocean, India itself, China's Sinkiang Province, and Outer Mongolia. Molotov still refused to be diverted. He used the opening Ribbentrop had given him on the status of the Straits to insist that Soviet security interests required much more than a new navigation agreement with Turkey and then pressed Ribbentrop to clarify Germany's position on all of Eastern Europe from the Baltic to Greece, thus broadening the discussion of that region far beyond its earlier bounds. Ribbentrop questioned Molotov on having said nothing about Soviet expansion southward to the Gulf. Molotov's response combined evasiveness with skepticism and wariness. He replied that spheres of influence would have to be specified but that he could say nothing binding on the subject without consulting Moscow. He further implied that Ribbentrop was offering vague promises that hinged on future developments that might not come to pass, like the defeat of England.[50] In summation, he stated that "all these great issues of tomorrow could not be separated from the issues of today and the fulfillment of existing agreements. The things that were started must first be completed before they proceeded to new tasks."[51]

Thus, the November 1940 talks do not provide an unusually frank admission of Soviet determination to take control of Iran and neighboring countries. What the talks do show is that two antagonists who were temporarily allies distrusted each other, were close to open rivalry in Eastern Europe, and wanted to use these talks to manipulate each other. Part of that manipulation was Berlin's attempt to distract Moscow from Germany's pursuit of European domination by proffering an adventuresome scheme for Soviet expansion in Asia. Not only were the Soviets not fooled, but the Germans did not take the scheme seriously either. A month after the talks ended, Hitler began to contemplate the invasion of the Soviet Union.

Difficulty in understanding the intentions of foreign countries' policymakers is a common enough problem in the history of international relations. It is an especially serious problem for those who have tried to deal with tsarist or Soviet Russia because of the sheer scarcity of accurate information. Under these conditions, history has often been used to fill in the gaps in the hope that it will reveal general patterns and long-term trends. But that is sometimes done in a way that mythologizes the history of tsarist and Soviet foreign relations. It is a disservice not only to Clio but also to other countries' diplomats because it restricts their own policy options. The mythic version of this history gives great weight to the role of quasi-instinctual obsessions. By their very nature, such irrational drives are not readily modified by the ordinary tools of conventional diplomacy. ·

Notes

1. K. A. Dunn, "'Mysteries' about the Soviet Union," *Orbis* 26 (Summer 1982): 361–62.

2. D. C. B. Lieven, *Russia and the Origins of the First World War* (New York: St. Martin's Press, 1983), 23–24.

3. For all the folly of the Iran-Contra imbroglio, the popular myths about Soviet designs on Iran seem not to have influenced those who supported the venture, at least as reflected by the information that has been made public thus far. Yet the perception of the Soviet role in Iran exhibited by two CIA documents used by advocates of the venture to support their case is just as disquieting as if ahistorical myths had guided the decision. At least the myths *attempt* to explain Soviet intentions and objectives. The CIA's "Special National Intelligence Estimate" and National Security Decision Directive on Iran (both of 1985), which policymakers used as part of their rationale for the dealings with Iran, do not consider such issues. This approach proceeds from the axiom that the Soviets pose the greatest danger to U.S. interests in Iran and that the Soviet threat is the most important reason for the United States to take an active interest in Iranian affairs. ("Special National Intelligence Estimate" by Graham E. Fuller, 17 May 1985, *Report of the Congressional Committees Investigating the Iran-Contra Affair* [Washington, D.C.: N.p., 1988], Appendix A, vol. I: 968; National Security Decision Directive [draft], ibid., 982, 986.) Ironically, within months of writing the pivotal "Special National Intelligence Estimate," Graham Fuller revised his interpretation, concluding that there was no pressing threat of Iranian domestic instability or extensive Soviet meddling. However, this view did not become widely known in government circles. (*New York Times*, 20 Mar. 1987, A12.) (The author would like to thank Dr. Eric Hooglund and Mr. Malcom Byrne, both of the National Security Archive, for their help in exploring the documents of the Iran-Contra investigation.)

4. H. Rawlinson, *England and Russia in the East* (London: John Murray, 1875), 145.

5. These included the need to expand further in order to secure territory previously conquered, fear of British competition for Central Asian trade, expansion toward India until stopped by some insurmountable obstacle, the influence of the military on government policy, and the use of increased strength in Asia to gain more influence in Europe. Ibid., 191–92, 197–98, 338–39.

6. Among the valuable modern works in English dealing with Russian and Soviet intentions toward Iran are F. Kazemzadeh, *Russia and Britain in Persia, 1864–1914* (New Haven: Yale University Press, 1968), and J. C. Campbell, "The Soviet Union and the Middle East 'In the General Direction of the Persian Gulf,'" *Russian Review*, in two parts: 29 (April 1970): 143–53; (July 1970): 247–61. M. E. Yapp's *Strategies of British India* (Oxford: Clarendon Press, 1980), examines the varied assessments of British officials of the possibility of a Russian threat to British India via Iran and Afghanistan. D. Geyer's 1977 study, *Der Russische Imperialismus,* now available in English as *Russian Imperialism,* trans. B. Little (New Haven: Yale University Press, 1987), discusses the motives for Russia's expansion in various quarters and the practical limits to its ambitions in the period from the reign of Alexander II to the outbreak of World War I. E. Sarkizyanz's "Russian Imperialism Reconsidered," in *Russian Imperialism from Ivan the Great to the Revolution,* ed. T. Hunczak (New Brunswick, N.J.: Rutgers University Press, 1974), 45–59, debunks several major Russophobic myths. In addition to these works, Muriel Atkin, *Russia and Iran, 1780–1828* (Minneapolis: University of Minnesota Press, 1980), chs. 3 and 4, discusses the objectives of Russian policy toward Iran in the late eighteenth and early nineteenth centuries. Professors Hugh Ragsdale and Hans Rogger have works in progress that look at different aspects of Western misperceptions of tsarist foreign policy.

7. Among the modern works in English on the subject are L. Lockhart, "The 'Political Testament' of Peter the Great," *Slavonic and East European Review* 14 (1935–36): 438–41; D. V. Lehovich, "The Testament of Peter the Great," *American Slavic and East European Review* 7 (April 1948): 111–24; O. Subtelny, "'Peter I's Testament': A Reassessment," *Slavic Review* 33 (Decem-

ber 1974): 663–78; H. Ragsdale, *Détente in the Napoleonic Era* (Lawrence: Regents Press of Kansas, 1980), 16–17, 20–21, 109–10; and A. Resis, "Russophobia and the 'Testament' of Peter the Great, 1812–1980," *Slavic Review* 44 (Winter 1985): 681–93. Professor Rogger has also debunked the Testament as part of a larger study of diplomatic Russophobia in "Origin of the Concept of the 'Russian Menace' " (paper presented at the Kennan Institute of the Woodrow Wilson Center on 7 Dec. 1987).

8. *Christian Science Monitor,* 31 Dec. 1979, 1.

9. Resis, "Russophobia and the 'Testament,' " 684.

10. *Time,* 15 Jan. 1979, 23n.

11. M. Rezun, *The Soviet Union and Iran* (Boulder, Colo.: Westview Press, 1988), 2.

12. A. T. Mahan, *The Problem of Asia* (Port Washington, N.Y.: Kennikat Press, 1970), 25–26, 42–45, 56–57, 117–19.

13. O. Hoetzsch, *Russland in Asien* (Stuttgart: Deutsche Verlags-Anstalt, 1966), 26–27.

14. R. J. Kerner's *The Urge to the Sea* (Berkeley: University of California Press, 1946) is a particularly well known exposition of the argument that Russian expansion has been linked historically to water routes. However, Kerner was not concerned with the question of warm-water ports per se. Rather, he focused on river routes leading to the Baltic, Black, and Caspian seas. In any event, Kerner makes two fundamental conceptual errors. By emphasizing the river system to the exclusion of all else as a factor in medieval Russian expansion, he came to the conclusion that the rivers were centrally important and that they were not only a means but also an end in themselves. He also treated river routes as uniquely important in the Russian context, without taking account of the great importance of riverine transportation in many parts of Europe before the development of the railroad.

15. A. J. Cottrell, "The Soviet Navy and the Indian Ocean," in *The Persian Gulf and Indian Ocean in International Politics,* ed. A. Amirie (Tehran: Institute for International Political and Economic Studies, 1975), 112.

16. *Wall Street Journal,* 4 Jan. 1979, 21.

17. *Washington Post,* 30 Dec. 1979, A16.

18. M. Hauner and J. Roberts, "Moscow's Iran Gambit: Railroading a Friendship," *Washington Post,* 16 Aug. 1987, D1.

19. Atkin, *Russia and Iran,* 4, 32–34, 37–40, 42.

20. G. N. Curzon, *Persia and the Persian Question* (London: Longmans, Green, 1892), 2:597.

21. Ibid., 1:236–37.

22. Zhurnal osobogo soveshchanie, *Krasnyi Arkhiv* 1, no. 56 (1922): 46.

23. Foreign minister [M. N. Murav'ev] to Nicholas II, *Krasnyi Arkhiv* 5, no. 18 (1926): 4–6, 9, 12–14; A. Kuropatkin [minister of war] to the minister of foreign affairs, 16 February 1900, ibid., 22; P. Tyrtov [naval minister] to the foreign minister, 14 February 1900, ibid., 19; Kazemzadeh, *Russia and Britain,* 334–39, 352, 436–40.

24. Kazemzadeh, *Russia and Britain,* 439–40.

25. S. Iu. Witte, *The Memoirs of Count Witte,* trans. and ed. A. Yarmolinsky (Garden City, N.Y.: Doubleday, Page, 1921), 433.

26. A similar proposal had been made in 1883 by a nobleman involved in the Baku oil industry. His motive, like Witte's, was competition with foreign oil companies in Asian markets. The government was completely uninterested in the plan. Kazemzadeh, *Russia and Britain,* 201.

27. The existing route, across Transcaucasia to the Black Sea port of Batum, already used a warm-water route, so the quest for one was not at issue in the pipeline project.

28. Kazemzadeh, *Russia and Britain,* 359–60, 378–84.

29. D. W. Mitchell, *A History of Russian and Soviet Sea Power* (New York: Macmillan Publishing, 1974), 373–75, 381–82, 408–10, 442, 469.

30. G. Guensberg, trans., *Soviet Command Study of Iran* (Moscow, 1941) (Washington, D.C.: Office of the Secretary of Defense, 1980). Almost all of the discussion of an invasion of Iran's Gulf coast is on pp. 190–93.

31. M. MccGwire, "The Turning Points in Soviet Naval Policy," in *Soviet Naval Developments,* ed. M. MccGwire (New York: Praeger Publishers, 1973), 195, 197, 202–04; G. E. Hudson, "Soviet Naval Doctrine, 1953–72," ibid., 285–87; R. G. Weinland, "The Changing Mission Structures of the Soviet Navy," ibid., 299–301; J. M. McConnell, "Doctrine and Capabilities," in *Soviet Naval Diplomacy,* ed. B. Dismukes and J. M. McConnell (New York: Pergamon Press, 1979), 1–29; C. C. Petersen, "Trends in Soviet Naval Operations," ibid., 38, 41, 45, 47; idem, "Showing the Flag," ibid., 89, 91; Mitchell, *A History of Russian and Soviet Sea Power,* 470; K. A. Dunn, "Constraints of the USSR in Southwest Asia: A Military Analysis," *Orbis* 25 (Fall 1981): 616.

32. Mitchell, *A History of Russian and Soviet Sea Power,* 583.

33. Hauner and Roberts, "Moscow's Iran Gambit," D1.

34. *Wall Street Journal,* 4 Jan. 1979, 21.

35. A. Y. Yodfat, *The Soviet Union and Revolutionary Iran* (London: Croom Helm, 1984), 68.

36. "Treaty of Friendship of December 1921 between Soviet Russia and Iran," in *Diplomacy in the Near and Middle East,* ed. J. C. Hurewitz (Princeton: D. Van Nostrand, 1956), 2:91.

37. R. K. Ramazani, *The Foreign Policy of Iran, 1500–1941* (Charlottesville: University Press of Virginia, 1966), 190, 236; Kazemzadeh, "Russia and the Middle East," in *Russian Foreign Policy,* ed. I. V. Lederer (New Haven: Yale University Press, 1962), 523.

38. "Note to the Iranian Foreign Minister from the Russian Representative in Tehran (12 December 1921)," in *Diplomacy in the Near and Middle East,* 2:91.

39. W. M. Reisman, "Termination of the USSR's Treaty Right of Intervention in Iran," *American Journal of International Law* 74, no. 1 (January 1980): 145, 148.

40. Ibid., 145, 149–53.

41. Ramazani, *Iran's Foreign Policy, 1941–1973* (Charlottesville: University Press of Virginia, 1975), 33–34.

42. *Pravda,* 19 Nov. 1978, 5.

43. R. G. Neumann, "Moscow's New Role as Mideast Broker," *Washington Post,* 25 Oct. 1987, C4.

44. C. M. Roberts, "Iran: In the Historical Middle," *Washington Post,* 16 Dec. 1979, B7.

45. Germany, Auswärtiges Amt, *Nazi-Soviet Relations, 1939–1941,* ed. R. J. Sontag and J. S. Beddie (New York: Didier, 1948).

46. This was shown clearly by J. C. Campbell in "The Soviet Union and the Middle East," pt. 1, 149–51; Alexander Werth also gave a vivid, accurate account in his well-known book on the Soviet role in World War II, *Russia at War, 1941–1945* (New York: E. P. Dutton, 1964), 105–06.

47. Memorandum of Ribbentrop-Molotov talks in Berlin, 12 November 1940 (dated 13 November 1940), in Germany, Auswärtiges Amt, *Nazi-Soviet Relations,* 218–21.

48. Ibid., 221–22.

49. Memoranda of meetings between Hitler and Molotov, 12 November 1940 (dated 16 November 1940), and 13 November 1940 (dated 15 November 1940), in ibid., 228–33, 238–45.

50. Memorandum of meeting between Ribbentrop and Molotov on 13 November 1940 (dated 18 November 1940), in ibid., 247–52.

51. Ibid., 252.

5

Gorbachev, Iran, and the Iran-Iraq War

ROBERT O. FREEDMAN

Mikhail Gorbachev would appear to be the most significant innovator in Soviet politics and foreign policy since the days of Nikita Khrushchev. His proposal for elections to the Soviet parliament; the increased glasnost (openness) in reporting problems in the Soviet Union; his release of well-known dissidents like Anatoly Sharansky, Ida Nudel, and Yuri Orlov; the rehabilitation of Boris Pasternak; and his efforts to improve Moscow's image in the West have all indicated that a new approach has replaced the *immobilisme* so apparent in Kremlin policy in recent years.

In many areas of foreign policy, too, Gorbachev has also made significant changes. Thus, by uncoupling the Strategic Defense Initiative from talks on intermediate-range ballistic missiles, the Soviet leader laid the groundwork for the INF treaty of December 1987. Similarly, by withdrawing Soviet troops from Afghanistan, helping to arrange a settlement in Angola, beginning a political dialogue with Israel, and undertaking a rapprochement with China, Gorbachev has made major alterations in a number of Soviet policies.[1] Underlying these changes has been what Gorbachev has called the "new thinking" in Soviet foreign policy. Essentially, the new thinking consists of the following five basic principles:[2]

1. The danger of nuclear war impels the superpowers to realize that human survival should take precedence over the interests of states, classes, and ideologies.

2. There is a need to abandon such concepts in international relations as the "zero-sum game" approach to the Third World, "vital interests," "spheres of influence," and "positions of strength."

3. A new concept should emerge—the pursuit of a "balance of interests" that would take into account the legitimate interests of the United States, the Soviet Union, and regional states.

4. Primary reliance should be placed on political means for the resolution of regional conflicts, with the United Nations playing a major role.

5. There is an organic connection between regional conflicts and super-power confrontation, and hence there is a need for joint action by the super-powers to settle the most serious regional conflicts.

Given the new thinking proclaimed in the Kremlin, one might have expected the Soviet Union to work actively with the United States to implement a cease-fire in the Iran-Iraq war once the possibility presented itself and to refrain from following a zero-sum game policy with the United States for influence in Iran. Interestingly, however, despite the new thinking and policy changes elsewhere in the world, in its policy toward the Iran-Iraq war, which lasted from 1980 to 1988, the Soviet Union under Gorbachev's leadership evidenced far more continuity than change when one compares Gorbachev with his three predecessors, Chernenko, Andropov, and Brezhnev. This chapter will discuss these main areas of continuity, placing Soviet policy toward the Gulf war in the larger context of Soviet policy toward the Middle East,[3] and will also suggest some of the areas in which change has occurred in Soviet policy toward the Gulf conflict.

On the eve of Gorbachev's accession to power in March 1985, the Arab world was badly divided, with Khomeini's Iran one of the primary causes of these divisions. There were, at the time, three main Arab camps. On the one hand was what might be called the Egyptian camp, consisting of Egypt, Sudan, Somalia, and Oman. All four states had either openly, as in the case of Egypt, or tacitly supported Camp David; all had denounced the Soviet invasion and occupation of Afghanistan; all had major military relationships with the United States that included joint military exercises; and all supported Iraq in its war with Iran. At the other end of the spectrum was the so-called Front of Steadfastness and Confrontation, which bitterly opposed Camp David, was generally supportive of Soviet foreign policy, and supported Iran in the Iran-Iraq war. Syria and Libya were the main countries in this alignment, although elements of the PLO, South Yemen, and Algeria also shared some of its policy perspectives and received arms from Moscow. In the middle of the Arab spectrum were such countries as Saudi Arabia, Jordan, Kuwait, Tunisia, Morocco, Iraq, the United

Arab Emirates, and the Yemen Arab Republic (North Yemen). Receiving weapons from both East and West, they had in common with the Egyptian-led camp an aversion to the Soviet invasion of Afghanistan and support for Iraq in the Iran-Iraq war, but they shared with the Steadfastness Front an opposition to Camp David, although they seemed more willing ultimately to sign a peace agreement with Israel than were Steadfastness Front members Syria and Libya. Moscow worried that this centrist grouping was moving toward Egypt, and Jordan's decision in September 1984 to resume diplomatic relations with Egypt and the frequent meetings between Mubarak and Hussein, as well as between Arafat and Mubarak, seemed to indicate such a movement had begun.

Consequently, as their Arab clients Syria and Libya were finding themselves increasingly isolated in the Arab world, Soviet diplomacy had an added incentive to try to end the Iran-Iraq war, which had adversely affected Moscow's position in the Arab world and especially in the Persian Gulf since it erupted in 1980. Not only had it badly divided the Arab world—thus making impossible the "anti-imperialist" Arab unity Moscow had wanted for so long— but it had also diverted the Arabs from their confrontation with Israel, an arena in which the United States was on the diplomatic defensive because of its support of Israel, which had become especially marked during the presidency of Ronald Reagan. Yet another problem for Moscow—and another benefit to Washington in the Soviet zero-sum view of the political competition in the Middle East—was the improvement in relations between Saudi Arabia and the United States that had occurred as a result of the war. Five U.S. AWACS aircraft had been stationed in Saudi Arabia to help monitor air traffic in the Gulf and prevent Iran from following through on its threat to close the Gulf.[4]

As a result, given the political benefits that had accrued to the United States because of the war, Moscow had a major interest in seeing it come to an end as quickly as possible, yet without a decisive victory for either combatant. Nonetheless, Moscow had a still higher priority and that was to prevent a rapprochement between Iran and the United States. The fall of the Shah and the hostage crisis that occurred when the U.S. embassy in Tehran was seized in November 1979 had driven a major wedge between the United States and its erstwhile "policeman of the Persian Gulf," Iran. Given the strategic position of Iran astride both the Persian Gulf and a long segment of the Soviet Union's southern border, Soviet leaders actively sought to prevent any rapprochement between the United States and Iran, and this was as evident under Gorbachev as it was under his predecessors.

In addition to its primary goals of preventing an Iran-U.S. rapprochement and prevailing on Iran to agree to end the Iran-Iraq war, Moscow had other elements on its political agenda with Iran. These included inducing Iran (1) to stop aiding the Afghan guerrillas, who were fighting against the Soviet-backed Kabul regime, (2) to resume shipments of oil and natural gas to the Soviet Union, while importing more goods from the Soviets, and (3) to increase its transit trade to Europe through the USSR. Moscow also was displeased about Iranian efforts to spread Islamic fundamentalism in the Arab world and the Khomeini regime's suppression of the Tudeh and other "progressive" forces in Iran.

For its part the Khomeini regime had a series of grievances with Moscow at the time Gorbachev took power. First and foremost were the Soviet arms shipments to Iraq—Moscow was Iraq's primary arms supplier. Second, Tehran was displeased by the Soviet invasion of Afghanistan, a development that enabled the Soviet Union to position troops on Iran's northern and eastern borders. Third, the Khomeini regime was angered by what it saw as Soviet support for the Tudeh Party and ethnic minorities in Iran's borderlands such as the Kurds and Azerbaijanis. Reinforcing Tehran's suspicion of the Soviet Union was Moscow's wartime occupation of Iranian Kurdistan and Azerbaijan and its attempts to maintain Soviet control there once World War II had come to an end.[5]

Thus, when Gorbachev took power, he faced a difficult task in improving ties with Iran. At the start of the war, Moscow had tilted toward Iran and stopped direct shipments of arms to Iraq until 1982, only to tilt back toward Iraq when Saddam Hussein offered to end the war in June 1982 but Khomeini refused. Soviet-Iranian relations hit their nadir in 1983, when eighteen Soviet diplomats were expelled from Iran,[6] and they continued to be strained through 1985. Thus, despite appealing for improved relations, Moscow took a critical stance toward the Khomeini regime not only because it continued to resist Iraqi offers to end the war but also because it was providing aid for the Afghan rebels and was repressing the Tudeh Party and other "democratic forces."[7] Indeed, although Iran and the Soviet Union shared a common interest in maintaining high oil prices and keeping the United States out of the Gulf, one of the senior Soviet specialists on the Middle East, R. Ulyanovsky, writing in the Communist Party journal *Kommunist,* went so far as to call the Khomeini regime a "political despotism reminiscent of the darkest times of the Middle Ages."[8] In addition, Moscow pulled its technicians out of Tehran, allegedly because they were threatened by the expanding war.[9]

Moscow's relations with Iraq were, however, not much better. Although two high-level Iraqi visits to the Soviet Union took place (Foreign Minister Tariq Aziz in March 1985 and President Saddam Hussein in December), Soviet references to an "exchange of views" during the March visit[10] and "a businesslike, frank and friendly atmosphere" during the December visit[11] clearly indicated disagreements, despite Soviet support of Iraq's efforts to end the war.

The Iraqis were displeased that the Soviet Union had permitted Libya (or Syria) to send Soviet-supplied ground-to-ground missiles to Iran that were then used to bombard Baghdad.[12] For its part, Moscow was unhappy at the steady improvement of Iraq's ties with the United States, which was exemplified by its purchase of forty-five U.S. helicopters that were initially developed as troop carriers for Iran.[13] Although the issue of Iraq's use of poison gas remained an irritant in U.S.-Iraqi relations,[14] commercial ties between the two countries continued to develop,[15] and Moscow may well have feared that Iraq, which made repeated calls in 1985 for Egypt's reintegration into the Arab world, was moving toward the pro-American camp despite its continuing dependence on Soviet arms.[16]

Elsewhere in the Gulf the Soviet record was mixed. Despite continuing efforts to establish diplomatic relations with Saudi Arabia, Moscow met with little success. In addition, the Saudi decision sharply to increase oil production, which had the effect of forcing down oil prices, was a major blow to the Soviet Union, which depended on oil exports for a large share of its hard currency earnings. Since the drop in oil prices came at a time when Moscow's own oil production had begun to decline, the negative impact of the Saudi action was intensified. In other areas of the Gulf, however, Moscow made gains, as both Oman in September 1985 and the United Arab Emirates in November of the same year established diplomatic relations with the Soviet Union. In both cases the escalation of the Iran-Iraq war appears to have been the primary motivation; both countries seem to have sought formal relations with the Soviet Union as another possible deterrent to an Iranian attack upon them. Indeed, in the words of Omani foreign minister Yousef bin Alawi, the escalation of the war had reached "a critical stage that was threatening the interests of states that are not party to the struggle."[17] A second possible reason for Oman's decision to establish diplomatic relations with the Soviet Union may have been related to the sudden burst of articles in U.S. newspapers earlier in the year that indicated that American-Omani defense ties were far greater than generally believed.[18] Oman's establishment of diplomatic ties with Moscow may have been intended to demonstrate to other states, especially fellow members of the Gulf Cooperation Council, that despite its close military ties with the United States, Oman had full freedom of action. As might be expected, Moscow warmly welcomed its new diplomatic ties with the two Gulf Arab states. A Soviet commentary, appearing in *New Times* after the establishment of Soviet-Omani diplomatic relations, gave Moscow's view of the significance of the event:

The decision to establish diplomatic relations with the USSR reflects the growing desire of Persian Gulf states to pursue a more balanced foreign policy. The Soviet Union's unchanging policy of supporting the Arab people of Palestine in their just struggle and the Arab nations in their fight against Israel's aggressive expansionist policy has earned it the respect of the monarchs in the region. The constructive Soviet stance with regard to issues bearing upon the situation in the Persian Gulf has also played a definite role.

Characteristic among press comment on Oman's decision is that of the British Guardian. According to this newspaper, the news came as a telling diplomatic blow to Britain and the U.S.A. which have military agreements with the present Oman regime. In this connection it would be in place to emphasize that the agreement to establish diplomatic relations with Oman in no way attests to Soviet desires to deal "diplomatic blows" at anyone or crowd anyone out. It merely demonstrates the Soviet Union's mounting international prestige and the striving of Persian Gulf states to pursue an independent policy according with their genuine interests.[19]

At the beginning of 1986 Gorbachev was to make a major effort to improve ties with Iran. Nonetheless, just as the Khomeini regime was later shown to have exploited U.S. efforts to improve ties during what became known as the Iran-Contra scandal,[20] so too did it appear to manipulate similar efforts by Moscow. Thus in early February 1986, the Soviet Union's first deputy foreign minister, Georgii Kornienko, traveled to Tehran—the highest ranking Soviet official to visit the capital since the ouster of the Shah. When Kornienko obtained an agreement in principle from Tehran to resume Aeroflot flights to Iran, and Iran's foreign minister accepted an invitation to visit Moscow, Gorbachev may well have felt he was making headway in improving the Soviet position in Iran.[21] Indeed, following Kornienko's visit, the Speaker of the Majles, Ali Akbar Hashemi-Rafsanjani, was quoted at a news conference as saying that Soviet-Iranian relations were improving and Kornienko's visit "will have a great effect on our relations with the Soviet Union and the Eastern world. One can be optimistic in fields such as technical, military, economic, and possibly political relations."[22]

Less than a week after Kornienko's visit, however, Iran embarked on a major offensive in its war against Iraq and seized valuable terrain around the city of Fao.[23] It may well have occurred to Moscow that Tehran had exploited the Kornienko visit and the impression of an improvement in Soviet-Iranian re-relations to deter the Soviet Union from increasing its aid to Iraq during the Iranian offensive lest Moscow lose the increased influence in Iran it had (or so it appeared) just obtained. In case Moscow did not see the significance of the Iranian ploy in February, Iran was to repeat the maneuver again later in the year. Thus in June, Iran announced its agreement to the first meeting in six years of the standing commission on Iranian-Soviet joint economic cooperation,[24] and in August there were visits to Moscow by the Iranian deputy foreign minister for economic and international affairs and the Iranian petroleum minister. (The latter stated that Iran was planning to resume natural gas sales to Moscow, something Moscow had long sought, and also stated, "we can cooperate with the Soviet Union as part of our defense strategy.")[25] Then, in December, during a Tehran visit by Konstantin Katushev, chairman of the Soviet committee for foreign economic relations, Moscow agreed to return the technicians it had pulled out of Iran in 1985.[26]

Yet once again Iran appeared to exploit the improvement of ties with Moscow by launching a major attack on Iraq, this one at the beginning of January 1987, less than two weeks after Katushev's departure. But its attacks on Iraq were not the only Iranian actions troubling Moscow. In September 1986 Iran had stopped two Soviet freighters in the Gulf and searched them before allowing them to continue—actions that drew a protest from the Soviet Foreign Ministry.[27] A second major irritant for Moscow, besides Iran's continued prosecution of the Iran-Iraq war and its unwillingness to accept Iraqi offers to settle it, was its aid to the Afghan guerrillas. Moscow changed leaders in Afghanistan in 1986, replacing Dabrak Karmal with Mohammed Najibullah; announced the withdrawal of six Soviet regiments in October and its readiness to withdraw the rest of its troops if external aid to the guerrillas ceased; and on 1 January 1987 offered a cease-fire and a general amnesty.[28] Iran did not appear to be impressed, however, and continued its aid to the Afghan insurgents.[29]

By far the most serious issue in Soviet-Iranian relations in 1986, however, was the revelation in early November that the United States had been secretly selling arms to Iran. On the surface, the scandal was a major boon for the Soviet Union. The Reagan administration lost credibility both in the United States and in Western Europe because its arms-for-hostages deal undermined the anti-terrorist policy Reagan had long been pursuing. Second, the Arab states of the Gulf, which had depended to a considerable degree on the United States for protection against Iran, were seriously discomfited by the revelation that the United States had been secretly courting Iran with the weapons that enabled it to wage its war against Iraq more effectively. Finally, not only had the Gulf Arabs lost confidence in the United States but, to a considerable extent, so too had Egypt and Jordan, nations on which the United States depended for support in its Middle East peace efforts. On the other hand, the fact that the United States was again shipping arms to Iran held out the possibility of a reconciliation between the two countries—something that Moscow had long feared and sought to prevent by improving its own position in Tehran. As the crisis unfolded, Soviet propaganda exploited it by claiming that the U.S. arms deal was a device both for prolonging the war (from which Moscow asserted that the United States benefited) and for interfering in the internal affairs of Iran.

Moscow's major concern about Irangate—that it would lead to a reconciliation between Iran and the United States—quickly proved unfounded as Secretary of State George Shultz publicly revealed in late January 1987 that there had been a secret U.S.-Iranian meeting in December 1986 in which the United States told Iran that any further improvement in relations would be based solely on Iran's "willingness to mend its ways."[30] Given Iran's active prosecution of the war with Iraq and its continued support for international terrorism, a change in its policy satisfactory to the United States must have seemed to Moscow to be an unlikely prospect. Indeed, Shultz on 29 January publicly stated that Iran had "very strong ties" to the group that kidnaped three American teachers from the American University of Beirut a week before.[31] The Iranian president, Ali Khamene'i, two weeks later ruled out any reconciliation with the United States unless America ended its "hostility and hatred."[32]

Meanwhile, however, Moscow was strongly castigating Iran for its January 1987 offensive against Iraq and began, for the next six months, to tilt toward Iraq in the war. Thus Moscow, on 9 January, issued its most detailed condemnation of the war to date, one clearly timed as a reaction to the Iranian offensive. It was, in its proposed solution to the war, far closer to the Iraqi than the Iranian position in that it called for a return to the prewar borders and "noninterference in each other's internal affairs," and asserted the right of every people "to independence and freedom" and "to choose its own way of life"—a clear rejection of the Iranian goal of deposing Saddam Hussein and setting up an Islamic republic in Iraq.[33] Moscow followed this up with a bitterly critical article in *Pravda* decrying the mistreatment of jailed Iranian communists.[34]

It was in this atmosphere that Iranian foreign minister Ali Akbar Velayati journeyed to Moscow in mid-February. Velayati met first with Andrei Gromyko, the president of the Soviet Union, who took a very tough line with the visiting Iranian (*Pravda* described the atmosphere of their talks as being "frank and businesslike"),[35] blaming Iran both for continuing the Iran-Iraq war and for aiding the Afghan insurgents from bases in Iranian territory. Gromyko warned that Iran bore "full responsibility" for allowing the Afghan guerrillas to use its territory and urged Velayati to influence the Afghans living in Iran to accept the Afghan government's offer of national reconciliation.[36] Velayati had an apparently more successful visit with Eduard Shevardnadze in which the Iranian, utilizing a ploy Iran had employed in the past to entice the Soviet Union into better relations, mentioned a number of economic projects in which it was interested in Soviet assistance. As in the past, Moscow apparently was willing to be enticed, with the *Pravda* report of the talks noting that the Soviet Union stated its readiness to consider Iran's requests "in a positive manner."[37] Trade was also a major subject of Velayati's discussions with Soviet prime minister Nikolai Ryzhkov, and *Izvestia* reported that both Ryzhkov and Velayati had agreed that the present level of Soviet-Iranian trade was below the "available opportunities."[38] Moscow's willingness to consider additional aid to Iran may also have been linked to its concern about a possible Iranian move back toward the United States, given the failure of the January offensive and Iraqi bombing of Iranian cities. According to a Kuwaiti report, Velayati told Soviet officials that the Iraqi bombardment of Iranian cities had caused great destruction and serious damage and that it was likely to make Iran turn openly to the United States.[39]

In examining the Velayati visit there are several issues of importance to note. In the first place, while Iran's agenda was to try to convince Moscow to stop supplying arms to Iraq, Moscow had two major objectives. The Soviet Union wanted both to end the Iran-Iraq war and, by 1987, to reach a settlement in Afghanistan. Given Iran's position as a major opponent of the Afghan regime and as a base of support for its enemies, Iranian help to Moscow in achieving a satisfactory settlement in Afghanistan would be very welcome. That Moscow received little support from Iran on the Afghan issue, however, became clear less than two weeks later when a Soviet Persian-language broadcast denounced Iran's leadership for holding "a special consultative meeting with leaders of Afghan counterrevolutionary bands who are ensconced in Iran," issuing "strict orders to prevent the return of Afghan emigrants to their homeland," and using the army to prevent their return.[40] Second, although Moscow was clearly angry with Iran for continuing to prosecute the war, it still had some hope of winning influence in the Khomeini regime (or positioning itself for good relations with a successor regime). For this reason, as well as its concern that Iran might yet gravitate back to the United States, Moscow continued to offer economic assistance to Iran, regardless of the serious problems in the two countries' relationship.

Nonetheless, by March 1987 it was clear that Moscow was tilting toward Iraq in the Iran-Iraq war, and this tilt was to continue until June 1987, when the U.S. reflagging of Kuwaiti tankers once again would prompt Moscow to court Iran. During the January–June period, Moscow sought to exploit the furor in the Arab world caused by the Irangate crisis by taking an increasingly public anti-Iranian stance. By agreeing to a Kuwaiti request to charter three of its ships, Moscow was demonstrating that, as in the case of the Arab-Israeli conflict, while the United States was arming the enemy of the Arabs, the Soviet Union was aiding the Arabs themselves. As a follow-up to the charter announcement on 14 April, Moscow stated that its deputy foreign minister, Vladimir Petrovsky, would visit Kuwait, Iraq, Oman, and the United Arab Emirates. Yet just as the United States was later to encounter problems with Iran because of its reflagging operation, so too was the Soviet Union. The day after the Soviet reflagging announcement, Iran's Foreign Ministry called the Soviet move "very dangerous,"[41] and three weeks later, on 6 May, a Soviet freighter was attacked in a daylight raid (so, presumably, the attackers knew it was a Soviet ship) by Iranian patrol boats (Tass called the attack an act of "piracy").[42] Less than two weeks after that attack, a Soviet oil tanker, which had been chartered by Kuwait, struck a mine in the Gulf.[43] These incidents elicited an angry Soviet response, with Deputy Foreign Minister Petrovsky, after returning from his tour of the Gulf Arab states, noting in an interview with *Moscow News* that the "USSR reserved the right to act according to international law [that is, use self-defense] if provocative actions with regard to Soviet ships were repeated."[44]

Iranian attacks on Soviet ships were not the only irritants in the Soviet-Iranian relationship in the late spring. Moscow also complained about pro-Iranian forces in Afghanistan rejecting the Afghan government's cease-fire appeal[45] and about an article in the Iranian newspaper *Jomhuri-ye Islami* that claimed that the Soviet republics of Tadjikistan, Turkmenistan, and Uzbekistan, as well as some districts in Georgia, were originally part of Iran's national territory and ought to be liberated.[46] The Soviet Union also emphasized its opposition to Iran's efforts to export Islamic fundamentalism. Gromyko, speaking to a visiting Arab delegation in late April, asserted that "no state had the right to interfere in the internal affairs of another, regardless of pretext,"[47] and a Moscow Radio Peace and Progress broadcast in Persian to Iran in early May noted sarcastically, "tomorrow Afghanistan or even Turkey may be attacked on the basis of nonsensical pretexts such as a threat against traditional Islamic dress."[48]

Yet, despite the sharp Soviet criticism of Iran, relations between the two countries were to take a major turn for the better in mid-June as Moscow once again sought to improve ties with Iran, although it appears that as in the past Iran was once again exploiting the Soviet Union for its own purposes. The cause of the Soviet policy change was the U.S. decision not only to reflag eleven Kuwaiti tankers but also to protect them with a flotilla of the U.S. Navy, which would convoy the ships from the Strait of Hormuz to Kuwait's territorial waters. Moscow saw in this a major American effort both to block growing Soviet influence in the Gulf and to improve its ties with the Arabs after Irangate. In a statement on 30 May, Reagan took a strongly anti-Soviet as well as an anti-Iranian position, vowing, "The use of the vital sea lanes of the Persian Gulf will not be dictated by the Iranians. These lanes will not be allowed to come under the control of the Soviet Union."[49] On the basis of its own experience with Iran, the Soviet Union may have seen the U.S. move as a source of U.S.-Iranian tension. Given Moscow's earlier concern that Iran's need for weapons would, as in the Irangate affair, lead it to a rapprochement with the United States, any U.S.-Iranian tension over American assistance to Kuwait, a major ally of Iraq, could only be welcomed. At the same time, however, as the Iran-Iraq tanker war escalated, Moscow may have worried that the United States would use the reflagging operation not only to redeem itself in the eyes of the Gulf Arabs after Irangate but also to obtain naval and air bases in the Gulf. Indeed, Moscow was to claim that the United States used the accidental attack by Iraq on the U.S. warship *Stark* in mid-May as a "Gulf of Tonkin" ploy to accomplish just such an objective.[50] In addition, were Moscow to back Iran overtly in the Iran-Iraq war, the Soviet Union ran the risk of alienating Gulf Arab states such as Kuwait and Saudi Arabia that it had been diplomatically courting. On the other hand, this must have appeared to Moscow to be an opportune time to win the influence in the Khomeini regime it had long sought. Iran was now isolated as never before under Khomeini with not only the United States pitted against Iran's regime but most of the Arab world and Britain and France as well. For this reason Moscow moved openly to improve relations with Iran while seeking to end the Gulf war and get the American fleet out of the Gulf. In doing this, Moscow nevertheless sought to avoid alienating either the Gulf Arabs or the United States, whose cooperation it had been soliciting in solving regional conflicts such as the Iran-Iraq war.[51] This was, however, to be a very difficult diplomatic task.

Moscow's first move to improve relations with Iran came during a Tehran visit by Yuli Vorontsov, first Soviet deputy foreign minister, in mid-June. As if to reassure the Iranians, who have tended to see the Persian Gulf as their area of dominant influence,[52] Vorontsov announced on 6 June, before his trip, that the Soviet Union would not augment its force of three warships in the Gulf.[53] During his visit to Tehran, Vorontsov reportedly emphasized four major points: (1) that the Soviet Union does not have parallel interests to the United States in the Gulf; (2) that the United States was planning projects against both the Soviet Union and Iran in the Gulf; (3) that the Soviet Union did not want foreign (non-Gulf) military forces in the Gulf; and (4) that the Soviet Union had a great deal of respect for the Iranian Revolution.[54] The Soviet representative also discussed a number of industrial projects Moscow was interested in helping Iran develop, including the expansion of the capacity of the Isfahan metallurgical complex to 1.9 million tons and the completion and expansion of the Montagen power station.[55] In discussing these issues Moscow appears to have again been seeking to broaden the level of state-to-state economic relations, which it hoped would lead to improved political relations, if not with the Khomeini regime, then with its successor.

Vorontsov's reception was a relatively warm one, although Iran's Speaker Hashemi-Rafsanjani reportedly told him that the United States used the Soviet Union's "small action" in the Gulf as an excuse for adventurism.[56] Nonetheless, in an English-language broadcast over Tehran Radio—a possible effort by Iran to signal the United States that if it pushed too hard Iran might move into the Soviet camp—Iranian prime minister Mir-Hosain Musavi noted that Iran wanted "clear-cut and friendly relations with the USSR within the framework of [Iran's] principles," and he expressed the hope that "the policies of the two anti-imperialist countries would be coordinated both at the regional and international levels."[57] It was clear, however, that on the issues of Afghanistan and the Iran-Iraq war, Tehran was not changing its position. A Tehran Persian-language broadcast reported that when Iranian president Ali Khamene'i met Vorontsov, he called for "an expansion of relations based on friendship and sincere cooperation" and endorsed Vorontsov's remarks about Soviet anxiety over U.S. hegemony and its presence in the Gulf. But Khamene'i repeated the "firm Iranian position on the evacuation of Soviet troops from Afghanistan." Khamene'i also stated that "our resolve to punish the [Iraqi] aggressor has become firmer in every way"[58]—a statement unlikely to give Moscow much encouragement that Iran was considering an end to the war.

Nonetheless, following Vorontsov's visit to Iran, and his subsequent visit to Iraq, Moscow on 3 July issued a major new policy statement on the Iran-Iraq war. In it, in a clear demonstration of the similarity of Soviet and Iranian views on the issue, the Soviet Union called for the withdrawal of all foreign ships from the Gulf. Moscow also called for Iran and Iraq to refrain from actions threatening international shipping and appealed for a cease-fire and the withdrawal of all forces to internationally recognized borders. The U.N. secretary-general, it was suggested, could play a "substantial role" in achieving a just settlement. That the Soviet effort was in large part an anti-American propaganda device, however, can be seen from the commentary accompanying the proposal:

> The United States wants to exploit the present alarming situation in the Persian Gulf area to achieve its long harbored plans of establishing military-political hegemony in this strategically important area of the world that Washington is trying to present as a sphere of U.S. vital interests.
>
> As to several Soviet warships staying in the Persian Gulf to which they in Washington refer, they have to stay in the Gulf for they accompany Soviet merchant ships and have nothing to do with the heightening of tension in the area.[59]

Interestingly, just before the Soviets issued the 3 July statement, a meeting took place in Moscow between U.S. special envoy Vernon Walters and Deputy

Foreign Minister Petrovsky to discuss the Iran-Iraq war. But the Soviet statement of 3 July made it clear that Moscow considered the tactical advantages of gaining influence in Iran to be more important than any cooperative efforts with the United States to pressure Iran to end the war—a policy Moscow would continue to follow. Thus Walters said after the talks that the United States could "count on Moscow's vote for a U.N. resolution demanding a ceasefire," but there was no mention then or later of any Soviet agreement to sanctions against Iran if it rejected the cease-fire.[60]

As might be expected, Iran called the Soviet proposal for foreign forces to leave the Gulf a "positive" step,[61] and during a visit to Moscow in mid-July, the Iranian deputy foreign minister, Mohammad Larijani, discussed the possibility of cooperation in economic areas, including oil and gas.[62] Soon after Larijani's departure, the U.N. Security Council, on 20 July 1987, unanimously adopted Resolution 598, which called for an immediate cease-fire in the Iran-Iraq war and the release of prisoners of war. Other articles somewhat reflected the Soviet view by proposing that the U.N. secretary-general act as mediator and urging all other states to "refrain from any act which may lead to further escalation and widening of the conflict." (Moscow later claimed that the United States had violated this article by building up its forces in the Gulf.) Finally, in deference to Iran's continuing demand that Iraq be condemned for starting the war, Moscow succeeded in inserting an article calling for the establishment of an "impartial body" of inquiry to determine responsibility for the conflict.[63] Given the document's accommodation to the Soviet position, it is not surprising that Moscow praised it.[64] The United States, however, simultaneously emphasized the need for sanctions against Iran if it failed to agree to a cease-fire.[65]

Following the passage of the U.N. resolution, Moscow adopted a strategy of delaying attempts to impose sanctions on Iran in an obvious effort to win Iranian goodwill.[66] Thus, as the United States began its convoy operation, Soviet propaganda claimed that the U.S. naval buildup in the Gulf was as much a cause of tension as the war itself,[67] and asserted that the United States was in violation of the Security Council resolution. At the same time, perhaps concerned that the United States was winning increased influence among the Arab states of the Gulf,[68] Moscow warned them that the Gulf could become a second Vietnam, intimating that just as Vietnam had suffered massive destruction at American hands, so too might the Arabs if they became too closely involved with Washington.[69] Moscow was also alarmed when America's NATO allies, at first hesitant about the U.S. naval escort program, started sending their own ships to the Gulf.

Moscow's tilt toward Iran continued with an evenhanded reporting of the Iranian riots in Mecca in late July[70] (something that did little to improve Saudi-Soviet relations as the Iranians, following the riots, called for the "uprooting" of the Saudi royal family),[71] and Vorontsov made another visit to Tehran in early August. According to the Iranian version of the visit, Khamene'i told Vorontsov "our people will continue the war on the ground borders until the downfall of the aggressive Iraqi regime"[72]—a blunt rejection of Soviet efforts to achieve a cease-fire. Still, Iran needed the Soviet Union to block any follow-up U.N. Security Council actions, including the imposition of sanctions. So the Iranians made further gestures designed to assure Moscow that it had won influence in Tehran. Thus, during the Vorontsov visit there were discussions about the export of Iranian oil through the Black Sea, a possible second railroad link, and other aspects of economic cooperation. Deputy Foreign Minister Larijani praised Iranian-Soviet relations as "progressing and developing at a very good level."[73]

Meanwhile, as Soviet-Iranian relations improved, so too did U.S.-Arab relations, as a result of the growing American military presence in the Gulf—something ruefully noted by *Pravda* in late August.[74] During this period Moscow sought to portray Iran as more moderate than it actually was, with a Tass broadcast on 9 August citing Iran's U.N. representative as saying Iran did not plant mines in international waterways[75] and saying that Iran had not specifically rejected Resolution 598.[76]

By late August, with tension in the Gulf rising and Iran still rejecting a cease-fire despite the mediating efforts of the U.N. secretary-general, Arab criticism of Moscow began to mount. Editorials in the Iraqi government newspaper *al-Thawra* called Soviet opposition to sanctions against Iran "short-sighted,"[77] and a delegation of the Arab League headed by a Kuwaiti official came to Moscow on 7 September. Although Moscow sought to blame the rise in tension on the U.S. buildup in the Gulf and proclaimed its full support for Resolution 598,[78] the final communiqué described the talks as having taken place in a "businesslike atmosphere" where a "frank exchange of opinions had taken place"—a clear indication of serious disagreement.[79] Moscow's sensitivity to Arab charges that it was protecting Iran was reflected in a *Pravda* article that condemned "attempts to cast a shadow on the Soviet Union's policy and drive a wedge in its relations with the Arab states."[80]

Yet at the same time Moscow was trying to reassure the Arabs, it was entertaining the Iranian deputy foreign minister Larijani, who had come for talks on 9 September. (Perhaps to demonstrate an "evenhanded position," Soviet officials met Iraqi foreign minister Tariq Aziz the same day.) Commentators in Tehran noted that the two countries had agreed in principle on several projects: running an Iranian oil pipeline through Soviet territory to the Black Sea, drawing up plans for a railway network in eastern Iran, and moving toward joint shipping in the Caspian Sea.[81] Clearly, Iran was offering Moscow an increased economic stake in the country in return for its support in the United

Nations against the United States, something Moscow continued to do. Indeed, when the United States destroyed an Iranian speedboat laying mines in international waters on 21 September, Moscow backed the Iranian version of the incident, claiming that the ship was carrying food.[82]

Still, as tension—and Arab criticism—rose, Moscow turned to yet another diplomatic device. This was a call, by Soviet foreign minister Shevardnadze at the United Nations in late September, for a U.N. force to replace the U.S. and NATO forces in the Gulf.[83] Such a move, if successful, might reduce Iranian-U.S. tension, but it would also reduce U.S. influence in the Gulf, an important plus for Moscow. In addition, it would deflect pressure for sanctions against Iran, another of Moscow's goals. Not surprisingly, therefore, the United States rejected the plan. Many U.S. observers pointed out that U.N. forces have historically been effective as peacekeepers after a war has ended, but not in the midst of an ongoing conflict, as the history of the U.N. force in Lebanon (UNIFIL) demonstrated. Moreover, such questions as command responsibility and rules of engagement would have to be worked out, clearly a time-consuming process that would further delay consideration of sanctions.

For its part, Iran was showing its appreciation for the pro-Iranian stance of Soviet policy. On 1 October the Iranian ambassador in the Soviet Union held a press conference in which he praised the Soviets' decision to pull their troops out of Afghanistan, while criticizing the United States for wanting the war to continue.[84] Two weeks later, the Soviet airline Aeroflot formally resumed flights to Tehran.[85] Then, in mid-October, as the United States was placing an embargo on virtually all imports from Iran, the Iranian oil minister visited Moscow and signed an agreement in principle to supply oil for processing at Soviet refineries.[86]

Meanwhile, the Soviet Union was also taking the Iranian side during two U.S.-Iranian military confrontations in October, with Soviet Foreign Ministry spokesman Gerasimov deeming the U.S. attack on Iran's offshore oil platform on 19 October to be "a violation of the U.N. charter."[87] But it also sought to shore up its relations with the Gulf Arabs, using, as it had in the past, its special relationship with Kuwait to accomplish this objective. Thus on 15 October during a Moscow visit by Kuwait's oil minister Ali Al Khalifa, the two countries signed a bilateral cooperation agreement.[88] If Kuwait had arranged Khalifa's visit to Moscow in the hope of deterring Iranian attacks, the attempt did not meet with success. Indeed, the day before the agreement was signed, on 14 October, Iran fired a missile into Kuwait and hit a tanker in its port. Moscow's response to the Iranian act took the form of a *Pravda* statement that condemned the attack as "unacceptable from the standpoint of international law, politics and morality."[89]

Nevertheless, Arab displeasure with the Soviet Union increased. Iraqi foreign minister Tariq Aziz, speaking at a U.N. news conference on 2 October, had rejected Soviet efforts to effect a cease-fire and set up a commission to determine responsibility for the war,[90] and an Iraqi official was quoted as saying, "There is a minicrisis in our relations with the Soviet Union."[91] Moscow in response tried once again to achieve an end to the war, and sent Yuli Vorontsov at the end of October to Iraq, Kuwait, and Iran for talks. But the Iranians signaled their reaction to his efforts by launching a missile at Baghdad while Vorontsov was still there.[92] Following Vorontsov's return to Moscow, Iranian prime minister Musavi appeared to put an end to expectations that Iran might accept Resolution 598 by publicly stating, "We have no hope that the U.N. can do anything about the war."[93]

Musavi's negative comment coincided with the opening of the Arab summit in Amman, Jordan, in early November. The Gulf war dominated the conference: its opening was marked by an Iranian missile strike against Baghdad and the Arabs strongly condemned Iran in most of their resolutions.[94] The central decision of the meeting—to allow each Arab state to decide independently whether to restore the diplomatic relations with Egypt broken off in the aftermath of Camp David—was a major defeat for Soviet efforts to keep Egypt isolated. The Arabs decided that, despite Camp David, Egypt was needed as a counterweight to Iran, and in rapid succession Saudi Arabia, Kuwait, the UAE, Bahrain, Qatar, North Yemen, Morocco, and Tunisia restored ties with it. Relatively little attention was paid to the Arab-Israeli conflict at the summit, for the threat from Iran transcended what until now had been the Arab world's primary preoccupation—and the lever used by Moscow to increase its influence in the region. *Pravda*'s Middle East commentator, Pavel Demchenko, sought to put the best possible interpretation on the conference, noting that it was a step toward Arab unity and that it had endorsed the Soviet proposal to convene an international conference on the Middle East.[95] Yuri Glukhov, also writing in *Pravda,* took a more negative view, observing that "the meeting's documents do not contain a single word condemning the policy of U.S. imperialism." He also noted that Egypt was given "an opportunity to emerge from isolation, but there was no rehabilitation of Sadat's policy of separate deals."[96] Perhaps more reflective of Moscow's true feelings about the summit was the *Izvestia* interview with Popular Front for the Liberation of Palestine (PFLP) leader George Habash on 28 November:

> We note with profound regret that for the first time in the history of inter-Arab summit meetings, the Amman meeting's final documents for some reason did not mention support for the Palestinian people's legitimate national rights, including their right to self-determination and the creation

of an independent sovereign state with its capital in East Jerusalem. Furthermore—the decision adopted in Amman to give each state the right individually to decide the question of restoring diplomatic relations with Egypt may lead to the involvement of other Arab countries in the Camp David cause. The meeting in no way condemned the build-up of the U.S. military presence in the Persian Gulf. And in general, it seemed to us that the influence of progressive, patriotic forces was less perceptible in the atmosphere of the summit meeting than at previous such meetings.[97]

Given the strong anti-Iranian position taken by the Arab summit (even Syria joined the Arab call to Iran to accept a cease-fire and withdraw from Iraqi territory), Moscow evidently felt it had to respond. Thus on 19 November Moscow Radio Peace and Progress, broadcasting to Iran in Persian, warned:

We see the formation of a U.S. Middle East strategy on the establishment of bases, as well as the extension of its ambitious hegemonism. In our opinion, this is exactly the very point which should be taken into consideration by those Arab circles that are opening the doors of their countries to U.S. military presence, as well as by those Iranian dignitaries who continue to maintain their stand of "war, war until victory," and who are— irrespective of their inclinations—working against the interests of their peoples and those of regional and international security.[98]

Then, in early December, following the signing of a protocol for the opening of joint shipping routes between Iranian and Soviet ports,[99] Andrei Gromyko held a meeting with the Iranian ambassador to the Soviet Union, Naser Hairani-Naubari. Gromyko took a relatively hard line with the Iranian envoy, saying that "you as an ambassador and the Iranian leadership made a great number of statements about the wish to end the war. But the war goes on. Iran is practically not carrying matters toward ending the war." Gromyko went on to warn that if Resolution 598 were not accepted, "the question of further steps toward ensuring the implementation of the decisions adopted by the Security Council might be put on the order of the day," and reminded the Iranian that at the Reagan-Gorbachev summit, which was a few days off, the Iran-Iraq war would be discussed.[100] The tension inherent in the meeting was reflected in *Pravda*'s notation that the talks took place in "a businesslike and frank atmosphere."[101]

In addition to its calls to Iran to bring the war to an end, Moscow began to move on the diplomatic front to compensate for the events at the Arab summit, which it saw as a gain for the United States. Thus, Foreign Ministry spokesman Genady Gerasimov in a press briefing on 30 November went beyond the previous Soviet position on the war by stating that the Soviet Union would be prepared to have the United Nations not only escort ships in the Gulf but also act to implement sanctions.[102] To be sure, Gerasimov coupled this statement with a demand that Western nations enact legislation to prohibit both overt and covert trade in arms with any nation that violated U.N. Resolution 598. To some Americans, mindful of the time it would take to get such legislation passed, this appeared to be yet another delaying tactic by Moscow. Other analysts again raised the problem of command and control inherent in any U.N. force.[103] Nonetheless, Iran took the Soviet policy change seriously—and in a highly negative manner. Thus, on the eighth anniversary of the Soviet invasion of Afghanistan, Iran permitted a group of Afghan demonstrators to attack the Soviet consulate in Isfahan.[104] Moscow lodged a "strong protest" with Iran, claiming that the attack had been carried out by a "group of fanatical elements from the Afghan counterrevolutionaries who are based in Iran."[105] One week later, a commentator on Iranian television took a highly caustic view of the change in Soviet strategy and warned Moscow not to continue its new policy:

> The Soviet Union feels that because of the possible threat to them posed by the continuation of the war, the reactionary Arab leaders are daily inclining more and more toward the United States and the West. The culmination of this inclination could be seen in the Amman conference and the GCC summit. The Russians feel that if they continue their previous line, they may lose the astronomic loans from the Arabs and their future economic-political presence in Arab countries. They also feel that if they do not react more strongly toward Iran, the Americans will become the only defender among the Arab reactionaries, and this will pave the grounds for the United States to take strategic steps where the future of the Middle East is concerned. At this juncture, the Soviet Union has altered its stand; it is gradually moving away from its previous position toward a more overt stand on the war. At the same time it is trying, as much as possible, to postpone the moment of decision.
>
> Moscow's request to the U.N. Secretary General to pay another visit to the region stems precisely from this. But is this a logical policy at a time when the Americans are still prepared at the slightest smile from Tehran to sell out all the Arabs for the sake of establishing a small relationship with Iran? What will the Russians gain from this stand? The United States understands very well Iran's sensitive role in the region and if, under such conditions, the Russians join in the arms embargo, they will destroy all the bridges that have been built so far. Moreover, because of their intrinsic fear of communism and the natural compatability between their systems and

capitalism, the Arabs will certainly not turn toward the Soviet Union. The only outcome of the Russians' act can be that the Americans will benefit and their position will be strengthened.

The strength that Iran has shown in the past year in the Persian Gulf proves the seriousness of the remarks by our officials that if such a plan is implemented, all Persian Gulf ports will become obsolete. If the Russians go along with the Americans in this, they will be repeating the same mistake they once made when they leased their tankers to Kuwait. The difference, though, is that it is easy to make up for some mistakes, but difficult or impossible to do so for others.[106]

In February 1988, Moscow made a major move to improve its position in the Middle East and throughout the Islamic world by announcing its decision to pull out of Afghanistan. Gorbachev sent special envoys to virtually every Arab state as well as to Iran to inform them of the withdrawal and seek their aid in assisting it, hoping they would influence Pakistan and the United States to agree to Soviet conditions for the withdrawal at the Geneva talks.[107] The Khomeini regime, while welcoming the Soviet move and calling it a "positive development," nonetheless expressed its suspicion that it might be a ploy to keep the Najibullah regime in power and prevent the "Afghan Muslim people and revolutionaries" from controlling their own country.[108] Soviet deputy foreign minister Vladimir Petrovsky flew to Iran on 11 February to explain the withdrawal to the country's leadership, but was told by Iranian foreign minister Velayati that Iran expected that the mujahedin would have a "fundamental and decisive" role in the future of Afghanistan, which should be "independent and non-aligned."[109] Majles Speaker Rafsanjani apparently went so far as to offer Petrovsky a deal on this point, noting that "if you are determined to pull out of Afghanistan, we are prepared to assist you, so that after your departure there will be no U.S. domination in Afghanistan."[110] Although Foreign Minister Velayati was to give an overall positive evaluation of the Petrovsky visit,[111] differences about the role of the mujahedin remained, and on 23 February the Afghan Moslem Council issued a strongly worded anti-Soviet statement in Tehran rejecting the idea of any compromise with "Soviet-inspired groups who are responsible for the social calamities in Afghanistan."[112] Yet another irritant in the Soviet-Iranian relationship at the time was what Tehran saw as Soviet acquiescence in U.S. attempts to achieve an arms embargo against Iran.[113]

What was to be the greatest blow to Soviet-Iranian relations, however, occurred at the end of February when Iraq launched a missile attack against Tehran. The Iranian leadership denounced the Soviet Union for supplying Iraq with the missiles, and Iranian protesters marched on the Soviet embassy in

Tehran and the Soviet consulate in Isfahan, shouting "death to Russia."[114] Although Moscow denied supplying the missiles, the Iranian leadership rejected the denials, with Rafsanjani warning that the Iranian people would "never forget the Soviet Union's impudence" in supplying Iraq with missiles and stating that this would "definitely affect our future relations" with the Soviet Union.[115] Rafsanjani also asserted at a news conference that the Soviet Union was "currently pursuing a policy of hypocrisy and duplicity" by putting the missiles at Iraq's disposal and providing parts to modify them and increase their range.[116] Meanwhile, Iran's deputy foreign minister Javad Larijani, also speaking at a press conference in Tehran, declared that on his recent trip to Moscow he "clearly told the Soviet President and Prime Minister that any missile or bomb given to the tottering regime of Iraq by the Soviet Union will first hit Tehran-Moscow relations before hitting Iranian soil."[117]

The Soviet Union, clearly troubled by the Iranian response, sought to assuage their anger by leading a drive in the U.N. Security Council to achieve an end to the "war of the cities,"[118] although the Soviet effort was to prove ineffective. One month later, Tehran denounced the U.S.-Soviet agreement on Afghanistan that was signed in mid-April because it did not include the mujahedin.[119] Meanwhile, Moscow used another tactic to improve ties with Iran just a few days after the signing of the Geneva agreement on Afghanistan. On 20 April it sought to exploit the U.S. attack on Iranian offshore oil platforms that followed the mining strike on a U.S. warship. Tass commentators denounced the American attack (which quickly escalated into a battle between the U.S. and Iranian navies) as "an act of aggression" and "gangsterlike."[120] A Soviet Foreign Ministry spokesman, Vadim Perfilyev, labeled it a "gross violation of international law" taken in "total disregard for world public opinion."[121]

This did not meet with too much success, as Tass news analyst Valery Vavilov somewhat ruefully acknowledged when he deplored Rafsanjani's claim that the U.S. attack was part of a "coordinated campaign of the United States, the Soviet Union and Kuwait."[122] A Radio Peace and Progress broadcast, in Persian, to Iran on 25 April made this point more strongly, asserting that the Iranian mass media were claiming that the Soviet Union was "hand-in-hand" with the United States in a coordinated effort to destroy the Islamic Republic, and that Iran was now a target of hostile actions agreed to by the Soviet Union and the United States.[123] Moscow also deplored Iran's role in splitting Muslim unity through its refusal to end the war (diplomatic relations between Iran and Saudi Arabia had just been broken by Riyadh), with Moscow Radio Peace and Progress going so far as to say: "Those who support a protraction of the Iran-Iraq conflict hide their spiteful programs under the shield of religious slogans. They regard war as a decisive means in the struggle for leadership in the Islamic world. Such a policy can yield the most dangerous results under current international conditions."[124]

The negative status of Soviet-Iranian relations was spelled out in detail by the Iranian newspaper *Kayhan International* on 27 June in an editorial:

The Iranian nation and leadership have been alarmed at the rate Iraq's arsenals have been stock-piled after Gorbachev took the helm of power. Long-range Soviet missiles have rained on innocent Iranian civilians. Soviet MIGs are responsible for a very large number of Iranian non-military casualties. And these inhumane events have unfolded parallel to Mr. Gorbachev's image-building efforts at home and abroad. . . . As things appear to be, the Soviets have failed to win substantial influence in Tehran. Nearly 10 years of diplomatic, political and economic relations with the Islamic republic has surely not placed the Kremlin in a better position than the White House in the eyes of 50 million Iranians.[125]

Moscow tried again to exploit a U.S.-Iranian clash in early July when a U.S. cruiser, in the midst of a battle with Iranian gunboats, accidentally shot down an Iranian civilian airbus. Soviet commentators, strongly endorsing the Iranian version of the incident, condemned the action, with one hinting that it was "premeditated aggression"[126] and others, including *Pravda,* calling it "cold-blooded murder" and an attempt to intimidate Iran.[127] Moscow also sought to use the airbus affair to mobilize diplomatic pressure on the United States to pull its naval forces out of the Gulf—a goal shared by Iran.

In any case, less than three weeks after its airliner was shot down, Iran agreed to a cease-fire in the Iran-Iraq war. Having suffered major losses on the battlefield in the April–July 1988 period, including the loss of the Fao Peninsula, and facing missile and gas attacks by Iraq, Iran changed its position and reluctantly accepted the cease-fire unconditionally.[128] As might be expected, the Soviet Union warmly welcomed an end to the war that had caused it so many problems in the Middle East for the past eight years.[129] Yuli Vorontsov immediately flew to Tehran to consult with Iranian leaders and reportedly took the opportunity to condemn the shooting down of the Iranian airliner as an "act of barbarity," as he sought once again to undermine the U.S. position in Iran and open a new page in Soviet-Iranian relations.[130]

Several conclusions can be drawn regarding Gorbachev's policy toward Iran and the Iran-Iraq war. In the first place, despite all the Soviet rhetoric about "new thinking" and "balance of interests" in solving Third World problems, there has been far more continuity than change in Soviet policy. Thus, as

Brezhnev first tilted toward Iran and then toward Iraq, Gorbachev was to tilt toward Iran in 1986, toward Iraq in the first six months of 1987, and then back toward Iran again. Like his predecessors, too, Gorbachev tried—and failed—to end the Gulf war, which caused numerous problems for Soviet strategy in the Middle East. The cease-fire that ended the war in August 1988 was due to Iranian war-weariness and defeats on the battlefield, not to Soviet diplomacy, although the weaponry supplied to Iraq by the Soviet Union played a role in the Iranian decision to accept a cease-fire.

To be sure, Gorbachev demonstrated more diplomatic flexibility than his predecessors in dealing with Iran, although it is an open question as to whether or not he has been any more successful. Thus in 1986, Iran made a series of gestures to the Soviet Union that Moscow eagerly reciprocated, only to find out that Iran had exploited the Soviet drive for influence in order to mount major offensives against Iraq. Then Moscow sought to exploit the Irangate crisis by denouncing Iran and championing the Arabs, going so far as to agree to charter three Kuwaiti tankers. Once the United States moved to redeem itself for Irangate by reflagging eleven Kuwaiti tankers and building up its naval armada in the Gulf, however, Moscow switched positions again, trying to exploit the rise in U.S.-Iranian tension to enhance its own position in Tehran. Its peace initiative of 3 July, which was marked by anti-American propaganda, and its efforts to delay the imposition of U.N. sanctions against Iran clearly reflected the pro-Iranian tilt in its policy. Moscow's policy alienated the Arab states of the Gulf, while winning it very little new influence in Iran. Indeed relations between the Soviet Union and Iran appeared to fall to their lowest point since Gorbachev had come to power, when, in March 1988, the Iranian leadership blamed Moscow for supplying Iraq with the missiles it used to bombard Tehran. The anti-American policy of the Soviet Union in the Gulf from the U.S. reflagging of Kuwaiti tankers in July 1987 until the cease-fire one year later could raise serious questions about Soviet claims to "new thinking" in the solution of such Third World crises as the Iran-Iraq war.

The tactics used by Moscow in seeking to improve ties with Iran also show more continuity than change. Just as his predecessors sought to exploit a perceived Iranian economic vulnerability to improve ties with Tehran, so too did Gorbachev. Although Iran was in need of economic assistance, the Khomeini regime cleverly exploited Soviet offers of economic cooperation to entice the Soviet Union into thinking it was on the verge of a political breakthrough in Tehran. On three occasions (before the 1986 Fao offensive, before the 1987 offensive, and during the U.S. naval buildup in the Gulf) Iran appears to have manipulated Moscow and achieved its own political ends without making any concessions. On such basic issues as the continuation of the Iran-Iraq war and aid to the Afghan mujahedin, Iran demonstrated that Moscow had little influence over it, although Gorbachev may have taken some satisfaction from the fact that Washington and Tehran remained very far from striking any political rapprochement—this was at least a negative achievement.

One new facet of Soviet policy toward Iran was observable in the period from Gorbachev's coming to power in March 1985 to the August 1988 cease-fire. This was Moscow's new emphasis on the role of the United Nations, and especially the U.N. secretary-general, in settling the dispute. Moscow's turn to the United Nations came at a time when the United States had made a major military commitment in the Gulf. Thus, by first working for the passage of U.N. Resolution 598 and then calling for a U.N. fleet in the Gulf to escort shipping, Moscow appeared to be trying to use the world organization to prevent the United States from making major political gains with the Arab Gulf states. At the same time, however, Moscow's refusal to agree to the implementation of sanctions against Iran deprived the resolution of any real political force. Similarly, the Soviet suggestion that the proposed U.N. Gulf fleet be the instrument to impose sanctions was so limited by qualifications that it seemed merely a propaganda move to assuage Arab opinion at a time when the Gulf Arabs were increasingly critical of Moscow's pro-Iranian tilt.

In sum, therefore, despite some new flexibility, and despite its attempts to use the United Nations as an aid in its Gulf policy, there was clearly more continuity than change in Soviet policy toward Iran under Gorbachev.

Notes

1. For an analysis of some of the initial foreign policy steps taken by Gorbachev, see Robin F. Laird, ed., *Soviet Foreign Policy* (New York: Academy of Political Science, 1987).

2. For Gorbachev's own discussion of the new thinking, see Mikhail Gorbachev, *Perestroika* (New York: Harper and Row, 1987), esp. chapters 3 and 5, and Gorbachev's December 1988 speech to the United Nations (*Pravda*, 8 Dec. 1988).

3. For recent studies of Soviet policy in the Middle East, see Robert O. Freedman, *Soviet Policy toward the Middle East since 1970*, 3rd ed. (New York: Praeger, 1982); Jon D. Glassman, *Arms for the Arabs: The Soviet Union and War in the Middle East* (Baltimore: Johns Hopkins University Press, 1975); Galia Golan, *Yom Kippur and After: The Soviet Union and the Middle East Crisis* (London: Cambridge University Press, 1977); Yaacov Ro'i, *From Encroachment to Involvement: A Documentary Study of Soviet Policy in the Middle East* (Jerusalem: Israel Universities Press, 1974); and Adeed Dawisha and Karen Dawisha, eds., *The Soviet Union in the Middle East: Policies and Perspectives* (New York: Holmes and Meier, 1982). See also Yaacov Ro'i, ed., *The Limits to Power* (London: Croom Helm, 1979).

4. Freedman, *Soviet Policy toward the Middle East*, 390–99.

5. For a discussion of Soviet-Iranian relations in the 1979–85 period, see Robert O. Freedman, "Soviet Policy toward the Persian Gulf from the Outbreak of the Iran-Iraq War to the Death of Konstantin Chernenko," in *U.S. Strategic Interests in the Gulf Region*, ed. William J. Olson (Boulder, Colo.: Westview Press, 1987), 43–80.

6. Ibid.

7. *Pravda*, 6 Mar. 1985, Moscow Radio, in Persian, 27 Mar. 1985 (Foreign Broadcast Information Service Daily Report [hereafter FBIS]: USSR, 28 Mar. 1985, H-2), and *Izvestia*, 26 Aug. 1985.

8. Rotislav Ulyanovsky, "The Fate of the Iranian Revolution," *Kommunist*, no. 8 (1985), translated in *Current Digest of the Soviet Press* (hereafter *CDSP*) 37, no. 36 (1985): 19.

9. AP report, *Washington Post*, 13 Dec. 1986.

10. *Pravda*, 30 Mar. 1985.

11. Ibid., 17 Dec. 1985.

12. Deutsche Presse-Agentur report, *Washington Post*, 30 Mar. 1985, and Celestine Bahlen, *Washington Post*, 17 Dec. 1985. Moscow may have allowed these shipments to gain credit in Tehran by allowing the Khomeini regime to obtain a strategic response to the Iraqi-initiated "war of the cities."

13. David Ottaway, *Washington Post*, 13 Sept. 1985.

14. Bernard Gwertzman, *New York Times*, 26 Mar. 1985.

15. Barbara Rosewicz, *Wall Street Journal*, 5 Mar. 1985, and AP report, *Jerusalem Post*, 6 Oct. 1985.

16. For a Soviet view of the problems it faced because of the war, see Dmitry Volsky, "The Hidden Springs of a Senseless War," *New Times*, no. 40 (1985): 26–28. Volsky has long been one of Moscow's most astute observers.

17. Cited by Christopher Dickey, *Washington Post*, 4 Nov. 1985.

18. *New York Times*, 25 and 26 Mar. 1985, and Gerald F. Seib, *Wall Street Journal*, 11 Apr. 1985.

19. D. Zgersky, "Establish Relations," *New Times*, no. 41 (1985): 9.

20. See *The Tower Commission Report* (New York: New York Times Co., 1987), esp. 36–39, and *Report of the Congressional Committees Investigating the Iran-Contra Affair* (Washington: U.S. Government Printing Office, 1987).

21. *Washington Post*, 5 Feb. 1986.

22. Reuters report, *New York Times*, 10 Feb. 1986.

23. AP report, *New York Times*, 11 Feb. 1986. For a Soviet view deploring the Iranian attack and urging a speedy end to the war, see *Pravda*, 14 Feb. 1986.

24. For a survey of Soviet-Iranian interactions in 1986, see Bodhan Nahaylo, *Radio Liberty Research Report No. 47/87*, 3 Feb. 1987.

25. Reuters report, *Jerusalem Post*, 19 Aug. 1986. See also Youssef Ibrahim, *Wall Street Journal*, 26 Aug. 1986. Iran also had its own interests in resuming natural gas sales, including the desire for hard currency to prosecute the war. Tehran would benefit from increased economic ties with the Soviet Union, but this does not appear to have been its primary motivation in entering into economic talks with Moscow.

26. AP report, *Washington Post*, 13 Dec. 1986.

27. AP report, *Washington Post*, 5 Sept. 1986.

28. For an overview of Gorbachev's efforts to end the Afghan war in 1986, see Bodhan Nahaylo, *Radio Liberty Research Report No. 16/87*, 11 Jan. 1987.

29. See *Izvestia*, 2 Dec. 1986, for a strong Soviet critique of "flagrant interference" by Iran in Afghanistan's internal affairs. The article claimed there were more than sixty attacks on Afghanistan by Iranian air and ground forces.

30. David Shipler, *New York Times*, 22 Jan. 1987.

31. Elaine Sciolino, *New York Times*, 30 Jan. 1987.

32. AP report, *Washington Post*, 12 Feb. 1987. See also Reuters report, *New York Times*, 12 Feb. 1987.

33. For the text of the Soviet statement, see *Izvestia*, 9 Jan. 1987 (FBIS:USSR, 9 Jan. 1987, H-1). *Izvestia*, on 16 January, condemned Iran for "stubbornly rejecting" appeals for a cease-fire and insisting on "war until victory" and replacing the Iraqi regime.

34. *Pravda*, 29 Jan. 1987.

35. Ibid., 14 Feb. 1987.

36. Ibid.

37. Ibid., 15 Feb. 1987.

38. *Izvestia*, 15 Feb. 1987.

39. *Al-Ray Al-Am* (Kuwait), 15 Feb. 1987 (FBIS:USSR, 24 Feb. 1987, H-5).

40. Radio Moscow, in Persian to Iran (Igor Sheftunov, commentator), 21 Feb. 1987 (FBIS:USSR, 24 Feb. 1987, H-4).

41. Cited in *Washington Post*, 16 Apr. 1987.

42. For descriptions of the attack and the Soviet response to it, see *New York Times*, 9 May 1987; *Le Monde*, 10, 11 May 1987 (translated in *Manchester Guardian Weekly*, 17 May 1987); and AP report, *Jerusalem Post*, 18 May 1987.

43. Tass, 25 May 1987 (FBIS:USSR, 26 May 1987, H-1).

44. Ibid., 3 June 1987 (FBIS:USSR, 4 June 1987, E-1).

45. See *Izvestia*, 1 June 1987.

46. Moscow World Service, in English, 20 May 1987 (FBIS:USSR, 20 May 1987, H-2). See also Moscow Radio, in Persian to Iran, 27 May 1987 (FBIS:USSR, 9 June 1987, E-7).

47. *Pravda*, 30 Apr. 1987.

48. Moscow Radio Peace and Progress, in Persian to Iran, 8 May 1987 (FBIS:USSR, 11 May 1987, H-3). This is a "nonofficial" Soviet radio that tends to reflect Soviet policy perspectives more clearly than the "official" Radio Moscow.

49. Reagan's statement explaining the reflagging was printed in the *New York Times*, 30 May 1987. For background analyses on the U.S. reflagging decision, see Don Oberdorfer, *Washington Post*, 29 May 1987, and Jonathan Randal, *Washington Post*, 5 June 1987. The U.S. Congress had become quite critical of the reflagging effort after the Iraqi attack on the USS *Stark* in May 1987.

50. See *Izvestia*, 29 May 1987.

51. As part of the new thinking now being proclaimed in Moscow, Soviet academics and other Soviet officials have urged the United States to join in efforts to control regional conflicts rather than engage in zero-sum game competition for influence. (See presentation by a Soviet academic delegation headed by Nodari Simoniya, of the Institute of Oriental Studies, and Aleksey Vasiliev, USA-Canada Institute, at the University of Maryland, 21 Oct. 1987.) This is also a point made by Gorbachev in his book *Perestroika*, ch. 3.

52. On this point, see R. K. Ramazani, "The Iran-Iraq War and the Persian Gulf Crisis," *Current History*, Feb. 1988, 63–64.

53. Cited by Flora Lewis, *New York Times*, 7 June 1987.

54. FBIS:NESA, 15 June 1987, AA-1, and Tehran Domestic Service, in Persian, 13 June 1987 (FBIS:NESA, 15 June 1987, S-1).

55. Tehran Domestic Service, in Persian, 14 June 1987 (FBIS:NESA, 15 June 1987, S-1).

56. Ibid., 14 June 1987 (FBIS:NESA, 15 June 1987, S-2).

57. Tehran *IRNA*, in English, 14 June 1987 (FBIS:NESA, 15 June 1987, S-2).

58. Tehran Domestic Service, in Persian, 15 June 1987 (FBIS:NESA, 15 June 1987, S-3).

59. *Pravda*, 4 July 1987 (translation in FBIS:USSR, 6 July 1987, E-1, E-2). The Soviet call for the United Nations to play a role reflects a new Soviet strategy in which it has sought to use the United Nations to help it out of untenable positions (Afghanistan) or to prevent the United States from scoring political gains in the Third World (Persian Gulf).

60. Cited in report by Gary Lee, *Washington Post*, 3 July 1987.

61. Tehran *IRNA,* in English, 18 July 1987 (FBIS:USSR, 20 July 1987, E-3).

62. Ibid., E-4.

63. For the text of the resolution, see *New York Times,* 21 July 1987.

64. *Pravda,* 22 July 1987.

65. See speech of U.S. Secretary of State Shultz at United Nations, in the *New York Times,* 21 July 1987.

66. Philip Taubman, in a report in the *New York Times* on 23 July 1987, cites an unnamed Soviet official who stated that Moscow's interest in maintaining good relations with Iran might preclude an arms ban to force Iran to comply with the cease-fire.

67. Tass (Moscow), in English, 22 July 1987 (FBIS:USSR, 23 July 1987, E-1), and Gorbachev's letter to Reagan, cited in report by Gary Lee, *Washington Post,* 22 July 1987.

68. See article by Alexander Bovin, *Izvestia,* 31 July 1987.

69. Radio Moscow, in Arabic, 1 Aug. 1987 (FBIS:USSR, 3 Aug. 1987, A-4).

70. *Pravda,* 4 Aug. 1987.

71. John Kifner, *New York Times,* 3 Aug. 1987.

72. Tehran Domestic Service, in Persian, 3 Aug. 1987 (FBIS:NESA, 4 Aug. 1987, S-11).

73. Ibid., 4 Aug. 1987 (FBIS:NESA, 4 Aug. 1987, S-12). See also the reports by Jackson Diehl, *Washington Post,* 5 Aug. 1987, and Phillip Taubman, *New York Times,* 5 Aug. 1987.

74. *Pravda,* 24 Aug. 1987.

75. Tass International Service, in English, 9 Aug. 1987 (FBIS:USSR, 10 Aug. 1987, A-4).

76. Tass, in English, 24 Aug. 1987 (FBIS:USSR, 25 Aug. 1987, E-3).

77. Cited in *New York Times,* 22 Aug. 1987.

78. Tass, in English, 8 Sept. 1987 (FBIS:USSR, 9 Sept. 1987, 24).

79. *Pravda,* 10 Sept. 1987. See also Paris AFP, 10 Sept. 1987 (FBIS:USSR, 11 Sept. 1987, 15). For a somewhat different view of Soviet policy toward the Iran-Iraq war, see Galia Golan, "Gorbachev's Middle East Strategy," *Foreign Affairs* 66, no. 1 (Fall 1987): 57. Golan's view is that Moscow took a "fully supportive role" in U.N. efforts to bring about an end to the war.

80. *Pravda,* 9 Sept. 1986.

81. Tehran Domestic Service, in Persian, 8 Sept. 1987 (FBIS:USSR, 9 Sept. 1987, 22–23).

82. Moscow Radio, in English, 23 Sept. 1987 (FBIS:USSR, 24 Sept. 1987, 35).

83. Moscow Radio, in English, 24 Sept. 1987 (FBIS:USSR, 25 Sept. 1987, 27).

84. Tass International Service, in Russian, 1 Oct. 1987 (FBIS:USSR, 2 Oct. 1987, 15).

85. *Izvestia,* 18 Oct. 1987.

86. Tass, in English, 20 Oct. 1987 (FBIS:USSR, 21 Oct. 1987, 5).

87. *Pravda,* 21 Oct. 1987.

88. The agreement called for the creation of a permanent Soviet-Kuwaiti commission on economic, scientific, and technological cooperation in the areas of oil, pipeline transport, irrigation, trade, health protection, and other fields (Tass, 15 Oct. 1987 [FBIS:USSR, 16 Oct. 1987, 35]).

89. *Pravda,* 17 Oct. 1987.

90. Elaine Sciolino, *New York Times,* 3 Oct. 1987.

91. Ibid.

92. *Washington Post,* 31 Oct. 1987.

93. Cited in AP report, *New York Times,* 6 Nov. 1987.

94. For the text of the Amman summit resolutions, see Baghdad INA in Arabic, 12 Nov. 1987 (FBIS:NESA, 13 Nov. 1987, 23–25).

95. *Pravda,* 15 Nov. 1987.

96. Ibid., 14 Nov. 1987 (translated in FBIS:USSR, 19 Nov. 1987, 20).

97. *Izvestia,* 28 Nov. 1987 (FBIS:USSR, 3 Dec. 1987, 39). Even under glasnost, Moscow

uses interviews with key foreign allies to make political points that the Soviet Union, for diplomatic reasons, is unwilling to make itself.

98. Translated in FBIS:USSR, 25 Nov. 1987, 29.

99. See Moscow Radio, in Persian, 28 Nov. 1987, Igor Sheftunov commentary (FBIS:USSR, 1 Dec. 1987, 47).

100. *Pravda,* 5 Dec. 1987 (FBIS:USSR, 7 Dec. 1987, 44).

101. Ibid.

102. Tass, 30 Nov. 1987 (FBIS:USSR, 1 Dec. 1987, 7).

103. For a discussion of the U.S. reaction to the Soviet offer, see the reports by David Ottaway, *Washington Post,* 16 Dec. 1987, and David Shipler, *New York Times,* 29 Dec. 1987.

104. Celestine Bohlen, *Washington Post,* 28 Dec. 1987.

105. *Pravda,* 28 Dec. 1987.

106. Tehran Television, in Persian, 8 Jan. 1988 (FBIS:NESA, 12 Jan. 1988, 83).

107. Tass, International Service, 19 Feb. 1988 (FBIS:USSR, 22 Feb. 1988, 39).

108. Tehran, in English, 10 Feb. 1988 (FBIS:NESA, 11 Feb. 1988, 56).

109. Tehran Domestic Service, in Persian, 14 Feb. 1988 (FBIS:NESA, 16 Feb. 1988, 61).

110. Tehran TV, in Persian, 12 Feb. 1988 (FBIS:NESA, 18 Feb. 1988, 61).

111. Tehran Domestic Service, in Persian, 18 Feb. 1988 (FBIS:NESA, 19 Feb. 1988, 44).

112. Tehran IRNA, 23 Feb. 1988 (FBIS:NESA, 23 Feb. 1988, 65).

113. Tehran Domestic Service, in Persian, 22 Feb. 1988 (FBIS:NESA, 23 Feb. 1988, 65).

114. For Iranian descriptions of the demonstrations, see IRNA, 4 Mar. 1988 (FBIS:NESA, 4 Mar. 1988, 55), and IRNA, 6 Mar. 1988 (FBIS:NESA, 7 Mar. 1988, 57).

115. Cited in FBIS:NESA, 21 Mar. 1988, 1.

116. Tehran TV, 24 Mar. 1988 (FBIS:NESA, 25 Mar. 1988, 37).

117. Tehran IRNA, in English, 6 Mar. 1988 (FBIS:NESA, 7 Mar. 1988, 59).

118. Ibid., 9 Mar. 1988 (FBIS:NESA, 9 Mar. 1988, 60).

119. Tehran, in English, 14 Apr. 1988 (FBIS:NESA, 15 Apr. 1988, 55).

120. Tass, 20 Apr. 1988 (FBIS:USSR, 20 Apr. 1988, 12).

121. Tass, in English, 20 Apr. 1988 (FBIS:USSR, 21 Apr. 1988, 3).

122. Ibid., 19 Apr. 1988 (FBIS:USSR, 20 Apr. 1988, 13).

123. Moscow Radio Peace and Progress, 25 Apr. 1988 (FBIS:USSR, 26 Apr. 1988, 22).

124. Ibid., 12 May 1988 (FBIS:USSR, 13 May 1988, 17).

125. *Kayhan International,* 27 June 1988 (FBIS:NESA, 13 July 1988, 54).

126. See Moscow Radio, in English, 7 July 1988 (FBIS:USSR, 8 July 1988, 29).

127. *Pravda,* 15 July 1988; *Krasnaya Zvezda,* 10 July 1988 (FBIS:USSR, 14 July 1988, 5).

128. See Khomeini's statement, Tehran Domestic Service, 20 July 1988 (FBIS:NESA, 21 July 1988, 41–53). See also James Bill, "Why Tehran Finally Wants a Gulf Peace," *Washington Post,* 28 Aug. 1988, Outlook sec.

129. Moscow Radio, in Persian, 18 July 1988 (FBIS:USSR, 20 July 1988, 22–23).

130. Tehran IRNA, 21 July 1988 (FBIS:NESA, 22 July 1988, 48).

III Iran and the United States

6

Security Relations between the United States and Iran, 1953–1978

MARK J. GASIOROWSKI

The security relationship between the United States and Iran during the reign of the late Shah is still a controversial subject, despite the passage of more than a decade since the Shah was overthrown. Critics of the U.S. security relationship with Iran charge that the United States turned Iran into a virtual police state and encouraged the Shah to spend large amounts of Iran's limited oil wealth on unnecessary weapons. The main evidence for this view is that the United States had a close relationship with the Iranian armed forces and with SAVAK, the Shah's notorious intelligence agency. Defenders of the U.S. relationship with Iran argue that this relationship was much more limited than is widely believed and that the United States exercised very little influence over the Shah and his security forces, especially in the late 1960s and 1970s. Although much has been written about this subject, the debate remains largely unresolved, in part because many of its key details are still shrouded in secrecy.

This chapter attempts to shed some light on the debate by examining the basic character of the security relationship between the United States and Iran during the Shah's reign. Three main aspects are given particular attention here. First, the broad strategic considerations that guided U.S. policy toward Iran in this period are examined. Next, the specific nature of the U.S. relationship with the Iranian armed forces and with SAVAK is discussed in some detail. Finally, the various U.S.-sponsored regional security organizations that Iran participated in during this period are examined.

Since these issues involve sensitive matters of U.S. national security, little reliable information has appeared publicly about them. This study therefore relies heavily on information obtained in confidential interviews with former U.S. and Iranian officials who were involved in the U.S.-Iran security relationship. Considerable efforts have been made to ensure the accuracy of the information obtained in this manner.[1]

U.S. Security Interests in Iran

Although the United States and Iran established formal diplomatic relations in 1856, contact between the two countries was minimal before World War II. During that war, U.S. involvement in Iran increased, with some thirty thousand U.S. soldiers stationed there to help operate a supply line to the Soviet Union. A major confrontation took place between the United States and the Soviet Union in Iran in the immediate postwar period over the continued presence of Soviet occupation forces in northern Iran. The United States played a key role in persuading the Soviet Union to evacuate these forces in 1946, and it was widely assumed that the United States would maintain a strong presence in Iran after the Soviet evacuation. Despite the continuing Soviet threat and Iran's growing economic problems in the late 1940s, however, U.S. officials repeatedly rebuffed Iranian requests for a large aid package and a formal security agreement, encouraging Iran instead to improve its relations with the Soviet Union. Although Iran was considered to be "of vital strategic interest"[2] to the United States at this time, U.S. officials were preoccupied with the deepening Cold War in Europe and Asia. Iran was comparatively stable and was, in any case, viewed as a British security responsibility.[3]

U.S. security interests in Iran began to increase in early 1950, when a new general strategy for containing Soviet expansionism was adopted by the Truman administration. This strategy, embodied in the National Security Council study NSC-68, was a response to the growing tension between the two superpowers during this period. The study called for "a renewed initiative in the cold war," beginning with a substantial U.S. military buildup and increases in military and economic aid programs.[4] Most of America's foreign aid previously had gone to countries in Western Europe, the eastern Mediterranean, and East Asia. But in a strategy that came to be known as Perimeter Defense, much of the increased aid called for in NSC-68 was to be given to countries located on the borders of the emerging Sino-Soviet sphere of influence. Under the Perimeter Defense strategy, a cornerstone of U.S. national security policy until at least the early 1970s,[5] the United States established close security relationships with a number of countries that soon became important allies, including Iran, Pakistan, Thailand, South Vietnam, Taiwan, the Philippines, and South Korea.

Because of its location between the Soviet Union and the Persian Gulf oil fields, Iran was clearly a prime candidate for U.S. aid under the Perimeter Defense strategy. Moreover, unrest was increasing in Iran at this time as a result of economic problems and the widespread desire for nationalization of the British-controlled Iranian oil industry. U.S. policymakers, however, still viewed Iran as a British security responsibility,[6] and the Truman administration quickly became bogged down in the Korean War after the adoption of NSC-68. Consequently, although a small amount of aid was given to Iran and greater efforts were made to monitor Iran's domestic politics, a close security relationship between the two countries did not immediately develop. Even after the nationalization of the Iranian oil industry and the appointment of the popular nationalist Mohammad Mosaddeq as prime minister in May 1951, the Truman administration made no real effort either to build Iran up as an anti-Soviet client or to subvert Mosaddeq's neutralist government.[7]

The United States began to take a much greater interest in Iran after Dwight Eisenhower was inaugurated in January 1953. The new president and his advisers brought to the White House a more activist foreign policy than that pursued by the Truman administration. Once in power, they quickly set about strengthening U.S. allies throughout the world and denouncing or actively undermining not only Soviet allies but also neutralist governments that appeared to sympathize with the Soviet Union. Although U.S. policymakers did not regard Mosaddeq as a communist, the Eisenhower administration began planning to overthrow him within weeks of its inauguration. Mosaddeq was finally ousted in a CIA-instigated coup d'état in August 1953.[8] Afterward, firm measures were taken to strengthen Mosaddeq's successor and bring Iran firmly into the Western camp. By the late 1950s, Iran had become a major U.S. ally, receiving large amounts of U.S. economic and security assistance and joining a U.S.-backed regional security organization known as the Baghdad Pact. Despite important changes in the character of U.S.-Iranian relations, Iran was to remain a key U.S. ally until the 1978–79 revolution.[9]

U.S. interest in Iran after the 1953 coup was due mainly to Iran's critical role in the Perimeter Defense strategy. The country's location between the Soviet Union and the Persian Gulf made it a prime target for Soviet subversion in peacetime and a likely Soviet military objective in the event of general war. U.S. policymakers therefore sought to build up Iran's military capabilities. Moreover, Iran's long border with the Soviet Union and its proximity to Soviet missile-testing facilities in Central Asia made it extremely valuable to the

United States as a base for staging cross-border espionage operations and, beginning in 1957, for electronic intelligence-gathering devices aimed at the Soviet Union. These devices became central to the U.S. security system after the Soviet Union began to deploy nuclear missiles in the late 1950s and after it demonstrated the ability to shoot down high-altitude U.S. surveillance aircraft in 1959. As U.S.-Soviet tension subsided in the 1960s and early 1970s, Iran became increasingly valuable to the United States in regional matters: it gave considerable assistance to certain governments and guerrilla groups fighting Soviet-backed forces; it cooperated closely with Israel in many ways; and it helped advance U.S. interests in the region through diplomatic initiatives of various kinds. The evolving U.S.-Iran security relationship left the United States increasingly dependent on cooperation from Iran in the 1960s and 1970s and therefore made U.S. officials steadily more reluctant to pressure the Shah on sensitive matters, such as political reform.[10]

For Iran to be useful to the United States in these various ways, strong measures were needed to enhance its national security. U.S. policymakers were concerned about two main threats to Iran's national security in the mid-1950s: domestic political unrest, which might bring a neutralist or pro-Soviet government to power, and an outright invasion by the Soviet Union or its allies in the region.[11] In order to minimize these threats, the United States established a strong cliency relationship with Iran in the years after the 1953 coup. Under this relationship, Iran was given large amounts of U.S. military, economic, and intelligence assistance and was encouraged to join the Baghdad Pact. These measures were intended both to reduce political unrest in Iran and to strengthen it against foreign threats. In return, the Shah cooperated with the United States on security matters such as those described above. Although the U.S.-Iran cliency relationship changed considerably in character between the mid-1950s and the late 1970s, a high level of security cooperation was maintained between the two countries throughout this period.

The Post-Coup Consolidation of Power in Iran

The overthrow of Mosaddeq in the 1953 coup and the subsequent installation of a staunchly pro-Western government under Prime Minister Fazlollah Zahedi marked the beginning of a close relationship between the United States and Iran that was to last for twenty-five years. Unrest remained high in Iran in the immediate aftermath of the coup, however, posing a serious threat to the Zahedi government and to U.S. security interests there. Consequently, the United States undertook a variety of measures after the coup to strengthen the Zahedi government and establish a strong client state in Iran.

The most visible measures of support undertaken by the United States in Iran in this period were a series of diplomatic initiatives intended to demonstrate U.S. approval for the Zahedi government and bring an end to the economic problems caused by the Anglo-Iranian oil dispute. Immediately after the coup, President Eisenhower sent a message of congratulations to the Shah on having weathered the crisis and U.S. officials stated that an aid request from Iran would receive prompt and favorable consideration. These statements were followed by frequent public expressions of support by U.S. officials, culminating in a visit to Iran by Vice President Richard Nixon in December 1953. The United States also began a major effort soon after the coup to settle the oil dispute. Herbert Hoover, Jr., a prominent oil industry consultant, was hired by the State Department in October 1953 to negotiate a new oil agreement. Under Hoover's leadership, the terms of the agreement were soon worked out and eventually approved by the Iranian Majles (parliament), giving a major boost to the Iranian economy and providing the Zahedi government with a much-needed source of revenue.[12]

The United States also provided Iran with large amounts of economic and military assistance after the 1953 coup. Within ten days of the coup, the existing U.S. aid program in Iran was augmented with $23.4 million and an emergency grant of $45 million. In addition, the CIA station in Tehran gave the Zahedi government roughly $1 million in cash shortly after the coup. Another $15 million in economic aid was given in May 1954, bringing the total for fiscal year (FY) 1954 to $84.5 million. Together with $25.6 million in military assistance in FY 1954, U.S. aid to Iran in this period accounted for over half of the estimated $200 million in oil revenue lost during Mosaddeq's premiership as a result of the oil dispute and for roughly 60 percent of Iranian government expenditures in 1954. In the decade after the coup, U.S. economic and military aid to Iran together averaged $121.4 million per year, accounting for 31 percent of Iranian government expenditures in FYs 1954–59 and 17 percent in FYs 1960–63. Large loans were also made to Iran by the U.S. Export-Import Bank in this period, and the United States helped arrange several large World Bank loans for Iran. The large amounts of U.S. aid to Iran in this period helped strengthen its government by promoting rapid economic growth and enabling it to increase its spending on domestic security, social services, and other politically useful matters.[13]

In addition to these overt actions, the United States undertook various covert measures after the 1953 coup to strengthen the Zahedi government. The CIA station chief in Tehran traveled to Shiraz shortly after the coup to meet with the leaders of the pro-Mosaddeq Qashqa'i tribe and warn them not to stage an uprising against the new government. The Tehran CIA station provided intelligence information on the communist Tudeh Party to the Zahedi government to facilitate the anti-Tudeh campaign it began after the overthrow of Mosaddeq.

Officers of the CIA may also have helped the Zahedi government put down large antigovernment demonstrations in Tehran in November 1953. A CIA propaganda operation was used to generate popular support for the government and the new oil agreement in this period, and CIA propaganda specialists helped Iran's Ministry of Information carry out a similar operation. The CIA also spent a limited amount of money to support certain candidates in the Majles elections held in early 1954. These covert measures played a relatively minor role in the Zahedi government's post-coup consolidation of power, however, and they were largely discontinued after early 1954.[14]

A more important covert U.S. effort to strengthen Iran's post-coup government began in September 1953, when a U.S. Army colonel working for the CIA was sent to Iran under cover as a military attaché to organize and train a new intelligence unit. This unit was established under the auspices of the Tehran military governorship, which was placed under the command of Gen. Taimur Bakhtiar in December 1953. The U.S. Army colonel worked closely with Bakhtiar and his assistants, advising them on domestic security matters and training them in basic intelligence "tradecraft," such as surveillance and interrogation methods, the use of intelligence networks, and organizational security. This unit was the first modern, effective intelligence agency to operate in Iran. As will be discussed below, it later evolved into the notorious secret police force SAVAK.[15]

The primary mission of Bakhtiar's intelligence unit was to seek out and eliminate threats to the Shah and to the Iranian government. These threats were expected to come mainly from the Tudeh Party, but nationalist groups and dissident military officers were also viewed as possible threats. The main achievement of the intelligence unit, which began to operate in early 1954, was to detect and dismantle a large network organized by the Tudeh Party in the Iranian armed forces. Although the U.S. Army colonel was working very closely with Bakhtiar's unit at this time, it was his Iranian subordinates who discovered and subsequently dismantled the Tudeh network.[16] The destruction of the Tudeh military network eliminated the Tudeh Party as a major force in Iranian politics and instilled greater respect for the government's security forces among both supporters and opponents of the new regime. The success of the unit in destroying the network was a primary reason for the Shah's subsequent decision to establish a modern, unified intelligence agency—SAVAK.

Although the new regime had been consolidated by the end of 1954 and organized opposition largely suppressed, U.S. and Iranian officials recognized that a considerable amount of U.S. assistance would be needed to enable the

Iranian government to withstand future threats from the domestic opposition. Similarly, a large amount of U.S. aid was clearly needed to strengthen Iran's security forces against foreign adversaries. The United States therefore began a long-term effort in 1954 and 1955 to strengthen the Iranian government through a large economic aid program, training and assistance programs for Iran's security forces, and regional security organizations of various kinds. These programs had a major impact both on Iran's general security posture and on Iranian domestic politics.

The U.S. Military Aid Program

The United States first established a military aid mission in Iran in 1942. The mission stayed on after World War II, training the Iranian armed forces and helping them assimilate equipment provided under a small U.S. military assistance program.[17] Despite the efforts of this mission, however, the Iranian armed forces in the early 1950s were barely able to contain tribal unrest and were capable of offering only token resistance in the event of a foreign invasion.

Soon after the 1953 coup, U.S. military planners began a thorough review of Iran's potential role in U.S. global defense strategy. As a result of this review, policymakers decided in early 1955 to strengthen the Iranian armed forces sufficiently to enable them to conduct defensive delaying actions in the Zagros Mountains (in southwestern Iran) in the event of a Soviet invasion, in conjunction with the Perimeter Defense strategy. This decision involved a fundamental change in the basic mission of the Iranian armed forces: the task of maintaining domestic security, which had previously been the army's main function, would gradually be turned over to the National Police and the Gendarmerie (a rural paramilitary force), and the military services themselves would concentrate mainly on national defense. Moreover, the strategy and tactics of the Iranian armed forces were to be coordinated with those of the United States, Britain, Turkey, Pakistan, and Iraq under the Baghdad Pact. The decision to deploy the Iranian armed forces in the Zagros Mountains in the event of general war meant that the northern and central regions of Iran, where most of the population lived, would essentially be abandoned to Soviet invaders.[18]

In order to accomplish this new mission, the Iranian armed forces needed a considerable amount of training and new equipment. But despite pressure from the Shah for a rapid military buildup, U.S. policymakers decided in early 1955 that a major effort to strengthen the armed forces should be put off until Iran had officially joined the Baghdad Pact (which occurred in November 1955) and its economy had become stronger. In the meantime, U.S. military aid to Iran proceeded at a moderate pace: five military training teams, consisting of a total of 65 officers and 125 enlisted men, were attached to the Iranian army at the divisional and brigade levels, and the United States agreed to provide Iran with modern military equipment, including advanced F-84G jet fighters.[19]

It was not until early 1957, as the winds of nationalism swept through the Middle East following the Suez crisis, that a decision was finally made to increase U.S. assistance to the Iranian armed forces. Military aid to Iran grew from $23 million in FY 1956 to $82.5 million in FY 1957 and $104.9 million in FY 1958, enabling Iranian military expenditures to double between 1956 and 1958. The number of U.S. military advisers in Iran grew from 403 in 1956 to 704 in 1960, and the number of Iranian troops being trained in the United States grew from 227 in 1956 to 947 in 1960. Of the $240 million in U.S. military aid earmarked for Iran in early 1957 for FYs 1958–60, 47 percent was to be spent on military equipment and supplies, including more F-84G fighters and other aircraft, various naval vessels, tanks, armored cars, trucks, artillery, communications equipment, small arms, and a thirty-day supply of ammunition. A further 39 percent was to be spent on military construction projects, including roads, barracks, and air bases in Tehran, Dizful, and Qom. (The remainder covered training and shipping costs.) U.S. military aid to Iran was further expanded after the July 1958 coup in Iraq: deliveries of previously committed equipment were speeded up; $28.6 million in U.S. economic aid was converted into military aid; and U.S. authorization was given to expand the size of the Iranian armed forces by thirty-seven thousand troops.[20]

Mounting economic problems and widespread frustration with the absence of democratic institutions produced growing popular unrest in Iran in the late 1950s. As a result, U.S. policymakers became increasingly concerned about the political and economic consequences of the rapid military buildup that had begun in Iran in early 1957. Moreover, congressional hearings in the late 1950s uncovered evidence of widespread corruption and mismanagement in the U.S. aid programs in Iran. As a result of these factors, a decision was made in 1959 to reduce U.S. military aid to Iran in FY 1960 and expand the U.S. economic aid program. This decision greatly angered the Shah, who had been pressing for several years for a much larger military aid package. U.S. concerns about Iran grew further after the Kennedy administration took office in 1961. A special task force on Iran recommended in May that military aid be kept at the current reduced levels and that economic aid be increased. In response to growing pressure from the Shah, U.S. policymakers also authorized the adoption of a Forward Defense strategy by the Iranian armed forces in this period. Under this strategy, Iranian army and air force units were redeployed into the northern regions of the country to defend Iran's borders (rather than simply a front in the Zagros Mountains) against a possible invasion by the Soviet Union or Iraq.[21]

Political unrest declined in Iran in the mid-1960s after the main opposition groups had been suppressed and a wide-ranging program of reforms known as the White Revolution had been launched. Moreover, the Iranian economy began to expand rapidly in this period as a result of growing oil revenues. Increasingly confident, the Shah continued to pressure U.S. officials to approve a large military buildup but took steps to distance Iran from the United States, threatening to sign a nonaggression treaty with the Soviet Union and making a large arms purchase from the Soviets in 1967. Although U.S. officials were concerned about the Shah's military buildup and the absence of meaningful political reform in this period, the growing U.S. strategic dependence on Iran made it increasingly difficult for them to exert influence over the Shah on these matters. With Iran's high economic growth rate and its apparent political stability, U.S. military and economic aid to Iran declined rapidly in the mid-1960s and both were discontinued altogether in November 1967. U.S. military aid to Iran was gradually replaced with direct arms sales, which grew from a negligible amount in 1964 to $127.7 million in 1970. The number of U.S. military advisers in Iran and Iranian military personnel being trained in the United States also fell in the mid-1960s.[22]

No longer dependent on U.S. aid, the Shah began a massive buildup of the Iranian armed forces in the late 1960s, purchasing advanced U.S. military equipment such as F-4 fighter-bombers and M-47 tanks. In May 1972, President Richard Nixon agreed to sell the Shah virtually any type of conventional weaponry in the U.S. arsenal, including advanced F-14 and AWACS aircraft, Phoenix and Maverick missiles, Spruance-class destroyers, and a $500 million IBEX electronic surveillance system. This decision, together with the quadrupling of world oil prices in late 1973 and early 1974, resulted in a 600 percent increase in Iranian military expenditures and a tenfold increase in U.S. military sales to Iran between 1972 and 1977. The rapid growth in Iranian military expenditures in this period alarmed many members of Congress and other U.S. officials and created considerable tension between the two governments; it also created serious management and supply problems in the Iranian armed forces and fueled growing unrest in Iran. Despite President Jimmy Carter's emphasis on human rights and his desire to reduce U.S. foreign military sales, the policy of unlimited Iranian access to U.S. conventional weaponry was continued under his administration.[23]

Domestic Security and Intelligence Cooperation

As part of its strategy of strengthening anti-Soviet governments along the Sino-Soviet periphery and elsewhere in the Third World, the Eisenhower administration had begun a major effort in the mid-1950s to train and equip paramilitary, police, and intelligence organizations in friendly Third World countries, including Iran.[24] Three domestic security organizations in Iran received extensive assistance of this kind from the United States: the Gendarmerie, the National Police, and the intelligence unit established in late 1953 under General Bakhtiar, which soon evolved into SAVAK.

The United States first began to provide training and assistance to the Iranian Gendarmerie in 1942, in conjunction with the military aid mission described above. The Gendarmerie training mission (known as GENMISH) was expanded along with the military aid mission in the mid-1950s and remained in Iran until 1976, when it was finally deactivated. The main task of GENMISH was to improve the mobility, firepower, and communications capabilities of the Gendarmerie. In this capacity, GENMISH provided the Gendarmerie with a wide variety of vehicles and weapons and with a sophisticated communications system that linked Gendarmerie headquarters in Tehran with the provincial headquarters and regional field stations. The mission also trained Gendarmerie personnel in the use of this equipment, in basic tactics, and in specialized areas such as counterinsurgency methods, border patrol, and narcotics interdiction, and it helped the Gendarmerie develop new tactics and capabilities, such as special mobile strike units and an intelligence branch.[25]

U.S. assistance to the Iranian National Police began in mid-1954, when a three-man advisory team was sent to Iran to conduct a review of police operations there. This team developed a detailed reorganization plan for the National Police that was gradually implemented over the next few years with U.S. help. Under this plan, the training program of the National Police was completely revised along the lines of U.S. police academies. The advisers supervised a thorough reorganization of National Police operations down to the precinct level and set up modern crime and photographic laboratories and an efficient records management system. The reorganization plan also began a major effort to improve the communications capabilities of the Iranian National Police, including a nationwide police telecommunications system and a linkage to INTERPOL headquarters in Paris. At least 218 Iranian police officers were also sent to the United States in this period for intensive training at the International Police Academy, the FBI Academy, the U.S. Border Patrol Academy, and other training facilities.[26]

The United States also expanded its assistance to Iran's intelligence service in the mid-1950s. The U.S. Army colonel who had been sent to Iran in 1953 to organize and train a new intelligence unit was replaced with a more permanent team of five career CIA officers. This team consisted of a chief of base, a deputy chief of base, and specialists in covert operations, intelligence analysis, and counterintelligence. In 1956 Bakhtiar's intelligence unit was reorganized and made an independent intelligence agency, which came to be known as SAVAK. The CIA training team continued to work with SAVAK after this change, remaining in Iran until 1960 or 1961 with occasional changes in personnel.[27]

The primary objective of the CIA training team was to turn SAVAK into a modern, effective intelligence agency. The training consisted of courses in the fundamentals of intelligence work, much like those given to CIA officers. The SAVAK officers were trained in the basic tools of spycraft, such as agent recruitment, the use of message drops and safehouses, surveillance and interrogation methods, and personal security. Intelligence analysts were taught modern analytical techniques, such as how to set up biographical files, how to judge the reliability of intelligence sources, how to integrate material from different sources, and how to write and disseminate reports. Counterintelligence specialists were given training in the basic skills of this field and in the organization and operational techniques of the Soviet bloc intelligence agencies. Many SAVAK officers were also brought to the United States in this period for specialized training in matters such as forgery detection, the Russian language, and the use of computers and special equipment for surveillance, interrogation, and communications. Other SAVAK officers were sent to Britain, France, and West Germany in the late 1950s for certain kinds of specialized training. By the time the CIA training program ended in the early 1960s, virtually all of the first generation of SAVAK personnel had been trained by this team.[28]

The CIA training team was removed from Iran in 1960 or 1961, as part of the Shah's effort in this period to reduce Iran's dependence on the United States. The CIA team was soon replaced by a team of instructors from Mossad, the Israeli foreign intelligence service. The Mossad team generally had between two and eight members and remained in Iran until 1965, providing SAVAK with training much like that provided by its CIA predecessor. It was now while the Mossad team was in Iran that SAVAK began to develop its own training program. Under the direction of Gen. Hosain Fardust, a top SAVAK official and intimate friend of the Shah, SAVAK acquired training manuals and other relevant material from the intelligence agencies of the United States, Israel, Britain, France, West Germany, India, Pakistan, and Taiwan. This material was studied carefully and used to develop a full-scale training curriculum for SAVAK personnel. By 1966 SAVAK had developed the capability to train all its personnel in the fundamentals of intelligence work, although SAVAK officers were frequently sent to the United States, Israel, Britain, France, and West Germany for specialized training after 1965, and instructors from these countries were occasionally sent to Iran on a temporary basis.[29]

The CIA and SAVAK also cooperated in other ways, although on a selective and rather limited basis. The two agencies maintained a close liaison relationship, especially in the 1950s and early 1960s: the CIA station chiefs in Tehran were in regular contact with the Shah and the various directors of SAVAK; a close, working-level liaison relationship was maintained with SAVAK by both the five-man CIA training team and a smaller CIA liaison unit that maintained an office in SAVAK headquarters for several years after the training team left Iran; and the main SAVAK representative in the United States, who worked under cover at the United Nations, met frequently with CIA officials and was actually a paid agent of the CIA. Through these channels, the CIA and SAVAK exchanged intelligence on a variety of subjects. The CIA provided SAVAK with considerable amounts of intelligence on other countries in the region, including the Soviet Union, the Arab states, and Afghanistan. This included intelligence on Soviet missile tests and other Soviet military activities in the areas north of Iran that was obtained from the CIA listening posts constructed in Iran in 1957. The CIA also gave SAVAK a certain amount of material on the Tudeh Party in the 1950s and early 1960s, but *did not* give SAVAK intelligence on other Iranian political organizations, such as the National Front, clerical activists, or the guerrilla groups that emerged in the late 1960s. In turn, SAVAK provided the CIA with a considerable amount of intelligence on regional matters and on the Tudeh Party, the guerrillas, and other political organizations. Much of this material was unreliable, however, or even deliberately deceptive.[30]

The CIA also carried out joint covert operations with SAVAK and with Iranian army units, although on a very limited basis. Joint cross-border intelligence-gathering operations were launched into the Soviet Union from Iran by the two agencies. Typically, SAVAK provided logistical support for these operations in exchange for some of the intelligence that was obtained. These cross-border operations occurred much less often after 1957, when CIA-operated electronic listening posts were installed in northern Iran. The CIA also occasionally helped SAVAK interrogate Soviet agents captured in Iran. Although the CIA offered to carry out joint operations with SAVAK against the Tudeh Party in the early 1960s, SAVAK refused. Conversely, the CIA turned down SAVAK requests to launch joint cross-border operations into Iraq in this period. The CIA did, however, provide arms and financial assistance to the Iranian-backed Barzani Kurds in their war against the government of Iraq, which began in the early 1960s and ended in 1975. As will be discussed below, Israel was also deeply involved in this effort. All these joint operations were directed against foreign targets. The CIA did not assist SAVAK in its operations against domestic targets in Iran, although SAVAK was given permission to operate in the United States, where a large number of Iranian students and dissidents were living, as long as it agreed not to violate U.S. laws.[31]

The relationship between the CIA and SAVAK became much more distant in the early 1960s: the CIA training team was removed from Iran; fewer SAVAK officers were brought to the United States for training; liaison and joint operations occurred less often; and contact between the two agencies' personnel was increasingly restricted. The deterioration in CIA-SAVAK relations in this period occurred mainly because the primary U.S. goal of strengthening Iran's intelligence capabilities had been accomplished and because the Shah wanted to reduce Iran's dependence on the United States. At the same time, SAVAK began to diversify its contacts with Western intelligence services. More significantly, as will be discussed further in the next section, SAVAK established a close relationship with Mossad, the Israeli intelligence agency, in the early 1960s.

Regional Security Cooperation

In addition to strengthening Iran's security forces, the United States encouraged Iran to establish a variety of formal and informal security arrangements with other U.S. allies in the region in the decades after the 1953 coup. The most important of these regional security arrangements was the Baghdad Pact, which was established in February 1955 when Iraq and Turkey signed a mutual defense alliance. Britain joined this alliance several weeks later, and Pakistan and Iran joined in September and October, respectively. Although the United States had been the major architect of the Baghdad Pact and remained the driving force behind it, America's deepening involvement in the Arab-Israeli conflict prevented it from formally joining the alliance at this time.[32]

The Baghdad Pact was mainly a defense alliance aimed at preventing a Soviet invasion and subversion in the Middle East. Its most important provisions called for security cooperation among the member states, including joint military planning and exercises and mutual pledges of nonintervention. The formal structure of the Baghdad Pact consisted of a Council of Ministers, which was located in Baghdad, and special committees for military planning, economic cooperation, communications, and countersubversion. Although the United States did not become a full member of the Baghdad Pact, it joined the economics and countersubversion committees and established a permanent liaison with the military planning committee. The United States also indirectly supported the Baghdad Pact by giving each of its regional members large amounts of military aid and training.[33]

The Baghdad Pact was beset with problems from its inception. Incensed at Iraq's decision to join the pro-Western alliance, President Gamal Abdul Nasser of Egypt began to foment unrest in Iraq and isolate the Iraqi government in the Arab world. Regional tensions increased further when Nasser concluded a major arms deal with Czechoslovakia in 1955 and nationalized the Suez Canal in 1956, leading Britain, France, and Israel to invade Egypt. The Soviet Union, strengthening its ties with Egypt, also expressed great hostility toward the Baghdad Pact and bitterly denounced Iran and the other pact members. The United States responded to these events in early 1957 by unveiling the Eisenhower Doctrine, which authorized the use of U.S. military force on behalf of any Middle Eastern country threatened by the Soviet Union or its regional allies. Privately, a special U.S. envoy assured the Shah that "if Iran were attacked, the United States would be at its side."[34]

The Baghdad Pact was dealt a severe blow in July 1958, when the Iraqi monarchy was overthrown in a bloody coup. The new government boycotted subsequent meetings of the Baghdad Pact and then withdrew from it altogether in March 1959, leading the remaining members to rename it the Central Treaty Organization (CENTO) and move its headquarters to Ankara. In an effort to bolster the alliance, the United States began to negotiate bilateral treaties with the three remaining regional members in late 1958. The Soviet Union bitterly denounced this effort and briefly tried to negotiate a nonaggression treaty with Iran. The three bilateral treaties, which were signed in March 1959, reaffirmed the willingness of the United States to intervene militarily in defense of these countries but stopped short of providing them with formal guarantees of U.S. support. U.S. policymakers in this period also quietly developed contingency plans to use tactical nuclear weapons in the region in the event of a general war.[35]

Although CENTO survived the crises of the late 1950s, it never really developed into an effective security alliance. The members of CENTO could not reach agreement in the 1950s and early 1960s on such basic matters as a joint military command structure or contingency plans for limited war. Although joint military planning and exercises did occur under the auspices of CENTO, the alliance's contribution to the military capabilities of the member countries was "marginal," according to a 1964 State Department study.[36] Similarly, while the countersubversion committee of CENTO provided an institutional basis for cooperation among the members' intelligence agencies, most of the cooperation that did occur was conducted outside of CENTO. The main functions of the CENTO countersubversion committee were to coordinate and disseminate intelligence on Soviet activities in the region and to develop plans for guerrilla warfare in the event of a Soviet invasion. Although Iran did cooperate on a limited basis with other CENTO members to suppress tribal uprisings and occasionally on other matters, this was done *outside* of the CENTO framework.[37]

As the Cold War receded in the mid-1960s and economic issues became more salient for the regional members, CENTO increasingly evolved into a forum for economic cooperation. Under the auspices of the CENTO communications committee (and with financing from the United States and Britain), railroad, highway, air, telecommunications, and postal links were expanded among the regional members. The CENTO economics committee held conferences and financed technical assistance projects in agriculture, public works, and nuclear power development. The regional members also established a Regional Planning Committee to foster economic cooperation among themselves. Although this committee made extensive plans to promote increased trade and joint economic planning among its members, little real progress was made in these areas. The organization continued to function in these limited ways until Iran and Pakistan withdrew in March 1979, bringing about its effective demise.[38]

Iran also maintained bilateral cooperative security relationships with several countries in the Middle East and participated in two informal regional security organizations in the 1960s and 1970s. Although the United States was not directly involved in any of these relationships, it generally approved of them and apparently encouraged the Shah to enter into them. Taken together, these informal regional security relationships probably made a larger contribution to Iran's security than CENTO did.

After its ties with the United States, Iran's most important bilateral security relationship in the post-1953 period was with Israel. Iran's security relationship with Israel began essentially in 1960 or 1961, when a team of Israeli intelligence officers was sent to Iran to train SAVAK personnel, apparently with U.S. encouragement. As discussed above, this team replaced a similar CIA team and remained in Iran until 1965, providing the main source of training for SAVAK in this period. At about the same time, Iran and Israel began to cooperate on joint covert operations against radical Arab states and organizations in the Middle East.

Using bases located in western Iran, the two countries carried out a variety of joint intelligence-gathering operations against Iraq in the 1960s and 1970s. Israel collaborated with Iran (and the United States) in assisting the Barzani Kurds in their uprising against the Iraqi government in this period. In the mid-1960s, Israel provided Iran with captured Soviet-made arms, which were then given to the royalist forces in the Yemeni civil war. Israel and Iran also exchanged considerable amounts of intelligence on the Arab world, including material obtained by Iranian agents located in various Arab governments and in the Palestine Liberation Organization (PLO). Close economic ties also emerged between the two countries. Israel sent agricultural advisory missions to Iran and sold large amounts of arms to the Shah. In return, Iran sold oil to Israel and helped finance the construction of the Eilat-Ashkelon oil pipeline.[39]

The Iranian and Israeli intelligence services also maintained an informal liaison organization with the Turkish intelligence agency in the 1960s and 1970s. This organization, which was known as Trident, served as a forum for exchanging information on Soviet and radical Arab activities in the Middle East, which were of obvious mutual interest to the three member countries.

Iran maintained cooperative security relationships with several other pro-Western countries in the region as well. Iran's security forces cooperated in various ways with the security forces of Saudi Arabia, which shared Iran's antipathy toward the Soviet Union and Arab radicalism. The most notable instance of security cooperation between Iran and Saudi Arabia was their joint support for the Yemeni royalist forces against the republicans in the Yemeni civil war that began in the early 1960s. Iran and Saudi Arabia also helped organize an informal intelligence organization known as the Safari Club. This organization, which also included France, Egypt, and Morocco, was established in the early 1970s to combat communist influence in Africa by providing arms, intelligence, and financial support to pro-Western African countries. Although the United States was deliberately excluded from the Safari Club, it strongly approved of the activities of this organization and was kept fully informed about them. Iran also provided extensive military assistance to the government of Oman in the mid-1970s in its effort to crush the Dhofar rebellion and provided training and assistance to the Egyptian intelligence agency in the mid-1970s. Iran occasionally cooperated with Turkey and Pakistan as well in operations against rebellious Kurdish and Baluchi tribal groups.[40]

Conclusion

What are the implications of this study for the debate over the merits of the U.S. security relationship with Iran during the reign of the late Shah? The principal underlying theme of this discussion has been that U.S. security considerations, which stemmed mainly from Iran's critical role in the Perimeter Defense strategy, dictated that the United States focus mainly on strengthening Iran's security forces in its policy toward Iran during the Shah's reign. This focus led the United States to give large amounts of security assistance to Iran in the 1950s and early 1960s, including extensive training and other assistance to SAVAK, Iran's notorious intelligence agency. U.S. security considerations therefore did lead the United States to help foster a highly repressive regime in Iran in the post-1953 period. U.S. officials, however, repeatedly brushed aside requests by the Shah in the 1950s and early 1960s to expand the security assistance program, and it was scaled back and then ended altogether in the mid-1960s. Consequently, there were clear limits to the U.S. security assistance program in

Iran. Moreover, although U.S. officials apparently made little or no effort to stop the Shah's extensive arms buildup in the late 1960s and 1970s, there is no evidence that they really encouraged the Shah to undertake this buildup.[41] Therefore, while the U.S. security relationship with Iran clearly did contribute to the repressive character of the Shah's regime, its contribution appears to have been more limited than many critics suggest.

Security considerations not only led the United States to strengthen Iran's security forces; they also severely limited the ability of U.S. policymakers to exert influence over the Shah's domestic policies. U.S. policymakers were generally quite concerned about the absence of democratic institutions and the high level of repression in Iran, both for humanitarian reasons and because political instability in Iran posed an obvious threat to U.S. security interests. But though some pressure was exerted on the Shah in the late 1950s and early 1960s to carry out political reforms, the growing U.S. strategic dependence on Iran placed clear limits on U.S. influence over him in this period and virtually eliminated it altogether in the mid- and late 1960s and 1970s.[42] Consequently, although many U.S. policymakers were quite concerned about domestic political conditions in Iran, U.S. security interests largely prevented them from acting on these concerns.

The U.S. security relationship with Iran under the late Shah therefore illustrates an important point: security considerations in certain cases can lead the United States to pursue policies that both conflict with basic human values and undermine U.S. security interests in the long term by promoting political unrest and instability. This general idea undoubtedly applies not only to the case of Iran but also to a number of other present or former U.S. allies in the Third World.

Notes

1. Because of the sensitive nature of this study, many of these interviews were conducted on the basis of strict confidentiality. In order to establish the credibility of these confidential sources in the notes below, I have tried to describe the positions they held or the roles they played in key events to the extent possible without revealing their identities. Except where noted, all material presented here that was obtained in interviews was corroborated by at least one additional source in order to establish its veracity. Nevertheless, despite this procedure, it is possible that some of this material remains distorted or incomplete.

2. U.S. Joint Chiefs of Staff, *United States Strategic Interests in Iran, JCS 1714/1*, 4 Oct. 1946, 6. This document and other U.S. government documents cited below are located in the U.S. National Archives in Washington, D.C., except where noted. For a good study of U.S. policy toward Iran during World War II and in the immediate postwar period, see Mark Hamilton Lytle, *The Origins of the Iranian-American Alliance* (New York: Holmes and Meier, 1987).

3. See U.S. Joint Chiefs of Staff, *Review of U.S. Policy Regarding Persia, JCS 1714/12*, 31 Oct. 1950, 84–85.

4. U.S. National Security Council, *United States Objectives and Programs for National Security, NSC-68,* 14 Apr. 1950, reprinted in *Containment: Documents on American Policy and Strategy, 1945–1950,* ed. Thomas H. Etzold and John Lewis Gaddis (New York: Columbia University Press, 1950), 434.

5. On Perimeter Defense, see John Lewis Gaddis, *Strategies of Containment* (New York: Oxford University Press, 1982), ch. 4.

6. Department of State, *Foreign Relations,* 190ff.

7. See Mark J. Gasiorowski, "The 1953 *Coup D'Etat* in Iran," *International Journal of Middle East Studies* 19 (August 1987): 266–69.

8. For a detailed account of this coup, see ibid.

9. For a good overview of U.S.-Iranian diplomatic relations in the post-coup era, see James A. Bill, *The Eagle and the Lion: The Tragedy of American-Iranian Relations* (New Haven: Yale University Press, 1988).

10. On U.S. security interests in Iran in this period, see U.S. National Security Council, *United States Policy toward Iran, NSC-175,* 21 Dec. 1953, and the subsequent NSC studies on Iran. On U.S. listening devices in Iran see James Bamford, *The Puzzle Palace* (Boston: Houghton Mifflin, 1982), 198–201. The vital importance of these devices was stressed to me in numerous interviews with retired U.S. officials. On regional cooperation between the United States and Iran, see Rouhollah K. Ramazani, *Iran's Foreign Policy, 1941–1973: A Study of Foreign Policy in Modernizing Nations* (Charlottesville: University Press of Virginia, 1975), chs. 11, 15.

11. For analyses of Iran's national security in this period, see the National Security Council studies referred to in n. 10.

12. *New York Times,* 25 Aug. 1953, 11; 28 Aug. 1953, 4; 10 Dec. 1953, 3; and Burton I. Kaufman, *The Oil Cartel Case: A Documentary Study of Antitrust Activity in the Cold War Era* (Westport, Conn.: Greenwood Press, 1978), ch. 3.

13. Yonah Alexander and Allan Nanes, eds., *The United States and Iran: A Documentary History* (Frederick, Md.: University Publications of America, 1980), 250–54; interview with Kermit Roosevelt, Washington, D.C., 5 June 1985; U.S. Department of State, *Iran White Paper, Section IV.D,* p. 3 (this document was obtained under the Freedom of Information Act); U.S. Agency for International Development (AID), *U.S. Overseas Loans and Grants, Series of Yearly Data,* vol. 1, *Near East and South Asia* (Washington, 1984); *New York Times,* 30 Sept. 1953, 8 : 3; United Nations, *Statistical Yearbook* (New York, various years). For a good overview of the U.S. aid program in Iran, see U.S. AID Mission to Iran, *Summary Highlights of A.I.D. Economic Assistance Activities in Iran* (N.p. [AID Library, Rosslyn, Va.], 1966).

14. These various activities were described to me in interviews with five of the participants. On CIA involvement in suppressing the November 1953 demonstrations, see Kennett Love, "The American Role in the Pahlavi Restoration on 19 August 1953" (manuscript, Allen Dulles Papers, Princeton University Library, 1960). I was unable to confirm CIA involvement in this incident in my interviews.

15. The material presented in this and the next paragraph was obtained in a confidential interview with the U.S. Army colonel (March 1984) and confirmed in confidential interviews with two retired CIA officers who were involved in Iranian affairs at this time.

16. On the Tudeh network, see Farhad Kazemi, "The Military and Politics in Iran: The Uneasy Symbiosis," in *Towards a Modern Iran: Studies in Thought, Politics, and Society,* ed. Elie Kedourie and Sylvia G. Haim (London: Frank Cass, 1980), 217–40.

17. See Thomas M. Ricks, "U.S. Military Missions to Iran, 1943–1978: The Political Economy of Military Assistance," *Iranian Studies* 12 (Summer–Autumn 1979): 168–77.

18. "Shah's Proposals Regarding Expansion of United States Aid to Iranian Armed Forces," 7 Apr. 1954, Record Group 59, Box 4117; National Security Council, *U.S. Policy toward Iran,*

NSC-5504, 7; National Security Council, Operations Coordinating Board, *Progress Report on NSC 5402 (Iran)*, 15 Oct. 1954, 6.

19. *Progress Report*, 11–12; Department of State, *White Paper*, Sec. I.B, 26; National Security Council, *U.S. Policy toward Iran, NSC-5504*, 15 Jan. 1955, 27–28.

20. National Security Council, *U.S. Policy toward Iran, NSC-5703/1*, 8 Feb. 1957, 7, and Financial Appendix, pp. 16–17; AID, *U.S. Overseas Loans and Grants;* Stockholm International Peace Research Institute (SIPRI), *World Armaments and Disarmament, SIPRI Yearbook, 1980* (London: Taylor and Francis, 1980), 26; U.S. Senate, Committee on Foreign Relations, *U.S. Military Sales to Iran*, 94th Congress, 2nd Sess., July 1976, 34–36; U.S. Department of Defense, Defense Security Assistance Agency, *Fiscal Year Series, 1980* (Washington, 1980), 82–83; Joint Chiefs of Staff, "Briefing Paper for Presidential Use in Discussions with the Shah of Iran," 9 June 1958, pp. 6–7 (Dwight D. Eisenhower [DDE] Library); National Security Council, *U.S. Policy toward Iran, NSC-5821/1*, 15 Nov. 1958, 12; Wailes to Herter, 19 Aug. 1958 (DDE Library).

21. National Security Council, *U.S. Policy toward Iran, NSC-6010*, 8 June 1960, 12; National Security Council, Operations Coordinating Board, *Report on Iran*, 9 Dec. 1959, 4–6; U.S. House of Representatives, Committee on Government Operations, *United States Aid Operations in Iran, House Report no. 10*, 85th Congress, 1st Sess., 28 Jan. 1957, 45–48; U.S. Department of State, Office of Director S/P, *A Review of Problems in Iran and Recommendations for the National Security Council*, 15 May 1961 (John F. Kennedy [JFK] Library); Holmes to Rusk, 22 Sept. 1962 (JFK Library).

22. Iran White Paper, section I.B, 39–49; interviews with Stuart Rockwell (Washington, 16 July 1985) and Armin Meyer (Washington, 29 July 1987); AID, *U.S. Overseas Loans and Grants;* Department of Defense, *Fiscal Year Series, 1980*, 82–83; U.S. Senate, *U.S. Military Sales to Iran*, 34–36.

23. U.S. Senate, *Military Sales*, viii–xiii, 13–32; *Washington Post*, 2 Jan. 1977, 1; SIPRI, *World Armaments and Disarmament, 1980*, 26; Department of Defense, *Fiscal Year Series, 1980*, 82–83; Gary Sick, *All Fall Down: America's Tragic Encounter with Iran* (New York: Random House, 1985), 13–18; Barry Rubin, *Paved with Good Intentions: The American Experience and Iran* (New York: Oxford University Press, 1980), ch. 5.

24. For the study that initiated this program, see National Security Council, *Report to the National Security Council Pursuant to NSC Action 1290-d*, 23 Nov. 1955 (DDE Library).

25. Col. Victor J. Croziat, "Imperial Iranian Gendarmerie," *Marine Corps Gazette* (October 1975): 28–31; U.S. President's Citizen Advisors on the Mutual Security Program, *U.S. Army Military Msn. with the Imperial Iranian Gendarmerie*, January 1957 (DDE Library).

26. USOM-Iran, *Review of U.S. Technical Assistance and Economic Aid to Iran, 1951–1957*, 4 vols. (N.p.: [AID Library], n.d.), 483; End of Tour Reports, Public Safety Advisors (AID Library); Michael Klare and Nancy Stein, "Police Terrorism in Latin America," *NACLA Latin America and Empire Report* 8 (January 1974): 20, 22.

27. The material presented here and in the remainder of this section was obtained mainly in interviews with four retired CIA officers who worked closely with SAVAK in this period, and with a top SAVAK official who was directly involved in SAVAK's training programs. All major details presented here that were obtained from one of these sources were corroborated independently by at least one other. Additional sources for specific details are cited in the following notes. The acronym SAVAK stands for Sazman-e Ettela'at va Amniyat-e Keshvar (National Intelligence and Security Organization).

28. It is often alleged that the CIA trained SAVAK in the use of torture. This allegation was vehemently denied by all my CIA sources, who generally maintained that torture training was explicitly prohibited for both CIA and "friendly" trainees and that SAVAK was, in any case, already well skilled in the use of torture. As a result of my research into this matter, I am personally

convinced that the CIA did not provide torture training to SAVAK. The CIA, however, did train SAVAK personnel in interrogation methods and in techniques for resisting interrogation. These subjects clearly approach the fine line separating torture from more acceptable methods, and particular instructors may have crossed this line on certain occasions, either deliberately or by accident, without informing their superiors. It is also possible that my sources were misleading me on this matter, although I am convinced that this was not the case.

29. Most of the material presented in this paragraph was obtained in an interview with the SAVAK official mentioned in n. 27. Although it was impossible to confirm many of the details of the SAVAK training program provided by this source, the general scenario he presented was consistent with that provided by the other sources mentioned in n. 27 and was specifically corroborated by one of these sources. After the Iranian Revolution, several top SAVAK officials testified at revolutionary tribunals that they had received training in Israel and had worked closely with Mossad. See, e.g., *Iran Voice* (Washington) 1, no. 11 (8 Aug. 1979): 1, 12; and 1, no. 22 (21 Jan. 1980): 1.

30. On the SAVAK representative in the United States, see Mansur Rafizadeh, *Witness: From the Shah to the Secret Arms Deal* (New York: William Morrow, 1987), ch. 12 and elsewhere. Although much of the material contained in this book is unreliable, a former CIA officer who knew Rafizadeh confirmed to me that he had been a U.S. agent. The listening posts were operated by CIA technicians on bases provided (and guarded) by the Iranian air force and were under the operational command of the CIA station chief in Tehran. Intelligence material obtained by these listening posts that was useful to Iran was given directly to the Shah by the CIA station chief, bypassing SAVAK and the Iranian armed forces. U.S. intelligence on domestic matters in Iran was not given to SAVAK because U.S. intelligence sources in Iran might have been compromised as a result, as the Shah might have become alarmed at the extent of U.S. intelligence-gathering activities in Iran, and because it was generally believed that SAVAK had better intelligence than the CIA on such matters anyway. The unreliable intelligence given by SAVAK to the CIA typically consisted of inaccurate reports indicating that SAVAK was making major gains against certain opposition groups. The former SAVAK officer mentioned in n. 27 described this material as "trash" and told me that the Shah himself had ordered that the CIA be given such material.

31. On the Barzanis' war with Iraq, see Edmund Ghareeb, *The Kurdish Question in Iraq* (Syracuse: Syracuse University Press, 1981). The CIA refused to run joint operations into Iraq because it already had adequate intelligence capabilities there. However, the United States did help arrange the joint SAVAK-Mossad intelligence operations against Iraq described below. Joint operations against Iranian targets were not carried out because SAVAK was unwilling to do so and because U.S. officials believed that SAVAK was capable of undertaking such operations by itself. On SAVAK operations in the United States, see Department of State, *White Paper*, sec. III.B.

32. John C. Campbell, *Defense of the Middle East* (New York: Praeger, 1960), chs. 4, 5; U.S. Department of State, *History of CENTO*, Jan. 1964, 1–23 (Department of State, *White Paper*, document I.B-45).

33. Campbell, *Defense of the Middle East*, 60–61, 233.

34. Ibid., ch. 6; Ramazani, *Iran's Foreign Policy*, 292–94; Department of State, *White Paper*, sec. I.B, 29.

35. Iran White Paper, sec. I.B, 31–32; U.S. Joint Chiefs of Staff, "Briefing Paper for Presidential Use in Discussions with the Shah of Iran," 9 June 1958, 3 (DDE Library).

36. Department of State, *History of CENTO*, 60.

37. The material presented in this paragraph was obtained in confidential interviews with a retired CIA officer, a retired U.S. Army officer who headed the U.S. MAAG mission in Iran for several years, and a former SAVAK official who served on the CENTO countersubversion committee in the 1960s.

38. Department of State, *History of CENTO*, 78–90; W. M. Hale and Julian Bharier,

"CENTO, R.C.D. and the Northern Tier: A Political and Economic Appraisal," *Middle Eastern Studies* 8 (May 1972): 217–26; Shirin Tahir-Kheli, "Proxies and Allies: The Case of Iran and Pakistan," *Orbis* 24 (Summer 1980): 344.

39. For an overview of Iran's ties with Israel, see Shahram Chubin and Sepehr Zabih, *The Foreign Relations of Iran* (Berkeley: University of California Press, 1974), 156–62. It is often said that Israeli intelligence officers trained SAVAK personnel in torture techniques and helped them interrogate political prisoners. Although I have seen no reliable evidence of this, several retired CIA officers who are knowledgeable about the Iran-Israel intelligence relationship in this period have described it to me generally as a "no-holds-barred" relationship, indicating that they believe such activities may well have occurred. Most of the material presented in this paragraph was obtained in an interview with the former SAVAK official mentioned in n. 27 and corroborated by one of the retired CIA officers mentioned in that note. On economic ties between Iran and Israel, see Muslim Students Following the Imam's Line, *Documents from the Nest of Spies*, vol. 36 (Tehran: N.p., n.d.).

40. The material presented in this paragraph was obtained mainly from the two interviewees mentioned in n. 39. On Iranian involvement in the Yemen war, see Chubin and Zabih, *The Foreign Relations of Iran,* 153. On the Safari Club, see Mohamed Heikel, *Iran: The Untold Story* (New York: Pantheon, 1981), 112–16. Although this book contains many inaccuracies, its description of the Safari Club was corroborated by the two sources mentioned above. On Iranian involvement in the Dhofar uprising, see Fred Halliday, *Arabia without Sultans* (New York: Vintage Books, 1975), 364–66.

41. For a good discussion of this issue, see Sick, *All Fall Down,* 24–27.

42. These observations are based mainly on interviews I have conducted with several dozen retired U.S. officials who were involved in U.S. policy toward Iran in the 1953–78 period. Many of these sources stressed the importance of the electronic listening posts installed in Iran in 1957. (See n. 10, above, and the accompanying text.) These installations were regarded as vital to U.S. national security in the 1960s and 1970s. Because the Shah was capable of shutting these installations down virtually at a moment's notice, the United States became highly dependent on Iran in this regard.

7

The U.S. Overture to Iran, 1985–1986: An Analysis

JAMES A. BILL

The revelations in 1986 and 1987 that the administration of President Ronald Reagan had made secret diplomatic overtures to the Islamic Republic of Iran by trading arms for American hostages held in Lebanon shook the American political system to the core. When it was later demonstrated that some of the profits from this operation had been transferred to support the rebellion in Nicaragua, the incident, which had been described as a national policy embarrassment, was now labeled a national policy scandal involving both improprieties and illegalities. This scandal dealt irreparable harm to the administration of President Reagan and destroyed the careers of many of his leading officials and advisers. While seriously damaging the credibility of the president himself, the scandal cast a shadow on the political career of Vice President George Bush as well. In the words of the authoritative U.S. congressional investigation of the overture:

> The Iran initiative succeeded only in replacing three American hostages with another three, arming Iran with 2,004 TOWs and more than 200 vital spare parts for HAWK missile batteries, improperly generating funds for the Contras and other covert activities . . . , producing profits for the Hakim-Secord Enterprise that in fact belonged to the U.S. taxpayers, leading certain NSC and CIA personnel to deceive representatives of their own Government, undermining U.S. credibility in the eyes of the world, damaging relations between the Executive and the Congress, and engulf-

ing the President in one of the worst credibility crises of any Administration in U.S. history.[1]

This chapter is an attempt to uncover the complex cluster of reasons that lay behind the actions taken by the Reagan administration in the Iran arms affair. The story is not a simple one and cannot be accurately understood from the explanations presented by the two major schools, each with its own vested interests, that dominate the debate that has swirled about the incident. The first school consists of the critics who attack the government by focusing their attention upon the arms-for-hostages dimension of the initiative. This position has been effective for two reasons. First, there is considerable evidence to support this interpretation: the arms-for-hostages plan was clearly an important integral part of the arrangement. Second, the proponents of this position span the entire political spectrum from left to right. The more liberal critics stress the secrecy, doubletalk, and antidemocratic nature of the overture. The more conservative side expresses great indignation at a policy that seems to deal cooperatively with what they consider to be hardened terrorists. As a result, the Reaganites found themselves caught in a withering political crossfire. Buttressing this entire position is the anti-Iran feeling that has pervaded much of the American public since the revolution of 1978–79 and the hostage incident that followed. The second school is embodied in the defensive stance taken by the president and his inner circle.[2] Key players who hold this posture either have stubbornly refused to admit that arms were being traded for hostages or, if grudgingly admitting this, have argued that the overriding goal of the venture was to establish ties to "moderate" Iranian factions to enable the United States to better pursue its long-term interests in the region.

As the politicians involved have sought to protect themselves, they have resorted to the destruction and alteration of documents, the misrepresentation and distortion of the truth, and the tactic of shifting and denying their own responsibilities. The incident was one in which the president of the United States "misspoke"; the vice president was "out of the loop"; the secretaries of state and defense were "not seriously consulted"; the national security advisers thought it was "not necessary" to consult the president; and the key operative in the scheme, a marine lieutenant colonel at the National Security Council, was, in his own words, "this kid" whom "people came to when they wanted something done." In speaking of "full-service" covert operations, "nonlogged and out-of-system documents," and "offline conversations," Oliver North explains much about the methodology of this foreign policy escapade. He also signals the difficulties involved in uncovering the actual motivations and reasons for that policy.

Oliver North was undoubtedly motivated both by personal ambition and by his own interpretation of patriotic behavior. In the view of an observant associate:

> Ollie was typical of so many military officers at the rank of major (0-4) and LTC (0-5). He wanted to get promoted as fast as possible and learned in the course of his career that such promotions came with extraordinary deeds and highly-placed patrons. Though he was a zealous flag-waver, who frequently called those of us who came to his attention "fine Americans," he was probably more motivated by his desire to get ahead. Ollie also saw how well General Haig succeeded with the right accord and important patrons.[3]

Despite the ever-present personal ambitions and the long, dark trail of subterfuge, it is possible to explore with some success the thicket of political reasoning that surrounds and obscures the overture. This can be done through the careful examination of published documents and through interviews with selected participants.[4]

The evidence suggests that there were ten different but interrelated reasons for the dramatic overture to Iran. Although U.S. decision makers obviously did not systematically and coherently formulate policy on the basis of an explicit awareness of these considerations, all ten factors surfaced with varying impact at different times in the process of the initiative. They can be divided into two major categories: strategic or contextual reasons, on the one hand, and tactical or proximate reasons, on the other. The proximate reasons can in turn be divided into two categories: internal and external.

The Strategic Contextual Reasons

The Reagan administration moved to approach the Islamic Republic of Iran in a contextual situation that contained a battery of strategic underlying realities. These realities could be considered determinants in that they involve persistent geopolitical factors that influenced the decisions of the major actors in Washington. There were four such determinants: (1) the desire to reestablish influence in Iran, (2) the felt need to counter Soviet influence both in Iran and in the Persian Gulf region, (3) the desire to protect the "moderate" traditional regimes in the Gulf, with primary attention paid to the issue of stability in Saudi Arabia, and (4) the goal of protecting economic interests, with a special focus on oil pricing. The documents repeatedly emphasize the clear concern that the major actors exhibited toward these four strategic realities.

Given the fact that Iran could in many ways be considered the superpower of the Persian Gulf, several important members of the administration felt that it was in America's long-term interest to seek a quiet but effective way to reestablish connections with the Islamic Republic. This position was particularly prevalent among middle-level specialists in the Central Intelligence Agency and National Security Council, such as Graham Fuller and Howard Teicher. These analysts felt that "we should at least be working towards an expanded policy towards Iran, expanded in the broadest sense, more than a purely negative one of no arms and slap down on terrorism." They argued that Iran was destined to remain a significant power both in the Middle East and in the Islamic world more generally. Furthermore, the proponents of this position postulated that it was possible to initiate contacts with more "moderate" elements within the Iranian government and even to help strengthen their position vis-à-vis the more extremist factions there. Also, they hoped in this way to exert some influence over the succession process once Ayatollah Khomeini disappeared from the scene. This position lamented the "powerlessness" that marked the U.S. stance toward Iran.[5]

In explaining why President Reagan decided to approach Iran, Chief of Staff Donald Regan stated that "he has this feeling, that we cannot allow Iran to fall into the Soviet camp."[6] It is clear from the documents that the president himself was the driving force behind the initiative. According to former NSC head Robert "Bud" McFarlane, when warned about the possible consequences of his Iran approach, Reagan himself stated that he "would take all the heat for that."[7] In his personal and political battle against the Soviet Union, the president was willing to take even the extraordinary risk of dealing privately with a government he publicly condemned as a source of terrorism.

This worldview was shared widely by the White House inner circle, who reflected the president's own perspective. The director of the CIA, William Casey, for example, realized that "Iran had a special role in the world, a special location on the map, right on the underbelly of Russia. The United States could not turn its back on Iran and allow it to fall under Soviet influence."[8] The Soviet-centric mind-set that prevailed among the Reaganites was a major force that lay behind the overtures to Iran. This preoccupation was sharpened by the Soviet occupation of Afghanistan. The White House decision makers explicitly discussed the need to reknit relations with Iran in order to apply increasing pressure on Soviet forces occupying Afghanistan. In particular, they sought to enlist active Iranian assistance in support of the Afghan resistance. In playing the Soviet card, the major U.S. actors sought to frighten the Iranians. As Adm. John Poindexter wrote in a note to Colonel North: "If they really want to save their asses from the Soviets, they should get on board."[9] This Soviet concern overlaps considerably with the first strategic reason—the need to reestablish contacts and influence in Iran.

Certain analysts in the administration believed that new contacts with Iran could serve as channels that could be used to check Iran's efforts to spread its revolutionary ideas through the region. These observers considered countries such as Kuwait and Saudi Arabia to be inherently unstable and deeply suscepti- ble to Iranian revolutionary messages and disruption. In a memorandum listing "talking points" for CIA director Casey in February 1986, it was argued that "the Arabs would cheer if Iran could be moderated."[10] In an earlier June 1985 National Security Decision Directive (NSDD) prepared primarily by NSC Middle East specialist Howard Teicher, it was argued that a principal U.S. interest was "ending Iranian sponsorship of terrorism, and [its] policy of destabilizing neighboring states."[11] The special relationship between the United States and Saudi Arabia was the reason many officials favored this strategy of seeking to deflect Iranian propaganda away from the kingdom. One consideration that rested behind this American sensitivity was economic in nature; it involved oil and oil prices.

One of the critical strategic contextual reasons that encouraged the Ameri- can approach to Iran is one that has received relatively little attention. In 1985– 86, a confluence of interest concerning oil prices developed between Iran and America. In the words of Oliver North himself, the United States and Iran had "similar interests with respect to oil."[12] By this time, the Islamic Republic had taken a position that stressed controlled production and higher prices. Although the United States had earlier and publicly pressed for low prices, this position changed dramatically after oil prices plunged to less than ten dollars per barrel in the spring and summer of 1986.

The sharp price decline dealt a devastating economic blow to oil-produc- ing states such as Texas, Oklahoma, and Louisiana. The political reverberations were soon felt in Washington, where Vice President George Bush and other influential national politicians from the Southwest were pressured by powerful independent oil interests who had supported them over the years. Although leaders such as Bush spoke to a national constituency that dictated price sta- bility over price increases, their political home bases represented the founda- tions of their support. As the economic exigencies began to drive the indepen- dent oil operators from the fields, they bluntly confronted their representatives in Washington. This campaign was especially effective with respect to the vice president, who clearly had aspirations for even higher office. He needed the economic and political support of these interests. It was in this context that

George Bush made his April 1986 visit to the Kingdom of Saudi Arabia, the country that had flooded the market with excess oil. And it was in this context that Iran and Saudi Arabia arrived at their surprise August 1986 production agreement within the halls of OPEC that brought prices back to the eighteen-dollar-per-barrel level.[13]

In a July 1986 letter written by Iranian middleman Manuchehr Ghorbanifar to his contact in Tehran, Ghorbanifar attempted to demonstrate American goodwill toward Iran partially through the use of the oil price argument. He emphasized American "opposition to the decrease in oil prices; so much so that Mr. George Bush, the Vice President, on two occasions during speeches and interviews announced that the reduction in oil prices would ultimately be harmful to the United States and that oil prices should increase."[14] From the official American side, the 1986 NSDD referred to above contained two points emphasizing the oil argument. Both were listed under the category "longer-term goals" and emphasized "restoration of Iran's moderate and constructive role . . . in the 'world petroleum economy' " and "Iranian moderation of OPEC pricing policy."[15] In August and September of 1986, Iranian oil minister Gholam Reza Aghazadeh acted as a major political and economic emissary to Saudi Arabia and the other oil-producing states in the Gulf.[16] Thus, besides the political and ideological factors that catalyzed the American approach to Iran, there was also an important economic ingredient.

The above four strategic contextual determinants were obviously intertwined with one another. The strategic need to regain influence in Iran overlapped with the deep fear of possible Soviet advantage, the hope that the United States could exert a restraining influence upon the exportation of revolutionary ideas, and the understanding that the United States and the Islamic Republic could cooperate quietly on oil prices. And by regaining influence in Iran while working to buttress stability in Saudi Arabia, the United States could better protect oil prices at a level acceptable to its own perceived national interests.

The Tactical Proximate Reasons

The sources reflect six more immediate reasons for the initiative. Four involve internal perceptions and immediate preoccupations; two concern the positions of two key external actors. The four internal proximate reasons included the concern for American hostages in Lebanon, the desire to end the Iran-Iraq war, the fear of the imminent collapse of Iran, and the perceived need to improve intelligence capabilities. Of these four reasons, the first stands out above the others and can be referred to as the linkage reason—the one that most closely relates the strategic determinants identified above with the cluster of tactical factors to be discussed below. There was indeed an arms-for-hostages component to the initiative and it was the most important immediate motivating factor.

Throughout the tortuous negotiations and complex deliberations involving the United States and Iran in 1985 and 1986, most attention was focused upon the attempt to gain effective Iranian support for the return of American citizens held hostage in Lebanon. The record demonstrates that in the cases of Benjamin Weir (released 15 September 1985), Lawrence Jenco (released 26 July 1986), and David Jacobsen (released 2 November 1986) this policy succeeded; in other cases it failed. There is strong evidence that President Reagan himself was preoccupied with the desire to gain the freedom of these Americans. The president and especially CIA chief William Casey desperately sought the release of Beirut CIA station chief William Buckley, who had been kidnapped in March 1984.

The reasons for such deep concern about the hostages are complex and go beyond the obvious humanitarian concerns, which were certainly genuine. There were political reasons as well. Chief of Staff Regan publicly admitted this when he stated that the president wanted the hostages released "not only for geopolitical reasons but also the fact that we weren't getting anywhere in getting more hostages out. And we were going to spend another Christmas with hostages there, and he is looking powerless and inept as President because he's unable to do anything to get the hostages out."[17] In the words of the Near East CIA chief: "And there is a lot of fear about the yellow ribbons going back up and that this President would have the same problems that the last President had had with Iranian hostages, Iranian control."[18] The Reagan White House was haunted by the specter of Carter's failed hostage policy.

Despite all the emphasis on the arms-for-hostages policy, the immediate goal of hostage release was only one, albeit important, part of the overall decisional mosaic. The preoccupation with American hostages is perhaps best viewed as the door through which the United States sought to reenter Iran in order to achieve a wide range of tactical and strategic goals. In the view of NSC officials such as Teicher and North, for example, the "ultimate objective" of the 25 May 1986 Tehran visit to trade arms for hostages was "to commence the process of improving U.S.-Iranian relations." In their opinions, resolution of the hostage issue would "improve the opportunities" for a new U.S.-Iranian relationship.[19] The CIA national intelligence officer Charles Allen also viewed the "original objectives of the NSC initiative—to open up a geostrategic relationship in the long term with Iran, to get the hostage situation out of the way as a stumbling block to any further relations with Iran."[20] The Israelis analyzed the hostage issue in a similar manner. Amiram Nir, for example, spoke of tactical and strategic layers. "The tactical layer was described as an effort 'to get the hostages out.' The strategic layer was designed 'to build better contact with Iran and to insure we are better prepared when a change [in leadership] occurs.'"[21] At one point in the initiative, American NSC operatives worried that the approach was "too much hostage to the hostage problem."[22]

Throughout 1987 and into 1988, the U.S. government continued to view any new warmer relationship with the Islamic Republic of Iran as contingent upon Iranian assistance in the release of the American hostages. In State Department circles, a new strategic relationship with Iran was desirable but had to be approached through the hostage issue. In this sense, the policies of 1985 and 1986 were quietly carried forward into later years. Despite the preeminence and greater permanence of the hostage factor, there were three other integral tactical reasons for the initiative.

In his 13 November 1986 speech defending the Iran initiative, President Reagan listed the Iran-Iraq war as one of the four reasons for the policy. He and his advisers apparently felt that contacts with Iran would provide the United States with needed leverage to end the war. Furthermore, U.S. intelligence had indicated that Iran might in fact prevail in the conflict. Although the administration was not completely unhappy with a stalemate on the front and strongly opposed a victory by either contestant, it basically sought a termination of the war.[23] Given its tilt toward the Iraqi side, the United States would be in an especially difficult position if Iran were to prevail. Therefore, in order to both hedge its bets and attempt to gain a modicum of influence over Iran's war policy, the Reagan administration pursued the 1985–86 overture.

A third proximate reason for the overture involved U.S. intelligence concerning the domestic political situation in Iran. At a critical early point in the deliberations in the summer of 1985, CIA and NSC Iran analysts prepared reports arguing that Khomeini's political position was weakening and that Iran was on the verge of disintegration. Analyst Graham Fuller of the CIA wrote: "In bluntest form, the Khomeini regime is faltering and may be moving toward a moment of truth; we will soon see a struggle for succession."[24] In the June 1985 NSDD prepared by NSC officials Howard Teicher and Donald Fortier, the first immediate U.S. interest is listed as "preventing the disintegration of Iran."[25] Primarily because of the nearby Soviet presence, the United States was alarmed at the prospect of any disintegration of the Islamic Republic. Thus, in this sense, the intelligence reports of 1985 (whether in hindsight accurate or not) helped motivate the Iran initiative. And resting immediately behind this tactical informational factor was the second strategic argument listed above, the deep and persistent fear of any Soviet gains in revolutionary Iran.

A fourth proximate reason for the covert initiative concerned the absence of intelligence both on Iran itself and on events in the geostrategic band of countries surrounding Iran. The lack of accurate and reliable data was bemoaned by leading U.S. foreign policy decision makers after the fall of the Shah. Efforts to insert intelligence agents into post-Pahlavi Iran had been largely unsuccessful, especially after the student takeover of the U.S. embassy in Tehran. The loss of sophisticated listening posts in Kapkan and Behshahr severely crippled American capacities to monitor Soviet missile and space activities and stood as a reminder of U.S. intelligence impotence. Accurate data were badly needed concerning hostages, the Iran-Iraq war, the Soviet Union, the situation in Afghanistan, and the Iranian internal political and economic situation itself. By quietly reestablishing relations with Iran, the administration determined that it could strengthen significantly its weakened intelligence capabilities.

Besides these four factors, there were two further immediate reasons that stood somewhat separately as external factors and acted primarily as catalysts for the Iran initiative. Two countries, Israel and Iran itself, welcomed the American approach. For reasons of its own perceived self-interest, Israel was a critical force, pushing and prodding the United States throughout the venture. Israel's own motivations involved both economic and political considerations. Arms sales to the Islamic Republic meant substantial and badly needed financial resources, and the Israeli leadership was continuing its traditional approach of seeking ties with non-Arab Iran (regardless of the complexion of its political system) in order to attempt to find a regional ally against its Arab enemies. In brief, Israel sought to continue to protect what it termed its "Iranian connection." By drawing the United States into the arrangement, Israel hoped, among other things, to legitimize and strengthen its own frayed postrevolutionary Iran connection.

Israel had been shipping arms and spare parts in spurts to Iran since shortly after the Shah was overthrown. In keeping its own policy alive and its own channels open, it played an extremely active role in promoting a somewhat similar operation by the United States. This was quite consistent with the Israeli policy of working diligently to align American interests and policies with its own interests and policies. The prominence of the Israeli effort is evident, for example, in the 25 May 1986 journey of Robert McFarlane and associates to Tehran in a failed mission to trade arms for hostages. When the Boeing 707 aircraft left Tel Aviv for Tehran, it carried among its passengers Israeli intelligence official Amiram Nir disguised as an American named Miller. Although high-ranking American officials had questioned the presence of Nir on this sensitive U.S. mission, Prime Minister Shimon Peres himself intervened on

Nir's behalf. Throughout the entire episode Peres intervened at critical moments at the White House level to ensure that the initiative was kept alive.[26] Other Israelis deeply involved at various stages in the venture included David Kimche, Adolph Schwimmer, and Yaacov Nimrodi. Michael Ledeen, an NSC consultant known to have extremely close ties with Israel, also was a major promoter of the initiative, and Manuchehr Ghorbanifar, the controversial middleman in the operation, was praised by the Israelis, who acted as his sponsors to the United States. Both William Casey and Oliver North considered Ghorbanifar to be an Israeli intelligence agent.[27]

In encouraging the 1985–86 initiative, Israeli operatives continually repeated all the arguments subscribed to by Reagan officials such as William Casey, Robert McFarlane, John Poindexter, and Oliver North. The Israelis particularly emphasized the strategic arguments, with special attention being paid to the specter of a potential Soviet takeover in Iran. This was, of course, language that the Reagan administration understood well.

The final external proximate reason for the American approach to Iran is found in the Islamic Republic itself. Here, it is almost certainly true that Ayatollah Khomeini himself quietly knew and approved of the venture. Iran was at the time under enormous economic and political pressure; Khomeini too was concerned about the succession process that would replace him; and leading members of the ulama feared the Soviet Union, whose occupation of Afghanistan stood as a constant reminder of the nearby communist threat. Pragmatic leaders such as powerful Majles Speaker Ali Akbar Hashemi-Rafsanjani encouraged the overture, and it was out of the Speaker's office that the so-called second channel of contact flowed. In the view of the Iranian leadership, correct relations with the United States could be established if America was willing to respect Iran's territorial integrity and national autonomy and would adopt a truly neutral position with respect to the Gulf war.

Oliver North and his associates were aware of these Iranian concerns, and in their discussions they made numerous promises in response. These included false representations concerning the United States' willingness to accept the demise of Iraqi leader Saddam Hussein, the sharing of intelligence that was partly accurate and partly bogus, the dissemination of false information concerning alleged Soviet troop movements, and elaborate promises concerning the provision of a wide variety of military supplies badly needed by Iran. When questioned about making inaccurate statements and false promises to the Iranians, North agreed and described them as "blatantly false." In his words, "I lied everytime I met the Iranians."[28] Although Bud McFarlane referred to the Iranians as "rug merchants," the Iranians must at times have wondered about American bargaining techniques as well.

The Depressing Diplomatic Legacy

The American approach to Iran in the mid-1980s was dictated by the complex web of interrelated reasons analyzed above. Tactical and strategic considerations reinforced one another throughout. Although all ten motivating reasons came into play, there were two that stood out among all the others. At the strategic level of analysis, the administration nursed an ideological preoccupation with a perceived Soviet threat. At the time, Iran was viewed through the lens of the Cold War. With its troops occupying Afghanistan, Reagan's "Evil Empire" was seen to have wrapped itself halfway around the Islamic Republic of Iran. Although revolutionary Iran was viewed with distaste as an extremist, uncontrollable loose cannon in the region, its significance as a direct threat to the United States paled beside that represented by the Soviet Union. The president himself had established the atmosphere for this mind-set, but it was deeply shared by the other key actors who played major roles in the arms affair drama. William Casey, Robert McFarlane, John Poindexter, Oliver North, and Donald Regan, among others, all viewed foreign policy from this unidimensional perspective. Although it was also shared by Secretary of State George Shultz and Secretary of Defense Caspar Weinberger, the latter two came to slightly different policy conclusions based on their exposures to a modicum of Iran expertise present in their respective organizations.

The primary proximate reason for the initiative, the hostage situation, was considered the principal doorway to a new strategic relationship with Iran. But it was a doorway that the Reagan administration was never able to open for several reasons. First, Reagan's operatives lacked the knowledge necessary to unlock the door and to establish the new relationships they sought. They understood neither the configuration of the doorway nor the psychology and power of the principal doorkeepers, the Iranians. Nor did the advisers they relied on have the proper keys and introductions. Second, the administration's team felt it necessary to work clandestinely. In so doing, they worked clumsily in the dark and were unable, therefore, to bring either public or private expertise to bear on their task. Third, whenever the U.S. team sought to retreat, regroup, and rethink their tactics, they were forced along by outside players such as the Israelis, who had their own reasons for forcing the policy. Fourth, the Iranians with whom they dealt were limited themselves in their capacity to deliver hostages held in Lebanon. The delicate political struggles underway in revolutionary Iran at the time clearly weakened their hand. And, of course, the Iranians were not the only doorkeepers. The hostage-takers were Lebanese extremists with their own agenda and their own ideas.

An examination of the complex rationale for the American overture reveals that there were a number of excellent reasons for trying to improve relations with Iran. Strategically, it made a good deal of sense slowly and carefully to seek ways to reestablish relationships with the most populous and powerful country on the Persian Gulf. Yet, the methodology was deeply flawed. The principal immediate reason for the overture—the release of the hostages—should have come toward the end of the process of rapprochement rather than at the very beginning. Arms and hostages should not have been linked. The episode can be summarized as follows: it involved the wrong people (McFarlane, North, Teicher) advised by the wrong "experts" (Ledeen, Ghorbanifar) supported by the wrong ally (Israel); they went to the wrong place (Tehran) at the wrong time (during the month of Ramadan and after the United States had tilted toward the Iraqi side in the Gulf war) carrying the wrong tactical plan.

The Iranian side, lacking the will and capacity to deliver on all the American expectations, dragged out the process until its existence was ultimately leaked to the public in November 1986. Nor did the American operatives always provide what they had promised the Iranians. Deception abounded. From the beginning, the process lurched and faltered, accelerated and floundered. The American side lost patience. In Tehran, McFarlane lost his composure and flew out of Tehran fuming because of delays; North became sarcastic and increasingly dissembled to the Iranians; middlemen of questionable competence were hired, dropped, and rehired; and, ultimately, when the key actors were forced to testify publicly, they blamed neither themselves nor the president, nor even the Israelis. Instead, they all suddenly turned on Iran and bitterly blamed the Iranians. The president of the United States, the man who more than any other was responsible for the arms initiative, led the chorus of accusations against what he called "barbarians."

Because of this methodology of ignorance and the failure that derived from it, American-Iranian relations have been set back many years. Although the strategic determinants identified in this chapter remain essentially the same, the chances of developing a new rapprochement with Iran have become considerably smaller since the aborted initiative. Iranians willing to risk their careers (and lives) by developing communication with official Americans have become fewer. The clumsiness and admitted deception engaged in by the Norths and McFarlanes will be long remembered in Iran. On the American side, the anti-Iranian tone of the hearings and the constant condemnations of Iran by the U.S. president and his cabinet officials have deepened Iranophobia among the American public—a public already traumatized by the hostage incident at the beginning of the decade. The less enlightened policymakers in Washington invite confrontation with Iran. The more enlightened, located at mid-levels of the Department of State and elsewhere, have not given up hopes of one day establishing a new long-term relationship with Iran. But they adamantly argue that they are willing to do so only with the release of hostages in Lebanon. While one group of American policymakers seeks to blow down the entire Iranian house, the other group is once again talking about gathering at the door to talk only about hostages. U.S.-Iranian relations have once again become hostage to hostages, and this important case of foreign policy failure continues to compromise the interests of both countries.

Notes

1. U.S. Congress, House of Representatives and Senate, Select Committee to Investigate Covert Arms Transactions with Iran, *Report of the Congressional Committees Investigating the Iran-Contra Affair* (Washington, D.C.: Government Printing Office, 1987), 280.

2. Different actors in the administration in fact held different positions concerning U.S. policy toward Iran. In this chapter, the policymakers referred to are the president and the McFarlane-Poindexter-North clique that planned and sought to implement the overture to Iran. For a discussion of three schools of thought in Washington regarding Iran policy, see Nikki R. Keddie's interesting article "Iranian Imbroglios: Who's Irrational?" *World Policy Journal* 5 (Winter 1987–88): 29–54. For a more recent and more elaborate analysis of three Reaganite views of Iran, see Eric Hooglund, "Reagan's Iran: Factions behind U.S. Policy in the Gulf," *MERIP Middle East Report,* no. 151 (March–April 1988): 29–31, and his chapter in this volume. Hooglund identifies the positions as "Soviet-centric," "Israel-centric," and "Arab-centric."

3. Personal communication of 19 November 1987 from an associate of Oliver North.

4. Among the major sources examined for the preparation of this chapter are the following: John Tower, Edmund Muskie, and Brent Scowcroft, *The Tower Commission Report* (New York: Bantam Books/Times Books, 1987); The National Security Archive, *The Chronology: The Documented Day-by-Day Account of the Secret Military Assistance to Iran and the Contras* (New York: Warner Books, 1987); *Secret Military Assistance to Iran and the Contras: A Chronology of Events and Individuals* (Washington, D.C.: National Security Archive, 1987); Oliver L. North, *Taking the Stand* (New York: Pocket Books, 1987); U.S. Congress, Select Committees, *Report of the Congressional Committees Investigating the Iran-Contra Affair;* and Congressional Quarterly, *The Iran-Contra Puzzle* (Washington, D.C.: Congressional Quarterly, 1987). Although all these sources have been consulted, the basis for most of the documentation is the National Security Archive chronology published by Warner Books, which will be referred to hereafter as *Chronology.* I am grateful to Aaron Shawn Collins, whose thorough and meticulous perusal of the *Chronology* helped me identify the multifaceted nature of the covert U.S. overture to Iran.

5. For evidence of this motivating factor, see *Chronology,* 47–48, 53, 63, 69, 74, 78, 93–95, 101, 103–04, 112–14, 123, 129, 131, 133–34, 174, 243, 247–49, 258, 262, 264, 268–74 (esp. 272), 300–02, 304–05, 331, 370, 377–78, 380, 387, 389, 418, 436, 442–43, 450, 458, 483-85, 489–90, 499, 504, 519, 554–55, 561, 572. The "expanded policy" quotation is found on p. 101, and the "powerlessness" argument is presented on p. 69.

6. *Tower Commission Report,* 226. For other references to the Soviet factor, see *Chronology,* 68, 78–79, 103–04, 113–14, 135, 248, 300–03, 313, 330–34, 358, 383, 483, 489–90, 517, 529–30.

7. *Tower Commission Report,* 27, 148.

8. Bob Woodward, *Veil: The Secret Wars of the CIA, 1981–1987* (New York: Simon and Schuster, 1987), 433. See also p. 408.

9. *Tower Commission Report,* 277.

10. *Chronology,* 301.

11. *Chronology,* 113. See also pp. 519, 554–55.

12. See U.S. Congress, Select Committees, *Report of the Congressional Committees Investigating the Iran-Contra Affair,* 252. For a rare article that displays sensitivity to the oil price component of the initiative, see Patrick J. Sloyan, "Iranamok and OPEC," *New Republic,* 9 Nov. 1987, 19–21. This perceptive article tends to overemphasize U.S. influence over Iran's oil production policy. It was American pressure (through Bush) on Saudi Arabia that helped bring about Iranian-Saudi alignment on prices beginning in August 1986.

13. The information provided in this paragraph is based upon numerous discussions with leading independent oilmen in Austin and Houston, Texas, during 1986 and 1987.

14. *Tower Commission Report,* 360–61. See also *Chronology,* 413.

15. *Chronology,* 113–14.

16. See, for example, National Security Archives, *Secret Military Assistance,* 685.

17. *Tower Commission Report,* 201–02. See also Woodward, *Veil,* 439.

18. *Tower Commission Report,* 261.

19. *Chronology,* 331.

20. Ibid., 519.

21. Ibid., 442.

22. Ibid., 377.

23. This position is laid out clearly in an April 1986 "Terms of Reference" for a "U.S.-Iran Dialogue." See ibid., 332–33.

24. *Tower Commission Report,* 112.

25. Ibid., 116.

26. For the crucial role played by Peres in the Iran arms affairs, see ibid., 25, 45, 109–10, 215–16, 376–77, 400, 404–05, and 422. Amiram Nir died in a mysterious plane crash in the state of Michoacan in Mexico on 30 November 1988.

27. See North, *Taking the Stand,* 203, and Woodward, *Veil,* 467. For a detailed, informed account of the Israeli involvement in the arms overture to Iran, see Samuel Segev, *The Iranian Triangle: The Untold Story of Israel's Role in the Iran-Contra Affair* (New York: Free Press, 1988).

28. *New York Times,* 10 July 1987, 8, and 11 July 1987, 7; and *Washington Post,* 11 July 1987, 13.

8

The Policy of the Reagan Administration toward Iran

ERIC HOOGLUND

Despite its reputation for having inflexible ideological positions on foreign policy issues, the Reagan administration came to office in January 1981 lacking any program for dealing with Iran. The revolutionary developments in that country during the preceding two years and the national ordeal of the hostage crisis caused conservatives, as well as liberals, to feel simultaneously antagonistic and confused about the Islamic Republic. The new officials were relieved that the hostage crisis was finally over—the hostages were released into Algerian custody and departed Tehran at the very hour Ronald Reagan was being sworn in as president, thus sparing the new administration the necessity of doing anything further regarding a diplomatic crisis that had preoccupied the Carter administration for over fourteen months. Nevertheless, the new administration was not prepared to reestablish ties with Iran, and it temporized for four weeks before announcing its willingness to implement all provisions of the Algerian-mediated agreement that had ended the crisis.[1] There was a pervasive sense that Iran had humiliated the United States, a feeling reinforced by the media, which had reminded the country of its impotence vis-à-vis Iran for 444 days. Now the official consensus seemed to be to let Iran fade from the spotlight of national media attention.

Given the perception of Iran's strategic position, however, the Reagan administration was not ready to ignore that country completely. It viewed the Islamic Republic as importantly linked to the three broad policy objectives it pursued in the Middle East: (1) containing the influence and perceived aggressive designs of the Soviet Union; (2) supporting the security of Israel; and (3) protecting U.S. and Western oil and economic interests in the Persian Gulf region. These policy objectives were not unique to the Reagan administration, but were the same goals the United States had pursued since the Truman administration.[2] The Iranian Revolution and the subsequent U.S.-Iran hostility, however, had overturned the way Iran historically fit into these policy objectives. Thus, it was necessary to redefine the American conception of Iran's role in the Middle East. Was the Islamic Republic an instrument of Soviet policy? Was it a threat to the security of Israel? Did it endanger U.S. economic and strategic interests in the region? Initially, the Reagan administration had no consensus view on these questions.

During its first six years, the Reagan administration failed to formulate a coherent policy for dealing with Iran. Consequently, there were seemingly contradictory policy fluctuations—from ignoring the country to trying to discourage third countries from selling it weapons to secretly wooing its leaders with arms sales. These different policies were the result of competing and often conflicting objectives among officials who viewed Iran with different emphases on the three broad objectives outlined above. Those officials who were preoccupied primarily with confronting the Soviet Union will be referred to as Soviet-centric; those who were concerned chiefly with the security of Israel will be called Israel-centric; and those who were interested principally in safeguarding American access to Middle East oil and investment opportunities, concentrated in the Arab states historically allied to the United States, will be referred to as Arab-centric. An examination of their perspectives regarding Iran can provide insight as to why the Reagan administration was not successful in devising a consistent policy toward the Islamic Republic.[3] As is often the case, group and individual lineups were not always clear-cut or permanent.

The Reagan administration's perceptions of Iran were shaped by its worldview.[4] In this regard, the major difference between the administration's foreign policy and that of its most recent predecessors (the Nixon, Ford, and Carter administrations) was the far greater emphasis that was placed on containing the Soviet Union. Reagan's advisers and policymakers possessed an unreconstructed Cold War view of the Soviet Union as an aggressive, expansionist state. Administration stalwarts were convinced that the policy of détente had been exploited by the Soviets to undermine American prestige and influence in the world.[5] They believed the revolutions in Afghanistan, Iran, and Nicaragua demonstrated the malevolent cleverness of Moscow. The failure of the United States to respond to these challenges had only further emboldened the Soviet Union. Consequently, when the Afghan people tried to resist the Marxist government, Moscow did not think twice about invading. At least some of the

Reagan team feared the Soviet Union might repeat its December 1979 invasion of Afghanistan by marching into Iran in order to seize control of the oil resources of the Persian Gulf.[6]

Soviet-centric officials viewed the Iranian Revolution of 1979 as a premier example of the real strategic disaster that can occur when the United States refuses to assist a friendly regime (that of the last Shah) threatened by "radical" domestic forces susceptible of being subverted by pro-Soviet elements. Iran had been a valuable ally; it was now "lost" owing to America's folly and resolve. Only the Soviet Union had benefited from this debacle. The Shah's fate caused other allies to doubt the U.S. commitment to their own political stability. These views were most thoroughly articulated by Michael Ledeen, who was brought into the State Department as its expert on terrorism and later moved over to the National Security Council, where, as a part-time consultant, he had a key role in the administration's covert arms sales to Iran during 1985–86.[7] It was a view shared by Alexander Haig, who served as secretary of state from January 1981 to June 1982, Jeane Kirkpatrick, the U.S. ambassador to the United Nations from 1981 to 1985, and most other Reagan appointees.[8]

Although these officials readily embraced the idea of Iran's loss being a major strategic setback for the United States, they were less convinced that the loss represented a significant strategic gain for the Soviet Union.[9] They interpreted both the rhetoric and the policies of the Islamic Republic as indications that Tehran deeply mistrusted the Soviets, although they acknowledged that Iran's anti-Sovietism paled in comparison to its anti-Americanism.[10] This perception encouraged some analysts to entertain hope that a shared opposition to Soviet expansion could serve as a basis for eventually restoring Iran to American influence. Winning back Iran was thus an important objective, but Soviet-centric policymakers did not have a unified strategy for accomplishing this goal.

There were at least three distinct perspectives on Iran among Soviet-centric officials. One view, shared at the highest levels of the administration by men such as Secretary of Defense Caspar Weinberger and Central Intelligence Agency director William Casey, perceived the Islamic Republic as being governed by a group of "religious fanatics" and "terrorists." This view was formed during the hostage crisis and was reinforced after 1981 by international terrorist incidents that were attributed to Iran, in particular the bombing of the U.S. Marine barracks in Beirut in 1983 and the kidnaping of foreigners in Lebanon beginning in 1984. Those who held this attitude believed that Iran, with explicit or implicit Soviet encouragement, purposefully used terrorism to subvert American interests in the Middle East. They also were convinced that it was unrealistic to expect to deal rationally with such a regime. They supported, albeit with varying degrees of enthusiasm, clandestine efforts to bring about its downfall. In practice this became a policy of providing covert financial aid to various Iranian monarchist groups committed to the overthrow of the republican government. Since the deposed Shah had died in exile in 1980, these monarchists generally advocated the restoration of the throne to his oldest son, Cyrus Reza Pahlavi. The CIA actually had begun to give monetary assistance to monarchists, as well as to other groups opposed to the regime, during the Carter administration, but that program had been focused on trying to obtain information about internal political developments and, after November 1979, the condition of the hostages.[11] This policy was expanded during the initial years of the Reagan administration with the objective of determining the feasibility of the various exiled leaders forming a political organization that could "win" back Iran. The monarchists failed, however, to create an effective resistance movement, and by 1984 there was general disillusionment with them.[12] Nevertheless, the CIA and other U.S. government agencies continued to rely upon the monarchists as intelligence sources.[13]

The second perspective, and probably the view shared by a majority of Soviet-centric officials, derived from a preoccupation with perceived Soviet influence in Iran. These analysts were particularly concerned about the role of the Tudeh, an Iranian Marxist political party which, they believed, served as the primary agent of Soviet subversion. The Tudeh had first been established in 1941 and was outlawed in 1949.[14] Nevertheless, it had continued to exist both underground and in exile, and over the years it had been the subject of numerous classified studies prepared by the CIA, the Bureau of Intelligence and Research at the Department of State, and the Defense Department's Defense Intelligence Agency (DIA).[15] The Tudeh reemerged following the revolution, proclaimed its support for the Islamic Republic, and was legally permitted to organize party cells and publish its newspaper. Its position seemed to strengthen when, only five months after the Reagan administration assumed office, the Tudeh refused to join the Mojahedin-e Khalq, an Islamic political party that espoused some socialist ideas, and several small leftist parties in an armed uprising against the regime.

Despite the Tudeh's support for the government, relations between the party and Iranian officials were tenuous from the inception of the Islamic Republic. Tudeh members were frequently harassed, and those who tried to organize labor unions and strikes were arrested. The party's publications were often confiscated, and in 1981 its newspaper's license was suspended; the paper was banned permanently in 1982, the same year a purge of suspected Tudeh sympathizers was initiated in all government institutions.[16] Analysts concerned about perceived Tudeh influence tended to overlook the growing antagonism between the Tudeh and the clergy-dominated regime. They were convinced that the Tudeh had infiltrated the army, the ministries, and even the clergy.[17] This perception was reinforced in the summer of 1982 after London informed Washington that a Soviet diplomat who had defected to the British embassy in Tehran had provided the names of several hundred Tudeh cadres whom he said reported regularly to the Soviets.[18] Alarmed by what they believed to be extensive penetration of the Iranian government by Soviet agents, U.S. intelligence officials concurred in Great Britain's decision to pass on the names to Tehran. According to one source, information was provided to the Iranian government as early as October 1982.[19] U.S. officials felt a sense of relief in February 1983 when the Iranian government arrested seventy top Tudeh leaders, who were charged with spying for the Soviet Union; in April, Iran expelled eighteen Soviet diplomats, presumably those who had served as liaisons between the embassy and the Tudeh; and in May, the government declared the party illegal and arrested several hundred more members.[20]

The suppression of the Tudeh only temporarily alleviated fears about Soviet subversive designs upon Iran. The arrests and show trials, which continued throughout 1983 and included revelations of a clandestine Tudeh network within the Iranian army, actually confirmed in the minds of those Soviet-centric analysts thus predisposed that the danger to Iran was serious. These officials were most influential within the CIA and the NSC. In 1984 they persuaded their colleagues of the need for a reappraisal of administration policy toward Iran. The most significant studies to emerge from this process were a May 1985 CIA memo by Graham Fuller and a June 1985 draft National Security Decision Directive (NSDD) document prepared by Donald Fortier and Howard Teicher of the NSC. Both of these classified documents concluded that Soviet influence was growing in Iran and that Moscow was poised to reap political benefits from an anticipated internal struggle for power following Ayatollah Khomeini's death. All three analysts deplored the lack of any U.S. influence in Iran but maintained that this situation could be reversed if the United States was willing to sanction weapons sales to Tehran.[21] These reports influenced the views of three key Soviet-centric officials: National Security Adviser Robert McFarlane, his successor John Poindexter, and CIA director Casey. These reports therefore became one basis for the 1985–86 overture to Iran (analyzed by James Bill in chapter 7).

In addition to the preoccupation with Soviet subversion and encouragement of Iranian terrorism, there was a third Soviet-centric perspective that focused on the Islamic Republic as a potential ideological bulwark against Soviet expansionism. This perspective came from officials who were concerned primarily with Afghanistan. They viewed the Soviet military intervention in Afghanistan at the end of 1979 as proof of Moscow's aggressive intentions toward the Persian Gulf region. They supported the provision of large-scale, covert assistance to the Afghan resistance fighters, the mujahedin, and the military buildup of Pakistan, the country where the mujahedin maintained their bases; they had little interest in any negotiated settlement as long as the mujahedin seemed to be effective.[22] These officials welcomed Iran's often stated criticisms of the Soviet Union's role in Afghanistan, and they considered the Islamic Republic's anti-Soviet rhetoric, assistance to some of the mujahedin groups, and sanctuary for fighters as useful complements in an overall strategy of containing Moscow's ambitions.[23]

These analysts did not share the view of most of their colleagues that Iran's export of "Islamic fundamentalism" was a threat to U.S. interests. On the contrary, they perceived it as a potential weapon against the Soviet Union. They appreciated the influence of "Islamic fundamentalism" among the Afghan mujahedin, and some of them hoped this influence would spread into the Soviet Union's Asian republics, which had predominantly Muslim populations with historical and cultural ties to Iran.[24] They also believed that many "Islamic fundamentalists" in Tehran were at least as "moderate" as the Afghan mujahedin they knew and that in time it would be possible for Washington to reach an accommodation with these moderates based upon a common interest in opposing Soviet expansion.

The contradictory perspectives among Soviet-centric analysts impeded development of a coherent view regarding Iran's role in containment policy. It was not until 1984 that those concerned about communist influence in Iran and those preoccupied with Afghanistan began to share similar hopeful attitudes about moderates in Tehran. Ironically, the notion of moderates as Iranians basically sympathetic to the West evolved simultaneously with the increase in anti-American terrorist incidents in the Middle East. Nevertheless, some of the U.S. officials most prone to see Iran's invisible hands directing Arab airplane hijackers and kidnappers—for example, CIA director Casey and Robert McFarlane, who was Reagan's national security adviser from 1983 to 1985—were also among the most receptive to arguments about the presence of moderates in the Iranian government.

The second major objective of the Reagan administration's Middle East policy was to safeguard the security of the state of Israel. Even though there was no explicit treaty of alliance between the United States and Israel, relations between the two countries were very close, especially in the area of national security. Reagan and his advisers viewed Israel as a major "strategic asset" that could be counted upon to help protect American regional interests.[25] Nevertheless, they had to confront the persistent obstacle that had frustrated United States policy since 1945, when Israel was created out of the then British-administered Mandate of Palestine: how to persuade Israel and the Arab states to stop regarding each other, rather than the Soviet Union, as the principal threat to their security. To complicate the situation, Iran was a "loss" not only for the United States but also for Israel. Under the Shah, Iran had been one of the few regional states that was not antagonistic to Israel. Indeed, before the revolution swept him from power, the Shah had been a de facto ally of Israel.[26] The Islamic Republic now proclaimed hostility toward "the Zionist entity" and even called for the reestablishment of pre-1945 Palestine as an Arab and Muslim state, a position long since abandoned by the "moderate" Arab countries. Despite its rhetoric, few officials seriously believed that Iran posed any real threat to Israel. On the contrary, most of them tended to think that Iran's anti-Israel posture was a temporary phenomenon that would pass as revolutionary zeal gave way to pragmatism. There was a general assumption that the rulers in Tehran would eventually realize that their enemy, "radical" Arab nationalism, was also Israel's enemy. Since years of cooperation between the United States and Israel had fostered similar attitudes among policymakers in both countries, these views in Washington were reinforced by those in Tel Aviv.

The Israel-centric policymakers included Richard Allen, national security adviser in 1981–82, assistant for Middle East affairs Geoffrey Kemp at the NSC, Assistant Secretary of Defense Richard Perle, and Michael Ledeen, who initially was at the State Department but became a consultant to the NSC in November 1984. All Israel-centric officials were interested in ways of inducing Iran to resume, even if clandestinely, its cooperation with Israel. Initially there were two perspectives on how to accomplish this goal. One focused on Iran's perceived involvement with terrorism. Analysts preoccupied with terrorism believed that Iran supported the Palestine Liberation Organization (PLO) and other Palestinian groups they viewed as terrorists. Some foresaw the overthrow of the republican regime and the restoration of the monarchy as the best way to reverse Iranian policy. They pushed not only for covert American assistance to Iranian monarchists but also for secret operations undertaken by Israel. One former Israeli intelligence officer has revealed details of an elaborate but abortive 1982 plan, reportedly approved by CIA director Casey, to provide equipment and training for Iranian counterrevolutionary plotters who would be based in a camp in the Sudan.[27]

By 1981 most Israel-centric analysts probably did not have much confidence in the chances for success of a monarchist coup d'état. Their perspective on Iran was influenced by the arguments of some Israelis who viewed the Iran-Iraq war as an opportunity for Tel Aviv to rebuild contacts with the regime in

Tehran. Indeed, Israel had begun secretly to send military spare parts to Iran soon after Iraq invaded Iran in September 1980. Israel was a natural supply source for Iran because both countries had large arsenals of American-made weapons. The official U.S. policy toward the war, enunciated by President Carter and subsequently continued by Reagan, was neutrality, however, and a ban was imposed on any sales of American military equipment to either belligerent. In addition, public opinion in the United States was unreceptive to providing Iran with weapons. The Iraqi invasion had occurred while the hostage crisis was still unresolved and during the 1980 presidential election campaign. Consequently, there was considerable speculation about an "October surprise," meaning a release of the hostages before election day in return for the United States releasing military equipment that Iran had already paid for but whose delivery had been suspended after the American diplomats had been taken hostage in November 1979.[28] The equipment in question had not been released, not even as part of the Algerian-mediated agreement that ended the hostage crisis, and continued to be a contentious issue between Tehran and Washington throughout the Reagan administration.

Policymakers in Israel did not need to worry about potential Israeli political fallout resulting from arms sales to Iran. Israelis had long regarded the Ba'athist regime in Iraq as hostile. Baghdad had been the leader in the movement diplomatically to isolate and punish Egypt for signing the Camp David peace agreement with Israel in 1979. Thus, there were few qualms in Tel Aviv about selling Iran weapons to use against Iraq. Even though these sales were secret—neither Israel nor Iran cared to publicize them—Israeli leaders felt Washington's understanding of their position was essential in order to avoid possible recriminations about violating agreements on transferring American-made weapons to third countries. Significantly, one of Haig's first decisions as secretary of state was to approve of Israel's selling some of its American-made equipment to the Islamic Republic.[29] Although Israel-centric policymakers defended the secretive Israeli arms sales as serving the national interests of the United States, the policy was controversial within the administration. Officials who opposed the very notion of providing weapons to Iran probably were primary sources of leaks to the press. Although journalists obtained considerable detail about several transactions, the main parties, Israel and Iran, always denied the reports.[30]

Secretary of State Haig's ambition to involve Israel in a "strategic consensus" to confront the Soviet Union was probably the major reason he acquiesced to its secret arms sales policy. His sudden departure from the State Department in June 1982 in the wake of the Israeli invasion of Lebanon was a temporary setback for the proponents of secret arms sales among Israel-centric analysts.

Haig's successor, George Shultz, was skeptical that Iran could be wooed back to the West through clandestine weapons deals. On the contrary, he believed that the Iran-Iraq war itself was a threat to U.S. interests and was concerned about the ease with which Iran had apparently obtained American-made spare parts and weapons to prosecute the war. Shultz, in fact, initiated a policy in 1983 of trying to persuade U.S. allies to stop supplying weapons to Iran (Operation Staunch, discussed below). Nevertheless, there is no evidence that Shultz rescinded Haig's approval for Israel's secret transactions with Iran; these continued and even expanded, eventually involving the United States itself.

During 1983 a third Israel-centric perspective on Iran began to emerge. Like the other two perspectives, this one was influenced by attitudes in Israel, where a breakdown of the national security consensus was occurring as a result of the unpopular occupation of Lebanon (1982–85). The Israeli experience in Lebanon, where Shi'i militia groups violently resisted the occupation, convinced some leaders that the principal security threat no longer was radical Arab nationalism but Islamic fundamentalism. This new view differentiated between the moderate Arabs, with whom Israel could hope eventually to reach an accommodation, as it had done with Egypt, and the radical Arabs allied with fundamentalist Iran. The latter were perceived as anti-Israel and pro-Soviet. One of the more interesting developments was the evolution of attitudes in Israel toward Iraq. Prior to 1984, virtually all Israelis regarded Iraq as militantly radical. Fears that Baghdad might acquire an atomic weapons capability had even prompted the Israeli air force preemptively to bomb Iraq's nuclear reactor construction site in 1981.[31] By 1984, however, some Israelis were beginning to view Iraq as one of the moderate Arab countries. In contrast, they saw Iran as promoting an ideology inherently inimical to Israel. They were especially alarmed about Iran's role in Lebanon, and they tended to believe that the Lebanese Shi'i groups, who opposed the Israeli occupation of their country, were mere puppets of Tehran.[32]

The Israel-centric Americans who shared these views emerged out of the two other Israel-centric perspectives. In stark contrast to the Soviet-centric perspective that viewed Islamic fundamentalism as a potentially valuable force for containing the Soviet Union, this new attitude perceived Tehran as manipulating Islam to orchestrate terrorist actions against U.S. and Western interests in Lebanon and elsewhere in the Middle East. The seminal incident in forging this perspective was the October 1983 suicide attack on the U.S. Marine barracks in Beirut, a sensational event that left 241 Americans dead. Subsequent incidents in Lebanon, especially the kidnaping of CIA station chief William Buckley in March 1984, the additional kidnapings of Americans and other Westerners, and the June 1985 hijacking of a TWA airliner, contributed to consolidating this perspective and fostered an anti-Islamic phobia. Like their counterparts in Israel, this group of Israel-centric analysts saw no value to be gained by trying to woo Iran. Instead, they advocated a tilt toward Iraq in U.S. policy.[33]

Those policymakers who were preoccupied with the safety of American hostages in Lebanon, especially that of CIA agent Buckley, investigated various strategies to secure their freedom. Since they believed that Iran controlled the Lebanese who held the hostages, it was perhaps inevitable that some of them would find arguments about moderates in Tehran appealing. Although many motives certainly played a role in the secret arms sales policy that was pursued in 1985–86, a few Israel-centric analysts probably genuinely believed that the weapons would help strengthen the position of Iranian moderates, who in turn could order the release of the captive Americans in Beirut.

The different perspectives on Iran among Israel-centric analysts hindered formulation of a unified policy line. What is significant, however, is that during 1984 some of those who were antagonistic toward Iran and some of those who believed in the commonality of interests between Iran and Israel began to share similar ideas about perceived moderates in the government of the Islamic Republic, albeit for very different reasons. This was also the time that some Soviet-centric policymakers became interested in Tehran's moderates. By 1985, then, there was a core base of support for a secret overture toward Iran. Even though important officials such as Shultz and Weinberger continued to believe that the arguments about moderates were, at best, wishful thinking, the ideological support, combined with the backing that others provided for the initiative for a variety of unrelated reasons including outright greed, was sufficient to push this effort forward.

The third major Reagan administration policy objective in the Middle East was the protection of U.S. vital interests, namely, oil and other important economic assets. This objective was necessarily intertwined with U.S. policy toward the Arab countries, especially the so-called moderate states of the Persian Gulf, which together possessed nearly one-half of the world's petroleum reserves. The governments of these countries—Bahrain, Kuwait, Oman, Qatar, Saudi Arabia, and the United Arab Emirates—along with those of Egypt, Jordan, and Morocco, had close ties with the United States. Washington considered all of these countries moderate because they supported overall U.S. policy goals. Specifically, they accepted the U.S. commitment to the security of Israel, although Egypt was the only Arab country that formally recognized the Jewish state. The other countries tolerated Israel's existence, but they were suspicious of Israel and insisted that it had to negotiate with the PLO about the fate of the Palestinians before they would consider the question of diplomatic relations. The failure of Israel and the moderate Arab states to reach an accommodation was a persistent problem for Washington, but generally the United States had learned to fashion its regional policy to keep a balance between the contradictory interests of its allies.

Like the Israel-centric analysts, the views of Arab-centric policymakers about Iran were influenced by the attitudes of their counterparts in the moderate Arab states. During the period 1981–86, Arab leaders in the Persian Gulf area were concerned about the Iranian Revolution's impact on their own societies and the effect of the Iran-Iraq war on oil exports and regional security. Iran's rhetoric about exporting revolution had receptive audiences among the Shi'i communities of Bahrain, Kuwait, and Saudi Arabia, although the strength of Iran's appeal probably was exaggerated both in Tehran and in the Arab states.[34] However much the conflict between Iran and Iraq was unwelcome, there was a general perception in early 1981 that the war had sapped Iran's ability to support subversive activities.

Thus, at the outset of Reagan's first term in office, Arab-centric policymakers did not sense a compelling need to deal with Iran. Beginning in late 1981, however, Iran and the war became a source of concern. In December, an unsuccessful coup attempt in Bahrain alarmed Washington and revived fears throughout the Persian Gulf about Iranian-inspired subversive movements.[35] At the same time, Iran demonstrated that it had recovered from the shock of the initial invasion by launching several limited but successful offensives. By the summer of 1982, Iran had pushed Iraqi forces out of most of the areas originally occupied early in the war and had then sent its own troops into Iraq. Even though Iraq eventually halted the Iranian advance, American officials did not believe that there was any realistic hope of Iraq's defeating Iran militarily.

During these critical developments in the war, Arab-centric analysts were in fact preoccupied with mitigating the effects of Israel's invasion of Lebanon on U.S. relations with its Arab allies. Thus, it was not until early 1983 that they focused on the situation in the Persian Gulf. They perceived the continuance of the war as a threat to the stability of the region, but there was no consensus on what would constitute an effective strategy for bringing about an end to the fighting. Two perspectives gradually emerged. The first viewed both Islamic Iran and socialist Iraq as potential long-term threats to U.S. allies. The preferred solution to the conflict, as stated by Assistant Secretary of State Richard Murphy in 1984, was one in which "a victory by either side is neither militarily achievable nor strategically desirable."[36] In other words, the best security shield for America's regional allies would be a peace that left both Iran and Iraq unvanquished but sufficiently exhausted that they would have little ambition to intimidate their smaller neighbors. This viewpoint interpreted Iraq's ability to withstand Iran's major offensives in 1982 and 1983 as evidence that the regime in Baghdad was at least as resilient as the one in Tehran. When Iraq survived further massive offensives in 1984 and 1985, Arab-centric analysts became convinced that both Arab Ba'athists and Iranian fundamentalists would be in power for some time. They believed that neutrality best served the interests of the Persian Gulf states and the United States and supported United Nations and other third-party efforts to mediate a cease-fire.[37] Directly confronting Iran, they argued, would probably only provoke Tehran into retaliating with terrorist actions that would be more destabilizing to the moderate Arab states than a policy of waiting for time and the realities of politics to moderate Iran's policies in the Persian Gulf.

The second Arab-centric perspective anticipated the possibility of an Iraqi defeat and feared that any outright Iranian victory would embolden Tehran to interfere in the Persian Gulf even more extensively and more directly than it already was suspected of doing. Analysts of this persuasion advocated a more assertive U.S. role in ending the war. They argued that the war had developed in response to Iranian provocations and that its continuation was due to Iran's intransigence.[38] Consequently, they advocated measures that would restrict Tehran's capacity to wage war. They were aware of the reports of secret Israeli arms sales to Iran and felt strongly that the United States should pressure Israel to stop them. They supported Operation Staunch, the effort initiated by the State Department in 1983 to curb the flow of weapons to Iran from third countries. Operation Staunch proved to be a frustrating policy, since it failed to dissuade several NATO allies, including France, Portugal, Spain, and Turkey, from semiclandestinely selling arms to Iran between 1983 and 1986; Israel simply ignored the program.

The Arab-centric officials were more effective with a second objective, namely, to tilt U.S. policy from neutrality to support for Iraq. This was a significant diplomatic development because the Reagan administration had come to office with the view that Iraq was an agent of Soviet subversion in the Middle East. This view had formed in the late 1960s and early 1970s when the Ba'athist regime had broadcast vitriolic anti-American rhetoric over regional airwaves, built up its military with Soviet arms and training, and applauded terrorist acts against Israeli and American interests in the Middle East. But in the early 1980s the same Ba'athist regime, albeit with some new faces, was eager for a rapprochement with the United States. This was a gradual process coaxed along by many midwives, including Egypt, Jordan, Kuwait, and Saudi Arabia and an atypical coalition of liberal and conservative politicians in Washington. A sympathetic study of Saddam Hussein and his regime by Christine

Moss Helms published by the Brookings Institution, a respected policy think tank, helped foster the budding relationship.[39] All these efforts bore fruit: in 1982 the Reagan administration dropped Iraq from the list of pariah countries that supported international terrorism; in 1983 the United States extended some $400 million in credits to Iraq to finance the purchase of American commodities; and in November 1984 Washington and Baghdad reestablished diplomatic relations after a hiatus of more than seventeen years.[40]

In tandem with the diplomatic tilt toward Iraq was a military effort to contain Iran. The outbreak of the "tanker war" (Iraqi attacks on third-country ships carrying Persian Gulf oil with some Iranian retaliation) provided an opportunity for U.S. military intervention beginning in early 1984. Plans directly related to this policy included allowing American warships in the Persian Gulf to shoot at any aircraft that approached within five miles; sending AWACS and Stinger antiaircraft missiles to Saudi Arabia; providing escorts in the Gulf for oil tankers chartered by the U.S. Navy for refueling its warships at sea; and pressing Arab countries for use of their military facilities.[41] The Arab-centric analysts who pushed for this policy were probably the officials most surprised by the November 1986 revelations of secret U.S. arms sales to Iran. Nevertheless, the military plans that were implemented in 1984, 1985, and 1986 greatly facilitated the highly publicized intervention that began in 1987.[42]

The Arab-centric perspectives on Iran were thus as contradictory as those of the Soviet-centric and Israel-centric analysts. The simultaneous coexistence of all these contradictory views prevented the Reagan administration from formulating a coherent strategic policy vis-à-vis Iran in the period 1981–86. Nevertheless, as the different nuances within these three perspectives evolved, two distinct policy trends had crystallized by early 1985. On the one hand, an ideological anti-Soviet policy viewed Moscow as the principal threat to U.S. interests in the Middle East. Iran, with varying degrees of enthusiasm, was perceived as a country whose leaders included some moderates with whom the United States might expect to cooperate in opposing Moscow's expansion in the Middle East. On the other hand, an ideological anti-Iran policy perceived the Islamic Republic as the principal threat to U.S. interests in the Persian Gulf region. This policy envisaged a containment strategy undertaken in collaboration with friendly Arab regimes. By the end of 1985 and throughout 1986 the administration was thus pursuing two official policies toward Iran: one track was the overt policy of confronting Iran diplomatically and militarily through such measures as Operation Staunch and the expansion of regional military forces; the second track was the covert one of selling arms to Iran in consort with Israel, and even proceeding with plans for secret high-level negotiations with Iran.

These contradictory policies were exposed in November 1986 when a Beirut newspaper published details of McFarlane's secret trip to Tehran five months earlier (see chapter 7 for an analysis of the overture that culminated in McFarlane's visit). The revelations about the covert policy undoubtedly shocked many Arab-centric analysts and caused severe dismay in Arab countries. The sensational aspect of the covert policy—the diversion of profits from the secret arms sales to Nicaraguan Contras and the pockets of arms dealers—intensified the general sense of embarrassment. Arab-centric officials in both the Defense and State departments feared that six years of efforts to develop a strategic relationship with moderate Arab states could be destroyed by the scandal. They consequently urged that contacts with Tehran be terminated as long as the Iran-Iraq war continued and that the United States involve itself more directly in efforts to end the conflict. They received crucial support for a reinvigorated containment-of-Iran policy from their Soviet-centric colleagues who were concerned that Moscow could exploit the situation to expand its own influence in the Persian Gulf region.

Soviet-centric fears about the Kremlin's influence seemed to materialize in February 1987 when the Soviet Union responded affirmatively to a Kuwaiti request to lease three of its oil tankers. Kuwait had been trying to obtain superpower protection for its shipping since the summer of 1984, when Iran began to retaliate for Iraqi missile attacks against its seaborne oil trade by striking tankers carrying the oil of Baghdad's Arab allies. Although the United States had avoided direct involvement in this tanker war, the Reagan administration was alarmed by what it perceived to be Soviet intervention. Washington consequently agreed to permit Kuwait to place eleven of its tankers under the American flag.[43] As Gary Sick explains (see chapter 10), events escalated so quickly during the spring and summer that by mid-1987 the United States was confronting Iran both diplomatically and militarily. Although this new policy of active containment was in stark contrast to the secret arms sales policy of 1985–86, both actually were prompted by a similar motive: desire to check expanding Soviet influence.

The containment-of-Iran policy acquired broad support within the administration. Soviet-centric officials believed that the naval flotilla dispatched to the Persian Gulf demonstrated American resolve to defend vital interests and reassured nervous allies.[44] Arab-centric analysts felt that the strong military presence showed moderate Arabs that Washington shared their goals of ending the war and valued their friendship. Some Israel-centric officials agreed with the views of Soviet and Arab specialists; others were relieved to have attention diverted away from Israel's role in the once secret but now infamous arms sales to Iran. The stated objective of the policy was to secure a negotiated settlement of the Iran-Iraq war. Privately, some officials acknowledged that the goal was to intimidate Iran.[45] In contrast to the 1981–86 period, there was no ambiguity: this was a clear anti-Iran policy. This explicit bias probably contributed to prolonging the war by as much as one year, since Tehran was reluctant to give the impression of surrendering to American pressure.

Iran's July 1988 decision, after a year of temporizing, to accept U.N. Resolution 598 (calling for an end to the war) surprised the Reagan administration. Nevertheless, officials were quick to attribute it to the American intervention; after the U.S.-supervised cease-fire went into effect, they expressed public satisfaction with the success of their policy. Undoubtedly, the U.S. intervention was a factor in Iran's decision, but many other factors, such as Iraq's intensified use of chemical weapons and general war-weariness after eight years of fighting, also were important.[46] More relevant was the effect of the intervention. Rather than teaching Iran a lesson as its supporters had hoped, it reinforced anti-American stereotypes among Iranian leaders. Thus, at the end of eight years, the Reagan administration's policy toward Iran was as unlikely to encourage a mutual accommodation as it had been in 1981.[47]

Notes

1. According to Reagan's first secretary of state, Alexander Haig, abrogation of the just-negotiated Algiers Accord was seriously discussed at the initial meeting of the new administration's National Security Council on 21 January 1981. Haig, who was appalled by the suggestion, names James Baker, Reagan's first chief of staff and eight years later George Bush's choice to be secretary of state, as one of those "in sympathy" with the "amazing proposition." See Alexander M. Haig, Jr., *Caveat: Realism, Reagan, and Foreign Policy* (New York: Macmillan, 1984), 78–79.

2. See Richard W. Cottam, *Iran and the United States: A Cold War Case Study* (Pittsburgh: University of Pittsburgh Press, 1988), 116–17, 244.

3. I have analyzed the influences of these three perspectives in "Reagan's Iran: Factions behind U.S. Policy in the Gulf," *Middle East Report*, no. 151 (March–April 1988): 29–31.

4. My analysis of Reagan administration policy toward Iran derives from my research as senior analyst from 1986 to 1988 at the National Security Archive in Washington, D.C. During this period I discussed aspects of policy and conducted interviews with both current and former officials and met regularly with foreign affairs analysts, journalists, and scholars interested in the Middle East. I am grateful to the archive's executive director, Scott Armstrong, for providing me with the opportunity to undertake this research. My sources within the U.S. government have requested anonymity, and I shall respect their wishes, trusting that they understand my appreciation for their assistance.

5. For an excellent summary of the Reagan administration's Cold War ideology, see Fred Halliday, *Soviet Policy in the Arc of Crisis* (Washington: Institute for Policy Studies, 1981), 7–25.

6. Claudia Wright, "Neutral or Neutralized? Iraq, Iran, and the Superpowers," in *The Iran-Iraq War: New Weapons, Old Conflicts*, ed. Shireen Tahir-Kheli and Shaheen Ayubi (New York: Praeger, 1983), 185–86.

7. The "loss" of Iran is the theme of the book Ledeen wrote with William Lewis, *Debacle: The American Failure in Iran* (New York: Alfred Knopf, 1981).

8. Haig, for example, believed that the Shah had been "seduced and abandoned by the American government" and that the Soviet Union could get control of the Islamic movement. See

his *Caveat*, 6, 30. For Kirkpatrick's view of how the United States lost Iran, see her article "Dictatorships and Double Standards," in *Commentary*, November 1979, 40–41.

9. Howard Teicher of the NSC was one official who argued that the U.S. "loss" was not nor need be a Soviet gain. See his "Strategy and Politics: A U.S. Perception," in *The Middle East in Global Strategy*, ed. Aurel Braun (Boulder, Colo.: Westview Press, 1987), 13–23.

10. The Reagan administration's early dilemma in trying to understand an Iran that was simultaneously anti-American and anti-Soviet is analyzed by Richard W. Cottam, "Iran and Soviet-American Relations," in *The Iranian Revolution and the Islamic Republic*, ed. Nikki R. Keddie and Eric Hooglund (Syracuse: Syracuse University Press, 1986), 230–39.

11. The Iranian students who seized the U.S. embassy in Tehran in November 1979 captured thousands of pages of classified State Department and CIA documents, which they subsequently published in more than sixty volumes. Most major libraries have sets of these volumes, and they are also available through distributors of Iran-related books. Some of the CIA cables, many reconstituted from shredded documents, pertain to contacts with monarchists and other opposition figures during the summer and fall of 1979. For examples of these cables, see volumes 31 and 32 of *Documents from the Nest of Spies* (Tehran: Muslim Students Following the Imam's Line, n.d.).

12. One scholar maintains that most Reagan administration officials were dubious about the monarchists' popular support in Iran and thus did not respond enthusiastically to their appeals for assistance in staging an anti-Khomeini coup. See Richard W. Cottam, "The United States and Revolutionary Iran," *Soviet-American Relations with Pakistan, Iran and Afghanistan*, ed. Hafeez Malik (New York: St. Martin's Press, 1987), 233, 243 n. 31.

13. For details, see Bob Woodward, *Veil: The Secret Wars of the CIA, 1981–1987* (New York: Simon and Schuster, 1987), 111–12.

14. For the history of the Tudeh, see Ervand Abrahamian, *Iran between Two Revolutions* (Princeton: Princeton University Press, 1982), 281–318.

15. In December 1979 and January 1980, the Department of State assembled thousands of pages of official documents for an official history of the U.S. relationship with Iran since the end of World War II. Known as the White Paper, much of this collection of reports and documents has been declassified. Originally, the White Paper was divided into major sections, one of which dealt with studies of the Tudeh that had been undertaken by different government agencies. Several declassified analyses of the Tudeh are included in the special microfilm collection of documents prepared by the nonprofit National Security Archive. See Eric Hooglund, ed., "DOS White Paper: Studies of the Tudeh," in *Iran: The Making of U.S. Policy, 1977–1980* (Alexandria, Va.: Chadwyck-Healey and National Security Archive, 1989).

16. For more detail, see Dilip Hiro, *Iran under the Ayatollahs* (London: Routledge and Kegan Paul, 1985), 226–27.

17. Some scholars accepted without question the alarmist views of the Tudeh's penetration of the government. See, for example, Said Amir Arjomand, *The Turban for the Crown: The Islamic Revolution in Iran* (New York: Oxford University Press, 1988), 159.

18. Aryeh Yodfat, *The Soviet Union and Revolutionary Iran* (London: Croom Helm, 1984), 132.

19. Sources in the departments of State and Defense confirmed to me that British intelligence shared information obtained from the Soviet defector Vladimir Kuzichkin from the earliest stages of his debriefing. These same sources, however, either did not know or were unwilling to disclose whether the proposal to share Kuzichkin's list with Iran originated in Washington or London, or when this proposal was first made and to whom it was passed. According to one British journalist, who does not cite a source, MI6 passed the names to Iran in October 1982. See John Simpson, *Inside Iran: Life under Khomeini's Regime* (New York: St. Martin's Press, 1988), 99. However, the *Washington Post* of 13 Jan. 1987 says the Americans passed the names to Iran in May 1983.

20. For details, see Hiro, *Iran under the Ayatollahs*, 227–30.

21. These documents were declassified by the special presidential commission established at the end of 1986 to investigate the scandal of U.S. arms sales to Iran and the diversion of profits to the Nicaraguan Contras. For their texts, see John Tower, Edmund Muskie, and Brent Scowcroft, *The Tower Commission Report* (New York: Bantam Books, 1987), 112–21.

22. On Reagan administration support for the Afghan mujahedin, see Steven Galster, "Rivalry and Reconciliation in Afghanistan: What Prospects for the Accords?" *Third World Quarterly* 10, no. 4 (October 1988): 1528–31.

23. For analyses of Iranian-Soviet tensions over Afghanistan, see Aryeh Yodfat, *The Soviet Union and Revolutionary Iran*, 111–12, and Malcolm Yapp, "The Soviet Union and Iran since 1978," in *The Soviet Union and the Middle East in the 1980s*, ed. Mark Kauppi and R. Craig Nation (Lexington, Mass.: D. C. Heath, 1983), 228–30.

24. An example of a scholarly study that influenced these officials' view of Islam as a potential source of political instability for the Soviet Union is A. Bennigsen and M. Broxup, *The Islamic Threat to the Soviet Union* (New York: St. Martin's Press, 1983).

25. Joe Stork, "Israel as a Strategic Asset," in *MERIP Reports*, no. 105 (May 1982): 7.

26. For a brief analysis of Iran's ties with Israel under the Shah, see Farhad Kazemi, "Iran, Israel, and the Arab-Israeli Balance," in *Iran since the Revolution: Internal Dynamics, Regional Conflicts, and the Superpowers*, ed. Barry Rosen (New York: Columbia University Press, 1985), 86–90.

27. See Samuel Segev, *The Iranian Triangle: The Untold Story of Israel's Role in the Iran-Contra Affair* (New York: Macmillan, 1988).

28. For details, see Gary Sick, *All Fall Down: America's Tragic Encounter with Iran* (New York: Random House, 1985), 313–15. Some writers have maintained that officials associated with the Reagan election campaign even tried to prevent a pre-election release of the hostages. See Jonathan Marshall, Peter Scott, and Jane Hunter, *The Iran-Contra Connection: Secret Teams and Covert Operations in the Reagan Era* (Boston: South End Press, 1987), 162–66. See n. 47.

29. *Washington Post*, 29 Nov. 1986.

30. For examples of detailed reports on Israeli weapons sales, see the *Washington Post*, 21 May 1982 and 20 Aug. 1982; *Aerospace Daily*, 18 Aug. 1982; and *Time*, 25 July 1983.

31. An article that argues that Iraq was developing a nuclear weapons capability at its Tuwaitha Atomic Center when Israel bombed the site in June 1987 is Jed Snyder, "The Road to Osiraq: Baghdad's Quest for the Bomb," *Middle East Journal* 37, no. 4 (Autumn 1983): 565–93.

32. Clinton Bailey, a Tel Aviv University professor who is an authority on Lebanese Shi'i politics, contends that groups such as Hizbollah and Islamic Amal are loyal to directives from Tehran. See his "Lebanon's Shi'is after the 1982 War," in *Shi'ism, Resistance, and Revolution*, ed. Martin Kramer (Boulder, Colo.: Westview Press, 1988), 220, 234 n. 2.

33. For an example of Israel-centric views sympathetic to Iraq, see Milton Viorst, "Iraq at War," *Foreign Affairs* 65, no. 2 (1986): 349–65.

34. For an overview of the impact of the Iranian Revolution on the Shi'i communities in the Arab states of the Persian Gulf, see R. K. Ramazani, "Shi'ism in the Persian Gulf," in *Shi'ism and Social Protest*, ed. Juan R. I. Cole and Nikki R. Keddie (New Haven: Yale University Press, 1986), 30–54.

35. Ibid., 49–51.

36. Excerpts from Murphy's testimony before Congress, *Christian Science Monitor*, 14 June 1984.

37. In March 1985 U.N. Secretary-General Javier Pérez de Cuellar had presented an eight-point proposal for ending hostilities. In April he visited both Baghdad and Tehran to discuss this peace plan.

38. For an example of this thinking, see Nita Renfrew, "Who Started the War?" *Foreign Policy*, no. 66 (1987): 98–108.

39. See Christine Moss Helms, *Iraq: Eastern Flank of the Arab World* (Washington: Brookings Institution, 1984).

40. The U.S. tilt toward Iraq is analyzed in Joe Stork and Martha Wenger, "U.S. Ready to Intervene in the Gulf War," *MERIP Reports,* nos. 125–26 (July–September 1984): 44–48.

41. Ibid., 46–47; and Fred Lawson, "The Reagan Administration in the Middle East," *MERIP Reports,* no. 128 (November–December 1984): 27–34.

42. For details on the U.S. military intervention of 1987–88, see the chapter by Gary Sick in this book.

43. See Eric Hooglund, "Iran," in *Intervention in the 1980s: United States Foreign Policy in the Third World,* ed. Peter Schraeder (Boulder, Colo.: Lynne Rienner, 1989), 311–12.

44. A good analysis of anti-Soviet attitudes as they pertain to the 1987 military buildup in the Persian Gulf is Nikki R. Keddie, "Iranian Imbroglios: Who's Irrational?" *World Policy Journal* 5, no. 1 (Winter 1987–88): 44.

45. Interviews with officials of Defense and State departments, September and December 1987, and January, February, and May 1988.

46. For an analysis of the war's impact on Iranian politics and society, see Eric Hooglund, "The Iranian Revolution at War and Peace," *Middle East Report,* no. 156 (January–February 1989).

47. A letter from Gary Sick, 30 November 1989, notes the continuing accumulation of circumstantial evidence that members of the election campaign of Reagan and Bush struck a deal with Iran to delay the release of the American hostages until after the elections in 1980. The evidence includes assertions that meetings involving supporters of Reagan, Israelis, and Iranians were held in Europe in September and October 1980. Hushang Lavi, an Iranian-American arms dealer who says he was present, told Sick that he understood the meetings to have been aimed at persuading Iran to delay its release of the hostages until after the elections, in return for which Israel would sell arms to Iran with the acquiescence of the United States. Although Richard Allen, foreign policy adviser to Reagan's campaign, emphatically denies that the campaign would have authorized this, he told Sick that he could not be sure "self-starters" in the campaign would not have made such efforts on their own. In January 1981, just after the hostages were freed, Israel resumed major arms deliveries to Iran, which continued for several years. Details of the deliveries were provided to the Reagan administration, which did not intervene to stop them. In Sick's view, this does "not prove that a deal was ever consummated or in fact resulted in the delay of the release of the hostages. However, the sequence of events is not inconsistent with such a possibility and has led some observers, myself included, to reconsider their judgment that such an eventuality was highly improbable."

IV | The Fateful Triangle

9

Rules of the Game: The Geopolitics of U.S. Policy Options in Southwest Asia

BRUCE R. KUNIHOLM

United States policy options in the Persian Gulf region are informed by the geopolitical dynamics of Southwest Asia during the nineteenth and twentieth centuries. The British historian Malcolm Yapp has characterized these dynamics as a product of the relationships among the local powers of the Gulf coast that were geographically isolated; regional powers centered in Baghdad, Riyadh, and Tehran; and international powers such as the Ottoman Empire, Egypt, France, Germany, Russia, Britain, and the United States.[1] Central to an understanding of the dynamics of these relationships is the fact that British predominance, more limited than many suppose, was confined generally to the lesser powers of the lower Gulf.

On the local level, the stability created by British control reinforced the paternalistic and authoritarian leadership of the small coastal states. It also helped preserve the region's traditional sociopolitical organization, which was characterized by a complicated and delicate balance of power among tribal dynasties. The ruling factions of the small city-states were generally protected by the British from absorption by their neighbors and such protection enhanced their prestige. Although engaged in a confusing complex of feuds, intrigues, raids, and wars, the tribal chiefs, most of whom in the early nineteenth century could hardly be called rulers, gradually came to acquire the authority sufficient to merit the title.[2]

Regional powers such as Iran, Iraq, and Saudi Arabia meanwhile had sufficient geographical advantages, resources, and energies to avoid complete domination and play various international powers off against one another. But until these countries were able to assert themselves, as they did later in the twentieth century, they were otherwise preoccupied, first, with the problem of survival and, subsequently, with the need to provide security for their oil, as well as with difficulties that accompanied internal modernization. Under these circumstances, the status quo prevailed and the illusion of British supremacy was perpetuated by the framework of consent within which the British exercised their influence.[3]

On the international level, British concern for the security of British India had been precipitated by perceptions of the threat posed by Russia, which was expanding eastward by land as Europe's maritime states had by sea. When Russia acquired valuable land from northwest Iran and eastern Turkey in the treaties of Turkmanchay and Adrianople (1828 and 1829), the British became anxious about the new Russian frontiers. Having failed to create protectorates in either Persia or Turkey, they sought to devise a counterweight to Russian influence. Eventually they attempted to construct a zone of buffer states from Turkey through Persia to Khiva and Bokhara—recognized by both Russia and Britain as independent, possessing recognized boundaries, and preserved by equal British and Russian pressures.[4]

The competition for influence in the region that separated these expanding imperial rivals was characterized in different ways—from the Eastern Question to the Great Game. Over time, the Great Game of advancing and protecting great power interests resulted in modi vivendi whose rules included the implicit assumption that there should be an equilibrium of forces in the region and that vital interests should not be threatened. When observed, these arrangements maintained the balance of power in the region and (if they were deficient in dealing with the region's emerging nationalist forces) were capable of mitigating tensions between the great powers. In the Anglo-Russian Convention of 1907, for example, Russia acknowledged British ascendancy in Afghanistan (although Britain agreed not to annex it), and Persia was partitioned into zones of political and economic influence: a northern zone, which was Russia's sphere; a southeastern zone, which was Britain's sphere; and a central zone, which was neutral. In 1915–16, in the course of attempting to resolve the Eastern Question, Britain and Russia contributed to plans to partition the Ottoman Empire. Among the agreements that were reached were Britain's acknowledgment of Russia's right to annex the Turkish Straits and the adjacent Ottoman territories as well as over sixty thousand square miles of eastern Turkey and Russia's concession of control of most of the neutral zone in Persia to Britain. Within a few years of these agreements, a number of factors (the Bolshevik Revolution, the final collapse of the Ottoman Empire, and the region's emerging nationalist movements) contributed to their obsolescence—at least in Turkey and Iran.

During World War II, however, the Soviet Union and Great Britain again divided Iran into spheres of influence when they occupied it in August 1941. In October 1944, Churchill and Stalin's "percentages" agreement did somewhat the same for the Balkans. The countries that were subject to these understandings, meanwhile, did what they could to survive. In the period between World War I and World War II, for example, they allied among themselves against threats from without. The Balkan Pact of 1934, signed by Turkey, Greece, Romania, and Yugoslavia and supported by Britain, was directed against an irredentist Bulgaria. The Sa'adabad Pact of 1937 among Turkey, Iraq, Iran, and Afghanistan was directed against Soviet interference in their affairs. As such, it constituted an attempt to escape from the traditional rivalries to which they were subjected. The only alternative to forming alliances was playing one power off against the other, balancing them in one form or another, or looking to third powers, such as Germany, for assistance.

After World War II, however, survival of these states was threatened by the relative disparity between Soviet and British power. If Afghanistan retained its traditional role of a buffer state, Turkey and Iran were subjected to Soviet pressures (which exceeded wartime understandings) and risked being drawn into the Soviet orbit. Given Britain's imperialistic legacy and postwar difficulties, Turkey and Iran sought U.S. assistance as a countervailing force to balance Soviet pressures. The end result of the series of crises that played themselves out in the region in the early postwar years was the Truman Doctrine, which constituted a qualified commitment by the United States to maintain the balance of power in the Near East.

Elsewhere I have examined the evolution of U.S. policy during the postwar years and described the process by which the United States assumed Britain's role in maintaining the balance of power in the Near East as the British inexorably withdrew from the region—from Greece, Turkey, India, and Palestine in the 1940s; from Suez in the 1950s; and from east of Suez in the late 1960s and early 1970s.[5] Suffice it to note that in the course of continuing Britain's traditional policy of containment, and its implicit notion of an equilibrium of forces in the region, the United States, because of limited resources, collaborated with the British, whose imperial legacy was seen as less of a problem than the threat posed by the Soviet Union. Anglo-American collaboration, however, impeded better relations with the region's emerging nationalist forces, whose differences with Britain threatened to undermine the very policy (containment of Soviet influence) that collaboration was designed to support. In the 1950s, for example, when developments in Iran forced the United States to choose between Britain and Iranian nationalism, the United States sided with the British. Instead of supporting a viable, more democratic alternative to the Shah, the Truman administration limited Prime Minister Mohammad Mosaddeq's options and forced him into a corner; the Eisenhower administration, using the pretext of a nonexistent alliance between Mosaddeq and the Soviet Union, violated the principle of sovereignty that previous administrations had pledged to uphold, overthrew Mosaddeq, and reinstalled the Shah. In the process, the United States assumed Britain's imperial role in the region.

The Truman administration's unrealistic rhetoric, meanwhile, which at the time of the Truman Doctrine mobilized public opinion in support of sensible policies, increasingly influenced U.S. policies in the region. Under Eisenhower, abstractions would justify security interests and impose themselves on a changing world for which those abstractions were increasingly irrelevant. The Eisenhower Doctrine, for example, was rooted in a misperception of regional problems and a mistaken assumption of a communist threat. Toward the end of the Eisenhower administration, meanwhile, the United States negotiated a series of bilateral agreements along the so-called Northern Tier of the Middle East that effectively institutionalized American military support to Turkey (already a NATO ally), Iran, and Pakistan.

Following Britain's decision in 1968 to withdraw from the Persian Gulf in 1971, the United States sought to bolster its policy of containment and to ensure stability in the Gulf through cooperation with Iran (which American officials recognized as the region's predominant power) and Saudi Arabia. But exclusive reliance on the Shah—to protect U.S. interests under the Nixon Doctrine—fed his megalomania as well as his obsession with security and contributed substantially to the Iranian Revolution. The revolution was motivated in considerable part by opposition to the monarchy, foreign control of Iran, and cultural domination by the West. Failure of the United States to abide by the rules of the Great Game of imperial rivalry in Iran, it has been suggested, inadvertently paved the way for the Soviets to break them in Afghanistan.[6] In any event, the Iranian Revolution and the Soviet invasion of Afghanistan left the "twin pillar" policy of the United States (which relied on Iran and Saudi Arabia for regional defense) in ruins.

The response of President Jimmy Carter to these developments was the Carter Doctrine, under which the president publicly emphasized the United States' vital stake in the Persian Gulf and, in a departure from the Nixon Doctrine, assumed responsibility for regional defense. The Carter administration subsequently began construction of a security framework for the Persian Gulf and Southwest Asia, complete with improved regional capabilities and facilities that would be accessible to the Rapid Deployment force (subsequently the Central Command). The Reagan administration, after flirting with the notion of "a consensus of strategic concerns," which ended when officials discovered (as their predecessors had in the 1950s) that there was no strategic consensus in the region, consolidated the security framework initiated by President Carter and reverted to the policy of supporting "regional influentials" such as Turkey, Saudi Arabia, and Pakistan.

This brief retrospect of U.S. policies in the Middle East underscores a continuing concern for geopolitical realities. It also suggests that a concern for geopolitical factors has made it difficult for the United States or the Soviet Union to respond constructively to the region's emerging nationalist forces. When the two have conflicted, and countries in the region have been treated as pawns or surrogates, both the United States and the Soviet Union have discovered, as did their imperial predecessors, that their control was far more limited than they imagined. Nationalist forces (benefiting in part from the constraints that the balance of power places on great power interference) have eventually triumphed. That, it seems, is the lesson of the Iranian Revolution and the Afghan resistance.

Insight into the reasons the United States and the Soviet Union have had such a difficult time in the region is suggested by L. Carl Brown, who argues that a distinctive system of international politics—which he calls "the Eastern Question system"—has emerged in the Middle East. This system, similar to that described earlier by Malcolm Yapp, is characterized by an international and a regional power system, each composed of a multiplicity of autonomous political entities whose efforts to attain hegemony over the region have provoked counterbalancing efforts that illustrate the region's "stubborn penchant for kaleidoscopic equilibrium." In fact, Brown contends, no outside power has been able to dominate and organize the Middle East, no state within the Middle East has been able to establish regional predominance, and neither the victories nor the losses of outside powers seem as impressive in the long run as they might first appear.[7] Brown's interpretation is not without problems; its restricted definition of the Middle East, moreover, excludes Iran. Nonetheless, the history of the so-called buffer zone between empires over the last two centuries, and more recently the experience of both the Americans in Iran and the Soviets in Afghanistan, would seem to support Brown's argument along the Northern Tier.

According to Brown's interpretation, since no great powers have been able to dominate and organize the Middle East and since they can generally maintain a minimal position in the system at a relatively limited risk and cost, they should recognize the limitations on their influence and act accordingly. In short, Brown suggests, great powers could benefit if they followed more circumspect foreign policies and sought more limited diplomatic commitments.

The "correlation of forces" in the Middle East described by Brown is similar to that in the rest of the world as a whole, which, as the historian John Gaddis has observed, "favors the hegemonial aspirations of no one." No nation, it appears, has been able to exercise preeminence over the combination of forces that can be marshaled against it. To the extent that U.S. and Soviet forces balance each other (and this, it seems, should be the thrust of any containment policy), another of Gaddis's observations is also pertinent: "The superpower that can bring itself to accommodate diversity now will be the one most likely to maintain its status and position over the long haul."[8] The West, Gaddis argues, is in a better position to accommodate diversity than the Soviet Union; he also asserts that the real threat to diversity is not communism but the Soviet Union. If he is right, and I think he is, then the central thrust of any containment policy in the Middle East should be a capacity to deter the Soviet military from imposing its will on others. That is what the balance of power is all about. But that is not sufficient, nor should we become so obsessed with it that we lost sight of a related concern. The key is to ensure that others, such as the Afghans and the Iranians, have the freedom to choose their own governments, and that we can distinguish those situations in which ensuring such a choice is vital to our interests.

The geopolitical lessons identified by Brown have been borne out by the fall of the Shah, the war in Lebanon, and even more recently by events that have led the Soviet Union to withdraw from Afghanistan. In the Persian Gulf, these lessons suggest that U.S. military strategy should be to deter a unilateral Soviet threat to, as well as serious attempts by regional powers to exercise hegemony over, the Gulf by maintaining a limited ability to project strategic forces in the region.[9] A sensitivity to the concerns of countries in the region, meanwhile, suggests that preparations to counter the most serious (and least likely) threats may encourage and even precipitate regional instabilities. Playing down the most serious threats and discounting the efficacy of military force, on the other hand, could leave some of the Gulf states open to intimidation; and intimidation, in turn, could encourage regional initiatives that increase a destabilizing regional or Soviet influence to the detriment of vital U.S. interests.

These dilemmas suggest that a symbolic equilibrium between Soviet land forces (in the Transcaucasus and Central Asia) and the U.S. Central Command (operating out of the Indian Ocean), though essential to the balance of power,[10] is meaningless unless conceived in the context of a political strategy that provides the region with a common vision of its priorities and stability. If appropriately nurtured, such a vision could provide the context for the gradual creation of a buffer zone between East and West—a zone for which there is a historical precedent of sorts. The difference here would be that the two super-powers would not seek to establish a condominium arrangement, which was generally associated with previous arrangements earlier in the century and which, aside from being anathema to Afghanistan and Iran, would be unwork-able; rather, it would be to establish new rules of the game: a "code of conduct" agreement about U.S. and Soviet policies toward both countries.[11]

Whether such an agreement is possible or not is subject to question. It was tried some years ago under President Richard Nixon, who signed the Basic Principles Agreement at the Moscow summit on 29 May 1972. Three of the most important principles that he agreed to included:

1. An undertaking to develop "normal relations based on the principle of sovereignty, equality, non-interference in internal affairs and mutual advan-tage."

2. An undertaking to prevent the development of situations "capable of causing a dangerous exacerbation of . . . relations." (Means of prevention included doing the utmost to avoid military conflicts, exercising restraint in mutual relations, and settling differences by peaceful means. Both sides recog-nized that "efforts to obtain unilateral advantage at the expense of the other" were inconsistent with those objectives.)

3. Recognition of a special responsibility not only to prevent situations that increase international tension but also to promote conditions that preclude interference in the internal affairs of other countries.[12]

Henry Kissinger saw these principles not as a legal contract but as "a standard of conduct by which to judge whether real progress was being made and in the name of which we could resist violations," whereas the Soviets, apparently, saw them as tantamount to a treaty.[13]

Raymond Garthoff, who has looked closely at the Basic Principles, has observed that to criticize and dismiss their significance because of the subse-quent impasse between the United States and the Soviet Union would be to overlook both their actual and their potential value. It is his belief that "there was too little attempt at the time and since to understand the views of the other side and to seek to reconcile, or at least identify, differences in understanding." As a result, there were profound misunderstandings, particularly over Afghan-istan, where the Soviets were motivated by "the shoring up of a slipping existing hegemony . . . rather than control over oil or anyone's vital sea lanes." In many ways the Soviets saw the situation in Afghanistan as compar-able to that in the Dominican Republic in 1965 (when the United States intervened without an invitation and, before departing, established a responsive government). Violations of the Basic Principles, Garthoff argues, to the extent that they occurred, were on both sides; and although the hastily prepared principles did not permit the clarification of any *real* rules of the game, the fact is that leaders on *both* sides were influenced by them "as a charter for détente." Since Nixon and Kissinger depended less on Soviet restraint and more on active American efforts to ensure that the Soviets would not take advantage of the principles, Garthoff sees the failure of the code of conduct as more a failure of their détente strategy than a failure caused by Soviet violations of the code.[14]

The problems with a comprehensive code of conduct on the European model being applied in Southwest Asia, Fred Halliday tells us, is that it presupposed "a political stability and a degree of control over local states that cannot exist."[15] He believes, however, that it is possible, if one works within a framework of realism and balance, to reach substantive mutual agreements on a wide range of issues. The essentials of this framework include:

1. a recognition of the internal causes of change in the Third World;
2. U.S. rejection of the notion that it can reestablish control over the politics of the "Arc" countries—which include those running from Afghanistan through Iran and the Arab Middle East down to the Horn of Africa;
3. recognition of the Western contribution to upheavals in the Third World; and
4. a reduced and more sober approach to what "rules" are possible.[16]

A modest approach to such a code of conduct may have been taken by the United States and the Soviet Union in their roles as guarantors of the Geneva Accords signed by Afghanistan and Pakistan on 14 April 1988. Then again, previous problems may be repeating themselves. A statement of the U.S. interpretation of its rights as guarantor, for example, submitted to the U.N. secretary-general before the signing ceremony, noted that "should the Soviet Union exercise restraint in providing military assistance to parties in Afghanistan, the U.S. similarly will exercise restraint." Whether the accords, worked out after six years of negotiations, will hold up or disintegrate into bitter recriminations in the aftermath of Soviet withdrawal from Afghanistan depends on the extent to which the parties attended to the kind of precision recommended by Garthoff—on whether they attempted to clarify the *real* rules of the game and hammered out their differences.

The problem with the way in which the agreement has unfolded, however, at least insofar as it is possible to understand from public discussion, raises questions as to the level of precision that was reached in private. The press, for example, commented immediately after the agreement on the "unreal quality" of the signing ceremony, "with two signatories of the accords stating publicly that they intend to violate some of the key provisions under certain circumstances and refusing to recognize the legitimacy of one of the other signatories."[17]

By 15 August 1988, the Soviets had halved their occupation force of 115,000, but there were differences in interpretation over the notion of symmetry (the right of each side to match the support activities of the other). The Soviets, meanwhile, deployed SS1 SCUD-B missiles, MiG-27s, and Tu26 Backfire bombers in Afghanistan—whether as a show of support for the Najibullah regime before the inevitable pullout or as a last-ditch attempt to effect a face saving coalition government in order to achieve a "decent interval" (such as that sought by the United States in Vietnam) prior to departure from Afghanistan. On 19 November 1988, President Mikhail Gorbachev charged that the United States and Pakistan were trying to scuttle the accords and warned of "grave consequences." As the Soviets temporarily suspended withdrawal, Gorbachev criticized the United States and Pakistan for what he characterized as their difficulty in accepting "new approaches to international affairs."[18] Following Soviet withdrawal in February 1989, differences of interpretation continued, with the United States and the Soviet Union exchanging accusations of hypocrisy, lies, and bad faith in the U.N. Security Council.

The Afghan case suggests the need for clarity in an accord and for determination by both superpowers to limit intervention if a code of conduct agreement is to work. While the difficulties are enormous, conditions in Afghanistan are at least somewhat favorable for conflict management: a military balance of sorts; an understanding of respective interests (both the United States and the Soviet Union wanted the Soviets to withdraw and both could probably accept a neutral, nonaligned government); and a recognition that the risks of unilateral action are greater than the rewards.[19] Afghanistan's traditional policy of *bi-tarafi* (nonalignment, or being "without sides"), which seeks to balance external influences, is one of the few policies that most Afghans could agree upon.

The situation in the Persian Gulf, meanwhile, will require time to resolve itself. Both the United States and the Soviet Union share an interest in the equilibrium of the Gulf. That is why, over the course of the nine-year Iran-Iraq war, when Iraq ran into serious difficulties, both superpowers, in spite of Iran's greater strategic importance, tilted toward Iraq. The United States was concerned with access to the Gulf's resources and with preventing any one country from dominating the region. The Soviets, for their part, desired good relations with all the Gulf states. From a Soviet point of view, an Iranian victory would have resulted in the defeat of an ally, given Iran hegemony over the Gulf, and created instabilities on the Soviet-Iranian border that it did not need—particularly as ethnic/religious differences play themselves out in the Transcaucasus. These reasons, in addition to U.S.-Soviet competition (and, for the United States, a serious credibility problem in the Middle East resulting from the Iran-Contra affair), also explain why both countries offered to reflag Kuwaiti tankers.

Iran for a long time was unwilling to agree to a formal cease-fire until its war aims were met. Although these aims varied, they generally included international acknowledgment of Iraq's responsibility for starting the war (or an international arbitration committee to determine the aggressor), reparations, and the overthrow of Saddam Hussein and his Ba'athist regime. Saddam, however, was not willing to step down and the Ba'athists believed that, even if he did, no Ba'athist would be acceptable to the Iranians anyway. Under these circumstances, Saddam sought to influence the outcome by perpetuating the tanker war. Since its inception in 1984, the tanker war had damaged well over four hundred ships and resulted in a total damage write-off estimated as equal to half the total tonnage sunk in World War II. The purpose of hitting Iranian tankers was to cut Iran's economic lifeline, internationalize the war, and so bring pressure to bear on Iran. Other means of bringing pressure on Iran included the use of poison gas and terrorizing Iran's urban population with SCUD-B missiles.

Given the stalemate at the front, Iran's options were few and the success of the Iranian Revolution eventually was threatened. Iran was unable to isolate the war from the Gulf, its offensive was stalled, and it had a relatively small air force. It could not retaliate at sea because, with the completion of the oil pipeline connecting Iraq to the Saudi pipeline at Yanbu, Iraq shipped all of its oil exports by pipeline through Turkey and Saudi Arabia. As a result, Iran attacked ships from Kuwait, which supported Iraq, and attempted to disrupt trade in the Gulf.

Iraq, meanwhile, needed peace. Faced with a war of attrition it could not win[20] and the prospect of a continued mobilization that it could not afford, it insisted on a formal cease-fire and resorted to drastic measures whose purpose was to internationalize the war. The problem posed for those attempting to mediate the war was that it was virtually impossible to be neutral. To support freedom of the seas or a cease-fire at sea supported Iran, since it kept Iran's economy going and allowed it to continue the war. To protect Kuwaiti tankers as nonbelligerents in fact supported the Iraqi war effort. To support a general cease-fire (as does U.N. Resolution 598) also supported Iraq, since it prevented Iran from delivering the final blow to Iraq and forcing it to the peace table short of its aims.

Although Iran may have had legitimate grievances against Iraq for starting the war and a legitimate grievance against the U.N. Security Council for adopting, at the beginning of the war, Resolution 479 (which did not link a cease-fire to a withdrawal of forces to recognized international boundaries),[21] there was little U.S. or Soviet sympathy for its point of view. Its willingness to sacrifice so many lives (most of which were lost while on the offensive) was seen as unnecessary and excessively vengeful.

From the U.S. government's point of view, the situation required that Iran be contained by Iraq and the Gulf Cooperation Council (GCC). As a result, U.S. policy sought mandatory enforcement measures against the side that was not willing to accept a cease-fire, negotiations, and a withdrawal to international borders. The United States did not believe it would be advantageous for either side to win. This perception (which makes sense if one looks to a viable resolution of the conflict) was consistent with the U.S. position during the October 1973 Arab-Israeli war when it opposed Israel's attempt to capture Egypt's Third Army after Israel crossed the Suez Canal. The United States, by supporting the sovereignty and territorial integrity of both Iraq and Iran, in effect supported the containment of Iran by Iraq and the GCC.

Ultimately, developments within Iran, coupled perhaps with a rapprochement between the Soviet Union and the United States (which inhibited Iran's ability to play one power off against the other), led the ailing Ayatollah Khomeini to accept a cease-fire—a step that he characterized as "more deadly than taking poison," but that made possible (if not easy) an end to one of the bloodiest wars of the century.[22]

Under these circumstances, Iran, while enormously suspicious (and with good reason) of any great power agreement, like Afghanistan could be amenable to a U.S.-Soviet code of conduct agreement. It has chosen to follow a nonaligned role, evident in the slogan "neither East nor West," which in part follows traditional policies and currently characterizes its foreign policy. In the context of a code of conduct agreement, Iran itself, as well as other regional states in the Gulf, could be relatively free of great power pressures and would be in a position to pursue genuinely nonaligned policies to the benefit of all parties, providing that the Iranians, too, respect certain rules (such as the sovereignty and territorial integrity of their neighbors) and do not threaten the regional balance. Until the cease-fire agreement of 20 August 1988 between Iran and Iraq, the Iranian threat to the regional balance was the sticking point to any regional understanding because Iranian policies threatened the equilibrium of the Gulf and forced others to look to external support (Iraq primarily to the Soviet Union, and the GCC—until recently—primarily to the United States).

In Afghanistan, much depends on the Afghans themselves. Their decentralized tribal system (along with outside support such as Stinger antiaircraft missiles) has enabled them to thwart the Soviets—lacking a single head, one observer has noted, they could not be defeated by a single stroke. But that very strength may also impede their capacity to organize themselves following the Soviet withdrawal—the many heads will not necessarily speak with one voice. Afghan scholar Louis Dupree, who died in 1989, believed that after the Soviets left, six or seven distinct ethnographic and regional units would eventually form an Islamic federation that would pursue a neutral, nonaligned policy.[23] Others believe that civil war between ideologically and ethnically diverse groups will continue.

The broader context of the Afghan agreement suggests that the Soviets have recognized the political and military limits of their capacity to project power in a hostile environment (even if Afghanistan is a contiguous state), just as the United States, through its restraint during the fall of the Shah and the ensuing hostage crisis in Iran, has recognized the limits of its power. President Gorbachev appears less concerned with the implications of Soviet withdrawal for the Brezhnev Doctrine and the credibility of communism as the wave of the future[24] than he is with stability abroad and the Soviet economy. His emerging policies toward the Third World (for example, Afghanistan, Angola, Cambodia, and Nicaragua) are consistent with the insight, articulated earlier by Gaddis, that the superpower that can accommodate diversity now will be most likely to maintain its status and position later.

Withdrawal from Afghanistan, it should be noted, will ultimately *enhance* the Soviet Union's international credibility even if, initially, this may not appear to be the case. Perestroka and glasnost are creating and revealing problems along much of the outer rim of the Soviet Union: from Estonia, Lithuania, and Latvia in the Baltic, to Armenia, Azerbaijan, and Georgia in the Transcaucasus, to Kazakhstan and Uzbekistan in Central Asia. These problems Gorbachev needs to attend to.[25] On the international scene, he is backing away from questionable commitments to lost causes and pursuing a more activist, pragmatic policy that reflects the triumph of his supporters in the Soviet hierarchy. The INF agreement and the START negotiations, meanwhile, will make it possible for Gorbachev to reduce conventional forces on both European and Chinese frontiers. Withdrawal from Afghanistan will facilitate troop reductions and help improve relations with China. Although competition between the United States and the Soviet Union will continue,[26] there appears to be a greater willingness to examine the concept of deterrence, to explore the principles of coexistence, and to negotiate on concrete issues.[27] Gorbachev's political initiatives, like Henry Kissinger's triangular diplomacy during the U.S. withdrawal from Vietnam, it should be noted, are both necessitated and made possible by the fact of withdrawal.

The probability of a U.S.-Soviet understanding in the Persian Gulf, meanwhile, is dependent in part on the degree of cooperation between them in the aftermath of the Soviet withdrawal from Afghanistan. It also depends on the question of whether it is plausible in the nuclear era to believe that the Soviets would seek to obtain control of Gulf oil by force of arms. Western vulnerability, to be sure, is profound: the Gulf supplies 25 percent of all oil being moved today; it possesses 63 percent of the world's known petroleum reserves; in 1986, 43 percent of OECD European oil imports and 60 percent of Japan's oil imports came from the Gulf.[28] Joseph Twinam, former deputy assistant secretary of state for Near East and South Asian affairs, has posed the question in a way that is worth quoting at some length. He asks:

> Would not the West, particularly the United States, consider such a Soviet move a cause for war? In a nuclear age, would the Soviet Union risk such a confrontation for the uncertain goal of seeking an energy stranglehold on the West? Is it possible that a line has indeed been drawn against Soviet strategic ambitions in the Gulf? Is it reasonable to calculate that the Soviet Union, without abandoning the Marxist faith that history will ultimately bring the revolution to Gulf societies, might come to recognize the limited nature of its realistic goals in the region, and come to see its own interests as requiring stability there?
>
> . . . Today—after Iraqi and Iranian revolutions and much experience with the limits of Anglo-American strategic influence in the rest of the Gulf—the Western challenge may seem less formidable to Moscow. Is it possible that the Soviets may come to recognize limits on realistic Western strategic goals in the region? In sum, could the superpowers come to see the Gulf as a delicate place of great importance to the world at large in which cooperation rather than competition would better serve both Soviet and Western interests?[29]

Although Twinam does not see the Soviets having much incentive to cooperate in the context of the Gulf itself, he believes that there is ample motivation for a constructive Soviet policy in the wider context of East-West relations and that there is merit in exploring with the Soviets, with due caution, the possibilities and limits of such cooperation.

Of crucial significance for the relative influence of the United States and the Soviet Union in the Gulf, meanwhile, is the fact that, though the Soviet departure from Afghanistan frees it from a major impediment in its relations with the Gulf states, U.S. relations with those states will continue to be impeded by the U.S.-Israeli relationship. Israeli policies in the West Bank and Gaza, where the *intifada* is in its second year, in conjunction with U.S. support for Israel, limit the extent to which the Gulf Arabs can become identified with the United States. Such identification runs against public sentiment and jeopardizes the legitimacy of the Gulf regimes.

The U.S.-Israeli connection also poses a serious impediment to the U.S.-Saudi arms relationship. In 1985, for example, pro-Israeli congressional pressures resulted in U.S. denial of a Saudi purchase of forty-eight F-15s and spare parts, which had been carefully studied and approved by the State and Defense departments. As a result, the Saudis turned to the British, from whom they purchased seventy-two Tornado jets, and to the Chinese, from whom they purchased as many as twenty css-2 (East Wind) missiles.

The purchase of the Tornados not only complicates interoperability with other F-15s that the Saudis already own but removes the United States' involvement in servicing, training, and supplying spare parts. In conjunction with a new Saudi-British agreement in July 1988 that brings the number of Tornados to 122 and includes the construction of two new air bases, the loss of trade amounts to $68 billion.[30] More important than the loss of trade is the loss of U.S. influence with the Saudi establishment. Purchase of the East Wind missiles, on the other hand, has concerned some in Israel who talk of preemption. Israel's strategic interest in supporting Iran in its differences with Iraq poses problems for the Arabs and occasionally creates problems for the United States. Whether denial of the legitimate defense needs of Israel's neighbors is in Israel's best interests, meanwhile, is questionable. In contrast to U.S. sales to Saudi Arabia, for example, the British and Chinese sales have none of the restrictions regarding Saudi deployment that have accompanied the sale of a number of American weapons systems.

The drift of events seems to suggest that forces in both Saudi Arabia and the United States will work to distance the two countries over the next decade. This is particularly true if the Palestinian issue is not addressed (results of the Israeli elections in November 1988 suggest that such a task will be difficult) and if the Saudi regime is responsive to public resentment over U.S. inattention to the Palestinian problem. If the security threats to Saudi Arabia come from outside the country (that is, Iran) and are of a military nature (that is, an air attack), U.S.-Saudi relations will improve commensurate with perceptions of the value of U.S. assistance. But to the extent that the Iran-Iraq cease-fire holds, and threats to Saudi Arabia are internal, subversive, religious in orientation, and directed at the legitimacy of the House of Saud, the United States will be of little help. Indeed, the U.S.-Saudi relationship will cause problems for the

Saudis unless the United States keeps a low profile and does something about the Arab-Israeli problem.

Given the difficulties of addressing the Palestinian question, it is probable that the United States will face a troubled decade in the Persian Gulf region as a whole. Fundamentalist Islam, particularly of what James Bill calls the populist variety,[31] will play itself out in the region, while the states of the Gulf (and particularly Saudi Arabia) will jockey to defuse and coopt it before it consumes them.[32] The Soviets have their own difficulties with Islam, but once the liability posed by their occupation of Afghanistan is removed, they will have greater freedom to maneuver.

In sum, there is substantial support for the suggestion put forward in this chapter: that the United States and the Soviet Union (not to mention the region itself) would benefit from an attempt to codify new rules of the game—a U.S.-Soviet code of conduct—in the Persian Gulf and Southwest Asia. Developments that support this suggestion include the constraints on Soviet policy dictated by internal preoccupations and a concomitant need for stability along Soviet borders, the constraints on U.S. policy dictated by the U.S.-Israeli relationship, the economic priorities and geopolitical interests of both the United States and the Soviet Union, and lessons learned from the recent history of attempts to overstep the rules of the game along the Northern Tier. Ironically, the most compelling argument for an attempt to codify new rules of the game may be that the proliferation of weapons and arms in the region—in considerable part the result of arms transfers from the competing superpowers—appears to have gotten out of hand.

Ultimately, the proliferation of poison gas and ballistic missiles risks causing far greater damage than the already enormous loss of life in Afghanistan and Iran. In the months before the cease-fire between Iran and Iraq, possession of chemical weapons resulted in their use by Iraq and, possibly, Iran (according to one expert, each country has a minimum of a hundred tons of stockpiled mustard gas). Iran and Iraq also resorted to ballistic missile warfare against each other's cities. The Saudis, meanwhile, concerned about their security and denied what they felt were legitimate defensive weapons by the United States, purchased from the Chinese a nuclear-capable missile, the css-2, with a range of 1,625 miles (capable of carrying either a nuclear warhead or a 750-kilogram conventional weapon, albeit with a target accuracy of only two kilometers). There are now at least seven countries in the Middle East and Southwest Asia—from Israel to India—that have ballistic missiles. Three countries in the region (Israel, Pakistan, and India), moreover, are capable of manufacturing nuclear weapons, and others (in addition to Saudi Arabia) have ballistic missiles that are capable of carrying nuclear weapons.[33] These developments all suggest that we need to give serious thought to arms control in the region and to the better management of affairs between states (on both international and regional levels) if we are to survive. A code of conduct agreement between the United States and the Soviet Union—particularly if it is crafted with the care that is necessary—would not be a bad place to start.

Notes

1. Malcolm Yapp, "The History of the Persian Gulf: The Nineteenth and Twentieth Centuries," in *The Persian Gulf States: A General Survey,* ed. Alvin Cottrell et al. (Baltimore: Johns Hopkins University Press), 41–42.

2. John Duke Anthony, *Arab States of the Lower Gulf: People, Politics, Petroleum* (Washington, D.C.: Middle East Institute, 1975), 4; Donald Hawley, *The Trucial States* (London: Allen and Unwin, 1970), 142–46; Rosemarie Said Zahlan, *The Origins of the United Arab Emirates: A Political and Social History of the Trucial States* (New York: St. Martin's, 1978), xi–xiii, 9–11, 196–99; Yapp, "The Persian Gulf," 66.

3. Yapp: "The Persian Gulf," 58–61, and "British Policy in the Persian Gulf," in Cottrell et al., *The Persian Gulf States,* 82, 88–89, 98; Zahlan, *The Origins of the United Arab Emirates,* 19, 21.

4. Edward Ingram, *The Beginning of the Great Game in Asia, 1828–1834* (Oxford: Clarendon Press, 1980), 4–5, 13–14, 17, 50, 328, 337–39. David Fromkin, "The Great Game in Asia," *Foreign Affairs* 58, no. 4 (1980): 936–51, convincingly argues that the so called Great Game in Asia "was played for real stakes, and not merely imaginary ones—the unjustified fears and mutual misunderstandings upon which historians tend to focus." A. J. P. Taylor suggests the interesting generalization that "the Anglo-Saxons and perhaps the French believe in buffer states and the Germans and perhaps the Russians believe in partition as the best way to peace between the Great Powers." *The Struggle for Mastery in Europe, 1848–1918* (Oxford: Oxford University Press, 1965), 239. This generalization may explain some of the problems between the Soviet Union and the West both in Eastern Europe and in the Near East after World War II.

5. See Bruce R. Kuniholm, *The Origins of the Cold War in the Near East: Great Power Conflict and Diplomacy in Iran, Turkey, and Greece* (Princeton: Princeton University Press, 1980), and "Retrospect and Prospect: Forty Years of U.S. Middle East Policy," *Middle East Journal* 41, no. 1 (Winter 1987): 7–25, from which parts of this essay are drawn.

6. J. B. Kelly, "Great Game or Grand Illusion," *Survey* 24 (1980): 118.

7. L. Carl Brown, *International Politics and the Middle East: Old Rules, Dangerous Game* (Princeton, N.J.: Princeton University Press, 1984), 12–15.

8. John Gaddis, "Containment: Its Past and Future," *International Security* (Spring 1981): 74–102.

9. See Bruce R. Kuniholm, "A Political/Military Strategy for the Persian Gulf and Southwest Asia," in *Security in the Middle East: Regional Change and Great Power Strategies,* ed. Samuel Wells and Mark Bruzonsky (Boulder, Colo.: Westview Press, 1987), 306–46, and "Strategies for Containment in the Middle East," in *Containment: Concept and Policy,* ed. Terry Deibel and John Gaddis (Washington, D.C.: National Defense University Press, 1986), 423–56.

10. The asymmetrical nature of power projection capabilities is noted by Shahram Chubin, who observes that "Soviet geographical proximity facilitates its land based power projection capabilities and lengthens the shadow of its military power in the region. This advantage encourages Soviet officials to look for constraints on naval activities that will asymmetrically inhibit the U.S. and her allies, while appearing 'equal.'" *Security in the Persian Gulf 4: The Role of Outside*

Powers (Totowa, N.J.: Allanheld, Osmun, 1982), 150. The key to such capabilities, of course, is their effect on the perceptions of local and regional powers.

11. The possibility of such a code has been discussed by a number of analysts. See Fred Halliday, *Soviet Policy in the Arc of Crisis* (Washington, D.C.: Institute for Policy Studies, 1981), 119–26, 138–43; Raymond Garthoff, *Détente and Confrontation: American Soviet Relations from Nixon to Reagan* (Washington, D.C.: Brookings Institution, 1985), 290–98, 338, 345, 386–93, 533, 536–37, 937, 960, 1077–78, 1103–04; Shahram Chubin, *Security in the Persian Gulf*, 132 ff.; and the articles by Harold Saunders and Alexander George in *American Enterprise Institute Foreign Policy and Defense Review* 6, no. 1 (1986).

12. Garthoff, *Détente and Confrontation*, 290–91.

13. Henry Kissinger, *White House Years* (Boston: Little, Brown, 1979), 1250; Garthoff, *Détente and Confrontation*, 292.

14. Garthoff, *Détente and Confrontation*, 298, 937, 960, 1103–04; see also Nikki R. Keddie, "Iranian Imbroglios: Who's Irrational?" *World Policy Journal* 5, no. 1 (Winter 1987–88): 42, who observes: "The idea that we could 'regain our position' in Iran is based on a distorted, Cold War vision of ourselves, the Soviet Union, and Iran. In this view, a government is expected to be either pro-American or pro-Soviet, not wary of or hostile to both as in Iran."

15. Halliday, *Arc of Crisis*, 124.

16. Ibid., 125–26.

17. See the discussions by Don Oberdorfer, *Washington Post*, 14 Apr. 1988, and David Ottoway, *Washington Post*, 15 Apr. 1988.

18. Richard Weintraub, *Washington Post*, 20 Nov. 1988.

19. As Shahram Chubin has observed, these "conditions for successful conflict management by outside powers are as simple to define as they are difficult to achieve." *Security in the Persian Gulf*, 142.

20. The number of people born in Iran since the revolution (11 million) is not much smaller than the total population of Iraq and is greater than the total number of citizens of all the other Gulf states combined. See Gary Sick, "Iran's Quest for Superpower Status," *Foreign Affairs* 65, no. 4 (Spring 1987): 712.

21. *The United Nations and the Iran-Iraq War*, Ford Foundation Conference Report (New York: Ford Foundation, August 1987), 30.

22. James Bill estimates casualties of the Iran-Iraq war at 700,000 deaths and almost 2 million wounded. *The Eagle and the Lion: The Tragedy of American-Iranian Relations* (New Haven: Yale University Press, 1988), 305. Eric Hooglund, "The Islamic Republic at War and Peace," *Middle East Report*, 156 (January–February 1989): 8, observes that preliminary statistics released by Iran in September 1988 indicate that at least 160,000 died in the war; the number of Iranian deaths commonly cited in the Western media is 300,000. Estimates of the number of Iranians wounded vary from 400,000 to 700,000. Estimates of Iraqi deaths range from 90,000 to 150,000, and estimates of the number of Iraqi wounded hover around 250,000. Edward Girardet estimates that 1.3 million Afghans have died and uncountable numbers have been wounded as a direct result of the Soviet occupation. One-third of the prewar population of 15 million has fled the country and 2.5 million are internally displaced. *Christian Science Monitor*, 24 Oct. 1988. For the quote by Ayatollah Khomeini, see *Time*, 1 Aug. 1988, 28.

23. Conversation with Louis Dupree, 20 Apr. 1988.

24. See the discussion by Graham Fuller, "Afghanistan: So Much for the March of History," *Washington Post*, 6 Mar. 1988. For more on Fuller's views, see Nikki R. Keddie, "Iranian Imbroglios: Who's Irrational?" 39, and *New York Times*, 20 Mar. 1988.

25. See Celestine Bohlen, *Washington Post*, 27 Mar. 1988, and Paul Quinn-Judge, *Christian Science Monitor*, 21 Sept. and 12 Oct. 1988, as well as the articles by David Remnick and Michael Dobbs in the *Washington Post*, April–August 1989.

26. John Gaddis observes that one of the problems with the Basic Principles agreement was that "it conveyed the false impression that détente meant a cessation of Soviet-American competition everywhere, and so made the measures necessary to counter Moscow's initiatives in those fields where competition was in fact continuing to appear both provocative and unnecessary." *Strategies of Containment: A Critical Appraisal of Postwar American National Security Policy* (New York: Oxford University Press, 1982), 318.

27. Détente, Henry Kissinger has written, was built on "the twin pillars of resistance to Soviet expansionism and a willingness to negotiate on concrete issues, on the concept of deterrence and a readiness to explore the principles of coexistence." *Years of Upheaval* (Boston: Little, Brown, 1982), 982.

28. *U.S. Policy in the Persian Gulf,* Special Report no. 166, U.S. Department of State, July 1987.

29. Joseph W. Twinam, "U.S. Interests in the Arabian Gulf," *American-Arab Affairs* 21 (Summer 1987): 14.

30. Molly Moore and David Ottaway, *Washington Post,* 22 Oct. 1988.

31. See James Bill, "Resurgent Islam in the Persian Gulf," *Foreign Affairs* 63 (Fall 1984): 108–27.

32. See Bruce R. Kuniholm, "The Carter Doctrine, the Reagan Corollary, and Prospects for United States Policy in Southwest Asia," *International Journal* 41 (Spring 1986): 342–61.

33. See Geoffrey Kemp, "Mideast Missile Madness: A Bazaar for Doomsday," *Washington Post,* 27 Mar. 1988; David Ottaway, "In Mideast, Warfare Takes a New Nature," *Washington Post,* 5 Apr. 1988; E. A. Wayne, "Undeclared A-Bombs Spread: Norms against Proliferation Eroding," *Christian Science Monitor,* 17 Nov. 1988; and Warren Richey, "Chemical Arms Race Speeds Up in Gulf," *Christian Science Monitor,* 29 Nov. 1988.

10 Slouching toward Settlement: The Internationalization of the Iran-Iraq War, 1987–1988

GARY SICK

A major turning point in the war between Iraq and Iran came in 1987. Fundamental changes occurred with respect to the fighting on the battlefield, the role of the United States and its allies, the role of the Soviet Union, and particularly the active engagement of the U.N. Security Council. These and other circumstances combined, in an environment almost totally devoid of goodwill and understanding, to produce a cease-fire in mid-1988.

This sequence of events did not follow a direct path. On the contrary, forward movement was halting and circuitous, as the various parties pursued seemingly incompatible goals. In the end, these countervailing forces were not so much reconciled as simply canceled out in a final burst of error and exhaustion. What follows is the account of those twenty eventful months, as the international community groped and stumbled toward peace.

The Ground War

On 9 January 1987, Iran launched Operation Karbala V at Basra. For months in advance, Iranian spokesmen had been predicting a "decisive offensive" that would extend their success of the previous year, when Iranian forces had crossed the Shatt al-Arab River under cover of night to take the Fao Peninsula. Although they carefully avoided defining the precise objectives of Karbala V, most observers believed that the winter offensive was intended to challenge the Iraqi army in a frontal attack at its strongest point. A decisive victory there would break the back of the Iraqi military, separate Baghdad from the southern capital, and possibly bring down the Ba'athist government of Iraqi president Saddam Hussein.

Karbala V was perhaps the best-prepared Iranian offensive of the war. Planning and intensive training exercises had been underway for nearly a year. The arms available to Iran were superior to those used in any previous battle of the war. Because of the Iran-Contra affair, Iran had received more than two thousand U.S. antitank weapons and spare parts for their Hawk surface-to-air missile batteries. These weapons, however, may have been less significant than the much larger quantity of unspecified matériel that Iran had received over the previous year from Israel.[1] Iran had also succeeded in establishing a military supply relationship with the People's Republic of China—perhaps also facilitated by Israel[2]—as well as a number of other countries and arms brokers.

Despite these advantages, and despite fierce and prolonged battle in the marshes before Basra, it was apparent to the Iranian leadership by 11 February, the seventh anniversary of the Iranian Revolution, that the offensive had failed to achieve a breakthrough. The Speaker of the Majles, Ali Akbar Hashemi-Rafsanjani, and others subsequently attempted to put the best face on the Iranian failure to break through Iraqi defenses, claiming that Karbala V had achieved its purpose by destroying a substantial part of the Iraqi army, thereby opening the way to new Iranian victories in the future.

The reality was more sobering. Iran had made a supreme military effort and had failed. Its leadership was therefore forced to ask itself whether still one more offensive the following year would yield results any different from those of early 1987. The answer came four months later in an interview by Mohsen Reza'i, military commander of the Islamic Revolutionary Guard Corps (IRGC), with *Kayhan,* a newspaper in Tehran. The plan for the coming year, he said, would be a "series of limited operations and a series of bigger ones. . . . we have plans to organize, train and arm popular forces inside Iraq. . . . this is the new front." The objective, Reza'i noted, would be to keep Iraq off balance, relying on a series of smaller attacks along the front and joint guerrilla operations in northern Iraq by dissident Kurdish forces and the IRGC.[3]

That statement proved to be an accurate description of Iran's strategy in the ground war for the remainder of the year. Significantly, during the summer of 1987, Iran did not undertake the elaborate training and logistical preparations that would have been required for a determined offensive in the winter. For the first time since 1982, the rhetoric of Iran's leaders contained no references to a prospective "decisive battle" or the coming "year of destiny."

Iran had not renounced its fundamental objective of defeating Iraq and overthrowing the regime of Saddam Hussein, but the evidence suggests that after Karbala V Iran no longer believed the war could be won in a single, decisive battle. Instead, relying on its strategic depth and overwhelming advantage in manpower, it seemed prepared to settle in for a long war of attrition.[4]

Given these realities, it appeared that there were individuals in senior leadership positions in Iran who were prepared—perhaps for the first time—to consider seriously the possibility of a negotiated settlement or cease-fire if the proper terms were available. That fact, plus the relative exhaustion and mutual frustration of both parties to the conflict, made it an interesting moment for international diplomacy.[5]

The War at Sea and in the Air

The tanker war was relatively insensitive to developments on the battlefront. As indicated in the first two columns of table 10.1, Iraq maintained a fairly consistent level of attacks on tankers and oil facilities in the first five months of 1987 in an attempt to choke off Iran's oil exports, and Iran responded sporadically with gunboat attacks against neutral shipping in the Persian Gulf.

This pattern was interrupted on 17 May, when Iraq announced successful missile strikes on two "large maritime targets." One of these attacks hit a Cypriot tanker, but the second was the frigate USS *Stark,* which was struck by two Iraqi Exocet missiles while on patrol in the central Persian Gulf outside the war zone in international waters. The ship was badly damaged and thirty-seven Americans were killed. Iraq apologized to the United States for the error and ceased its shipping attacks for more than a month, resuming only on 20 June after a U.S. military team visited Baghdad to develop procedures intended to prevent a recurrence.[6]

In early July, Iraq resumed its previous level of shipping attacks, but terminated them again as the U.N. Security Council approached a vote on a cease-fire resolution on 20 July. After Resolution 598 was adopted, Iraq observed a self-imposed cease-fire in the Gulf for a month, awaiting an Iranian response to the resolution.

When the shipping cease-fire expired on 29 August without Iranian acceptance of Resolution 598, Iraq resumed its shipping attacks at the highest level of intensity in the history of the tanker war. Attacks on cities and industrial sites were also stepped up. This new level of activity was sustained into the second half of December, when attacks on cities and industrial sites tapered off sharply, probably in anticipation of the summit meeting of the Gulf Cooperation Council (GCC) on 29 December.

Iraqi bombing attacks against nonmilitary targets—the "war of the cities"—followed a more complex pattern. These attacks were sustained at a

Table 10.1 Strikes against Shipping and Nonmilitary Targets, 1987

		Shipping Attacks		Residential/Economic Targets[a]		
		Iraq[b]	Iran[c]	Iraq	Iran	(SCUD)[d]
Jan.	1–15	5	3	30	3	
	16–31	2	2	18	15	(3)
Feb.	1–15	4	3	27	5	(5)
	16–28	5	3	8	—	—
Mar.	1–15	3	1	—	—	—
	16–31	5	3	4	—	—
Apr.	1–15	2	2	5	—	—
	16–30	3	3	2	—	—
May	1–15	4	4	4	1	—
	16–31	2	6	1	1	—
June	1–15	—	1	—	—	—
	16–30	1	3	1	—	—
July	1–15	5	3	6	—	—
	16–31	—	2	—	—	—
Aug.	1–15	—	2	2	—	—
	16–31	—	1	13	7	—
Sept.	1–15[e]	22	10	35	8	—
	16–30	19	7	19	3	—
Oct.	1–15	15	0	12	6	—
	16–31	9	1	4	8	(4)
Nov.	1–15	18	3	14	9	(1)
	16–30	12	7	10	2	(2)
Dec.	1–15	8	5	7	2	—
	16–31	9	10	1	—	—
	Total	153	93	223	70	(15)

[a]Bombing and missile attacks on cities and economic, nonmilitary targets, as reported in daily war communiqués and other sources
[b]Aircraft strikes on Iranian maritime targets and offshore oil terminals as reported in Iraqi daily war communiqués
[c]All-source reporting of Iranian gunboat attacks against neutral shipping
[d]Iranian SCUD-B missiles fired at Baghdad (included in figures for Iran)
[e]Data from 29 August, when the self-imposed Iraqi cease-fire on shipping terminated

very high level during the first two months of 1987, when Iran was conducting a major ground offensive; and, as indicated in table 10.1, they tapered off sharply once that threat had disappeared. For the remainder of 1987, Iraqi attacks on Iranian cities seemed to be associated almost exclusively with political, rather than military, developments. Iraq escalated its city raids in August, immediately after Iran submitted to the U.N. secretary-general its response to Resolution 598, which Iraq regarded as "invalid." The raids continued at a relatively high level throughout the remainder of the year, except for a lull in the weeks prior to the Arab League summit in early November and the GCC summit in late December.

From this brief review, several conclusions can be drawn about the nature of the fighting between Iran and Iraq. The tempo of ground combat along the fronts, at least after 1982, was determined by Iran. The intensity of the tanker war, however, was determined entirely by Iraq. Operations were based primarily on strategic economic considerations, as Iraq attempted to shut off Iran's oil exports and thereby cripple its economic capacity to sustain the war, but were also affected by political considerations, such as the suspension of operations after the *Stark* incident and Iraq's self-imposed cease-fire during and after the U.N. Security Council vote on Resolution 598.

The so-called war of the cities was also dictated exclusively by Iraq. Given Iraq's overwhelming air superiority, attacks on residential and economic targets had both a military and a political or psychological dimension, reminiscent of the strategic bombing campaigns of World War II. On the military side, these bombing attacks were linked to the ground war and were intended to punish and deter Iran during periods of heavy fighting along the fronts. On the political and psychological side, they were intended to undermine Iranian civilian morale, to affect Iran's ability to sustain its war effort, to punish Iran for its military or political actions against Iraq, to bring pressure on Iran to modify its negotiating position, and, on occasion, to focus international attention on the war when it began to shift to other issues.

The intensity of Iraq's bombing campaign against nonmilitary targets consequently was extremely sensitive to political developments and provided a useful barometer of Iraq's political strategy at any given time. The bombing campaign was opposed by many of Iraq's friends and allies, including the United Nations,[7] so Iraq often suspended its attacks while it was attempting to build official international support in the United Nations or the GCC. Attacks typically resumed once the diplomatic issue had been resolved.

The United States

At the beginning of 1987, U.S. Persian Gulf policy was in a state of absolute disarray. Revelations about covert U.S. arms deals with Iran had surfaced in November of the previous year and had ignited a political crisis that bore comparison to the Watergate scandals of the 1970s. The United States' credibility with the Arab Gulf states plummeted to its lowest level since the Arab-Israel war of 1973 because of the perceived U.S. breach of faith in covertly shifting its support to Iran.

The United States had two key foreign policy questions to resolve. First, what was to be the U.S. position on future relations with Iran in the wake of the scandal? Second, and more urgent, how could the United States reassure its Arab friends in the Persian Gulf and restore a measure of trust and confidence?

The first question was answered by Secretary of State George Shultz in a statement on 6 January while en route to Africa:

> We recognize the Iranian revolution. It is a fact of life. But Iran's behavior with respect to the Iran-Iraq war, with respect to terrorism, with respect to hostage-taking, with respect to its threat in the region particularly represents problems. And at the same time, Iran is a critical piece of geography. . . . There is an inherent aspect to Iran's geographic position that causes them to look to other countries for some support. They have a long border with the Soviet Union, they see the Afghan problem on their doorstep, and so those are things that perhaps we can work with them on.[8]

This statement sent signals to many different audiences. To Iran, it indicated that the United States accepted the revolution and, by inference, would not attempt to overthrow it. On the contrary, the United States was prepared to continue contacts through normal diplomatic channels (Shultz said that official contacts with Iran were being maintained through the Swiss protecting power) and even to work with Iran on issues of mutual interest. To the Arabs, it said that the United States recognized the importance of Iran's position in the region but would take a tough position on issues of terrorism and security. It recognized the legitimacy of a certain level of contacts between Iran and the Soviet Union, which had been one of the justifications for the covert opening to Iran. And, to the American people and the world, it indicated that Shultz and the Department of State were now in charge of U.S. Iranian policy.

Iran never replied directly to the Shultz statement, but some weeks later Rafsanjani outlined Iran's position: "With regard to the United States, we do not believe that our relations with that country have to be cut forever. . . . If we can be sure that the United States plans no mischief, we are willing to establish relations with the United States. But I think it will be very hard."[9]

The second problem of restoring Arab confidence was more complex. In late 1986, as Iranian attacks on shipping to and from Kuwait began to mount, Kuwait had asked the United States to register a number of its tankers under the U.S. flag for protection. Over the winter, the United States took no action on the request. Then in May, the Soviet Union agreed to lease three Soviet-flag tankers to Kuwait, increasing the pressure on the United States.

Assistant Secretary of State for Near East Affairs Richard Murphy visited Iraq shortly thereafter and met with Saddam Hussein on 11 May. Murphy reportedly promised Saddam that the United States would lead an effort in the

U.N. Security Council for a resolution calling for a mandatory halt of arms shipments to Iran. According to these reports, the U.N. resolution would not name Iran directly. Rather, it would first call on Iran and Iraq to cease fire and withdraw their forces to the international boundaries. Then "enforcement measures," such as a worldwide arms embargo, would be imposed on the party that rejected the demand. Iran was expected to reject and Iraq to accept the demand.[10]

Murphy's promise was part of a package of U.S. actions, including reflagging, that was intended to mollify Arab concerns after the Iran-Contra revelations and to prove America's good faith. Over the following months, this pledge was to become a dominant factor in U.S. policy-making on the war.

Six days after Murphy's visit to Baghdad, the USS *Stark* was struck by Iraqi missiles. That event dramatized the military threat in the Gulf and effectively silenced congressional critics who had been resisting a U.S. naval buildup there. The irony of the United States responding to an Iraqi attack by virtually declaring war on Iran was not lost on some observers, but it was soon forgotten in the flood of reports about ship movements, Iranian missile emplacements, and an upsurge of Iranian gunboat and mine attacks on neutral shipping.

In the weeks after the *Stark* incident, the United States acted quickly to reflag eleven Kuwaiti tankers and to move into place the necessary naval forces to provide convoy protection.[11] Discussions had been underway among the five permanent members of the U.N. Security Council since January about a new resolution on the war, and the United States took the lead in these discussions beginning in May.[12] In early July, U.S. Ambassador to the United Nations Vernon Walters traveled to the Soviet Union, China, and other countries to press for early U.N. action. Resolution 598 was approved unanimously by the Security Council on 20 July.

Iran's decision to deploy mines in the Persian Gulf was a serious miscalculation. Although several ships were hit, Iran paid a heavy political and military price for its actions. International public opinion was alarmed and outraged at the indiscriminate attacks, removing whatever sympathy Iran may have enjoyed and drowning the voices of those who were calling for a negotiated settlement. European nations such as Belgium, the Netherlands, and Italy, which had been reluctant to get involved in the Gulf war, decided to join France and the United Kingdom in sending minesweeping forces to the Gulf in self-defense.

Eventually, the floating mines embarrassed Iran by striking a ship carrying its own oil, and Iran had to send minesweepers into the Gulf to clear a path for its own shipping. Many of the mine explosions occurred during the month of August, when Iraq was observing a cease-fire in the tanker war, thus placing full responsibility on Iran for continuing the hostilities. Another major impediment to serious negotiations during that month was the rioting in Mecca on 1 August that resulted in the deaths of more than three hundred Iranian pilgrims. The shock of that event and its negative impact on Iran's reputation in the Islamic world was not conducive to accommodation or quiet diplomacy. As a result, one of the most promising moments for negotiations was lost.

Mines were also responsible for touching off the retaliatory exchange between Iran and the United States in late 1987. On the night of 21 September a U.S. Army Special Forces helicopter from the frigate USS *Jarrett* sighted an Iranian amphibious ship, the *Iran Ajr,* laying mines fifty miles north of Bahrain at an anchorage used by ships of the United States and other nations. The helicopter opened fire with machine guns and rockets, setting the Iranian ship on fire. The attack killed four and wounded three members of the crew. Another twenty-six were taken into custody by the U.S. Navy.[13]

This was the first direct clash between United States and Iranian military forces since the Iranian Revolution. It occurred on the night before Iranian president Khamene'i was to address the U.N. General Assembly in New York. Khamene'i had come to the United Nations with the intention of asserting that Iran had been unfairly treated by the Security Council at the beginning of the war and to convey Iran's willingness to observe a cease-fire on the basis of a modified version of Resolution 598. These objectives, however, were overwhelmed by the dramatic news from the Gulf, and Khamene'i spent most of this visit answering questions about Iran's attacks on shipping.

Secretary of Defense Caspar Weinberger arrived in the Gulf three days later to visit U.S. forces. At a dinner in Bahrain on 27 September, while gloating over the *Iran Ajr* incident, Weinberger expressed his own view of U.S. policy: "There must be a totally different kind of government in Iran," he said, "because we cannot deal with the irrational, fanatical government of the kind they now have."[14]

That view was sharply at odds with the position taken by Shultz, and it was also contrary to the efforts of the State Department, which had attempted to defuse the situation by an exchange of messages with Iran.[15] The Iranian response was predictable. Prime Minister Mir-Hosain Musavi vowed, "We will make the United States sorry for these remarks."[16]

On 15 October, an Iranian Silkworm missile[17] fired from the Fao Peninsula struck a U.S.-owned Liberian flag supertanker anchored in Kuwaiti territorial waters. The following day, the reflagged Kuwaiti tanker *Sea Isle City* was hit and severely damaged in the same general location.

On 19 October, the United States bombarded and destroyed the Iranian Rostam oil drilling platform in the central Persian Gulf. On 22 October, an Iranian missile hit a floating oil terminal in Kuwaiti territorial waters, setting off an explosion and fire that disabled the facility for a month. Rafsanjani said that Kuwait should regard this attack as retaliation for the earlier U.S. bombardment, "since the United States does not possess oil platforms in the Persian Gulf under the American flag."[18]

The United States did not respond. A senior U.S. official commented, "We have never assumed responsibility for the security of all the littoral states of the Persian Gulf. We have no defense treaty with the Kuwaitis."[19]

This ended the exchange, but the retaliatory cycle had set in motion a political process in Tehran that had to play itself out.[20] The Supreme Defense Council on 13 November announced a new mobilization campaign, fueling speculation that Iran intended to conduct a major winter offensive against Iraq.

Such an offensive was never very likely, since Iran had failed to put in place the necessary infrastructure to sustain such an operation, but it did reflect the renewed prominence in the Iranian leadership of those favoring a hard-line military policy. That perspective was reflected in a speech by Hojjat al-Islam Mohammad Musavi Khoeiniha, the state public prosecutor and former spiritual leader of the students holding U.S. hostages in Tehran. He denounced "certain corrupt, ill-intentioned people and ignorant, weak-kneed irresponsible groups frightened by America's show of force," who believed the war should end. Instead he proposed "continuous jihad" as "the only factor that guarantees the continuation of Iran's Islamic Revolution."[21] Although these pronouncements did not produce a new major offensive, they served to harden Iran's negotiating position and dampened any prospects of fruitful negotiations through the end of the year.

The Role of the Soviet Union

According to Naser Hairani-Naubari, the Iranian ambassador to Moscow, "The exposure of the [Robert C.] McFarlane visit [to Tehran as part of the U.S. arms-for-hostages deal] was shocking for the Soviets. . . . They said clearly the Americans had been playing games with them."[22] Since Moscow probably viewed the U.S.-Iran arms deal as an effort by Washington to restore its relationship with the revolutionary leaders in Tehran that were severed when the Shah's regime collapsed in 1979, it may well have been a shock.

Moscow responded with a two-pronged strategy. On one hand, the Soviet Union initiated a series of high-level diplomatic contacts with Tehran that was intended to put Soviet-Iranian relations on a more businesslike and cooperative basis. On the other, the Soviet Union permitted pro-Soviet, anti-Khomeini groups such as the Tudeh Party and Feda'iyan-e Khalq (majority) to make propaganda broadcasts from a clandestine radio station in Afghanistan.[23]

These broadcasts often provided a more barbed version of Soviet policy views toward Iran than the official Soviet media. Thus, the Soviet Union invited Iranian foreign minister Ali Akbar Velayati to pay an official visit to Moscow on 12 February 1987. In the weeks before the visit, the clandestine radio broadcast a statement by the Tudeh Party calling for the overthrow of the "medieval religious dictatorship" of Ayatollah Khomeini. "The wretched regime of the Islamic Republic," it stated, "is trying to turn our country once again into a U.S. appendage and to place the yoke of dependence and slavery upon your necks."[24]

This carrot-and-stick approach reflected a fundamental ambivalence in Soviet relations with Iran. A senior Soviet foreign policy official described this to an American visitor in early 1988 as a debate within the Kremlin between two competing views.[25] One body of opinion focused on the fact that "Russian-Persian relations go back a very long way" and that any direct clash with Tehran could have disagreeable long-term consequences. Proponents of this point of view did not necessarily exclude pressure tactics in dealing with Iran's revolutionary leaders, but they counseled caution and argued in favor of a longer view of history that would take account of Iranian sensitivities, since Iran and the Soviet Union were fated by geography to live side by side.

A second group was more interested in short-term political gains. They believed that it was impossible for the Soviet Union to cooperate in any meaningful way with the theocratic regime in Tehran, and they were prepared to incur the wrath of the mollas in order to register gains with the Arab states of the Persian Gulf. They argued, according to one Soviet observer, that "we should be more like the Americans."

These policy choices were complicated by several factors. First, Iran's revolutionary politics were so volatile and unpredictable that today's policy judgments could prove embarrassingly wrong tomorrow when the winds shifted in Tehran. Second, the Soviet Union was Iraq's principal arms supplier, and the substantial Soviet investment there over many years could not lightly be put at risk. Third, the Soviet military presence in Afghanistan constituted a constant point of irritation and conflict with Iran. Although this problem began to ease somewhat in late 1987 as the Soviet Union signaled its intention to withdraw, the Soviets were aware that Iran could complicate the process if it chose to increase its support for the Afghan fundamentalists. Similarly, Iran could stir up trouble with the Soviet Muslim nationalities in the south if it chose to do so. Finally, the Soviet Union was anxious to prevent the buildup of a permanent U.S. military presence in the Gulf, but it was also pursuing a policy of closer cooperation with the United States on strategic arms control issues that could be disrupted by a policy clash in the region.

These conflicting interests and objectives were never satisfactorily reconciled during 1987. Instead, Soviet policy tended to fluctuate with changing events. The Soviets cooperated with the United States in passing Resolution 598 in the Security Council, but resisted U.S. efforts to move to a second resolution on an arms embargo. Iranian foreign minister Velayati was received in Moscow, and a series of Soviet delegations were sent to Tehran for talks on areas of economic cooperation, but the talks produced no major breakthroughs.

The Soviet Union agreed in early May to lease three of its ships to Kuwait. Immediately thereafter, a Soviet cargo ship was hit by small Iranian gunboats, and Iran denounced the Soviets for collaborating with the United States against Iran. Tass in turn complained about Iran's "unfriendly campaign" and its "distortion" of Soviet policy on the war. A few days later, on 16 May, one of the Soviet tankers leased to Kuwait was hit by a mine off the Kuwaiti coast. The tension eased after the Soviet Union announced that it had no intention of augmenting its small naval force in the Gulf and criticized the U.S. naval buildup.

At the United Nations, Soviet foreign minister Eduard Shevardnadze in September supported the Iranian position that a cease-fire in the Iran-Iraq war should be accompanied by the formation of a commission to investigate the origins of the war. But when Iran hardened its negotiating position in November and postponed a scheduled visit to Moscow by Majles Speaker Rafsanjani, clandestine broadcasts charged that the failure to put an end to the war was, "first of all, due to the obstinacy" of the Khomeini regime and pointed to the dangers of "religious militarism," which had "taken root in all economic, social and political sectors" of Iranian society.[26] The Soviet Foreign Ministry warned that a second resolution imposing an arms embargo on Iran would be adopted "immediately" when "all other possibilities have been exhausted," and Soviet president Andrei Gromyko warned the Iranian ambassador that Iran was "practically not carrying the matters toward ending the war."[27]

Soviet frustration with Tehran was expressed most clearly at the end of the year in an obscure Communist Party newspaper article that probably was not intended for Western eyes. It criticized the "total incompetence of the Iranian theologians in social and economic development," and asserted that "the war . . . is a form of political existence" for the leaders in Tehran. The end of the war, it suggested, would likely "lead to the collapse of the Islamic regime in its current form, unless, that is, it starts a new war elsewhere to distract Iranians from unresolved internal problems."[28]

At the same time that this scathing critique appeared, a senior Soviet official was touring several Arab capitals, defending the Soviet position in the United Nations against the imposition of a second resolution, explaining that it was natural for the Soviet Union to maintain good relations with Iran "because they are our neighbor," and drawing attention to the fact that "the Soviet Union is one of the few countries that do not supply Iran with arms."[29] So the year ended as it had begun, with the Soviet Union attempting to straddle the issues and finding the position more than a little awkward.

Negotiations at the United Nations

During the first six years of the Iran-Iraq war, most of the actions of the Security Council varied between leaving things much as they were and making them worse. The Security Council first met to discuss the war several days after Iraq invaded Iran on 22 September 1980. On 28 September the council adopted Resolution 479 calling for a cease-fire. This resolution was notable on two accounts. First, it failed to mention Iraq's aggression and, second, it called for no withdrawal of Iraqi forces, which by then had penetrated well into Iran's Khuzistan Province.[30] When both parties ignored it, the council put the subject aside and did not raise it again for nearly two years.

The council's lackadaisical approach to its responsibilities on issues of international peace and security was more than oversight. Iran, which was still holding fifty-two American hostages in flagrant disregard of the United Nations and international law, had no support from any quarter. A number of members of the Security Council quietly hoped that Iraq's attack, which was originally intended to inflict a crushing defeat on Iran in the first few days, would succeed in bringing down the Khomeini regime.[31] When that failed to materialize, there was a reluctance, especially among the Arab states, to chastise an Arab government while it was fighting the Persians. Moreover, once the initial shock had subsided, the superpowers and others concluded that their interests could best be served by letting these two abominable regimes exhaust themselves on the battlefield.

Efforts at negotiation and mediation were left principally to individual states and to U.N. Secretary-General Javier Pérez de Cuellar. He personally negotiated a seven-month truce in the "war of the cities" in mid-1984 and dispatched fact-finding teams to the region to investigate treatment of prisoners of war and charges of Iraqi use of chemical weapons. These efforts won him the respect of the parties and facilitated the negotiation efforts in 1987.

The most promising mediation effort occurred in early 1982 when the foreign minister of Algeria led a delegation on a secret peace mission to the region. On 3 May, while his aircraft was in Iranian airspace en route from Turkey to Tehran, the plane was shot down by an air-to-air missile from an Iraqi fighter, killing the foreign minister and all the members of his entourage. An Iraqi pilot captured by Iran years later indicated that the Iraqi objective was to blame the shootdown on Iran and thereby exacerbate its relations with Algeria.[32] Whatever the motive, the practical effect of the shootdown was that the entire Algerian team of experts who had worked on Iran-Iraq issues since 1975 was killed at a single stroke, and Algeria was effectively removed from the diplomatic scene for more than five years.

By the beginning of 1987, two developments combined to put the Iran-Iraq war back on the agenda of the Security Council. The first was the tanker war, which had escalated to a dangerous level. As indicated in table 10.2, not only had the absolute number of shipping attacks increased sharply but the frequency of Iranian attacks outside the war zone was, by the end of 1986, approaching parity with Iraq.

The second development was U.S. involvement in the sale of arms to Iran. As noted previously, reaction to the scandal led the United States to undertake a series of commitments to redeem itself in the eyes of the Arab Gulf states, including a promise to undertake a major initiative at the United Nations. Shortly after Assistant Secretary Murphy's visit to Baghdad in mid-May, a draft resolution was circulated among the permanent members of the Security Council. As Murphy had promised Saddam Hussein, it was deliberately written in a form that Iran could not accept and included a provision for mandatory sanctions against any party that rejected it.

By 21 June, the five permanent members had agreed on a resolution calling for a cease-fire in the war, but they had failed to agree on mandatory sanctions. During the following month, Security Council discussions were expanded to include the nonpermanent members, and several changes were introduced, including a provision favored by Iran for establishing an impartial commission to investigate the origins of the war.

One of the most controversial provisions in the draft resolution was in the first operative paragraph, which demanded that both sides observe "an immediate cease-fire . . . and withdraw all forces to the internationally recognized boundaries." Iran, of course, was the only party holding substantial territory at the time, and no one believed that it would withdraw its forces and relinquish its most important bargaining leverage before negotiations began on the terms of a

Table 10.2   Shipping Attacks in the Persian Gulf

	1981	1982	1983	1984	1985	1986
Iraq	5	22	16	53	33	66
Iran	—	—	—	18	14	41
Total	5	22	16	71	47	107

Source: *New York Times*, 22 May 1987; Lloyd's Shipping Intelligence Unit

settlement. One senior U.N. diplomat characterized this demand as "unprecedented and unrealistic."[33] A European delegation proposed that the word "subsequently" be inserted before "withdraw" to acknowledge the fact that instant and simultaneous compliance was impractical, if not impossible. This change was accepted by the delegations of all five permanent members of the Security Council; however, after an Iraqi intervention in Washington, this modification was rejected in the final moments by the U.S. delegation in response to instructions from Washington.[34]

Resolution 598 was passed unanimously by the Security Council on 20 July 1987. The first paragraph, referring to the mandatory provisions of Articles 39 and 40 of the United Nations Charter, stated that the Security Council:

> DEMANDS that, as a first step towards a negotiated settlement, Iran and Iraq observe an immediate cease-fire, discontinue all military actions on land, at sea and in the air, and withdraw all forces to the internationally recognized boundaries without delay.

Subsequent operative paragraphs 2 through 9 were worded as requests, not demands. Thus, paragraph 6:

> REQUESTS the Secretary General to explore, in consultation with Iran and Iraq, the question of entrusting an impartial body with inquiring into responsibility for the conflict and to report to the Security Council as soon as possible.

According to paragraph 10, the Security Council:

> DECIDES to meet again as necessary to consider further steps to ensure compliance with this resolution.

Paragraphs 1 and 6 became the center of the diplomatic controversy between Iran and Iraq through the end of the year and beyond, with paragraph 10 as the point of pressure. The positions of the two sides were drawn almost immediately. Iraq welcomed the resolution and stressed that the resolution must be accepted as an "integral and indivisible whole."[35] Iran issued a blistering criticism of the past efforts of the Security Council, but concluded that "grounds have been laid so that the Islamic Republic of Iran would continue its cooperation in a manner that would lead the Security Council to a just position. Undoubtedly, clear-cut pronouncements on the responsibility of Iraq for the conflict . . . constitute the most important element in the just resolution of the conflict."[36]

Iraq immediately denounced the Iranian reply as "invalid" and on 10

August launched bombing raids against industrial targets. There were, however, no Iraqi attacks against shipping until a self-imposed deadline expired on 29 August.[37] Unfortunately, during this relative lull in the fighting immediately following the adoption of Resolution 598, Secretary-General Pérez de Cuellar went on vacation and diplomatic activity was essentially at a standstill.

On 29 August, as the informal Iraqi cease-fire expired, Saddam Hussein gave a speech denouncing Iran's failure to give a clear answer to the Security Council, asserting, "We will attack them at sea."[38] On that date, Iraq launched at least five raids on ships and offshore oil facilities in Iranian waters and conducted extensive bombing of nonmilitary targets. The United States, Great Britain, and other countries protested to Iraq about the resumption of attacks, but Iraq dismissed these complaints and the bombing campaign continued unabated into December.

Two weeks after the bombing resumed, the secretary-general traveled to the area for direct talks with both parties. When he returned to New York, he outlined the positions of the two sides in a statement to the Security Council.[39] The secretary-general said that he had discussed with Iran and Iraq a nine-point plan for implementation of Resolution 598 starting with a cease-fire on a designated day ("D-Day"), when U.N. observers would be dispatched to verify the cease-fire, and "an impartial body to inquire into responsibility for the conflict would start its work." He proposed that "on a specific date after D-Day, which would have to be agreed upon, the withdrawal of all forces to the internationally recognized boundaries would start" to be completed within an agreed time-frame.

The secretary-general's understanding of the position of the two sides was summarized as follows:

A) Iran accepts the implementation of Resolution 598 on the basis of an integrated approach which would include a cease-fire as a first step;
B) Iran insists that a link should be established between the cease-fire and the identification of responsibility for the conflict: The observance of a formal cease-fire must be preceded by the process of the identification of the party responsible for the initiation of the conflict;
C) Iran would accordingly be prepared to accept an implementation plan in which the announcement of the identification of the party responsible for initiating the conflict and the beginning of the observance of a formal cease-fire would take place on the same date.

. . . I was also given to understand that, if this approach were to be accepted by both sides, an undeclared cessation of hostilities could come into effect. . . .

The Iraqi authorities emphasized repeatedly that Iraq believes that the various provisions of the resolution should be implemented in the order of their sequence in the resolution itself. . . . under no circumstances would Iraq accept an undeclared cease-fire.[40]

The Security Council endorsed the secretary-general's efforts. When Iranian president Khamene'i spoke to the U.N. General Assembly on 22 September, he specifically endorsed the secretary-general's report. Secretary of State Shultz met with Foreign Minister Shevardnadze on 24 September and agreed to postpone any call for sanctions to allow more time for the secretary-general to pursue his plan with Iran. This dual approach was officially approved in a luncheon meeting of the foreign ministers of the five permanent members of the Security Council the following day.

On 26 September, Iraqi foreign minister Tariq Aziz responded, "We will not discuss the resolution's clauses with the secretary general except in their natural order. He is free to discuss what he pleases with the Iranian side. However, Iraq is a party to a process which cannot continue without Iraq's agreement." He added that he had told Foreign Minister Shevardnadze that Iraq rejected the plan to link the cease-fire with a commission on the origins of the war.[41]

Pressure on Iran mounted when the Arab League convened a special summit meeting in Amman, 8–11 November. The Arab states had earlier threatened to break diplomatic relations with Iran if it did not comply with Resolution 598 and cease attacks on neutral shipping in the Gulf. But, perhaps owing to Syria's intervention on Iran's behalf, the final communiqué stopped short of a diplomatic break.

Pérez de Cuellar met with Iranian deputy foreign minister for economic and international affairs Mohammad Javad Larijani and Iraqi foreign minister Tariq Aziz during the first week of December, but he made no progress. The secretary-general was forced to report to the Security Council that the talks were at an impasse, and he asked the Security Council to provide him with a "fresh and resolute impulse" to guide his next steps. On 24 December, after two days of talks, the Security Council again expressed its support for the secretary-general's outline plan and his efforts to implement Resolution 598. The council instructed him to continue his efforts and declared its determination, in accordance with paragraph 10 of the resolution, to consider further steps to ensure compliance.

The year ended with the summit meeting of the Gulf Cooperation Council (GCC) on 29 December. The summit declaration noted "with great regret Iran's procrastination regarding accepting [Resolution 598] and urged the international community, led by the Security Council, to shoulder its responsibility to adopt the necessary steps to implement Resolution 598 as soon as possible." Again, this resolution was much less harsh than anticipated. Prince Saud al-Faisal, the foreign minister of Saudi Arabia, indicated in a press conference after the summit that "a dialogue" was underway between the GCC and Iran, and said that "there will be talks with Iran after the GCC summit."[42]

Changing Signals

The words of the Saudi foreign minister presaged a series of new political and diplomatic developments during the first three months of 1988. Iran expressed interest in participating in talks with the GCC, and the Syrian vice president and foreign minister began shuttling between the Gulf capitals and Tehran in an effort to find common ground. On 10 January, an official of the UAE Foreign Ministry was designated to travel to Tehran as the representative of the GCC states. Six days later, Hosain Lavasani, director-general for Arab-African affairs in the Iranian Foreign Ministry, traveled to Abu Dhabi to meet the UAE foreign minister. Reportedly, he relayed a pledge that Iran would cease attacks on ships flying the flags of GCC states.[43] This new era of good feelings culminated in mid-March at the GCC foreign ministers' meeting in Riyadh. The final communiqué of that meeting, unlike its predecessors, did not criticize Iran and did not praise the Iraqi position.[44]

This new environment of conciliation between Iran and its Gulf neighbors was enhanced by several external developments. In the United States, Caspar Weinberger resigned in November and was replaced as secretary of defense by Frank Carlucci, the former national security adviser. Carlucci spent a week in the Gulf in early January. While in Kuwait on 5 January, he said that the United States had no plans to expand its escort role in the Persian Gulf, noting that "we are not policing every area of the high seas for every country" and denying any U.S. interest in acquiring bases in the area.[45] He also let it be known that the United States intended to reduce the level of its military presence in the Gulf by withdrawing the battleship USS *Iowa* and the helicopter carrier USS *Okinawa*. These moves were interpreted as positive signals by Iran, which responded with approval.

During this same period, the Soviet Union announced its intention to withdraw its military forces from Afghanistan by the end of 1988. This resulted in the signing of an accord between Afghanistan and Pakistan on 14 April in Geneva, with the United States and the Soviet Union as coguarantors. The Soviet decision was welcomed in Tehran, where Rafsanjani assured the Soviet Union, "If you are determined to leave Afghanistan, we are prepared to help you leave so that the United States does not dominate Afghanistan after your departure."[46] Soviet deputy foreign minister Vladimir Petrovsky visited Tehran in February for talks described by Velayati as "the friendliest and most positive talks held between the two countries."[47]

Not everything went smoothly, however. The bitter dispute between Iran and Saudi Arabia over Iran's participation in the annual hajj deepened the distrust between these two states, even as Iran's relations with the other GCC states were improving. Saudi Arabia stepped up its direct support for Iraq, apparently permitting Iraqi aircraft to utilize Saudi airfields during raids on Iranian oil facilities in the southern Gulf.[48] On 26 April, Saudi Arabia broke diplomatic relations with Iran.

The United States also chose to ignore the new signals coming from Iran. As president of the Security Council during February, the United States announced its intention to move toward a showdown on sanctions against Iran. President Reagan told Saudi foreign minister Saud in Washington that the United States was "committed to a major effort this month while we serve as president of the Security Council."[49] Secretary of State Shultz reportedly raised this with the Soviets during his visit to Moscow in late February, presenting a plan that would involve a quick vote on the second resolution but with a thirty-day delay in implementation to permit more time for the secretary-general to pursue negotiations.[50] Despite this effort, the United States was unable to muster the necessary support in the Security Council, and the effort failed.

President Khamene'i spelled out the Iranian position on 29 February—the last day of the U.S. council presidency. The passage of a resolution of sanctions, he said, would mean the

> end of all political solutions to the Iraqi-imposed war. . . . The U.S. and other powers which are hypocritically talking of an amicable settlement are, in fact, closing all avenues for an amicable rapprochement by such a step. . . . We had previously accepted the UN secretary general's method of implementing Resolution 598 and we reiterate that we will stand by it. . . . If they wish to resolve the matter through political means, there is a way. The first step is to declare that the Iraqi regime is the aggressor. This must be done. . . . There is no other way.[51]

The Iraqi Response

Iraq took a very different view of these developments. As Iran adopted a more accommodating position and as the GCC began to consider talks with Tehran, pressure built on Iraq to modify its own position concerning a cease-fire. President Saddam Hussein responded in a major speech on 6 January, asserting that "Iraq will not accede to any tampering with the resolution, whether with regard to sequence, contents, or results. . . . We still see and hear statements and behavior that stem from weakness, shortsightedness, selfishness, and other factors which call for compromises with the enemy."[52]

Three weeks later, as the Syrian foreign minister traveled to Tehran, Iraqi deputy prime minister Taha Yasin Ramadan denounced Syrian mediation efforts as "a dirty attempt to divide brothers" and accused the U.N. Security Council of yielding to blackmail.[53] On 5 February, Ramadan was even more explicit: "The resolution represents the will of the international community and, together with the five principles declared by President Saddam in August 1985, constitute the correct basis for ending the war. We will reject all that we believe is incompatible with our view of peace, even if the war should continue for many years."[54]

The implication of Ramadan's words—that Iraq was confident of its military position and preferred a continuation of the war rather than compromise on its interpretation of Resolution 598—was confirmed by many observers during this period. Patrick Tyler, the *Washington Post* correspondent covering the war, quoted high Iraqi officials as telling him, "For the first time in our history, we want the Iranians to attack"—since Iran was believed unable to broach Iraqi defenses and a defeat would demonstrate Iranian weakness. Moreover, these officials felt that such a defeat would put the war back into international consciousness and revive diplomatic efforts to isolate Iran. Regional diplomats reported that Iraq was frustrated with the GCC talks and the absence of an Iranian offensive, which tended to remove any sense of urgency.[55]

Iraqi frustration may have been evident in the events of 12 February. On that date, an Iraqi TU-16 bomber fired two air-to-surface missiles toward the destroyer USS *Chandler,* which was convoying reflagged Kuwaiti ships in the central Persian Gulf. One missile passed astern, the other along the starboard side.[56] The same aircraft apparently also fired on the Danish tanker *Kate Maersk* off the United Arab Emirates, hitting the superstructure and wounding at least three crew members. This ship was on its way out of the Persian Gulf with a load of oil from Saudi Arabia.[57] These attacks, which were reminiscent of the *Stark* incident in May 1987, may have been due to simple pilot error. They may also, however, have been intended to remind the international community of the dangers of the Gulf war at a time when military activities were settling into a relatively comfortable routine and the Security Council was resisting U.S. efforts to impose an embargo on Iran.

Iraq Resumes the War of the Cities

On 29 February, as the United States relinquished the presidency of the Security Council without a vote on the second resolution, Iraq dramatically escalated the war. On that evening, Iraq fired eleven modified SCUD-B missiles at Tehran.[58] As indicated in table 10.3, a total of more than one hundred such missiles were fired in the following two weeks at Tehran, Qom, and Isfahan, together with extensive bombing raids against thirty-seven Iranian cities, after which the frequency of attacks began to decline.

During the same two-week period, Iran responded by firing approximately twenty-six of its own SCUD missiles at Baghdad and by extensively shelling Iraqi border towns. Iran's most serious retaliation, however, occurred on 16

Table 10.3 Strikes against Shipping and Nonmilitary Targets, 1 January 1988 to 20 August 1988 (Date of Cease-Fire)

		Shipping Attacks		Residential/Economic Targets[a]			
		Iraq[b]	Iran[c]	Iraq	(Long-Range)[d]	Iran	(SCUD)[e]
Jan.	1–15	5	2	1	—	—	—
	16–31	11	6	—	—	1	—
Feb.	1–15	13	5	3	—	—	—
	16–29	—	—	5	—	3	—
Mar.	1–15[f]	5	—	215	(101)	73	(31)
	16–31	14	15	130	(36)	143	(14)
Apr.	1–15	2	1	78	(40)	96	(11)
	16–30	2	5	33	(26)	63	(5)
May	1–15	12	—	2	—	—	—
	16–31	2	5	2	—	—	—
June	1–15	3	3	—	—	—	—
	16–30	—	—	13	—	1	—
July	1–18[g]	5	5	3	—	—	—
	19–31	—	—	4	—	—	—
Aug.	1–20	—	1	5	—	—	—
	Total	74	48	494	(203)	380	(61)

[a]Bombing and missile attacks on cities and economic, nonmilitary targets, as reported in daily war communiqués and other sources
[b]Aircraft strikes on Iranian maritime targets and offshore oil terminals as reported in Iraqi daily war communiqués
[c]All-source reporting of Iranian gunboat attacks against neutral shipping
[d]Long-range missiles fired at Iranian cities outside the border region (included in figures for Iraq)
[e]SCUD-B missiles fired at Baghdad and other Iraqi cities outside the border region (included in figures for Iran)
[f]Includes Iraqi missile attacks begun on the evening of 29 February
[g]From beginning of month to Iranian acceptance of Resolution 598

March, when it launched the Val-Fajr 10 offensive in Iraqi Kurdistan. This surprise attack in a weakly defended region where the population was already in near rebellion against the Iraqi government achieved substantial gains in the first few days: four thousand Iraqi prisoners were taken, a number of villages and substantial territories were occupied, and troops pushed close to the Darband-i Khan Dam that provides electric power to Baghdad.

The resumption of the war of the cities interrupted the trend toward improved Iran-Soviet relations. On the first day of the renewed attacks, Iran summoned the Soviet ambassador to protest Iraqi use of Soviet missiles. Three days later, unruly crowds demonstrated in front of the Soviet embassy in Tehran and the consulate in Isfahan. Iran also began to harden its stance regarding the Soviet withdrawal from Afghanistan, calling for the Soviets to pull out unconditionally. The Soviet Union quickly introduced an emergency resolution to the U.N. Security Council calling for an end to the war of the cities, stressing that Iraq was not authorized to employ scud missiles at the extended range. Rafsanjani summed up the Iranian reaction in a press conference on 24 March:

> The Soviet Union is currently pursuing a policy of hypocrisy and duplicity. Yes, the Russians put these missiles at Iraq's disposal. We have studied some of them, which we recovered intact. Most of them were manufactured in 1985 and 1986. They used new parts produced by the Soviet Union to modify the missiles and increase their range. . . . We are talking with them. Due to the fact that we are neighbors and have no desire for a crisis in relations, the issue is controlled to a point. However, it remains a serious matter for us.[59]

The other new element in this escalation of the war was the expanded use of chemical weapons by Iraq against civilian targets. Iraq had used poison gas extensively in earlier campaigns, but the targets had been Iranian military forces. On the evening of 16 March, Iraq conducted two bombing raids against the village of Halabjah, which Iranian forces were about to enter. The bombs caught the local Iraqi Kurdish villagers in their homes and in the street, killing at least two thousand civilians. This raid attracted intense media attention, and grisly pictures of the massacre filled television screens around the world.

The United Nations dispatched an investigating team that confirmed the atrocity. But Iraq was unrepentant. Tariq Aziz wrote to the secretary-general that "in their legitimate, moral, and internationally approved self-defense, our people are determined to use all available abilities and means against the criminal invaders."[60] In fact, in the succeeding months Iraq used poison gas more frequently and against a wider range of targets, including civilians, than at any previous time in the war. The U.N. Security Council passed Resolution 612 on

9 May, mandating an immediate end to the use of chemical weapons in the war and holding out the prospect of sanctions against violators, but it had no effect.

Iran Succumbs

Throughout this period, evidence accumulated of growing factional disputes within the Iranian leadership. Elections for the third Majles in early April were extremely contentious and resulted in the replacement of many conservative representatives from the bazaar and clergy with more radical individuals. In the days immediately preceding the election, a Kuwaiti airliner was hijacked to Mashhad, severely embarrassing those elements of the leadership who were attempting to cleanse Iran's image as a "terrorist state." Several days later, mines again appeared in the central Persian Gulf, one of which struck the USS *Samuel B. Roberts* and set off a new round of clashes with U.S. forces. Rafsanjani characterized this incident as "an accident . . . which appears to be rigged by elements we cannot yet identify."[61]

This was only the beginning of a series of blows that Iran experienced over a period of three months. Iraq went on the offensive against Iran's disorganized and disheartened military forces, recapturing the Fao Peninsula in a lightning attack on 18 April and then pushing back Iranian forces all along the front. In mid-May, Iraq carried out a devastating attack on the Iranian oil transfer site at Larak Island in the southern Gulf, destroying five ships, including the world's largest supertanker. Antiwar sentiment began to appear openly in demonstrations in major Iranian cities. And, most disturbing of all for the divided leadership, persuasive evidence began to accumulate that Khomeini was severely ill and virtually incapacitated.

Iran desperately attempted to stem the tide, appointing Rafsanjani as the acting commander in chief in an effort to halt the disarray and disintegration of the armed forces and starting a new peace offensive at the United Nations. But this was interrupted on 3 July by the tragic shootdown of a commercial Iranian aircraft by the USS *Vincennes,* killing all 290 passengers and crew.

This terrible accident, coming at the end of a seemingly endless series of defeats, underscored the despair of Iran's position. Despite the enormity of the mistake, Iran was unable to muster sufficient support at the United Nations to condemn the U.S. action. Its isolation and weakness had never been more apparent. As Rafsanjani noted just before the airbus incident, "We created enemies for ourselves" in the international community. "We have not spent enough time seeing that they become friends."[62]

On 18 July, the Iranian foreign minister sent a letter to the U.N. secretary-general formally accepting Resolution 598. Two days later, Khomeini sent a "message to the nation," read by an announcer, associating himself with the decision, which, he said, was "more deadly than taking poison."[63]

Although Iran did not spell out the reasons for this decision, the key factor was probably the changed conditions at the battlefront. Iran had always balked at withdrawing its forces from Iraqi territory without some quid pro quo. That consideration had now been rendered moot by Iraq's recapture of virtually all of its own territory. Resolution 598 had originally been written to favor Iraq, which in mid-1987 was perceived as being in danger of losing the war. With the change of fortune on the battlefield, the resolution now offered the prospect of international support and protection for Iran in the face of an effective and determined Iraqi offensive.

Iraq was taken by surprise and initially resisted accepting a cease-fire while continuing its mopping-up operations. Iraq also continued to demonstrate a contemptuous disregard for the Security Council and for world opinion on the use of chemical weapons. A U.N. investigative team presented its report to the Security Council on 1 August, finding that "chemical weapons continue to be used on an intensive scale" by Iraq. Only hours later, Iraq launched a massive chemical bombing attack on the Iranian town of Oshnoviyeh. As international pressure mounted, however, Saddam Hussein finally agreed to accept a cease-fire on 6 August, on condition that the cease-fire would be followed immediately by direct talks.

A U.N. observer force was rushed to the region, and a cease-fire went into effect on 20 August. Formal talks began in Geneva on 25 August, under the aegis of the U.N. secretary-general. Although the war was not officially over, for the first time in eight years fighting was suspended.

Backing into a Truce

There are many lessons to be drawn from the events of these twenty months from the perspective of each of the participants, the regional states, the superpowers, and the United Nations. That must be the subject of another study. There is, however, one interpretation of the complex process leading up to the cease-fire that is not intuitively obvious and therefore deserves at least brief mention.

If it is true, as the evidence strongly suggests, that Iran concluded in early 1987 that the war was not winnable, the subsequent events can be viewed as an internal debate within Iran—with substantial external involvement—about how to disengage. There was a consistent thread throughout Iran's many maneuvers over these twenty months suggesting an underlying willingness to reach a compromise settlement. But there is also evidence that such an outcome was vigorously opposed by factions within Iran who were committed to the war for reasons of ideology or interest and who were prepared to undercut and embarrass their own national leadership if necessary to sabotage such an outcome.

Viewed from this perspective, the interesting question is: what actions by external actors encouraged the peacemaking process and what actions impeded that process? Certainly the role of the U.N. secretary-general was crucial. He kept the negotiating process alive and developed alternatives that kept options open for those in Iran who wished to disengage.

The role of the United States was ambiguous. The introduction of substantial U.S. forces into the Gulf and their direct military clashes with Iran certainly raised the stakes for Iran and dramatized its isolation. But the U.S. focus on punishing Iran—first by drafting Resolution 598 in a form known to be unacceptable to Iran and later by its singleminded pursuit of an arms embargo despite Iran's offers of a compromise settlement—may have prolonged the war for many months by closing off acceptable avenues to an agreement, thereby strengthening the hands of the hardliners in Tehran.

Iraq, particularly from mid-1987, was less interested in a cease-fire than in a clear-cut victory in the war. With the support of the United States and several other countries, Iraq was prepared to use Resolution 598 to keep Iran isolated and on the defensive. Iraq, however, repeatedly rejected the efforts of the secretary-general to develop a compromise implementation plan that could have provided the basis for an early cease-fire. That attitude became unmistakable after Iran finally accepted the cease-fire and Iraq began to stall and resist. Nevertheless, it was Iraq's brutal but effective series of offensives in 1988 that turned the tide and finally persuaded Iran to "drink the poison" of political concession.

These external forces were obviously very important in pressing Iran to accept a cease-fire. In the final analysis, however, the crucial turning point may have come in the spring of 1988 as internal opposition to the war began to mount in Iran, as it became evident that Khomeini might be dying, and as the political infighting began to run out of control. At that point, the Iranian leadership had to confront the possibility that the revolution itself might be in jeopardy.

Given the choice between an ideologically appealing but increasingly futile war and the survival of the revolutionary system itself, the pragmatists in the leadership asserted themselves and stopped the war.

Notes

1. According to the Danish Seamen's Union, nine to twelve shiploads (more than five thousand tons) of military equipment were delivered to Bandar Abbas from Elath in 1986. A

reasonable estimate of the value of these cargoes would be more than $500 million, or roughly ten times the value of U.S. arms delivered by air to Iran.

2. See Anthony H. Cordesman, *The Iran-Iraq War and Western Security, 1984–87* (London: Jane's, 1987), 57 n. 19.

3. *Kayhan,* 29 June 1987, cited in Foreign Broadcast Information Service, Daily Report: Near East and South Asia (hereafter FBIS), 7 July 1987.

4. Both Iran and Iraq announced census results in 1987. Iraq reported its population as 16.3 million (FBIS, 19 Oct. 1987); Iran said its population totaled 52 million, 25 percent of whom were under six years old (FBIS, 18 Nov. 1987). The number of people born in Iran since the revolution was roughly equal to the entire population of Iraq.

5. The possibilities of a negotiating effort were visible at the time, as well as in retrospect. See Brian Urquhart and Gary Sick, "Douse the Spreading Iran-Iraq Flames," *New York Times,* 19 May 1987.

6. Since this event galvanized U.S. public opinion about the need for a more capable U.S. naval presence in the Gulf, many observers suspected that the Iraqi attack was done deliberately to draw the United States into the Gulf. The evidence for this view is not persuasive. The United States' reaction was not predictable, and it is unlikely that Iraq would have risked destroying its relationship with the United States in an uncertain gamble. Iraqi pilots were notorious for their imprecise navigation and for firing at radar images without verifying the nature of the target. A senior U.S. naval official with extensive experience in the Gulf told me more than a year before the *Stark* incident that Iraqi carelessness was "a mistake waiting to happen." On 17 May it did.

7. U.N. Secretary-General Pérez de Cuellar had personally arranged a truce in the war of the cities in 1984. Although the truce broke down after some seven months, both sides were technically still on record as renouncing such attacks. Both Iran and Iraq continued to issue occasional protests to the United Nations about egregious breaches of the understanding through 1987.

8. *New York Times,* 7 Jan. 1987.

9. Press conference with foreign and local correspondents, 20 Apr. 1987 (FBIS, 4 May 1987).

10. *Washington Post,* 30 and 31 May 1987. These reports were based on a background briefing at the State Department, apparently with Murphy.

11. The first convoy of reflagged ships transited the Strait of Hormuz on 22 July. Two days later the reflagged tanker *Bridgeton* struck a mine near the Iranian Revolutionary Guard base on Farsi Island. That was the only damage sustained by any of the convoys during 1987.

12. Consideration of a major new U.N. initiative on the war had begun through the efforts of the secretary-general in 1985. The British delegation took the lead in promoting such an initiative in early 1986, until the United States became directly engaged in May, about the time of the Murphy trip to Baghdad.

13. On the same day, Iranian gunboats attacked the British tanker *Gentle Breeze,* killing one crew member and wounding thirty-three others. British foreign secretary Sir Geoffrey Howe condemned this attack as "the last straw." He called for the imposition of sanctions against Iran and closed the Iranian military purchasing office in London. The *Iran Ajr* was scuttled on 25 September, and the captured Iranian crew members were returned to Iran via Oman on the twenty-sixth.

14. *New York Times,* 28 Sept. 1987, 3.

15. During an interview on the CBS television program "Face the Nation" on 13 September, Shultz confirmed that the United States and Iran exchanged messages regularly through the Swiss protecting power. I was told in a private interview that a conciliatory message was sent to Iran by the United States immediately after the *Iran Ajr* affair in an effort to "put this behind us as quickly as possible."

16. FBIS, 1 Oct. 1987.

17. The so-called Silkworm (HY-2) is a Chinese copy of the Soviet Styx antiship missile. It is

a subsonic surface-to-surface missile with a 1,100-pound high explosive warhead and a range of about twenty-five miles. It can be fired from coastal sites or from ships. See Cordesman, *The Iran-Iraq War and Western Security,* 133.

18. FBIS, 26 Oct. 1987.

19. *New York Times,* 23 Oct. 1987.

20. A Silkworm missile was fired into Kuwaiti waters on 7 December, possibly in response to newspaper stories that the United States intended to locate a barge there to support U.S. forces. The missile struck a decoy platform and did no damage (*Washington Post,* 8 Dec. 1987).

21. Broadcast of a speech on 22 Dec. 1987, cited in FBIS, 23 Dec. 1987.

22. Interview of 5 Apr. 1987, cited in FBIS, 15 Apr. 1987.

23. For many years, during and after the Shah's rule, the Soviet Union sponsored a Persian-language broadcasting station near Baku, north of the Iranian border. Called the National Voice of Iran, it broadcast statements by the banned Tudeh Party. That operation was closed down in the mid-1980s, probably as a political gesture to Iran. It began again in 1986 from Afghanistan under the name Radio of the Iran Toilers.

24. FBIS, 3 Feb. 1987.

25. The following description of Soviet policy is based on my discussions in Moscow in mid-January 1988 during a meeting of U.S. Middle East specialists with their Soviet counterparts, sponsored by the International Research and Exchanges Board (IREX).

26. Tudeh Party statements of 27 and 29 Nov. 1987 (FBIS, 2 Dec. 1987).

27. Tass, 4 Dec. 1987. These remarks were not mentioned by Tehran radio in its report of the meeting.

28. Article by M. Krutikin in the Armenian party newspaper *Kommunist,* reported in *Washington Post,* 26 Dec. 1987, 25.

29. Statement by Karen Brutents, deputy chief of the Communist Party Central Committee International Department, in Kuwait, 28 Dec. 1987 (FBIS, 7 Jan. 1988).

30. For a concise summary of U.N. activities during the war, see the paper by Ralph King in *The United Nations and the Iran-Iraq War* (New York: Ford Foundation, August 1987), 7–27, the proceedings of a conference, 20–21 Apr. 1987.

31. The Iraqi ambassador to the United Nations was able to delay the first formal Security Council meeting on the war by promising that Iraq would quickly solve the problem. See Ford Foundation, *The United Nations and the Iran-Iraq War,* 29.

32. Iraqi Mirage pilot Capt. Zuhayr Mohammed Said al-Audisi was captured by Iran on 2 February 1987, when his plane crashed in Iranian territory. He reportedly told Iranian interrogators that an Iraqi MIG-25 fighter piloted by Lt. Col. Abdullah Faraj was ordered in early May 1982 to fly toward the Iranian-Turkish border where the Iraqi government knew that Algerian foreign minister Benyahya's aircraft would pass. The aircraft was shot down with a Soviet air-to-air missile (FBIS, 22 May 1987).

33. Personal interview in February 1988. The problem was alluded to by several speakers during the formal Security Council debate on 20 July. The most explicit reservation was voiced by German foreign minister Genscher, who remarked that "the cease-fire, the ending of all military actions, and the withdrawal of troops cannot take place simultaneously; they will follow in succession" (U.N. document S/2750, 28).

34. Personal interview with a U.N. diplomat in January 1988.

35. Iraq's formal reply to the secretary-general was dated 23 July (S/19045).

36. S/19031, 11 Aug. 1987, 5.

37. On 24 July, Iraqi foreign minister Tariq Aziz reportedly informed the secretary-general unofficially that his country would cease all shipping attacks for thirty days beginning 29 July pending the Iranian reply (see FBIS, 27 July 1987). Although the report was officially denied by Iraq, it proved to be precisely accurate.

38. FBIS, 1 Sept. 1987. Other Iraqi spokesmen were more explicit. On 3 October, Iraqi minister of culture Jasim said in an interview with *Al-Tadamun* in London: "When 100 Iraqi planes fly over Iran, Iran can afford to send one and if it is lucky two. . . . We are capable of demolishing Iran brick by brick. . . . We have decided to return Iran to the stage of relying on 'rugs' rather than oil" (FBIS, 21 Oct. 1987).

39. The secretary-general's report to the Security Council on 16 September represented the most authoritative statement to date of the positions of the two parties. Although the report was confidential, it circulated widely at the United Nations and was published verbatim by the Kuwait News Agency on 19 September (FBIS, 22 Sept. 1987, 45).

40. Ibid.

41. Recorded interview with Radio Monte Carlo (FBIS, 28 Sept. 1987).

42. FBIS, 30 Dec. 1987.

43. See the statement by the Syrian minister of information on 16 January (FBIS, 21 Jan. 1988) and a similar report by Patrick Tyler in the *Washington Post*, 7 Mar. 1988, A27. This was not a major concession by Iran, since relatively few ships traveled under the flags of the Gulf states. However, there had been two attacks on Saudi flag ships in December, and Kuwait had, of course, reflagged eleven of its tankers after repeated attacks. There were no Iranian attacks on GCC flag ships in the first quarter of 1988.

44. See the press conference of the Saudi foreign minister on 16 Mar. 1988 (FBIS, 17 Mar. 1988).

45. *Washington Post,* 6 Jan. 1988, 17.

46. Tehran radio, 30 January, following a meeting between Rafsanjani and the Soviet ambassador (FBIS, 1 Feb. 1988). This position was subsequently hardened after the war of the cities heated up in March. See below.

47. FBIS, 19 Feb. 1988.

48. See Iran's letter to the U.N. secretary-general of 2 July 1988 (FBIS, 6 July 1988).

49. *Washington Post,* 10 Feb. 1988, 32.

50. Ibid., 25 Feb. 1988, 36.

51. FBIS, 1 Feb. 1988.

52. Ibid., 7 Jan. 1988.

53. Speech of 30 Jan. 1988 (FBIS, 3 Feb. 1988).

54. Interview in *Al-Watan Al-Arabi.*

55. *Washington Post,* 2 Mar. 1988, 16. These same views were reflected in the private comments of Soviet officials to me in Moscow during January.

56. *New York Times,* 14 Feb. 1988, 1, 16.

57. *Washington Post,* 23 Feb. 1988, 18.

58. Over the years, Iraq had received substantial numbers of SCUD-B missiles from the Soviet Union. The nominal range of these weapons did not permit them to reach Tehran or other cities in central Iran, although they had been used extensively in the past against border towns. Iraq modified the missiles by increasing the fuel capacity and reducing the size of the warhead, thereby extending the range by about one-third. These modifications severely degraded the already poor accuracy of the SCUDs, making them useful only as a terror weapon against large targets such as cities, comparable to German use of V-2 rockets against London in World War II.

59. FBIS, 25 Mar. 1988.

60. Letter to the secretary-general of 28 March (FBIS, 30 Mar. 1988).

61. Interview on 18 April (FBIS, 19 Apr. 1988).

62. Interview on 2 July (FBIS, 6 July 1988).

63. FBIS, 21 July 1988. On 25 July, Khomeini made a six-minute appearance on television from the balcony of his residence. He appeared extremely frail and did not speak.

11

The Iranian Revolution and Great-Power Politics: Components of the First Decade

FRED HALLIDAY

Delegation arrived Tehran Sunday morning. Absence of anyone to receive us for over an hour and recurrent evidence anxiety ineptitude in even the most straightforward discourse makes it clear that we must take a step backward from the history of the past 8 years and put our task in a different light.

It may be best for us to try to picture what it would be like if after nuclear attack, a surviving Tatar[1] became Vice President; a recent grad student became Secretary of State; and a bookie became the interlocutor for all discourse with foreign countries.

—Robert McFarlane to John Poindexter, 25 May 1986

The Iranian Revolution has posed acute problems for both the United States and the Soviet Union, problems that, a decade later, still appear to be far from resolution. Neither Moscow nor Washington has been able either to develop a stable relationship with the Islamic Republic of Iran (IRI) or to ignore and oppose it outright. It would appear that, in addition to the foreign dilemmas posed by *all* revolutions, that of Iran has presented the great powers with particular difficulties. If this was so during the eight-year Iran-Iraq conflict, it may be equally so in the ensuing uneasy peace.

This is not the first time in modern history that Iran has been at the center of such international conflict: it was so in the period from the early 1890s to 1921, when a combination of international economic pressure on the Qajar dynasty, strategic rivalry between Britain and tsarist Russia, and internal upheaval within Iran led to the disintegration of the Iranian state and the entry of foreign troops—Russian and British—onto Iranian territory. The military coup of 1921, encouraged if not organized by Britain, brought this period of turmoil, internal and international, to an end. The second phase of crisis surrounding Iran was in the period 1941 to 1953. This had a more abrupt beginning than the first, being the result of an Anglo-Russian invasion in August 1941 rather than of any internal crisis, but it opened up a period of even more profound and internationalized uncertainty surrounding Iran. With the end of World War II, Soviet forces were compelled to leave Iran in March 1946, as they had been in 1920; but it took seven more years before, in the coup of August 1953, the internal and international alignments of Iran were resolved. The 1946 crisis over Azerbaijan is, in the opinion of many, the point at which the Cold War started; the coup of 1953 ended a long period of international uncertainty over Iran. In western Asia 1953 marked a final drawing of the lines of battle inherited from World War II comparable to those drawn in the same year in Korea and, a year later, in Vietnam.

The consequences of these two earlier periods have been relevant to, if not determinant of, the course of events since 1979. For many Iranians three lessons in particular were evident. First, the precondition of Iran's ability to resist external pressure and maintain its independence is that there exist a strong government in Tehran, one able to control its own armed forces, administer the provinces, manage social discontent in the major cities, and resist external machinations. It was the weakness of the Qajars and the flux of the Constitutional Revolution of 1906 that laid Iran so open to intervention in the 1900s. It was the vacuum of the war period leading to the uprising in Gilan, in which Islamic nationalists and communists formed a temporary alliance, that prompted the intervention of Bolshevik forces after 1917 and the British attempt to impose a protectorate in 1919. Although internal turmoil did not occasion the invasion of 1941, such turmoil followed the invasion and did prolong the consequences of that invasion to 1953: it provided a context in which Britain and, later, the United States were able to weaken and ultimately to oust Mosaddeq.

The second lesson of these earlier crises is that Iran's importance does not lie primarily in its economy. Its products other than oil are of little international importance—it is not carpets, opium, or pistachio nuts that have concerned Curzon, Churchill, or Reagan. Even in the case of oil Iran is not so important: in the 1951–53 period AIOC/BP was able to replace Iranian output by boosting that from Kuwait and building a substitute Abadan in Aden. The revolution of 1979 contributed to the second great oil price rise, but the related threats to Gulf oil supply, the subsequent reduction of Iranian output from 6 million to under 2 million barrels a day, and the uncertainties of the war did not prevent a fall in the world price. Iran's importance was evident long before oil was first struck in Masjid-i Suleiman in 1908. Its significance is above all strategic—where Iran is located. It is this that causes its neighbor Russia, and Russia's distant foes, the most concern.

Here, however, a third and recurrent problem arises. Faced with such intrusive concern from both blocs, Iran has often been attracted to a policy of neutrality or equidistance between the blocs. Governments in Tehran have sought to balance the pressures of two rivals in order to maximize the benefits they offer Iran while reducing their influence upon the country itself. This is what the Qajars did in the late nineteenth century, hoping to use British influence to offset tsarist Russia. It was Reza Shah's hope to use German influence to offset his British imperial neighbor to the west (in Iraq, the Gulf) and southeast (India). It was Mosaddeq's hope to pursue a policy of "negative" balance between East and West and so gain acceptance for his nationalist policies. Khomeini, of course, followed this with his own version, *nah sharq, nah gharb,* "neither East nor West." Whatever the outcome of this latest balancing policy, the record of the other two attempts is clear: in the end, they failed. If this can be ascribed in part to internal dissension within Iran (the enabling factor), it must also be due in part to the sensitivity of where Iran is. Policies of equidistance are easier to pursue when a state is removed from the immediate vicinity of either great power. When a state is on one or the other's frontier, both blocs have particular cause for alarm—the neighboring bloc because it fears its enemy will consolidate there, the distant bloc because it fears, or claims to fear, that the adjacent power will extend its influence into this weaker neighbor. The temptations to intervene, therefore, are all the greater. In nationalizing oil, Mosaddeq in 1951–53 only did what Cárdenas in Mexico had done in the 1930s, but he did it in a country bordering the Soviet Union. It was, therefore, all the more important for the West to stop him.

Iranians, like others, are to a considerable degree influenced by these earlier outcomes, and since 1979 the aspiration to equidistance has been revived, albeit in Islamic guise. The political culture of modern Iran, one in which myths about the power and motives of foreign states have a vivid life, is in part a product of these earlier, and by no means imagined, external interventions. This supposedly paranoid streak in Iranian nationalism has its historical rational roots, just as the anxiety and illusions of individuals can have roots in their own earlier traumatic experiences. Equally, the Soviet Union and the United States have approached the post-1979 crisis with concerns that derive from the past; these shape and, in part, distort the present.

For the Soviet Union Iran is a country through which threats may advance. Russia was invaded through its southern Caucasian frontier during World War I, first by the Turks and then by British forces, who left only in 1920. The Square of the Twenty-six Commissars in Baku commemorates the murder of Bolshevik officials in that period, allegedly with British complicity. The Soviet intervention in August 1941 was undertaken for military reasons: to prevent a German consolidation in Iran, then a remote but not impossible eventuality, and to protect the lines from the Gulf through which, in the end, over half of all U.S. military supplies to the Russian front were transported. The Soviet Union had a reserved policy toward radical forces in Iran after 1945: it abandoned the Azerbaijani and Kurdish republics in 1946, allowed the Tudeh Party's influence to be chiseled away by the Shah, and did little to help Mosaddeq until it was too late.

The underlying Soviet aim was not revolution in Iran but a stabilization of the situation there and some limitation of the military presence that the United States could maintain in Iran. With the Tehran-Moscow understanding of 1962, under which the United States pledged not to station nuclear forces in Iran, the Soviet Union was able to regain that measure of stability on its southern frontier that it had lost in June 1941. It is this, above all, that accounts for the tardy and ambivalent Soviet response to the Iranian Revolution itself. The gist of Brezhnev's statement of November 1978, the first official Soviet declaration on the revolution, was that the United States should not intervene. For the Soviet Union, the Iranian Revolution, though positive in some respects (end of U.S. influence in Iran, dissolution of CENTO), also opened up new strategic uncertainties, both because of the fluid situation within Iran itself and because of the subsequent destabilizing regional consequences (Gulf, Afghanistan).

For the United States, Iran has been one of the most difficult Third World countries to deal with, not least because the understandings of what constitute "reasonable" behavior or "good intentions" notoriously differ in the two countries. This conflict reflects not just misunderstanding or policy mistakes, let alone some impersonal "tragedy," but a clash of interests between a nationalist Iran and a United States concerned to maintain, via Iranian partners, a degree of domination in that country. The first real encounter between the two came in the late 1940s and the Mosaddeq period. For many Iranians, the United States replaced Britain as the main imperial enemy, responsible from 1953 onward for the maintenance of the Pahlavi dictatorship. In U.S. perceptions, two images remained from that period—the threat of a Soviet thrust southward, toward the oil fields of Saudi Arabia in particular, and the image of an Iranian nationalist leadership prone to theatrical negotiation tactics and anti-imperialist declamation. By the time the Iranian Revolution came about in 1978–79 the United States was already alarmed about upheavals in the Third World (Vietnam, Angola, Ethiopia), and the shock of the revolution was all the greater because it appeared to clash with the received perception of Iran as a secure modernizing ally. If the revolution itself—that is, the fall of the Shah—did not place Iran in the center of U.S. concern and demonology, this deficiency was made up in no uncertain terms on 4 November 1979 when the Muslim Students Following the Imam's Line (SFIL) occupied the U.S. embassy in Tehran. No single event in modern history since the outbreak of the Korean war in June 1950 has so concentrated U.S. attention on a Third World crisis.

The Aftermath of 1979

The fall of the Shah in January 1979 ushered in the third major phase in modern history of internal and international crises focused on Iran. In some respects, the coordinates of the crisis were similar to those of its two predecessors: an undermining of the Iranian state occasioned external interventions and concern; the strategic overshadowed the economic; both blocs proceeded, with asymmetric interests and resources, to react—seeking advantage and trying to limit the influence and advance of the other.

Yet the post-1979 complex of problems surrounding the Iranian Revolution is, in some important respects, distinct from that which characterized earlier crises and is in many ways more intractable. In the first place, the situation within Iran is markedly different. The last two decades of the Qajar dynasty and the 1941–53 interregnum were marked by great instability within Iran, by a weak state, and by organized opposition political movements. It was this that enabled outside influence—covert and overt, together with economic pressure—to have its effects. The situation since 1979 has been very different. For all its factionalism, the Islamic Republic of Iran has to date been a strong state, largely resistant to outside political enticements, in control of its armed forces, and able to mobilize significant sections of the population within. Since 1981 it has faced no major opposition forces, and it has weathered the supreme test of foreign invasion. It is marked by factionalism, which could provide an occasion for external influence, now that Khomeini is gone; but to date this factionalism has been a sign of political health more than of weakness, allowing a degree of public debate and electoral uncertainty rare in any postrevolutionary state or in a country at war.

Second, the post-1979 international context is very different, not so much because of the policies of the United States and the Soviet Union, but because of the changed regional context. In the earlier two crises the other states of the region were, to a considerable extent, insulated from what happened in Iran: during Iran's Constitutional Revolution Iraq was under Ottoman rule, and from 1920 until 1958 it was subject to British influence; the Persian Gulf was, until 1971, under predominantly British naval influence: Afghanistan experienced brief periods of upheaval, as in the 1919–29 period and after 1946, but was only slowly beginning to be integrated into the international economic and strategic systems and was not visibly affected by events in Iran. Iranian radicalism, for its part, had its international links, notably through Sufi sects and clerical contacts, but neither the constitutional revolutionaries of 1906 nor Mosaddeq saw foreign policy in predominantly regional terms.

The situation since 1979 has, of course, been very different. Afghanistan has, since the early 1970s, been increasingly linked to events in Iran—indeed Pahlavi pressure on the Daud regime was one component in the 1978 communist seizure of power—and up to one million Afghans have worked as migrants in Iran.[2] Britain has withdrawn from the Gulf, its departure symbolized by the lame-duck response to the Iranian seizure of the islands of Tumbs and Abu Musa on 30 November 1971 in the last hours of imperial protection. Iraq has, since 1958, been governed by radical military regimes that are both more exposed to Iranian influence, monarchical and clerical alike, and more intent on rivaling Iran in the Gulf. On the margins, Pakistan, occupying the area adjacent to southeast Iran that was formerly part of the British raj, has come to play a significant regional role, most of all as instigator of rebellion in Afghanistan, but also as a regime seeking to straddle the Gulf divide by maintaining close and profitable links with both Iran and the Arabs. The quiet reentry into the Middle East of another power, Turkey, betokens an analogous revitalization of postcolonial concerns; Ankara's policy has been motivated by a quest for economic advantage and strategic gain and by the need to keep the Gulf conflict from activating communal and ethnic conflicts within its own frontiers.[3] A precondition for stability in eastern Turkey is peace between Iran and Iraq.

For its part, the IRI has seen a militant foreign policy as one of its justifications: in contrast to the passive or constrained neutralism of Mosaddeq, Khomeini activated an international revolutionary movement, with arms, money, training, and radio broadcasts, and sought, as determinedly as Lenin and his associates ever did, to spread the revolution to neighboring states and organize an international following. Tempered, much as Lenin was, by diplomatic and strategic constraints, Khomeini was still, a decade after coming to power, actively promoting opposition in three Middle Eastern states—Iraq, Afghanistan, and Lebanon. Few can believe that periodic proclamations of coexistence from Tehran will be permanent, not least because such foreign policy initiatives often reflect the temporary priorities of factional competition at home. The demise in late 1986 of the Hashemi brothers, who were linked to the more militant exporters of revolution in the Islamic Guards, signaled an end to one kind of promotion of revolution. But the angry Iranian response to the Saudi massacre of Iranian pilgrims in July 1987, when Rafsanjani and Khomeini called for the overthrow of the Saudi monarchy, and the endorsement given to

Islamist critics of secularism in Turkey, suggest that the parameters of Islamic internationalism may expand, as well as contract, in the coming years.[4] The end of the war, in August 1988, may release these internationalist energies in novel ways.

The result of this second major difference is that what happens in Iran has much more impact on the regional, as distinct from East-West, balance than was earlier the case. The Iran-Iraq war lasted for seven years and eleven months, only two months shorter than the longest interstate war of the twentieth century, the Sino-Japanese. Not only was Iran involved for almost eight years in war with Iraq, but the war also affected the international and internal processes of Turkey, Pakistan, Kuwait, and Saudi Arabia. More dramatically, it placed the Iranian Revolution and the Gulf war at the center of a triplet of regional crises stretching from the Wakhan corridor in Afghanistan bordering China to the eastern shores of the Mediterranean—that is, tying in a reinforcing and mutually enflaming manner the Afghan conflict, the Gulf war, and the Arab-Israeli dispute. Iran's revolution also had its effects on at least four other long-established regional conflicts—the Indo-Pakistani, the Syrian-Iraqi, the Greek-Turkish, and that in the Horn of Africa (Ethiopia–Somalia/Sudan). Some of these interlockings were evident. Iran was an actor in Afghanistan through its support for the Shi'i guerrillas; it not only opposed the Soviet Union but also in the longer run challenged Pakistan for hegemony. At the same time Iran became an actor in the Arab-Israeli dispute both by distracting the Arab world from Israel and by inspiring and helping to organize the Hizbollah in Lebanon.

Such interlockings made it much more difficult to find solutions to these problems and also made it harder for those outside to calculate their policies. The United States supported the same side as Iran in Afghanistan, yet it backed Iraq against Iran in the Gulf war. Israel is pitted against Iran in southern Lebanon, yet sees Iran as an objective ally because of its threat to the Arabs. The Soviet Union had to calculate how far to pursue favor with Iran in order to ease the situation in Afghanistan, and in the last year of the war it risked Arab displeasure by appearing to appease the IRI and expressing reservations about a U.N. boycott. Such dilemmas were not, of course, unknown in Washington, and they underlay some of the confusions of the Irangate affair.

To these two novel features of the latest, post-1979, Iranian crisis can now be added a third: the internal politics of the two great powers themselves have been affected by the Iranian Revolution. The Constitutional Revolution of 1906 was itself in part a reaction to the 1905 revolution in Russia, and there was some interaction of revolutionaries as between Tabriz and the Caucasus. Stalin began his career organizing Persian migrants in the oil fields. But neither this nor the

1941–53 crisis had much impact on Soviet politics. The fact that the August 1953 debacle came soon after the death of Stalin prevented the new leadership from being blamed for Soviet miscalculations. For the U.S. polity, the earlier crisis had no salience, beyond the exertions of the economic adviser Morgan Shuster. The successful outcome of the 1953 coup was to become one of the points of honor in the CIA's history, contributing to U.S. interventionist as well as Iranian nationalist mythology by excluding both the British role and the importance of other social and political preconditions within Iran itself.[5] Yet 1953, too, had little impact on U.S. politics. With the 1979 revolution this insulation ended. Iran became a factor influencing both Soviet and U.S. polities at several levels, thus making it far more difficult for the leaderships of these countries to handle the crisis adequately. The ways in which Iran influenced the domestic affairs of the two countries were very different, but the shared result was that in both Moscow and Washington policy-making on the IRI and the Gulf war acquired new areas of complexity.

For the Soviet Union, the Iranian Revolution affected domestic politics in at least three respects. First, as in the United States, the revolution occasioned disagreements within the foreign policy–making apparatus. We know only a restricted amount about this process, but the available evidence indicates that Iran has been a subject of dispute. Soon after the revolution, during 1979, there was evidently one faction that was critical of Khomeini and, as seen in articles by Brezhnev's speech writer Aleksandr Bovin, pointed to the medieval and chauvinist elements in his thinking; another faction, for strategic reasons, wanted to win sympathy in Tehran.[6] In the turmoil of the hostage crisis, when the focus was on preventing an intervention by the United States, it was the latter strategic current, championed by Gromyko, that prevailed. But differences of evaluation regarding Iran persisted, some of them expressed elliptically in discussion of the class character of the Islamic movement; and with the suppression of the Tudeh in 1983 it became more legitimate to criticize the IRI. By 1986 it was possible for a Soviet writer to say that, overall, the Iranian Revolution had been a negative development, creating a situation worse than that under the shahs.[7] In January 1988 the senior Middle East expert Igor Belyaev wrote a strong attack on Khomeini in *Literaturnaya Gazeta*. In some ways reminiscent of earlier debates on Nasser, which sought to weigh his progressive against his regressive characteristics, this debate evidently had important foreign policy implications.

The second internal repercussion of the Iranian Revolution was in regard to Soviet Muslims. There is a lot of speculation about this question, on the basis of scant evidence, to the effect that an Iran-style Islamic revolt is brewing within the Soviet Union. Events regarding Nagorno-Karabakh should have served to underline that where there is a multiplicity of ethnic minorities their desire to revolt or secede from the dominant group may be tempered by a comparable or even greater dislike of other minorities. Secession apart, however, there are major problems among the Soviet Muslim republics relating to the quality of military recruits, employment, corruption, and Islamic practices themselves. Although the social institutions sustaining traditional Islam have been abolished (schools, endowed lands, courts, taxation systems), many Islamic ideas and personal practices remain, and there has undoubtedly been a revival of interest in some aspects of Islam since the 1970s. For the Soviet authorities the dilemma is evident: to confront Islamic movements outside, whether in Iran or Afghanistan, may exacerbate the situation within the Soviet Union; to appease them may seem to endorse their spread to the Soviet Union itself. The Soviet Union had evidently been concerned to insulate its Muslim areas from Iran as much as possible: when, in 1982, Iran asked to be allowed to transfer its consulate from Leningrad to Dushambe, capital of Persian-speaking Tajikistan, the decision went to the CPSU Politburo before it was turned down, and the authorities have been annoyed by Iranian radio broadcasts to the Soviet Union. They also sought to turn the Iran-Iraq war to advantage, asserting that this kind of slaughter, and the medieval practices of the IRI, would follow from an Islamic revival in the Soviet Union itself. One thing that every Russian knows about Khomeini is that he forbade the playing of chess.

There is, however, a third domestic component of the Iranian Revolution, namely, the specific implications for Moscow-Tehran relations of perestroika. Perestroika is above all an attempt to transform the Soviet economy and galvanize society from above. It requires a period of détente with the United States and, by extension, a reduction of Third World tension. From this has followed the more active, businesslike approach of Gorbachev to regional issues. For relations with the IRI, two consequences followed from perestroika; one is obvious, the other less so. The first consequence was that from 1985 onward Moscow was more concerned than ever to end the Iran-Iraq war—to remove a justification for friction with the United States and to demonstrate Soviet flexibility and "new thinking." Moscow was less likely than it would have been in the early 1980s (as, for example, in the U.S. hostage affair) to use uncertainties in Iran or the Gulf to win advantage vis-à-vis the West—hence the cooperation on naval deployments, U.N. Security Council Resolution 598, condemnations of terrorism, and a de facto joint policy of shoring up Iraq. This is not to say that an element of competition and disagreement with the United States did not persist, but that it was tempered by the search for common ground.

The second, less obvious, consequence of perestroika has been that, for largely domestic reasons, Gorbachev has initiated a much tougher policy vis-à-vis the Islamic republics and Islamist ideologies in general. The Central Asian republics of the Soviet Union have been targeted for perestroika because they are seen as riddled with corruption and inefficiency; the inflation of cotton production figures in Uzbekistan under Rashidov and the corruption in Kazakhstan under Kunayev are outstanding examples. In February 1986 the twenty-seventh CPSU Congress finally voted *not* to divert Siberian rivers to Central Asia: this was a decision interpreted as detrimental to the Central Asian republics, where the possibility of increased employment in agriculture rests on the extension of the cultivable area. In November 1986, on his way home from India, Gorbachev stopped in Tashkent to deliver a speech containing a particularly tart attack on Islamist practices. The importance of this speech was later played down, but the post-1985 tone in Moscow has been in general less indulgent than formerly toward Third World rhetoric in its Iranian, Libyan, or Cuban guises, and this has had an impact on policy toward the IRI. The perception of Khomeini among post-1985 Soviet leaders is unlikely to have been much more sympathetic than it was in Washington.

For the United States, Iran has had equally significant internal consequences. These have complicated the making of policy toward Tehran, even though Iran is many thousands of miles away. As in the Soviet Union, the Iranian Revolution produced divisions within the foreign policy–making apparatus. It exacerbated an already existing chasm between hawkish and dovish elements within the Carter administration. In the way that such crises can focus underlying differences, it generated two competing myths about what might have been possible—a military clampdown for the hawks, a working relationship with the IRI for the doves. These differences are evident in the subsequent accounts of the participants: the writing of memoirs constitutes the continuation of bureaucratic politics by other means.[8] Such divisions, moreover, resurfaced in the mid-1980s, once the Irangate initiative got underway, with well-known consequences and led to the greatest scandal of Reagan's administration. The implications of the Iranian Revolution itself were not, however, confined to the foreign policy–making apparatus but, enhanced by the hostage crisis, had an important impact on U.S. public opinion. That opinion was already alarmed about the Third World before 4 November 1979, as the factitious argument about the Soviet "combat brigade" in Cuba had shown a few months earlier; but the seizure and public humiliation of U.S. diplomats brought on an important shift in American opinion that underlay the Reagan victory in 1980.

The public alarm had two results, although it was not until Reagan's second term that this became clear. The first, enhanced by later terrorist attacks, was that anti-Iranian sentiment became an enduring feature of U.S. politics in the 1980s. The callous response among U.S. politicians and the public to the airbus incident in July 1988 was a sign of this attitude, and it made any dealings with the IRI almost impossible, whatever strategic (anti-Soviet) reasons Reagan was to offer for any initiatives. The second consequence was that, with a composite Third World/terrorist enemy identified as the main threat to U.S. interests, it became politically safer to deal with the Soviet Union. Whereas in the early 1980s Moscow was often blamed for what the PLO or Khomeini did, this had changed by 1986–87. The shift, encouraged by a smiling Gorbachev, constituted an enabling factor in Reagan's Soviet policy. By becoming the most prominent enemy, Khomeini unwittingly contributed to the improvement in Moscow-Washington relations that characterized Reagan's second term.[9]

The anger that IRI policies engendered in the United States was, however, to have a third consequence for the United States—namely, to provide opponents of Reagan's Central American policy with a convenient pretext for reducing aid to the Contras. They thereby made it more difficult for the Reagan administration to pursue its Central American policy. Congressional attitudes earlier had shifted significantly toward favoring covert action in the Third World. Although the full exposition of the Reagan Doctrine did not come until 1985, this policy change dated from the first Reagan election and led to American involvement in counterrevolutionary guerrilla movements in at least four countries—Cambodia, Afghanistan, Angola, and Nicaragua. (Some covert action in others—Ethiopia, South Yemen, Surinam—was also reported.) In the case of Afghanistan, by far the largest in terms of financial outlay and strategic importance, there was no congressional dissent. But many opposed aid to the Contras in Nicaragua, and this widespread sentiment, which predated Irangate, was enhanced by revelations about the Iran-Contra link. Congressional critics used the dislike of Khomeini to compound the opposition to aid for the Contras. At the same time, the administration, stung by domestic and Arab criticism of its Iran policy, adopted a more active anti-Iranian stance. In one of those lurches characteristic of foreign policy–making, the quiet overtures to Iran in 1985 led in 1987 to the deployment in the Gulf of over forty ships that acted, in effect, as protectors of Iraq.

Such was the dislike of Iran as evidenced by the Irangate affair that a selective moralism came into play, and two striking paradoxes went unremarked. The first was that in Afghanistan the CIA was aiding people many of whom had an outlook not dissimilar to that of Khomeini and some of whom were major narcotics traffickers to boot; the second was that U.S. ships went into the Gulf in July 1987 after an *Iraqi* attack on a U.S. ship in which thirty-seven Americans lost their lives. The strategic legacy of the Irangate affair, therefore, was that it had made any new openings to Tehran unfeasible in light of the revitalized tide of anti-Khomeini feelings, at least as long as the war with Iraq lasted.

Managing Relations with Tehran

All revolutions present special problems of international policy–making that take decades rather than months to resolve. This is as true of Iran as it was of France, Russia, China, Vietnam, Ethiopia, or any other. Even the apparently least internationalist of modern revolutions, that in Mexico, sent reverberations throughout Latin America that were to be of significance in the decades ahead—not least in Guatemala, Cuba, Nicaragua, and Peru. There have been over twenty Third World revolutions in the post-1945 period, and they have become intertwined with, though not solely determined by, East-West relations, in some cases leading to major confrontations—as in Korea in 1950, Cuba in 1962, and Vietnam in 1972. But by the same token, they have been amenable to some degree of diplomatic management by the United States and the Soviet Union: this was true of Korea, Vietnam, Ethiopia, and Cuba. Indeed much of the history of Third World revolutions has been marked by the countries' attempts to use great-power protection to cover their own internationalist initiatives, whatever the wishes of the great power might be: Kim Il-sung in 1950, Castro after 1962, and Ho Chi Minh all pursued military initiatives against the West in the face of Moscow's unhappiness. In the end, it was the strain of managing this tension between local revolutionary priorities and those of its great-power ally that led China and Mao Zedong to break finally with Moscow in 1963.

The Iranian Revolution, however, has been less embroiled in East-West relations than any other in modern times. This has not prevented Iran from becoming an issue between East and West, but it has made it more difficult for Moscow and Washington to manage relations with the country. Each would like to contain the Iranian Revolution and prevent its challenging their interests in the region; each would like to keep its options open and avoid driving the IRI into the arms of the other; each is nervous that, if factionalism explodes now that Khomeini is dead, the other's allies within Iran, with some discreet assistance, may take power in a replay of 1921 and 1953. If all revolutions are difficult to handle on the international level, that of Iran has proven even more intractable than most, given its autonomous character and ideology and the conflicting goals that both Moscow and Washington have in the region.

For Washington, there have been severe restrictions on what it could, in practice, achieve. The initial hope that friendly relations with the postrevolutionary government could continue was dashed on 4 November 1979 when the American hostages were seized. If this was a result of factional conflicts within the IRI and the radicals were using the embassy seizure to oust Bazargan, it reproduced a postrevolutionary pattern in which an initial period of grace is followed by a more confrontational relationship with the outside world. The

first months of the French, Russian, Chinese, Cuban, and Nicaraguan revolutionary regimes were temperate, but, for a combination of internal and external
reasons, in each case war ensued. The hostage crisis itself made any resumption
of U.S.-Iranian ties more difficult, although, as Gary Sick has pointed out, the
final outcome was less catastrophic for both parties than might have been the
case.[10] The United States did not take military action apart from the failed
rescue attempt of April 1980. The hostages were freed and the arbitration
procedures set up under the Algiers agreement have continued to function in
The Hague. Nor did the United States organize Iranian Contras. For its part, the
IRI needed military supplies from U.S. sources, whether officially sanctioned or
not, and in Afghanistan the United States and Iran had a common interest in
aiding the guerrillas.

The obstacles to a revival of U.S.-Iranian ties, then, were not insuperable.
The resumption of U.S. ties with China, a country that, in Korea, spilled more
U.S. blood than Khomeini ever tried to do, set a precedent that seems to have
been in the minds of Oliver North and Robert McFarlane when they flew to
Tehran in May 1986. Given the goals of U.S. strategy at that time, there were
very good reasons for establishing relations with Iran, four of them clearly
spelled out by Reagan in his November 1986 speech: the restoration of ties to a
traditional ally; the need for coordination vis-à-vis the Soviet Union; the tem-
pering of Iran in the Gulf war; and the question of the hostages in Lebanon.
Even after Irangate broke, Secretary of State George Shultz said on 8 January
1987 that the United States and Iran had common interests, in particular with
regard to Afghanistan. The issue of Afghanistan may have played a more
important role in the U.S. perception of its interest in developing relations with
Tehran than the selectively declassified documents published by the Tower and
Iran-Contra committees have so far revealed; the emphasis in the minority Iran-
Contra report on strategic concerns regarding Afghanistan may be significant.[11] The repeated affirmations by Reagan in public and McFarlane during his
Tehran visit that the United States accepts the legitimacy of the Iranian Revolution would fit such a policy. The desire to open contacts with the IRI and to
increase U.S. presence in an area to which the Soviet Union had diplomatic
access provided the strategic rationale for the 1984–86 initiatives. It became
convenient to blame the initiative on irresponsible elements within the U.S.
government and to scapegoat the Israelis, but the opening to Tehran made sense
as part of an overall anti-Soviet strategy; the flurry of concern over the pro-
prieties of "diversion" and "congressional notification" served to distract attention from the more fundamental policy premises that Congress and the president shared.

The problems, however, have prevented this strategy from being sustained. Three have already been mentioned: the comparative lack of openness of the Iranian regime to covert enticements, the regional repercussions of any Iranian policy, and the resistance within the United States itself, particularly in Congress, to dealing with the IRI. To these must be added other difficulties that have impeded even the most minimal dialogue between Tehran and Washington. The first is that if relations with Iran are controversial in Washington, they are equally so in Tehran. The factionalism within the regime has made any sustained policy of discussion with the United States unlikely: none of the factions is, on the evidence, potentially pro-Western in the traditional sense—there are no Razmaras or Zahedis waiting to seize power. But men like Rafsanjani who favor some discussions with the United States must be careful to avoid the fate of Bazargan and Yazdi, who, in November 1979, fell from power because factional rivals used their meeting with Brzezinski in Algiers to launch an offensive against them. Rafsanjani's response to the failure of the 1984–86 dialogue is instructive; facing criticism in the press and the Majles, he embarked on a preemptive campaign of denouncing the United States.

At the same time, while the IRI continued to promote revolution in Lebanon and in Saudi Arabia after the Mecca killings in July 1987, those most clearly associated with the international activities of the Revolutionary Guards, Mehdi Hashemi and his followers, were tried and executed, albeit on charges that bore little relationship to their activities outside Iran. If the full story of the U.S. mission in April 1986 is ever told, it will probably emerge that jostling within the regime added to the difficulties of the negotiation procedures, just as they served to spin out the negotiations over the hostages in 1980. In the end, however, it was possible for the IRI to control internal squabbling over the initiative in ways that the U.S. administration could not. In this, as in other matters, the Ayatollah showed more decisiveness toward his executive officials than his counterpart on Pennsylvania Avenue.

The second major obstacle to continuing the U.S.-Iranian dialogue has concerned U.S. policies in the region. The Iranians criticize U.S. policy on Israel, for example, although this is probably not an insuperable problem. More substantial has been Iranian resentment of U.S. policy toward the Gulf itself. For one thing, the United States, angered by the hostage crisis, clearly hoped that the September 1980 Iraqi invasion would succeed in "punishing" Khomeini if not in overthrowing him. The Iranians neither forgot nor forgave this, leading in part to their insistence throughout the war on a clear international condemnation of the Iraqi invasion. Second, U.S. policy after the passage of the U.N. Security Council resolution of July 1987 was, in effect, to enter the war on Iraq's side. Iran was opposed to the tanker war—it was not that country that attacked the USS *Stark*. The fact that U.S. forces protected Iraq so that it could attack Iranian ships with impunity, while Iran was restricted in its targets, was greatly resented. Just as the multilateral force sent to Lebanon in 1982–84 degenerated into a partisan corps, so the U.S. force in the Gulf became an adjunct of Saddam's war effort. This U.S. intervention on the side of Iraq in 1987 therefore complicated any resumption of U.S. discussions with Iran.

The Soviet Union, which superficially is in a better position vis-à-vis Tehran, has nonetheless found itself in analogous difficulties. Unlike the United States, it does have diplomatic and trading links with Tehran, but there have been countervailing tensions. Up to 1988, Tehran helped three of the smaller, Shi'i, guerrilla movements in Afghanistan, giving Moscow more difficulties than the IRI has given the United States in the Arabian Peninsula. If the West was concerned to shore up Iraq, it was the Soviet Union that provided up to 80 percent of Iraq's arms, foreseeing the danger of this long-standing ally's turning to the West as Egypt and Somalia did earlier. The economic opening within Iraq accompanying the war bore ominous resemblances to the *infitah* of the Egyptian economy that underlay Sadat's change of international alignment.[12]

Moscow nonetheless has been able to maintain a dialogue with Tehran, despite Afghanistan and the suppression of the Tudeh Party and its ally the Feda'iyan Majority. After the end of the war with Iraq and the Soviet withdrawal from Afghanistan in February 1989 there was considerable improvement in relations. Even before this Tehran was, for its part, willing to continue talking to Moscow despite the Soviet Union's provision of arms to Iraq. In 1985 Iran appeared to have secured agreement from the Soviets not to supply Baghdad with missiles capable of reaching Tehran, an understanding that lasted until 1988. But the Moscow-Tehran relationship has been an unstable one and could be changed for the worse by either side. The Russians were angry about the Iranian role in Afghanistan and, from 1982, were critical of their continuation of the war with Iraq: they repeatedly characterized the war as "senseless" and backed U.N. Resolution 598. In 1987 and 1988, while dragging their feet on the issue, they kept open the option of supporting an arms embargo at some point. The Iranians have little love for the Soviet Union and have calibrated their relations with Moscow in response to U.S. pressure and to prospects of concerted international action through the United Nations. In this regard, the Iranians have used pro-Soviet political prisoners from Tudeh and the Feda'iyan Majority as, in effect, Soviet hostages and have, at moments of crisis in their relations with Moscow, carried out selected retaliatory executions. This occurred after the February 1988 Iraqi missile attacks on Tehran, for which the Iranians held the Soviet Union responsible, and again in August 1988, after the Iranian acceptance of the U.N. cease-fire amidst widespread resentment in Tehran at great-power, including Soviet, pressure. Despite the improvement in relations in 1988–89, no one can imagine that any permanent IRI–Soviet Union axis can be constructed; the Russians know this very well.

There are at least three factors underlying this Iranian calculation. The first is that, for all its predominant concern with the West, the Islamic Revolution is also directed against the Soviet Union: both the Islamic internationalist and the Persian nationalist components of the IRI's propaganda pose a challenge to the Soviet Union. In the list of countries where, in IRI propaganda, Muslims are "struggling," Afghanistan, Uzbekistan, and Eritrea figure alongside Palestine, Kashmir, and the Philippines. Second, the Soviet hope that sooner or later the mollas would "come to their senses" has not to date been realized: "coming to their senses" meant, above all, pursuing internal policies of the kind adopted by states of socialist orientation, like Syria, Iraq, Algeria, and Egypt under Nasser, with a predominant state role in the economy, a measure of planning, and control by a ruling party. The Soviet fear was that overtly pro-American elements would emerge in Tehran, and that has not, to date, come to pass; but the consolidation of the IRI under a clerical leadership that pursues such unappetizing socioeconomic policies has considerably disappointed Soviet policymakers.

This abuts a third issue, that of economic relations between the two countries. Trade between Iran and the Soviet Union has continued at substantial levels since 1979, and the Soviet Union has transshipped some of Iran's imports to avoid blockages in the south. But despite many encouragements, the Iranians did not hasten to reopen gas supplies through the IGAT-I pipeline, or complete work on IGAT-II, which was under construction in 1979: indeed they made a political point of their refusal to do so. The fate of Iranian imports from the Soviet Union since 1979 is evidence of this *political* character; they rose from $419 million in 1979 to $794 million in 1982, but dropped after the souring of relations in 1983 to $296 million in 1984. The economic agreement signed by Iran and the Soviet Union in 1987 envisages new areas of cooperation: joint exploration for oil in the Caspian, a conversion of IGAT-I from gas to oil over a three-year period, and the building of a railway from Askhabad in Soviet Turkmenia through Sarakhs, Mashhad, and Zahedan to the Indian Ocean. All three of these are important projects. The first two would make Iran less vulnerable to pressure from the West, and the last would give the Soviet Union a strategic route it has long desired. But such are the political uncertainties on both sides that construction could well be delayed, and at times of crisis, either side could exert pressure on the other: the Soviet Union could stop importing Iranian oil, and the Iranians could cut oil exports or block the railway system. There is no reason, therefore, to expect that increased economic ties will resolve the deeper political differences and remove distrust between the two.

Iran's Options

A provisional assessment of the foreign policy record of the Iranian Revolution can in some measure complete this picture by showing how far Iran has been able to take advantage of the policy difficulties of the great powers. It is conventional wisdom in much of the Western and Arab discussion of the IRI to say that the revolutionary regime has failed in its foreign policy goals. It has not fostered a second Islamic revolution in another country; the war with Iraq ended in stalemate with Saddam and the Ba'ath Party still in power; and Iran has isolated itself from much of the international community by its intransigence. The cost of the war, in economic and human terms, was high, and by the mid-1980s the revolution had stalled at home, as debates about state power under Khomeini in early 1988 showed. Iran has had far fewer international sources of support than Iraq. In addition, at the United Nations the IRI has brought the United States and the Soviet Union together on a Third World issue to a degree not yet seen in any other regional conflict.

These assertions are all, to some extent, valid, but they must be offset against other factors that suggest a greater measure of success on the part of the IRI. In the first place, Iran has maneuvered the United States and the Soviet Union into competing for its goodwill, in part because of its strategic position, in part because of the concern to contain Islamic internationalism. The United States has been less hostile in dealing with Iran than the public mood over the hostages affair or Lebanese hostages might suggest. In the end Washington knows it will have to deal in the future with Iran, and probably a clerical Iran at that, and the end of the war makes this more possible. The Soviet Union cannot ignore its southern neighbor or lightly cede Iran, any more than it can Iraq, to the West. Second, Iran has to a remarkable degree sustained the policy of *nah sharq, nah gharb* (neither East nor West); it has tacked this way and that, and given both Moscow and Washington false expectations at times when the other has pressed it especially hard. But more than any other revolution in modern times it has evaded the East-West spectrum and profited by so doing: Moscow continues to court it; there are, as already noted, no Iranian Contras.

Iran's ability to maneuver itself vis-à-vis Moscow and Washington has been enhanced by the decision taken in July 1988 to end the war. This will enable the regime to reduce the great-power pressures exerted on it through the war itself and the attendant U.N. Security Council processes, and it will also provide an opportunity for the IRI to consolidate its domestic position by diverting resources to reconstruction. The international and internal preconditions for an autonomous foreign policy may, therefore, have been increased. At the same time, Tehran may be able to take advantage of another consequence of the war's end, namely, the erosion of support for Iraq in the Arab world. Although peace may lessen tensions in one respect, it will also make the Arab world more nervous about Iraqi ambitions and about the "pan-Arab" intentions of the Ba'ath Party. The Arab world has to live with both the Iraqi and the Iranian regimes as they have survived the war, but the Arabs may also seek to improve relations with Tehran as a means, over time, of offsetting the regional policies of Baghdad. This Iranian role in the region, something that began to emerge under the Shah in the late 1960s and that, appropriately transformed, continued under Khomeini, will necessarily attract the interest of both the Soviet Union and the United States. In peace as much as in war, the interlocking of Iranian developments with other conflicts in the region, one of the hallmarks of the third phase of international crisis concerning Iran, will complicate great-power policy toward the IRI.

In sum, it is far too early to assess the longer-run consequences of the Iranian Revolution. It took the Bolshevik Revolution nearly three decades, until the end of World War II, to spread eastward and westward. It took Castro until 1979, two decades after he entered Havana, to secure an ally in Central America. The Iranian regime has had to temper its goals and seek some interlocutors internationally. But, as its involvements in Afghanistan and Lebanon show, it has the capacity and will to organize an international revolutionary following where and when this becomes a possibility. Whatever their current goals may be, Moscow and Washington will have to live with this for quite some time, and certainly longer than they would wish.

For all three actors, the outcome will, in part, depend upon timing—upon making, at the right moment, a strategic decision about how to act in this situation. For both the United States and the Soviet Union the right timing involves knowing when it is possible to make a bid for closer relations with the IRI: so far, neither has been successful in finding stable interlocutors in Tehran. For the leadership of the IRI, with or without the Ayatollah, the issue has been of deciding at what point to seek more substantial dialogue, with either *sharq* or *gharb* or both. The person in this whole imbroglio who showed the best sense of timing was Khomeini himself both in 1978–79 and in the 1988 decision to stop fighting: the least that can be said of him is that he never judged that the moment for strategic compromise with East or West had arrived. Khomeini and his successor, Rafsanjani, have, however, been careful to keep their options open: Rafsanjani must know, as well as anyone else, that in 1906 and 1953, the two previous occasions when Iranian leaders sought to maintain such an opening, they, in the end, misjudged the international situation.

Notes

1. A congressional report has this as "tailor" (*Report of the Congressional Committee Investigating the Iran-Contra Affair* [Washington, D.C.: GPO, 1987], 238). The quotation is from *Tower Commission Report* (New York: Bantam, 1987), 296.

2. On Iranian precipitation of the 1978 crisis in Afghanistan, see Selig Harrison, "The Shah, Not Kremlin, Touched Off Afghan Coup," *Washington Post,* 13 May 1979.

3. For the economic side of Turkey's reentry to the Middle East, see Halis Akder, "Turkey's Export Expansion in the Middle East, 1980–1985" *Middle East Journal* 41, no. 4 (Autumn 1987).

4. I have gone into this in greater detail in "Iranian Foreign Policy since 1979: Internationalism and Nationalism in the Iranian Revolution," in *Shi'ism and Social Protest,* ed. Juan R. I. Cole and Nikki R. Keddie (New Haven: Yale University Press, 1986). See also chs. 2 and 3 of R. K. Ramazani, *Revolutionary Iran: Challenge and Response in the Middle East* (Baltimore: Johns Hopkins University Press, 1988).

5. On the 1953 intervention, see, among other recent accounts, James Bill, *The Eagle and the Lion: The Tragedy of American-Iranian Relations* (New Haven: Yale University Press, 1988), 86 ff.; and Gregory Treverton, *Covert Action* (London: I. B. Tauris, 1987), ch. 2.

6. Bovin in *Nedelya,* 3–9 Sept. 1979, quoted in *Current Digest of the Soviet Press,* 26 Sept. 1979.

7. "The regime that was taking shape constituted a step backwards, compared with the Shah's rule, from the point of view of accomplishing historical economic and social tasks." Artyom Arabajan [A. Z. Arabadzhyan], "Iranian Revolution: Causes and Lessons," *Asia and Africa Today,* no. 4 (1986).

8. I have discussed the retrospective U.S. literature on the Iranian Revolution, and the mirror illusions of doves and hawks, in "Iran and the Reagan Doctrine," *MERIP Middle East Report* no. 140 (May–June 1986). The myth sustained by the latter—that the Iranian army could, with prompt steering, have checked the revolution—was matched by the underestimation by the doves of the incompatibility of U.S. and Islamic Iranian goals.

9. "Mention Russia, and the US Heartland No Longer Sees Red," *International Herald Tribune,* 7 Dec. 1987. This story, by Haynes Johnson and Claire Robertson, was originally published by the *Washington Post.*

10. Gary Sick, *All Fall Down: America's Tragic Encounter with Iran* (London: I. B. Tauris, 1986), 174.

11. In the words of the minority: "The majority report systematically downplays the importance of strategic objectives in the Iran initiative. We believe, to the contrary, that the record is unambiguous on the following facts: (1) that strategic objectives were important to the participants at all times; (2) that the objectives were credible; (3) that they were the driving force for the initiative at the outset; and (4) that without such a strategic concern, the initiative would never have been undertaken." *Report of the Congressional Committee Investigating the Iran-Contra Affair,* 523. The *Report* at several points mentions the importance of the Soviet Union and Afghanistan in Iranian-U.S. contacts (254, 531). See also Bill, *The Eagle and the Lion,* 310–11.

12. On Iraqi *infitah,* see Roderic Pitty, "Soviet Perceptions of Iraq," *MERIP Middle East Report,* no. 151 (March–April 1988).

12

U.S. and Soviet Responses to Islamic Political Militancy

RICHARD W. COTTAM

Soviet-American rivalry in the early 1950s began to take shape in the Middle East, as elsewhere, in what came to be called the Cold War. An essential expression of that conflict in the Middle East and in the Third World generally was a struggle for influence in the internal political developments of states that were viewed as strategically important to the competing superpowers. Coincidentally, during that early period of the Cold War in the Middle East, secular nationalism was well established as the sociopolitical movement that was the primary focus of populist appeal and the foremost instrument of rapid political change. It was inevitable, therefore, that Soviet-American rivalry in the area would find expression in terms of differing responses to the forces of nationalism.

In the 1980s, however, another major sociopolitical movement in the Middle East began to replace nationalism as the primary focus of populist appeal and as the primary instrument of rapid political change: the force of politically resurgent Islam. It follows that the continuing Soviet-American rivalry in the area now would be defined very much in terms of the differing responses to this major force. Would the response patterns that developed in the 1950s for dealing with nationalistic forces find their parallel in the responses to Islamic resurgence? If not, could it be argued that the differing patterns reflect a major alteration in the nature of Soviet-American relations? These are the questions this chapter will explore.

U.S. Policy Choices Prior to 1978

There is little reason to doubt that the contours of both Soviet and American policy in the Middle East and in the world generally were determined in the first degree by the response of each power to the perceived challenge from the other. In the case of the United States in particular, the challenger, the Soviet Union, was perceived as following a highly aggressive policy that reflected an intention to bring to the world the blessings of Marxism-Leninism as interpreted by Moscow. The pattern of Soviet expansionism that was expected was a variation on those acts of expansion that had been noted at the conclusion of World War II in Eastern Europe and in Greece, Turkey, and Iran. Expectations were that the primary mode of Soviet advance would be through the subversion and manipulation of target regimes. When, as in Eastern Europe and northern Iran at the termination of World War II, Soviet troops were in occupation of target territories, the intervention was seen as crude, brutal, and hardly concealed. When, as in Greece, Turkey, and central and southern Iran, Soviet armies were nearby, the pattern was viewed as a combination of military threat and active subversion. The American strategic response quickly became one of helping the regimes that appeared to be Soviet targets stand up to the Soviet military threat and to understand and avoid Soviet efforts at subversion.

But if containment of perceived Soviet aggression was the central American strategic concern, there were two other vital objectives of American policy in the Middle East. One of these, to ensure the free flow of Middle Eastern oil to Western industry, was closely related to the goal of containing the Soviet Union. If the West were to have the capability to meet the Soviet challenge, the recovery and health of Western industry was essential and required a stable source of oil. But Middle Eastern oil was also a major concern of vested economic interests in the United States and Western Europe and a source of significant political pressure on Western governments. The other objective, only distantly related to the containment task, was nevertheless a major American governmental concern: the independence and security of the state of Israel. This objective, reflecting deeply held attitudes within sections of the American public, Jewish and non-Jewish, was a product of the American foreign policy process and could be ignored by political leaders only at their peril.

American policy as it evolved in the late 1940s and early 1950s would, of necessity, reflect a reconciliation of these three major objectives: Soviet aggressiveness must be contained but in a manner that would secure the flow of oil and the independence of Israel. There would appear, over time and as a consequence of many discrete decisions rather than of a conscious strategy, a formula for reconciling these objectives in a manner that appeared for many years to approach the optimal. The dimensions of a policy formula that would counter Soviet aggression in the Middle East and at the same time ensure the free flow of oil and the security of Israel were anything but self-evident, however. The Middle East was in the throes of a process of change that was proceeding at a revolutionary tempo and hence was inevitably destructive of stability. An acceptable policy formula, therefore, had to be one that in the first instance would be capable of dealing with this rapid process of change in such a way as to be effective for achieving the three objectives.

It quickly became apparent that the specific focus for attention must be the forces of nationalism in the region. In much of the area those political elites who favored rapid change and could attract the support base to effect that change were secular nationalists. How then should the United States deal with the force of nationalism in the area? The argument that such a force should be supported was easily made. Nationalists could be expected to resist fiercely any effort to impose external control on their area. Since, in American eyes, the Soviet Union strongly desired to establish such control, an alliance with regional nationalisms should serve American containment interests. On the other hand, the chaos that is associated with extremely rapid change was a threat to an essentially favorable regional status quo and could be viewed as increasing the vulnerability to subversion in the area.

The dilemma was far less compelling with regard to Turkish nationalism than it was with Iranian and Arab nationalism. Turkey was at least a generation ahead of the most highly developed Iranian and Arab areas. Under the leadership of Ataturk, the forces favoring rapid change had effectively won the battle in Turkey. Traditional elites had been dealt with harshly and a nationalistic, secular elite had emerged victorious. Fiercely jealous of any infringement on Turkish sovereign independence and seeing the most likely challenge as one emanating from the Soviet Union, the Turkish governing elite was a natural ally for the primary American purpose. Furthermore, such an alliance would not adversely affect the effort to achieve the other two objectives. But in the Iranian and Arab world the battle with traditional elements had not been won. The forces of rapid change here also were led by nationalists, although frequently in alliance with more radical clerical leadership. They, like their Turkish counterparts, were fiercely determined to establish and defend sovereign independence. The case could be and was made within the U.S. government that an alliance with the nationalistic leadership of Iran and the Arab states was congruent with American interests. Throughout the Truman administration years, in fact, policy seemed to incline toward dealing with the rapid change phenomenon by tying into the nationalistic part of it. To advocates of such an alliance, that policy appeared well and again the most effective means for containing a Soviet move southward, especially with regard to its subversive potential.[1]

Almost immediately with the advent of the Eisenhower administration and the primacy of Secretary of State John Foster Dulles in the foreign policy arena, this policy changed. Now Iranian nationalism led by Dr. Mohammad Mosaddeq was viewed as serving the Soviet, not the American, purpose. Nonalignment in the East-West struggle and tolerance for a vigorous communist press and communist political activity did not add up, to Dulles and his brother Allen, the director of Central Intelligence, as a strong concern for Iranian sovereign independence. To the contrary, it appeared to grant to the Soviets a happy hunting ground for a strategy of communist subversion. The suspicion that Mosaddeq and his allies were in fact a witting part of the conspiracy gained currency with extreme cold warriors such as Kermit Roosevelt.[2] A community of purpose quickly developed with the British, who were far more concerned with the question of oil than with the Soviet threat. The administration drifted within a few months of Eisenhower's inauguration in 1953 into a truly historic policy decision,[3] although they would not have defined it that way: to oust the nationalist political elite and replace it with an essentially traditional elite under the dictatorial leadership of Gen. Fazlollah Zahedi. The choice had been made. A government would be imposed on Iran and then given full support, which would first slow the rate of change and then control and manage it. But as events would demonstrate a generation later, the effect of this decision was to eliminate from leadership a nationalist elite that might have served to socialize and mobilize the Iranian mass public in support of liberal and secular institutions. In its stead would appear an Islamic counterelite that was fully prepared to socialize and mobilize Iranian mass public support for Islamic political institutions.

American support for Arab nationalism led by Gamal Abdul Nasser persisted for two years after the overthrow of Mosaddeq. Indeed, the self-proclaimed leader of the Anglo-American-sponsored coup in Iran, Kermit Roosevelt, was a major advocate of support for Nasser.[4] The easiest explanation for this inconsistency lies in the authoritarian quality of the Nasser government. Nasser did embrace nonalignment but he did so while accepting an informal cooperation with the American intelligence agency. Even more significantly, he did not permit the kind of internal chaos tolerated by the liberal Mosaddeq. Communism and the Moslem Brotherhood in Egypt were tightly constrained. The shift in American policy away from Nasser came more as a consequence of his confrontation with Israel following the humiliating Gaza Strip raid in February 1955 in which an Egyptian garrison was one of the targets. Even then the "policy decision" to turn against Nasser and Arab nationalism was not really a decision at all. Nasser, reacting to American indecision with respect to his request for a sale of arms to prevent a recurrence of the Gaza Strip incident, turned to the Soviet Union for arms. That decision set into motion a series of events culminating in the Suez crisis and a few months later in the Eisenhower Doctrine, which amounted in essence to a move to isolate and destroy Nasser and other leaders of Arab nationalism.[5] An American alliance developed with traditional Arab leaders who were opposed to the rapid change favored by Arab nationalists. The pattern that had appeared first in Iran of opposing progressive nationalist elements now developed in the Arab world. The major difference was that within the fragmented Arab world there were always leaders who could claim with some credibility to speak for the Arab nation, those usually referred to as belonging to the rejectionist front. But by and large the Arab nationalist elite, like the Iranian nationalist elite, was weakened and discredited to the point that it would have difficulty dealing effectively with the external challenge from Israel and, later, with the internal challenge from an Islamic counterelite.

The policy choices to turn against the nationalist leaderships of Iran and of the Arab world were in substantial degree the products of responses to different disturbances. Iranian nationalism with its liberal leadership was opposed primarily because of a perceived vulnerability to Soviet subversion. Arab nationalism with a more generally authoritarian leadership was viewed as an asset in the struggle against Soviet subversion but as a major threat to the state of Israel. At the public level, the rationalization that Israel was America's one reliable ally in the area and hence a vital component in dealing with the Soviet threat was widely accepted, and political leaders adapted their decisions to this view. But within the professional bureaucracy the contrary conclusion, that close relations with Israel added to the vulnerability in the area to Soviet expansion, especially through subversion, was widely accepted. There was, therefore, in the dimension of support for Israel an implicit tension in the foreign policy process with bureaucratic and public elements favoring different policies.

Nevertheless, by 1957 a policy formula had developed that proved to be remarkably stable, enduring without major alteration for twenty years. It consisted of constructing alliances, whether formal or de facto, with a number of local actors: Israel, Turkey, the Shah's Iran, and a number of Arab regimes that saw a community of interests with the United States in opposing the more nationalistic and progressive elements.[6] The American definition of the situation in the Middle East from 1957 until 1978 was similarly stable. Symbolic representations, such as "pro-West," "moderate and responsible," "Westernized," and "modernizing," were applied to friendly regimes, whereas "pro-Soviet," "satellite," "radical," and "terroristic" were applied to the unfriendly. Israel, Turkey, the Shah's Iran, and conservative Arab regimes were described as essential and sincere allies. Syria, Nasser's Egypt, Qaddafi's Libya, and, until recently, Saddam Hussein's Iraq were viewed as close to, if not fully within, the Soviet satellite category. When Sadat, after three years of trying to change sides in the Cold War arena, finally was taken seriously, Egypt began moving from the negative to the positive category. In 1978, with Sadat's full embrace of the Camp David peace process and the beginnings of Saddam Hussein's migration into alliance with the Arab conservative camp, success for the American formula had reached its apex. But, coincidentally with this great success, the Iranian Revolution began to take shape as a manifestation of a major challenge from Islamic political resurgence to what had become for Americans a very comfortable status quo. The policy formula, so long an apparent success, would have to adapt to a radically changing environment.

Soviet Policy Choices Prior to 1978

The rhythm of Soviet policy choices regarding the Middle East resembled very little that of the United States. In the closing years of World War II, in fact very soon after the decisive Soviet victory at Stalingrad, Soviet policy in the region became highly activist. The Soviet occupation force in Iran was used to encourage ethnic separatism of Iranian Kurds and Azerbaijanis, and threatening demands were levied on Turkey.[7] But even in this period there were signs that this spurt in Soviet activism did not rest clearly on expansionist intentions. Soviet verbalizations of the situation followed a consistent defensive pattern, describing Soviet policy as a response to the capitalist encirclement policies of the United Kingdom, with support from the United States and the capitalistic West in general.[8] But, far more significant, after the Soviets had engineered a separatist military coup in Iranian Azerbaijan and had set up a puppet regime in the city of Tabriz, they negotiated with the Iranian government an agreement by which Soviet troops would be withdrawn, thus leaving the puppet leaders to defend themselves. The Soviets did this even though there was no real possibility that the United States would engage in military confrontation to compel them to leave.[9] Then, when the Iranians moved an army toward Tabriz, the city liberated itself of the presence of the puppet government and the Soviets did nothing to defend this government. Shortly thereafter, the vigorous media campaign against Turkey was dropped and demands levied against the Turks for territorial adjustments were abandoned.

Americans such as George Kennan and the ambassador to the Soviet

Union, Walter Bedell Smith, who were early advocates of a Cold War view of the situation, were mystified by this Soviet behavior.[10] The Soviet move in Azerbaijan occurred simultaneously with the sovietization of Eastern Europe and apparent Soviet involvement in the Greek civil war. These were the three major actions that precipitated the Cold War. Of the three, the Azerbaijan occupation was, for geopolitical reasons, the least easily challenged and the one least likely to produce deleterious consequences for the Soviets. International opposition was confined largely to condemnatory statements and resolutions made in the U.N. Security Council. Assuming that Soviet intentions were to expand their influence and spread Marxist-Leninism, as they were perceived increasingly by American leaders to be doing, it is difficult or impossible to explain Soviet behavior. George Allen, the American ambassador to Iran, suggested a number of possible explanations, including the need to rebuild a ruined industrial base.[11] Yet, despite the contrary views held by those Americans most concerned with Iran, within months the explanation accepted generally was that the Soviets had indeed left because of an American show of will and determination in the Security Council. That explanation, in fact, would be generalized to account for apparent Soviet passivity in the Middle East for the next generation, and indeed it has yet to be seriously challenged within the American foreign policy community. *The central proposition of this chapter, however, is that, though official American rhetoric regarding Soviet intentions has altered very little, American policy has adjusted to the fact of Soviet passivity. Thus, whereas the intensely perceived threat from the Soviet Union led to American hostility toward Iranian and Arab nationalism, the weakening of that perception of threat has prevented thus far the development of a parallel hostility toward resurgent Islam.*

Examples of Soviet policy passivity in the Middle East are easy to come by, especially regarding Iran. If the passivity of the Soviet response to the ousting of the Azerbaijani and Kurdish autonomous regimes is surprising, the Soviet response to Mosaddeq's ouster is astonishing. Placed in stark outline, what occurred was the removal of a nonaligned government of a state with a twelve-hundred-mile land border with the Soviet Union by a coup in which the Soviets' most deadly rivals, the United States and United Kingdom, were deeply and conspicuously involved and the imposition of a new government that was entirely dependent for its survival on military and financial support from the United States. The extraordinary quality of the challenge one would expect the Soviets to feel can be gleaned by imagining the American response to a parallel Soviet move in Mexico. Add to this the fact that the ousted regime was regarded in Iran as the purest manifestation to date of Iranian aspirations for full sovereign independence. Furthermore, the leader of the regime, Mosaddeq, was viewed by politically attentive Iranians overwhelmingly as the leader of a national movement. One would think the Anglo-American action would have the effect of virtually compelling the Iranian national movement to turn to an alliance with the Soviet Union, even considering the historic suspicion in Iran of Russian intentions. In so doing it could well give the Soviets the opportunity to advance the very subversive purpose the action was supposedly designed to oppose. Yet within months the Soviet government had established reasonably good relations with the Zahedi regime in Iran. The Tudeh Party did call for a united front with the nationalists, but the Soviet Union made no serious visible effort in this direction.[12]

There are two major puzzles regarding this exceedingly important event. First, why did the American authors of the coup assume there would not be a violent Soviet response to their action? Second, why was the Soviet response so acquiescing and essentially in tune with American expectations?

The answer to the first question lies deep in the ethos of Cold War thinking. In the first place, the American government assumed nonattributability for their actions. The operation was clandestine and the illusion that a major operation of this dimension could be conducted without a serious danger of attribution characterized that era. In the second place, as mentioned earlier, by this time the assumption was widely held that if the U.S. government were seen as fully determined to stand up to the aggressive enemy, that enemy, in full rationality, would avoid confrontation and ultimately acquiesce in what amounted to a fait accompli.

The second puzzle, the passive Soviet acquiescence, is more perplexing. But the conclusion that the Soviets even in this period, five months after Stalin's death, in fact saw little serious threat from the United States in the region is difficult to avoid. Soviet imagery of the United States in this period was not at all parallel in its simplicity to that held in the United States of the Soviet Union. There was a picture of some American leaders being highly imperialistic, but the American government was not seen as monolithic. Any tendency to see the United States, as the American government saw the Soviet Union, in the diabolical enemy image, seems to have died with Stalin.[13] On the other hand, there is nothing to indicate that the Soviets were viewing the situation as one that offered them an opportunity to impose their will on Iran and the region. Surely the opportunity was there at least to explore the possibility of an alliance with the leaders of Iranian nationalism with their large and enthusiastic base of support within the populace. But the Soviets inexplicably passed it up.

A not unreasonable conclusion from this is that the intensity of Soviet concern for its security from challenges emanating from its Middle Eastern borders was at most only moderate. But, of course, this was not the conclusion drawn by those making American policy. The very passivity of the Soviet response in the face of extremely aggressive American behavior in overturning the neutralist regime of a Soviet neighbor and replacing it with an American dependency reinforced an image grounded in the assumption of highly aggressive Soviet intent. According to that image, if one behaves with sufficient will and determination the aggressive but rational foe will avoid confrontation. By 1953 this imagery was well established and it persisted for a generation. It could be seen possibly most clearly of all in 1974 when an American-Iranian-Israeli operation was carried out to destabilize the Iraqi regime.[14] The operation called for triggering a rebellion by Iraqi Kurds against an Iraqi regime perceived to be a Soviet satellite. The tactical plan of the United States and its allies involved an ethnic group, the Kurds, more than 100,000 of whom lived in the Soviet Union itself. It was carried out against a close Soviet ally and occurred within two hundred miles of the Soviet border. Furthermore, the Kurds were supplied with Soviet arms that had been captured by the Israelis and were secreted across the Iranian border into Iraq, presumably with the idea of suggesting to infinitely gullible Iraqis that the operation was Soviet. The entire operational plan, amazingly, was premised on the assumption that the Soviet Union would respond passively even when challenged with such provocative audacity. Furthermore, these expectations proved to be correct. The operation was a military failure, but not because of Soviet assistance to Iraq. The Soviet response was what American policymakers had come to expect: rhetorically strongly negative.

The pattern of Soviet passivity in the face of American challenges that appears in the above examples is at the extreme end of a scale of Soviet responses.[15] If the occupation of Afghanistan is at the other end of the scale, much of Soviet behavior toward the Arab world is closer to the center. The 1955 Soviet decision to respond favorably to Nasser's request for a sale of arms represented a major shift in Soviet policy. Comparing the Soviet response to two opportunities involving two nationalisms, that of 1953 with Iran and 1955 with the Arabs, suggests a move in the direction of greater activism. But the circumstances were very different. To take advantage of the Anglo-American direct attack on the Iranian nationalist movement and its primary leaders would have required a major Soviet effort in the realm of clandestine politics. Iranian nationalist suspicions would have to be allayed and an organization created that could operate covertly inside Iran. Responding favorably to Nasser's request for arms, in contrast, could be handled in a virtually routine diplomatic fashion, as could his later request for financial assistance in constructing the Aswan Dam. Commitment was low and the arrangement was, in essence, a commercial one. Nor was Nasser at the time this first commitment was made a serious target of

American hostility. Thus the risks of confrontation with the United States were fairly low.

Nevertheless the decision that Czech arms be sold to Nasser carried with it implications regarding the dynamics of the situation that the Soviets must have been aware of. The Arab bargaining position with Israel was improved substantially and the likelihood of Soviet-American competition within the Arab world was strengthened. The stage was set for the crystallization of alliance patterns clustered around the two superpowers. But the pattern of Soviet association with Arabs was not one of gravitating toward the most radical of the Arab regimes. Rather, the choice was more likely to center on those regimes that could be described as change-oriented at a progressive rather than radical rate. With few exceptions, the Soviets seemed to encourage the Arabs to be less, rather than more, confrontational. And there was at no time any serious suggestion that the Soviets would renege on their decision to support Israeli independence.

Responses to the Appearance of Islamic Resurgence

The Iranian Revolution

The argument presented thus far is that the United States far more than the Soviet Union saw the Middle East as a central Cold War arena. The prevailing American view reflected an intensely perceived threat from the Soviet Union and was close to the diabolical-enemy stereotype.[16] American policymakers, in their efforts to deal with that threat, had to come up with a policy formula that reconciled the need to contain and deter the Soviet Union with two major regional disturbances: the efforts to establish and secure a Jewish state in the face of Arab hostility and the destabilizing effects of sociopolitical change in the region. The formula that developed was that of an alliance with Israel, Turkey, the Shah's Iran, and conservative Arab regimes. The climactic year for this policy was 1978. It marked the consolidation of Egypt's departure from Arab ranks and the beginning of a parallel move by Iraq. But it also saw the destabilization of the Shah's regime that by the end of the year was beyond remedy.

Far less dramatic, but in terms of consequences far more profound, were indications that the Cold War was no longer for American decision makers the primary source of disturbance in the region. The case has been made above that a diabolical-enemy view of the Soviet Union persisted throughout the 1957–78 period in spite of an actual Soviet policy that was frequently passive, usually moderate, and only occasionally highly assertive. This persistence, it was argued, was possible because of the expectation of those holding the stereotypical view that if they showed the requisite will and determination the Soviet Union would behave passively. But most policymakers, and especially those at the working level of the bureaucracy, deal at a concrete level and are little influenced in their day-to-day work by public imagery. For them, over time, the persistent Soviet passivity/moderation meant that the Soviets would be taken decreasingly into account in the formulation of specific policies.

The American response to the Iranian Revolution and in particular to its Islamic dimension illustrated these changes. Most concerned officers in the Department of State tended to see the Iranian Revolution as a product of indigenous forces and not necessarily detrimental to American policy interests. Furthermore, there was a sharp contrast to 1952, when Dean Acheson and others in the Truman administration had argued that a good relationship with the Iranian national movement and its Islamic allies was essential for the purposes of containing Soviet expansionism through subversion. There was no argument from the Department of State now that an association with a popular movement would serve well the American anti-Soviet purpose. The goal of containing Soviet expansionism simply was not raised by those who saw the force of change in 1978 as compatible with American interests.

If there was no parallel in 1978 to the view of the Truman administration regarding Iran in 1952, however, there was a close parallel in 1978 to the view of John Foster Dulles regarding Iran in 1953. Zbigniew Brzezinski, Carter's national security adviser, saw a serious degree of Soviet orchestration in the Iranian Revolution.[17] Furthermore, Brzezinski and his allies, men such as James Schlesinger and Harold Brown, were able to persuade Carter to follow a policy congruent with this view. The three endorsed the idea—even in January 1979 when the enlisted personnel of the Iranian armed forces were deserting their commands—that as a last resort a military coup d'état should be executed and the revolution put down by brute force.[18] This policy was in full harmony with a view that the revolutionary forces in Iran were, just as Dulles had seen the Mosaddeqists in 1953, at least a functional instrument of the conspiratorial plans of the diabolical enemy.

Following the success of the revolution, two aspects of postrevolutionary Iran were too visible for American officials, including Brzezinski, to deny: first, the revolutionary government of Iran was fully independent of any external control and this included Soviet control, and, second, a struggle for leadership of the revolutionary regime was underway between secular and religious liberals, on the one hand, and a rapidly crystallizing radical Islamic leadership on the other. This struggle soon focused on government institutions. Mehdi

Bazargan, as prime minister, was fighting a losing battle to gain control of a set of revolutionary institutions that had formed spontaneously with the victory. By November 1979, with the taking of American diplomats as hostage, the battle had really been won by the religious radicals and Iran had polarized around intransigently opposed core groups favoring and opposing the domination of Iranian politics by a clerical governing elite.[19]

Two tendencies in American policy began appearing at that time that have proved to be strongly persistent. The first appears to have emanated primarily from the State Department. It took the specific form of subtle and nonobtrusive support for Bazargan, who was seeking to avoid polarization. Reflecting a sensitivity to Iranian suspicions of the United States, this policy was a quiet effort to normalize diplomatic and economic relations with Iran. The underlying assumption appears to have been that a rapid economic recovery from the disruption of the revolution and a diminution of fears of an American-backed effort to restore the Pahlavis would be essential for a restoration of stability in Iran. Implicit here was a sense that a victory for radical Islamic forces would be highly destabilizing and quite possibly move well beyond the borders of Iran. And why should there be a concern for the maintenance of stability? There is no reason to suspect that either then or now this abstract question was or is explicitly addressed by decision makers whose preoccupation, it has been argued, is with immediate and concrete issues. A propositional answer can be suggested, however. American policy in the Middle East had been remarkably successful prior to the Iranian Revolution. It had resulted in a web of economic and security relationships with Israel, Turkey, and "moderate" Arab states around which had evolved a great many private and public vested interests. The development of these relationships had been intended primarily to serve an *instrumental* purpose in accomplishing the main objective: that of containing perceived Soviet expansionism. That instrumental purpose had now been forgotten and the happy status quo that had evolved involving these friends and allies was now seen as an end in itself. Furthermore, it gradually became accepted, although again only occasionally and then only partially articulated, that the primary threat to that stability emanated not from the Soviet Union but from the force of Islamic political resurgence.

But what of those officials who, like Brzezinski, continued to see all major regional policy in the context of a perceived Soviet threat? For them the loss of Iran was indeed catastrophic, even if the Soviets had been unable to capitalize on it directly. Iran, Turkey, and Pakistan had been the major regional allies of the United States in containing and deterring Soviet aggressiveness. The "moderate" Arab states were useful allies. They were anti-Soviet and could be relied upon to oppose those political and social elements in the Arab world that would be vulnerable to Soviet subversive efforts. They were useful economic partners, providing oil and using their petrodollars to the advantage of the economies of the United States and its allies. And they could be relied on to limit their hostility toward Israel largely to the rhetorical level. In addition they were willing to cooperate in helping the United States deal with security concerns, particularly in the Gulf region. But it was not conceivable that, even collectively, they could serve a role in containment strategy comparable to that of the Shah's Iran.

Logically, there were really two options that such individuals would consider. The first would be to overturn this Iranian regime as had been done a generation earlier and replace it with an Iranian Pinochet. The second would be to make the effort to establish a de facto alliance with the forces of Islamic resurgence generally and with the regime of the Islamic Republic of Iran in particular. There were indications within a few months of the success of the Iranian Revolution that the second option would be the one advocated specifically by Brzezinski. He was contemptuous of the view that the secular and religious liberals, led by Bazargan, could remain in control of the Iranian government with Khomeini playing something of a passive legitimizing role.[20] Stability was not even implicitly his objective. His primary concern was to form an effective anti-Soviet alliance in the region he described as the "arc of crisis." By the summer of 1979 Brzezinski was convinced of the sincerity of Khomeini's fierce anticommunism. He seemed interested in exploring the possibility of convincing Khomeini that his regime's strong concern with independence from external control was fully in tune with American objectives and that there was in reality a genuine community of purpose of the two governments. The taking of hostages by Iran destroyed any possibility of developing this option, but the logic of the Brzezinski case would persist long after the termination of the hostage crisis. Ironically, it was the same logic that those who opposed the coup against Mosaddeq had followed a generation earlier: seeing an alliance with a populist leader, fiercely determined to maintain Iranian sovereign independence and fully cognizant of the threat from the Soviet Union, as in the American interest.

Soviet relations with the Shah's Iran had been generally good in the years of the Shah's absolute control of his country. Economic relations with Eastern Europe were particularly valuable to Iran, and there were no indications that the Soviet Union felt any real threat from an Iran viewed commonly as a primary regional surrogate of the United States. The willingness of the Soviet Union to sell artillery and military transport to an American "surrogate" with which they had a very long land border gave testimony to that point. The Shah's book, *Answer to History,* written in exile, is a reflection of the ambivalence in the relationship.[21] The evidence that to Brzezinski indicated a major Soviet role in the destabilization and overthrow of the Shah has yet to surface in any convincing form. The easy relations between the two, regardless of the CIA listening posts in Iran, is fully in tune with the picture presented above of a Soviet Union that did not perceive a threat from the United States and its friends, allies, and surrogates with more than a moderate intensity.

In November 1978 the Soviet government warned the United States not to interfere in the Iranian Revolution. This seems to have been the point at which an estimate of probable success for the revolution finally gained currency in the Soviet Union. But even then official descriptions of events did not suggest any serious awareness of the importance of the Islamic dimension in the revolution, including Khomeini's extraordinary popularity. Analyses of the revolution including the Islamic dimension by Nureddin Kianuri, the head of the pro-Soviet Tudeh Party, were highly sophisticated, however. Unlike much of the liberal and left-secular community, which grossly underestimated and was essentially contemptuous of the Islamic leadership, Kianuri from the beginning accepted Khomeini's charismatic attraction as the central ingredient of the revolution. He recognized clearly that the Islamic religiopolitical leaders had become the focus of populist appeal for this generation of Iranians. But he appeared to see the clerical elite as too thin and too incompetent in terms of an understanding of the needs of an advanced economy and society to be successful in the long run.[22] The strategy of forming an alliance with such an elite and gaining a position to assert leadership as that elite failed to provide the necessary programs to satisfy the utilitarian needs of its mass following, therefore, was logical and compelling. Kianuri's active support for the religious element in the struggle with Bazargan was equally logical. The defeat of Bazargan meant the defeat of an elite element that could have competed in terms of competence with the Left. There is little reason to suspect that Kianuri was giving expression to the thinking of his Soviet mentors in espousing this strategic line. Indeed, it is far more likely that Soviet diplomacy, which was generally correct in this period, was more influenced by the advice received from Kianuri. But evidence for such a conclusion can only be negative—the lack of any indication that the Soviet Union made an effort to compel Kianuri to follow a different line.

The Islamic Rebellion in Afghanistan

Since the withdrawal from Azerbaijan, there have been two major occasions in Soviet policy in the Middle East in which the Soviet Union seemed to risk losing control of their own policy to the dynamics of the situation. The first of these was in October 1973 after the initial Arab successes in the Egyptian-

Syrian attack on Israel. The second was the decision to send an occupation force into Afghanistan in December 1979. The Soviet decision to occupy Afghanistan was in the short term the least dangerous of the two, but in the longer run it posed a greater danger of loss of control. The Soviets had become involved in the internal affairs of Afghanistan in response to a request for assistance from a Marxist government that had come into power in the coup of April 1978. By the autumn of 1979 it was apparent that the Marxist government could not long survive without direct Soviet armed forces support. Furthermore, it was apparent that the most effective and militant opponents of the regime were Islamic religiopolitical leaders, some of whom clearly fit the mold of Islamic political resurgence. When the Soviets did intervene, they did so in a particularly brutal manner, eliminating the Afghan prime minister, Habibollah Amin, whom they blamed for a failure to broaden the regime's base of support. The Soviets thus chose to follow in Afghanistan a very different policy with respect to Islamic resurgence than they were following in Iran. Furthermore they pressured Kianuri and the Tudeh in Iran to defend Soviet policy in Afghanistan and in so doing effectively countered Kianuri's efforts to present himself as an independent agent sincerely interested in cooperation with the Islamic Republic.[23]

Whatever expectations the Soviets had that the Marxist regime in Afghanistan would be able to effect a reconciliation within the country to secure the regime's survivability were quickly shattered. The Soviets then had to choose between two unattractive options: to pacify the country directly or to find some way to withdraw. The choice was soon apparent. The Soviets were not willing to pay the price in terms of either resource allocation or the impact on their foreign relations to pacify Afghanistan. External, particularly American, support for the so-called mujahedin opposition escalated and Soviet relations with the People's Republic of China, the United States, and the Islamic world deteriorated. Fairly early on, the Soviets telegraphed a willingness to seek some face-saving formula for extricating themselves from this situation, but were generally rebuffed by the Reagan administration. The most militant of Islamic leaders and their organizations proved to be the most effective military of the opposition and the most likely leaders of a postoccupation Afghanistan. Nevertheless, Soviet policy continued to move in the direction of unconditional and unilateral withdrawal, and implicitly this appeared to reflect a willingness to risk living with an Afghani Islamic republic on their southeastern border. As severe as the Soviet defeat has been, it apparently has not precipitated a policy of direct hostility to the forces of Islamic resurgence either in Afghanistan or more broadly in the Middle East.

The American response to this situation was initially close to panic. The occupation of Afghanistan was the first really strong evidence of a Soviet aggressive intent in the Middle East region since the Azerbaijani crisis. Fears that this was likely to be merely the first in a series of aggressive moves were commonly expressed. But when these expectations were not realized, American attitudes returned to the old norm. Expectations of a Soviet aggressive advance were replaced by expectations of passive acquiescence in American assistance to a rebellion against a Soviet satellite that was halfway around the world from the United States and bordered directly on the Soviet Union! There was now once again apparently no consideration given to the possibility that the Soviet Union would regard this as an intolerable affront and provocation. Aid to individual units of the mujahedin coalition predictably strengthened the most militarily effective and also the most militantly Islamic elements. The consequence was to add to the internal bargaining position of the Party of Islam and its anti-American leader, Gulbadin Hikmatyar. There is no indication that the inconsistency of an Afghanistan policy that strengthened the most militantly Islamic of the Afghan factions and a policy of increasing hostility to the Islamic Republic of Iran was seriously noted.

The Iran-Iraq War: Phase One

When Iraq attacked Iran on 22 September 1980, a struggle for power inside Iran between President Bani-Sadr and the leadership of the Islamic Republic Party was well underway. But the response of all parties was unanimous in attributing the Iraqi attack to the United States. The case was based on logic rather than evidence. As viewed from Tehran, the United States, humiliated by its failure to save the Shah and effect the release of a handful of hostages, had struck out at Iran through the agency of one of its stable of Arab puppets. It had to do this in order to restore some credibility for the myth of American omnipotence in the area. Available evidence suggests that, to the contrary, the response of American officials involved in the effort to free the hostages was one of extreme annoyance.[24] The attack came ten days after a speech by Khomeini in which he outlined a formula for a settlement of Iranian-American differences and the release of the hostages. It was a formula that at least provided a basis for negotiations. Now all of that was on hold.

After the hostages were released, an event that coincided with Ronald Reagan's first inauguration as president, American policy toward the war seemed to be one of neutrality if not unconcern. But gradually a drift toward what was called a "tilt" toward Iraq developed and gained force. It was underlined by a statement by Under Secretary of State Richard Murphy in 1984 in which Murphy asserted the American intention of not permitting an aggressive Iran to destabilize Arab regimes that were long-term friends of the United

States.[25] But it should be noted that in this statement, as in others from administration spokespersons, the government of Iran rather than the forces of Islamic resurgence was identified as the target. Diplomatic relations with Iraq were restored in November 1984, and relations with Iraq began appearing more and more like those of de facto allies.

Viewed in stark outline this policy was a startling break with the past. It incorporated these features: (1) the United States was tilting toward a government that had, and maintained, a friendship agreement with the Soviet Union, whose weapons system was essentially Soviet in base, and whose leaders visited Moscow on a regular basis and continued to purchase arms from the Soviet Union—a government the United States and the Shah of Iran had attempted to destabilize in 1974; (2) the United States was tilting against a government that represented a major populist force, that of resurgent Islam, that was adamantly opposed to the projection of Soviet influence in the region, that had taken the lead among Islamic states in opposing the Soviet occupation of Afghanistan, and that was supporting some of the same elements of the Afghan mujahedin the United States was supporting; (3) the United States was tilting toward a government that Israel had regarded as one of its most serious enemies and a long-time member of the rejectionist front and against a government that was purchasing arms from agents of the Israeli government; and (4) the United States was tilting toward the government that initiated attacks on oil shipping in the Gulf and against the government that was on record with the promise to cease retaliatory attacks whenever Iraq ceased attacking shipments of Iranian oil. In other words, on the surface, the American policy seemed to contravene all three of the major objectives of the United States in the Middle East—to contain the Soviet Union, to secure the borders of Israel, and to provide for the free flow of oil to Western industry.

How, then, is this American policy to be explained? Central to any explanation is the functional decline of the intensity of threat perceived from the Soviet Union. Despite the occupation of Afghanistan, a diabolical-enemy image of the Soviet Union was difficult to sustain given actual Soviet behavior in the region. In tilting toward Iraq, American policy was in fact closely paralleling Soviet policy—to the point indeed that an observer from Mars might well conclude that the two governments were allies. But anyone familiar with the history of American policy in the region would be aware of the recent, continuing dislike for the intensely repressive Saddam Hussein regime. The regimes the American policymakers were concerned to protect were those long characterized as "moderate" and "responsible," particularly Saudi Arabia and Kuwait. These regimes saw a terrible threat but one that emanated from resurgent Islam, both in the form of the Islamic Republic and as an internal force. Yet the vested interest web that had evolved from the long-term American alliance with the "moderates" included strong security ties, and those ties were established for the purpose of dealing with a potential Soviet expansionist move. As suggested earlier, an alliance system that was designed to be instrumental in containing a Soviet threat had become an end itself. Verbally, the alliance was still defended as anti-Soviet in design. Functionally, however, it was really opposed to the forces of resurgent Islam, especially as represented by the Islamic Republic of Iran. But at the very time that Richard Murphy was making his statement to Congress, and apparently unknown to him, another policy was beginning to take shape in the White House, a policy that would be known as Irangate. That policy would be much more in harmony with dealing with a Soviet Union characterized as a diabolical enemy, one that would tilt toward Iran.

Soviet policy toward the Iran-Iraq war was far less complicated. Although guarded, Soviet statements regarding the war seemed to imply a conclusion that it was Iraqi in initiation. Soviet statements, in fact, paralleled in several respects those of Hafez al Asad of Syria. Whatever the Iranian provocation, the war served the purposes only of Israel and the United States. It should be ended and if the Iraqis were at fault in its initiation, Iran was at fault in its prolongation. Soviet diplomacy overall clearly favored Iraq, but there was a persistent effort to improve relations with Iran throughout the early years of conflict.

The Israeli Invasion of Lebanon

The fourth major arena in which American and Soviet responses to the forces of resurgent Islam should be examined is that of the 1982 Israeli invasion of Lebanon culminating in the occupation of Beirut. In its initial stages, the invasion was viewed more or less favorably by the U.S. government because it would likely cripple two entities perceived as Soviet clients, the PLO and the government of Syria. In tune with the patterns identified in this chapter, there was no serious expectation on either the Israeli or the American part of a Soviet response other than one of verbal denunciation, a sale of arms to the Syrians after their inevitable defeat, and a virtual abandonment of a crippled PLO. An additional expectation was that a more responsible Lebanese government would emerge that would follow essentially the path of Anwar Sadat in making peace with Israel.[26] As events turned out, expectations were not realized in three of the four areas. The resistance of the PLO was somewhat greater than expected, the Syrian defeat less decisive, and the new Lebanese government less strong than expected. But the expectations of Soviet behavior were fully realized. The American government, though really a close ally of one of the parties to the conflict, assumed the role of mediator and facilitator after the violence subsided, and in view of the passivity of their supposed mentor, even the Syrians for a time had no option other than to cooperate.

Both the Israelis and the Americans, however, were suddenly confronted with an extremely hostile response from elements indigenous to Lebanon. These included in particular Druze followers of Walid Jumblatt, the primarily secular Shi'i organization, Amal, and a largely Shi'i resurgent Islamic movement. Both Israel and the United States ultimately chose to withdraw from most of Lebanon rather than pay the price of remaining. American commentators generally concluded that the Syrians had gained a great victory and through them their mentor, the Soviet Union. There were few indications of an awareness that the victory was due far more to the actions of the three indigenous forces, including especially that of resurgent Islam. But, as the activities connected with what has come to be called Irangate indicated, there was indeed some understanding of the strikingly enhanced position of Iran in the balance of power in the eastern Mediterranean.

The Iran-Iraq War: Phase Two

The Irangate episode was unquestionably initiated by the strong desire of Ronald Reagan and some of his associates to free the second generation of American hostages, those captured in Lebanon. From the point of view of this chapter, however, the relevant aspect is the spillover into Iran. The episode began with the revelations of secret official American contacts with Iranian leaders. Statements made by Robert McFarlane[27] and by Vice President George Bush[28] shortly thereafter disclosed another major current of thought regarding relations with the forces of Islamic resurgence in Iran. In marked contrast to the assumptions underlying a policy of tilting toward Iraq, these statements pointed clearly to the critical strategic importance of Iran for Americans who continued to see the Soviet Union in diabolical-enemy terms. Both statements reflected a strong desire to discover and advance the political fortunes of officials in the Islamic Republic of Iran who could be described as moderate and who would be willing to ally with the United States in a containment strategy. They reflected a yearning for a regime much like that of the Shah but one with both legitimacy and popular support. Col. Oliver North went so far at one point as to indicate to Iranians that President Reagan understood that a settlement of the conflict with Iraq required the replacement of the Iraqi president, Saddam Hussein.[29] Irangate clearly reflected the continuing strength of the policy tendency identified earlier with Zbigniew Brzezinski: a willingness to associate with forces of resurgent Islam as a natural ally in the objective of containing the aggressive intent of the Soviet Union. But there was as well a clearly expressed wish that the regime could be moved in a direction that was less threatening to America's Arab friends. The deep concern with the moderate Arab regimes that seemed to pervade the Department of State was lacking, however. In effect, the moderate Arab regimes were seen to have lost their instrumental purpose and hence could be offended and disregarded. The move toward Iran indicated that for this group the status quo was no longer highly favorable and hence the objective of stability had little appeal.

A confrontation between advocates of these diametrically opposed policy approaches to the Islamic Republic of Iran did not take place, however. The apparent cynicism of an arms-for-hostages policy by an administration that had described such activities as essentially appeasing became the focus of discussion, and the logic of the case, well presented by Vice President Bush, for a return to an alliance with Iran was not seriously debated. Then when the extralegal transfer of funds to the Nicaraguan Contras became known, discussions concerning policy toward Iran virtually disappeared. With the collapse of the political position of those advocating rapprochement with Iran, the Department of State preferences prevailed and there was a rapid move toward a much more vigorous tilt toward Iraq. This led ultimately to the movement of large naval forces to the Gulf for the ostensible purpose of defending freedom of navigation. So parallel were Soviet and American policies in the Gulf that Americans and Soviets were reportedly warning each other about the proximity of Iranian naval vessels. Yet the operation was described as one to prevent the Soviet domination of the Gulf. Iran was playing a new surrogate role. It was the surrogate enemy against which American policy was directed, given the unwillingness of the Soviet Union to play the enemy role convincingly.

On the surface, Soviet policy toward Iran and toward the forces of Islamic resurgence had changed little in the decade of the 1980s. Even though the Soviet Union had fought Islamic forces in Afghanistan throughout those years, a clear policy had yet to crystallize. There is, however, verbal evidence suggesting that some well-placed Soviet citizens are beginning to view Iran and its Islamic allies in the region stereotypically. Konstantine Kapitonov, writing in the *Literaturnaya Gazeta,* presented a picture of an imperial Iran orchestrating an elaborate conspiracy in the internal affairs of Lebanon.[30] Also writing in *Literaturnaya Gazeta,* Igor Belayaev wrote, "Khomeini is the enemy of Israel. Verbally. In five years of the Iran-Iraq War, also with his knowledge, Israel supplied Iran with 5 billion dollars' worth of weapons. Last August Ahmad, son of the great Ayatollah, conducted talks in Geneva with the Americans and Israelis on problems of common interest."[31] There is no substantiated evidence supporting either statement, but the conspiratorial behavior the two writers describe mirrors a growing view among left secularists in the Arab world. It is not the typical picture of Islam appearing in official Soviet statements. But the fact that it is gaining some currency suggests a heightened sense of threat.

Conclusions

Whatever its long-term prospects, Islamic political militancy is certain to be a major disturbance in the immediate future for the Middle East region. Virtually every Arab regime in the region is to some degree destabilized by its populist appeal, an appeal that appears to be much greater than that of secular national-ism. It is a significant factor in the Palestinian uprising, especially in Gaza, and has altered seriously the boundaries of maneuverability of those attempting to find some solution to the Arab-Israeli conflict. And it is a highly complicating factor in the rapidly evolving relationship of the United States and the Soviet Union. In the Arab summit conference in Amman in November 1987, a tacit agreement emerged that the primary threat to the stability of the area was now that emanating from Iran. And by "Iran," everyone understood, was meant the force of Islamic political militancy. Within a few days, however, the beginnings of the Palestinian uprising occurred and the role of the mosques in that develop-ment was obvious to everyone. Arab leaders were forced to return their primary attention to the Palestinian demand for control of their own destiny and to moderate their attacks on the Islamic Republic. There is little doubt, however, that Islamic political militancy is a major preoccupation of Middle Eastern political leaders. But the policy behavior of both the United States and the Soviet Union suggests the lack of a parallel crystallization of objectives regard-ing political Islam on the part of either superpower.

A case-by-case survey, such as that done in outline above, of Soviet and American responses, reflects inconsistency, uncertainty, and the absence of any serious strategic focus on Islamic political militancy. American policy in the 1985–86 period, in fact, reflected simultaneous diametrically opposed re-sponses in the same arena: members of the National Security Council were probing the possibility of harnessing political Islam to the American anti-Soviet purpose, whereas the Department of State was advancing a policy that appeared to treat Islamic militance and the Islamic Republic of Iran as *a,* if not *the,* preeminent negative target of the United States.

The proposition advanced earlier in this chapter suggests that the policy confusion in the American government regarding political Islam is rooted in a changing attitude toward the Soviet Union. As long as a deeply perceived threat from Soviet expansionism in the Middle East prevailed among Americans, policy was dominated by the objective of containing that threat. Now, however, a generation and a half after the crystallizing of a policy formula for the area, that threat has lost its strongly determining force. To be sure, there is a persisting rationalization of the purpose of American policy in terms of a Soviet threat. Yet the policy itself, especially that of tilting toward Iraq in the Iran-Iraq war, is impossible to justify in those terms. The current American policy in the Gulf conflict is a defense of so-called moderate Arab regimes and the economic and military alliance structure that developed with them over the past generation and a half. But that alliance structure was created for the purpose of containing a Soviet threat and that threat is perceived today with such slight intensity that a functional alliance with a Soviet ally, Iraq, could become a core feature of American policy in the region. The real threat to that status quo is from political Islam, but American decision makers are not yet prepared to confront that fact, preferring to describe it as from Iran. It is difficult to believe, however, that treating Iran as the locus of threat without credibly tying that threat into a larger one from the Soviet Union can suffice for long in inducing Congress and the American people to maintain a heavy commitment in the area. Unless a renewed perception of threat of great intensity from the Soviet Union appears, serious adjustments in overall American policy are inevitable. Sooner or later the adjustment process may necessitate the evolving of a policy toward Islamic political militancy. But in the present regional environment, it is difficult to see a threat to basic national interests in that movement that could lead to a sustained policy of hostility that would be at all comparable to the earlier hostility toward Arab and Iranian nationalism.

The case presented above regarding the Soviet Union is that its intensity of concern with Cold War manifestations in the Middle East was far more moderate than that of the United States. This resulted in turn in a less sharply crystallized Soviet policy toward major disturbances in the Middle East such as the appearance of strong nationalist movements in Iran and the Arab world. In conformity with this pattern, the Soviet Union has made a much more persistent effort to remain on good terms with the Islamic government in Iran than has the United States. In particular in the Iran-Iraq war, the Soviet Union, in contrast to the United States, carefully avoided drifting into a position of extreme hostility toward Iran. The direct conflict with Islamic political militancy in Afghanistan was a consequence of the Soviet decision to send an occupation force into that country to save a faltering Marxist regime. Presumably the Soviet Union could avoid a major confrontation with political Islam by allowing events to take their natural course following the withdrawal of the occupation force.

Of far greater future concern, however, is a demand for control of their own destiny by the Islamic peoples within the Soviet Union. The probabilities of such demands occurring will likely vary directly with the persistence of a glasnost policy by the Soviet government. The early signs of a development of a negative conspiratorial view of the Islamic movement in Iran, described above, may well suggest that a perception of threat from Islamic political militance is intensifying in the Soviet Union. If that should indeed occur, the system disturbance represented by Islamic political resurgence may begin to give major definition to Soviet policy in the Middle East. In contrast to the point made regarding the national interests of the United States, it is possible to see developments from Islamic militance that could be construed as threatening to Soviet national interests.

Notes

1. Dean Acheson summarizes this well in his *Present at the Creation* (New York: Norton, 1969).

2. Roosevelt's view of Mosaddeq is both contemptuous and conspiratorial. See Kermit Roosevelt, *Countercoup: The Struggle for Control in Iran* (New York: McGraw-Hill, 1979).

3. Mark Gasiorowski is producing the definitive work on this subject. See his "The 1953 Coup d'Etat in Iran," *International Journal of Middle East Studies* 19, no. 3 (August 1987): 261–86.

4. For a description of Nasser's relationship with the CIA, see Miles Copeland, *The Game of Nations: The Amorality of Power Politics* (London: Weidenfeld and Nicolson, 1969).

5. For the best account of the dynamics of the policy shift away from Nasser, see Kennett Love, *Suez: The Twice Fought War* (New York: McGraw-Hill, 1969).

6. For a good overview of U.S. policy that captures this picture, see Seth P. Tillman, *The United States and the Middle East* (Bloomington: Indiana University Press, 1982).

7. For the best account of this episode, see Bruce R. Kuniholm, *The Origins of the Cold War in the Middle East: Great Power Conflict and Diplomacy in Iran, Turkey and Greece* (Princeton: Princeton University Press, 1980).

8. Lancelot Pyman, the Iranian desk officer of the British Foreign Ministry in this period, described Soviet attitudes convincingly to his American counterparts. See U.S. Department of State, *Papers Relating to the Foreign Relations of the United States* (Washington, D.C.: U.S. Government Printing Office, 1947), 5:927.

9. See the blunt statement made to the American embassy in Tehran in 1947 indicating U.S. government acceptance of this point in U.S. Department of State, *Foreign Relations of the United States*, 5:924.

10. Ibid., 7:565.

11. Ibid.

12. The Tudeh Party printed a pamphlet, *28 Mordad,* which was sharply self-critical and called for a united front with the Mosaddeqists.

13. For an excellent analysis of Soviet imagery in the 1970s, see Richard K. Herrmann, *Perceptions and Behavior in Soviet Foreign Policy* (Pittsburgh: University of Pittsburgh Press, 1985).

14. The case was investigated by the House of Representatives' Pike committee in its study of clandestine diplomacy. The report of the committee was leaked and published in the *Village Voice,* 16 Feb. 1976, 85.

15. For a sharply different interpretation of Soviet behavior, see Alvin Rubinstein, *Red Star on the Nile: The Soviet-Egyptian Influence Relationship since the June War* (Princeton: Princeton University Press, 1977).

16. For a good application of the diabolical-enemy stereotype, see David J. Finlay, Ole R. Holsti, and Richard Fagan, *Enemies in Public* (Chicago: Rand McNally, 1967).

17. For evidence of this contention, see Gary Sick, *All Fall Down: America's Tragic Encounter with Iran* (New York: Random House, 1985).

18. Zbigniew Brzezinski, *Power and Principle: Memoirs of the National Security Adviser, 1977–1981* (New York: Farrar, Straus, and Giroux), 371–82.

19. For an account of the dynamics of postrevolutionary developments, see Shaul Bakhash, *The Reign of the Ayatollahs* (New York: Basic Books, 1984).

20. For Gary Sick's similar appraisal, see *All Fall Down,* 134–36.

21. Mohammad Reza Pahlavi, *Answer to History* (New York: Stein and Day, 1980).

22. See the following interviews with Kianuri: *Horizont* (East Berlin), no. 9 (1979): 11 (Foreign Broadcast Information Service [hereafter FBIS], 11 Mar. 1979); *L'Humanité,* 4 Apr. 1979 (FBIS, 11 Apr. 1979); *Horizont,* no. 16 (1979): 14–15 (FBIS, 24 Apr. 1979); *Unsere Zeit* (East Berlin) (FBIS, 23 Apr. 1979).

23. On Afghanistan, a good account is Henry S. Bradsher, *Afghanistan and the Soviet Union* (Durham: Duke University Press, 1983).

24. Gary Sick in *All Fall Down* indicates the American response to the attack was one of dismay since it could complicate the release of the hostages. For similar views, see Hamilton Jordan, *Crisis: The Last Year of the Carter Presidency* (New York: G. P. Putnam's Sons, 1982), and Jimmy Carter, *Keeping Faith: Memoirs of a President* (New York: Barton, 1982).

25. See *New York Times,* 12 June 1984.

26. For an excellent journalistic account of these expectations, see Ze'ev Schiff and Ehud Ya'ari, *Israel's Lebanon War* (New York: Simon and Schuster, 1984).

27. *New York Times,* 11 Nov. 1986, 1:6

28. *New York Times,* 4 Nov. 1986, 14:1.

29. *Report of the President's Special Review Board,* 26 Feb. 1987 (Tower Commission), 3:18.

30. FBIS-Soviet Union, 9 Dec. 1987, 46–47.

31. FBIS-Soviet Union, 13 Jan. 1988, 37.

Index